MEMOIRS
OF A
REVOLUTIONIST

The Cresset Library

The Best Circles
Leonore Davidoff

Britain by Mass-Observation
Arranged and written by Tom Harrisson and Charles Madge

Byron: A Portrait
Leslie A. Marchand

Captain Bligh and Mister Christian
Richard Hough

China: A Short Cultural History
C. P. Fitzgerald

The Eighteen Nineties
Holbrook Jackson

A Farmer's Year
H. Rider Haggard

Four Portraits: Boswell, Gibbon, Sterne and Wilkes
Peter Quennell

The Four Voyages of Christopher Columbus
Edited and translated by J. M. Cohen

The General Strike
Julian Symons

The Home Front
E. Sylvia Pankhurst

Irish Affairs
Edmund Burke

Ishi in Two Worlds
Theodora Kroeber

Japan: A Short Cultural History
G. B. Sansom

The Making of the Middle Ages
R. W. Southern

Memoirs of a Revolutionist
Peter Kropotkin

Mutiny: The Floating Republic
G. E. Manwaring and Bonamy Dobré

From Ploughtail to Parliament: An Autobiography
Joseph Arch

The Pub and the People
Mass-Observation

Russia Perceived: A Trans-Siberian Journey
Elizabeth Pond

A Short History of Ireland
J. C. Beckett

The Social History of the Machine Gun
John Ellis

The Spanish Conquistadores
F. A. Kirkpatrick

It Takes a Thief: The life and times of Jonathan Wild
Gerald Howson

War Factory
Mass-Observation

Wittgenstein
W. W. Bartley III

Front cover: *A Revolutionary throws a bomb into a group of advancing Cossacks in 1905* by N. Nikonov. Reproduced by courtesy of John Massey Stewart.
Back cover: *Prince Peter Alexeivitch Kropotkin.* Reproduced by courtesy of the BBC Hulton Picture Library.

MEMOIRS OF A REVOLUTIONIST

Peter Kropotkin

EDITED BY
JAMES ALLEN ROGERS

THE CRESSET LIBRARY

London   Melbourne   Auckland   Johannesburg

The Cresset Library

An imprint of Century Hutchinson Ltd

62–65 Chandos Place, London WC2N 4NW

Century Hutchinson Australia Pty Ltd
P O Box 496, 16–22 Church Street, Hawthorn,
Victoria 3122, Australia

Century Hutchinson New Zealand Ltd
P O Box 40–086, Glenfield, Auckland 10,
New Zealand

Century Hutchinson South Africa (Pty) Ltd
P O Box 337, Bergvlei 2012, South Africa

First published 1962
This edition first published 1988

Made and printed in Great Britain by
Richard Clay Ltd, Bungay, Suffolk

ISBN 0 09 173198 4

CONTENTS

PREFACE

The *Memoirs* of Peter Kropótkin occupy an unusual place in world literature. Although now an eminent part of Russian letters, they were originally published in English in 1899. Three years later a Russian edition *translated* from the original English text was published (because of Tsarist censorship) in London.[1] To explain to his Russian reader why a book about Russian affairs by a Russian was translated from English, Kropótkin wrote a special preface to the 1902 Russian edition:

> "I began to write these *Memoirs,* naturally, in Russian. The first part, "Childhood," was already written when I went to America in the autumn of 1897. In America I became acquainted with a very likable man—Walter Page —who was then the editor of the *Atlantic Monthly.* He persuaded me to continue my memoirs, to finish them and to begin to publish them in his journal."

Besides writing each installment in English for the *Atlantic Monthly,* Kropótkin attempted to write another copy directly in Russian, in order to have a complete and original text in both languages. But this demanded too much effort and for most of the *Memoirs* he had time only to prepare an English text.

The curious result is that a complete and original text of Kropótkin's *Memoirs* exists only in English. After its publication, Kropótkin began to write additional notes in Russian, planning to bring out an original and larger Russian edition of the *Memoirs.* But by the time he died in 1921, he had managed only to write revisions of two chapters and a number of fragments of varying length and quality.

These Russian additions to the *Memoirs* fall generally into two categories: the first consists mostly of more anecdotal material about certain events in Kropótkin's life or about persons who appear in the *Memoirs;* the second and more important contains information which he intentionally avoided using in his original English edition because it would have expressed too strongly his differences with the Russian revolutionary movement at a time (1899) when that movement was still struggling against the Tsarist autocracy.

The significant part of this additional material, which has never before appeared in English, has been used in the present edition. But I have followed Kropótkin's advice to the Russian editors of the *Memoirs,* not to intermix the original English edition and the incomplete Russian text, as this would destroy the style of the integral English version. The reader will consequently find translations of the important fragments left by Kropótkin, as well as extracts from his letters and other writings that clarify various points of his autobiography, in the notes appended to the end of the text.

Kropótkin used a number of pseudonyms in the original edition to avoid compromising his friends still living in Tsarist Russia. These pseudonyms have been replaced in the present edition wherever possible by the actual names. Kropótkin's account of his geographical explorations and his travels in Western Europe, which are of less interest to the reader today, have been abridged because of considerations of size.

A short epilogue based upon extracts from Kropótkin's letters carries the story of his life from the 1890s (when he wrote the *Memoirs*) to his death in 1921. His letters from Soviet Russia describing his reactions to the Bolshevik regime, his quarrel with Lenin, and nonetheless his protests against Allied intervention are especially significant in view of his own revolutionary past.

For permission to use the letters of Kropótkin to Professor S. P. Turin, edited by the late historian, S. Melgounóff, I am indebted to the kindness of Madame P. Melgounóff. The editor of *The Russian Review* has graciously consented to the use of the letters from Kropótkin to Lenin first published in that review. Permission to make use of the letter from Kropótkin to Georg Brandes has been kindly allowed by *The Nation.*

In preparing this new edition for publication, I found particularly helpful the services of Widener Library of Harvard, the Library of the Institute of Slavic Studies of Paris, and the Lenin Library of Moscow. I would also like to express a special debt of gratitude to the late Professor Michael Karpovich of Harvard who first guided my studies of Kropótkin.

JAMES ALLEN ROGERS

INTRODUCTION

To the student of Russian history or literature, Kropótkin's *Memoirs* of his life in Russia are indispensable. To others, the *Memoirs* will appeal by their high literary quality and by the intrinsic attraction of Kropótkin's life. While belonging to the highest rank of Russian aristocracy, Kropótkin became a revolutionary and later an exile, only to find himself after the October Revolution of 1917 as tragically opposed to the Bolsheviks as he had been to the Tsarist autocracy. The story of his life, which spanned the reigns of the last four Románov tsars and the first four years of Soviet rule, contains all the elements of great drama. Prince Mirsky, that *doyen* of Russian and Soviet littérateurs, described these *Memoirs* as "a first-class autobiography, the most remarkable work of its kind since Hérzen's *My Past and Thought*."

Kropótkin's autobiography, like that of Alexander Hérzen, owes its remarkable quality to the brilliant presentation of an unusual story by an original and gifted personality. More interested in describing his contemporaries than himself, Kropótkin created such a portrait gallery of his friends in the Russian revolutionary movement that his *Memoirs* transcend his own life and become the social history of an era.[2]

Born in 1842 of an ancient and noble Russian family, Kropótkin witnessed during the course of his life (he died in 1921) cataclysmic changes in his own country and in Western Europe. His own birth date of December 12, 1842, fell in one of the quiet periods, a trough between the revolutionary crests of 1830 and 1848. In 1842 the twenty-four-year-old Karl Marx had just become editor of the *Rheinische Zeitung* of Cologne, which he soon turned into a vehemently radical journal. Six years later, with the collaboration of Friedrich Engels, his ideas on the inevitable fall of capitalism and the rise of communism took vivid form in *The Communist Manifesto*.

The summer of 1842 found Charles Darwin, age thirty-three, sketching a theory of evolution which he had been mulling over in his mind. Seventeen years later (1859) his *Origin of Species by the Means of Natural Selection* burst upon a startled Victorian society and brought the war of science and religion to its highest pitch on the question of the origin of man. In 1842, the later famous Russian anarchist, Michael Bakúnin, age twenty-eight, was becoming a convert to socialism in Berlin. There he began to work out his revolutionary and anarchist equation of destruction and creation, arguing that man should put his trust in the eternal spirit which destroys and annihilates because it is also the spirit of all creation.

Within the boundary of this network of revolutionary ideas created by Marx, Darwin, and Bakúnin, Kropótkin began to develop his ideas on socialism. His own experience soon led him across the boundaries of these ideas in the name of his philosophy of anarchism. But the theories of Marx, Darwin, and Bakúnin remained the most important ideological influences in his life, even when he strongly opposed them.

The Russia into which Kropótkin was born in 1842 lay under a shroud of repression. The revolution of December 1825, which greeted the accession of Nicholas I (d. 1855), had been ruthlessly suppressed, setting the keynote of this reign. But if Nicholas' motif was a vigorous defense of the status quo in all aspects of Russian life, he was not insensible to the weak points of Russian society:

> "There is no doubt that serfdom in its present form is a flagrant evil which everyone realizes" [Nicholas declared to his State Council in 1842]. "Yet to attempt to remedy it now would be, of course, an evil even more disastrous."

These words from a tsar whose reign experienced more than 550 major peasant uprisings expresses the untenable position of the Russian autocracy toward the middle of the nineteenth century. While all of Russia gave mute evidence of a desperate need for profound reform, the tsar was inhibited from any real change by his inability even to consider any modification of the sanctified foundations of the autocracy and the existing social order. All reform activity and discussion were strictly confined to the governmental bureaucracy. The result was piecemeal improvement in a few areas but not Reform.

Kropótkin's reminiscences of the last years of the reign of Nicholas I are presented to us in his *Memoirs* in a series of unforgettable vignettes of his childhood, contrasting the privileged life of the Moscow nobility with the debased existence of their serfs. His father, with twelve hundred serfs on various estates, fifty serf servants in his Moscow house, seventy-five in his country house at Nikólskoe, and a genealogy going back to the nobility of medieval Russia, moved easily in the highest circles of the Russian aristocracy.

But Kropótkin was never close to his father, and he became conscious early in life of the social injustice upon which their leisurely life depended. His earliest memory was of the death of his mother (he was three and a half), and of the loving care the family serfs lavished upon him and his older brother, Alexander. "I do not know what would have become of us," he later wrote, "if we had not found in our house, among the serf servants, that atmosphere of love which children must have around them." It gave him a feeling of gratitude and affection for the broad mass of Russian people which permeates everything he ever wrote about them.

When Nicholas I died in 1855, his successor, Alexander II (d. 1881) began a reign full of hope and promise of great reform. The new reign also marked a new step in Kropótkin's life. In 1857 he entered the aristocratic Corps of Pages in St. Petersburg. With his brother, Alexander, who had remained in Moscow, he began a lively correspondence which reflects in a youthful and delightful form many of the questions that agitated the young Russian thinkers of the late 1850s and early 1860s.

In the beginning, Alexander, as the older brother, took the lead in the correspondence and impelled Peter to develop himself intellectually.

"With this in mind" [Peter Kropótkin wrote later] "he raised one question after another, philosophical and scientific, sending me whole scholarly dissertations in his letters, advising me to read and to study. How fortunate I am that I had such a brother who loved me dearly. To him, more than to anything or to anyone, I am indebted for my development."

For the two young Kropótkin princes, the overriding question was: "What sort of philosophy should we have?" The manner in which they asked the question was primarily moral, and it is not surprising that they turned at first to religious books. Alexander secretly abandoned the Russian Orthodox faith and embraced Lutheranism. The correspondence temporarily grew heavy with a lugubrious discussion of theology, until Peter found he did not know what to believe:

"I find that at least it is better to be a Lutheran like you than an Orthodox like me because I have no religion" [Peter wrote to Alexander]. "I find that even now I believe that God exists, that Jesus Christ exists, but meanwhile this is all so unclear in my mind that I am confused. I experienced what you wrote about being unable to pray. I even involuntarily laughed several times while passing by people praying on the square near the doors of our church. Why? I think it is because I read several works concerning religion, for example, the philosophical dictionary of Voltaire, then myself rejected several dogmas of our faith and many traditions which seemed to me absurd. I finally reached the point that there is almost nothing to believe."

The question of "what to believe" profoundly troubled many of the young thinkers of Kropótkin's generation in the early 1860s. In reaction against the romantic idealism and German metaphysics of the previous generation, they called themselves "critical realists" and searched for a new and absolute guide to life. Many refused to accept any conclusion that could not be verified by the methods of the natural sciences. Turgénev brilliantly portrayed this type of young nihilist through the character of Bazárov in his famous novel, *Fathers and Sons,* which appeared in 1862.

Isolated from direct contact with the nihilist 'movement by the thick gray walls of the privileged Corps of Pages, Kropótkin felt nonetheless the veneration for the natural sciences that had seized his generation. He and Alexander enthusiastically discussed the spectacular scientific discoveries of those years, and Peter decided to follow a career in science.

His religious anxiety disappeared before the seemingly confident truths of nineteenth-century science, and he soon found an outlet for his moral temperament when he came across a copy of *The Polar Star* of the famous exile, Alexander Hérzen (1812–70). Although published in England and forbidden in Russia, this review had a wide circulation among Russian thinkers and reached the throne itself. The breadth of Hérzen's ideas and his deep love of Russia made a profound impression upon Kropótkin and produced an unexpected political attitude in the conservative Corps of Pages.

> "Here in the Corps everyone is so greatly retarded that the idea came to me to help their development" [Peter wrote to Alexander]. "With this in mind, I began to edit a paper [secretly] under the title, *Echoes from the Corps*. My main goal was to awaken in the Corps a realization of the erroneous outlook by which we are ruled, that is, that it is wrong to think that autocracy is the best form of government, that a military career is the best way of life, and that it is only possible to be a good fellow by being in the Preobrazhénsky Regiment and in the Horse Guards."

Reading Hérzen gave form to Kropótkin's growing political awareness. When he became personal page to the tsar at the age of nineteen, Kropótkin idolized Alexander II, seeing in him Russia's great hero defending reform against the reactionary elements in Russian society. But close attendance at the Russian Imperial Court soon eroded this passionate devotion. It was not that the era of promised reforms did not come. The emancipation of the serfs was achieved in 1861, and other reforms followed. But, as in all such cases where a period of reform follows a period of repression, heightened expectations demanded more. Every compromise by Alexander II was interpreted by Kropótkin as a step backward toward reaction. This attitude remained and colored his entire account of the reign of Alexander II in the *Memoirs*.

When he graduated from the Corps of Pages in 1861, Kropótkin passed by the opportunity for a fashionable military career to help implement the Alexandrian reforms in Siberia. But after two years of rather disappointing results (which he blamed on corruption and interference by the St. Petersburg bureaucracy), he turned his energies instead to geographical explorations in East Siberia. While he traveled, his past experiences continuously sifted through his mind, seeking meaning and pattern. His personal disillusionment with Alexander II and his disappointing experiences with reform in Siberia had convinced him that reform could not successfully come from above, that the administrative machinery of a centralized government could do nothing really useful for the people.

Everywhere that Kropótkin traveled in Siberia he was impressed by the quiet and constructive work of the people. He observed the complex and successful social organization of primitive tribes amidst all the failures of state colonization. He began to doubt not only the State in its Russian form, but centralized government in any form, although these misgivings had not yet given birth to any alternative system.

This new tendency in Kropótkin's thought was strengthened, strangely enough, by observations he made in Siberia on Darwin's theory of the origin of species by natural selection. With a friend, the zoologist Poliakóv, Kropótkin explored the Vitím region of Eastern Siberia looking for the keen competition between animals of the same species that Darwin's theory of evolution had prepared him to expect. But he could find no struggle for existence among animals of the same species. Reflecting on this experience over the years, Kropótkin concluded that the animals he had seen in Siberia had survived because of an inherent sense of mutual aid within the species which was far more important for the progressive evolution of the species than the Darwinian struggle for existence. He began to see in mutual aid the possible basis for a new society, if man could break free of those forms of society that discouraged by their very structure the expression of mutual-aid tendencies.[3]

The primary purpose of Kropótkin's geographical explorations, however, had been to collect data on the basic mountain structure of Siberia which was still an unsolved problem. After returning to St. Petersburg in 1867, he worked over his data for several years and then presented his new theories to the scientific world. He had a resounding success, and his reputation as Russia's brilliant young geographer was firmly established. But at the very moment when he was offered the high honor of the secretaryship of the Russian Geographical Society, Kropótkin decided to give up his scientific work:

"What right had I to these highest joys" [he recalled later] "when all around me was nothing but misery and struggle for a moldy bit of bread; when whatsoever I should spend to enable me to live in that world of higher emotions must needs be taken from the very mouths of those who grew the wheat and had not bread enough for their own children."

Following this decision at the age of twenty-nine, Kropótkin made a trip to Switzerland to study firsthand the international socialist movement. There he was at first attracted to a group of socialists who had sided with Marx in the quarrel between Marx and Bakúnin that was soon to split the socialist movement. Later, dismayed by the political opportunism among the leaders of this group, he transferred his allegiance to the Jura Federation, oriented toward Bakúnist anarchism. "After a week's stay with the watchmakers [of the Jura Federation]," he noted, "my views on socialism were settled. I was an anarchist."

His stay with the Jura watchmakers had not so much converted Kropótkin to anarchism as it had brought to crystallization almost a decade of frustration by presenting in very favorable surroundings what appeared to him as a clear answer to tyranny in any form. Like many of his generation, Kropótkin looked hopefully in the direction of socialism for an answer to Russia's problems. But unlike most of them, he had had the experience of attempting to apply governmental reforms in Siberia under an autocracy strongly centralized in St. Petersburg. The frustrating result placed him squarely against all centralized governments, whether they called themselves monarchist or socialist.

Here lay the strongest source of his implacable opposition to Marxism in which he began to see only the seeds of another authoritarian and centralized state, but more dangerous because it came in the guise of democratic socialism. When he later became the theoretician of the anarchist movement, Kropótkin attempted to reshape its ideology more effectively against Marxism. Although he had a profound admiration for Bakúnin, he explicitly repudiated Bakúnin's collectivist anarchism and conspiratorial methods as contradictory and obsolete. What is needed, said Kropótkin, is for the anarchists to hold their own in the domain of theory, to establish their ideal of the society of the future, and to prove that it is in accord with the historical progress of culture.

Kropótkin had in effect mapped out his own lifework. The result was an enormous number of articles and books on anarchism, nearly all of which are forgotten today. The *Memoirs* have continued to live because in them Kropótkin completely subordinated his passion for anarchism to tell instead the exciting story of his life in Russia and of his generation's struggle against the Tsarist autocracy.

What is significant for an understanding of the *Memoirs* is consequently not Kropótkin's theory of anarchism itself,[4] but the experiences sketched here which led him toward anarchism. These experiences are the origin of the values that eventually brought Kropótkin into the Russian revolutionary movement and that permeate his interpretation of it in the *Memoirs*.

Kropótkin was an anarchist before he became a revolutionist. He had known the young radicals of his generation only through literature until he returned from Switzerland in 1872. He was then thirty years old, and his own particular views on socialism had already begun to focus around the concept of anarchism. At that point he was invited by a friend to join a group of young radical thinkers known as the Chaikóvsky Circle. His new thought was bringing him closer to the radicals of his generation at the same time that it distinguished his ideas from theirs. This marked the entrance of Kropótkin into the Russian revolutionary movement. That story, however, belongs properly to the *Memoirs of a Revolutionist*.

MEMOIRS OF A REVOLUTIONIST

* * * * * * * * * * * * * * * * *

PART ONE

CHILDHOOD

I

Moscow is a city of slow historical growth, and down to the present time its different parts have wonderfully well retained the features which have been stamped upon them in the slow course of history. The Trans-Moskva River district, with its broad, sleepy streets and its monotonous gray-painted, low-roofed houses, of which the entrance-gates remain securely bolted day and night, has always been the secluded abode of the merchant class, and the stronghold of the outwardly austere, formalistic, and despotic Nonconformists of the "Old Faith." The citadel, or Kremlin, is still the stronghold of church and state; and the immense space in front of it, covered with thousands of shops and warehouses, has been for centuries a crowded beehive of commerce, and still remains the heart of a great internal trade which spreads over the whole surface of the vast empire. The Tverskáia and the Smiths' Bridge have been for hundreds of years the chief centers for the fashionable shops; while the artisans' quarters, the Pluschíkha and the Dorogomílovka, retain the very same features which characterized their uproarious populations in the times of the Moscow Tsars. Each quarter is a little world in itself; each has its own physiognomy, and lives its own separate life. Even the railways—when they made an irruption into the old capital—grouped apart in special centers on the outskirts of the old town their stores and machine-works, their heavily loaded carts and engines.

However, of all parts of Moscow, none, perhaps, is more typical than that labyrinth of clean, quiet, winding streets and lanes which lies at the back of the Kremlin, between two great radial streets, the Arbát and the Prechístenka, and is still called the Old Equerries' Quarter,—the Stáraia Koniúshennaia.

Some fifty years ago, there lived in this quarter, and slowly died out, the old Moscow nobility, whose names were so frequently mentioned in the pages of Russian history before the times of Peter I., but who subsequently disappeared to make room for the newcomers, "the men of all ranks," called into service by the founder of the Russian state. Feeling themselves supplanted at the St. Petersburg court, these nobles of the old stock retired either to the Old Equerries' Quarter in Moscow, or to their picturesque estates in the country round about the capital, and they looked with a sort of contempt and secret jealousy upon the motley crowd of families which came "from no one knew where" to take possession of the highest functions of the government, in the new capital on the banks of the Nevá.

In their younger days, most of them had tried their fortunes in the service of the state, chiefly in the army; but for one reason or another they had soon abandoned it, without having risen to high rank. The more successful ones obtained some quiet, almost honorary position in their mother city,—my father was one of these,—while most of the others simply retired from active service. But wheresoever they might have been shifted, in the course of their careers, over the wide surface of Russia, they always somehow managed to spend their old age in a house of their own in the Old Equerries' Quarter, under the shadow of the church where they had been baptized, and where the last prayers had been pronounced at the burial of their parents.

New branches budded from the old stocks. Some of them achieved more or less distinction in different parts of Russia; some owned more luxurious houses in the new style in other quarters of Moscow or at St. Petersburg; but the branch which continued to reside in the Old Equerries' Quarter, somewhere near to the green, the yellow, the pink, or the brown church which was endeared through family associations, was considered as the true representative of the family, irrespective of the position it occupied in the family tree. Its old-fashioned head was treated with great respect, not devoid, I must say, of a slight tinge of irony, even by those younger representatives of the same stock who had left their mother city for a more brilliant career in the St. Petersburg Guard or in the court circles. He personified for them the antiquity of the family and its traditions.

In these quiet streets, far away from the noise and bustle of the commercial Moscow, all the houses had much the same appearance. They were mostly built of wood, with bright green sheet-iron roofs, the exteriors stuccoed and decorated with columns and porticoes; all were painted in gay colors. Nearly every house had but one story, with seven or nine big, gay-looking windows facing the street. A second story was admitted only in the back part of the house, which looked upon a spacious yard, surrounded by numbers of small buildings, used as kitchens, stables, cellars, coach-houses, and as dwellings for the retainers and servants. A wide gate opened upon this yard, and a brass plate on it usually bore the inscription, "House of So-and-So, Lieutenant or Colonel, and Commander,"—very seldom "Major-General" or any similarly elevated civil rank. But if a more luxurious house, embellished by a gilded iron railing and an iron gate, stood in one of those streets, the brass plate on the gate was sure to bear the name of "Commerce Counsel" or "Honorable Citizen" So-and-So. These were the intruders, those who came unasked to settle in this quarter, and were therefore ignored by their neighbors.

No shops were allowed in these select streets, except that in some small wooden house, belonging to the parish church, a tiny grocer's or greengrocer's shop might have been found; but then, the policeman's lodge stood on the opposite corner, and in the daytime the policeman himself, armed with a halberd, would appear at the door to salute with his inoffensive weapon the officers passing by, and would retire inside when dusk came, to employ himself either as a cobbler, or in the manufacture of some special snuff patronized by the elder male servants of the neighborhood.

Life went on quietly and peacefully—at least for the outsider —in this Moscow Faubourg Saint-Germain. In the morning nobody was seen in the streets. About midday the children made their appearance under the guidance of French tutors and German nurses who took them out for a walk on the snow-covered boulevards. Later on in the day the ladies might be seen in their two-horse sledges, with a valet standing behind on a small plank fastened at the end of the runners, or ensconced in an old-fashioned carriage, immense and high, suspended on big curved springs and dragged by four horses, with a postilion in front and two valets standing behind. In the evening most of the houses were brightly illuminated, and, the blinds not being drawn down, the passers-by could admire the card-players or the waltzers in the saloons. "Opinions" were not in vogue in those days, and we were yet far from the years when in each one of these houses a struggle began between "fathers and sons,"—a struggle that usually ended either in a family tragedy or in a nocturnal visit of the state police. Fifty years ago nothing of the sort was thought of; all was quiet and smooth,—at least on the surface.

In this Old Equerries' Quarter I was born in 1842, and here I passed the first fifteen years of my life. Even after our father had sold the house in which our mother died, and bought another, and when again he had sold that house, and we spent several winters in hired houses, until he had found a third one to his taste, within a stone's throw of the church where he had been baptized, we still remained in the Old Equerries' Quarter, leaving it only during the summer to go to our country-seat.

II

A high, spacious bedroom, the corner room of our house, with a white bed upon which our mother is lying, our baby chairs and tables standing close by, and the neatly served tables covered with sweets and jellies in pretty glass jars,—a room into which we children are ushered at a strange hour,—this is the first half-distinct reminiscence of my life.

Our mother was dying of consumption; she was only thirty-five years old. Before parting with us forever, she had wished to have us by her side, to caress us, to feel happy for a moment in our joys, and she had arranged this little treat by the side of her bed, which she could leave no more. I remember her pale thin face, her large, dark brown eyes. She looked at us with love, and invited us to eat, to climb upon her bed; then all of a sudden she burst into tears and began to cough, and we were told to go.

Some time after, we children—that is, my brother Alexander and myself—were removed from the big house to a small side house in the court-yard. The April sun filled the little rooms with its rays, but our German nurse, Madame Búrman, and Uliána our Russian nurse, told us to go to bed. Their faces wet with tears, they were sewing for us black shirts fringed with broad white tassels. We could not sleep: the unknown frightened us, and we listened to their subdued talk. They said something about our mother which we could not understand. We jumped out of our beds, asking, "Where is mamma? Where is mamma?"

Both of them burst into sobs, and began to pat our curly heads, calling us "poor orphans," until Uliána could hold out no longer, and said, "Your mother is gone there,—to the sky, to the angels."

"How to the sky? Why?" our infantile imagination in vain demanded.

This was in April, 1846. I was only three and a half years old, and my brother Sásha not yet five. Where our elder brother and sister, Nicholas and Hélène, had gone I do not know: perhaps they were already at school. Nicholas was twelve years old, Hélène was eleven; they kept together, and we knew them but little. So we remained, Alexander and I, in this little house, in the hands of Madame Búrman and Uliána. The good old German lady, homeless and absolutely alone in the wide world, took toward us the place of our mother. She brought us up as well as she could, buying us from time to time some simple toys, and over-feeding us with ginger cakes whenever another old German, who used to sell such cakes,—probably as homeless and solitary as herself,—paid an occasional visit to our house. We seldom saw our father, and the next two years passed without leaving any impression on my memory.

III

Our father was very proud of the origin of his family, and would point with solemnity to a piece of parchment which hung on a wall of his study. It was decorated with our arms, —the arms of the principality of Smolénsk covered with the ermine mantle and the crown of the Monomáchs,—and there was written on it, and certified by the Heraldry Department, that our family originated with a grandson of Rostisláv Mstislávich the Bold (a name familiar in Russian history as that of a Grand Prince of Kíev), and that our ancestors had been Grand Princes of Smolénsk.

"It cost me three hundred rubles to obtain that parchment," our father used to say. Like most people of his generation, he was not much versed in Russian history, and valued the parchment more for its cost than for its historical associations.

As a matter of fact, our family is of very ancient origin indeed; but, like most descendants of Rurik who may be regarded as representative of the feudal period of Russian history, it was driven into the background when that period ended, and the Románovs, enthroned at Moscow, began the work of consolidating the Russian state. In recent times, none of the Kropótkins seem to have had any special liking for state functions. Our great-grandfather and grandfather both retired from the military service when quite young men, and hastened to return to their family estates. It must also be said that of these estates the main one, Urúsovo, situated in the government of Riazán, on a high hill at the border of fertile prairies, might tempt any one by the beauty of its shadowy forests, its winding rivers, and its endless meadows. Our grandfather was only a lieutenant when he left the service, and retired to Urúsovo, devoting himself to his estate, and to the purchase of other estates in the neighboring provinces.

Probably our generation would have done the same; but our grandfather married a Princess Gagárina, who belonged to a quite different family. Her brother was well known as a passionate lover of the stage. He kept a private theater of his own, and went so far in his passion as to marry, to the scandal of all his relations, a serf,—the genial actress Semiónova, who was one of the creators of dramatic art in Russia, and undoubtedly one of its most sympathetic figures. To the horror of "all Moscow," she continued to appear on the stage.

I do not know if our grandmother had the same artistic and literary tastes as her brother,—I remember her when she was already paralyzed and could speak only in whispers; but it is certain that in the next generation a leaning toward literature became a characteristic of our family. One of the sons of the Princess Gagárina was a minor Russian poet, and issued a book of poems,—a fact which my father was ashamed of and always avoided mentioning; and in our own generation several of our cousins, as well as my brother and myself, have contributed more or less to the literature of our period.

Our father was a typical officer of the time of Nicholas I. Not that he was imbued with a warlike spirit or much in love with camp life; I doubt whether he spent a single night of his life at a bivouac fire, or took part in one battle. But under Nicholas I. that was of quite secondary importance. The true military man of those times was the officer who was enamored of the military uniform, and utterly despised all other sorts of attire; whose soldiers were trained to perform almost superhuman tricks with their legs and rifles (to break the wood of the rifle into pieces while "presenting arms" was one of those famous tricks); and who could show on parade a row of soldiers as perfectly aligned and as motionless as a row of toy-soldiers. "Very good," the Grand Duke Michael said once of a regiment, after having kept it for one hour presenting arms,— "only, *they breathe!*" To respond to the then current conception of a military man was certainly our father's ideal.

True, he took part in the Turkish campaign of 1828; but he managed to remain all the time on the staff of the chief commander; and if we children, taking advantage of a moment when he was in a particularly good temper, asked him to tell us something about the war, he had nothing to tell but of a fierce attack of hundreds of Turkish dogs which one night assailed him and his faithful servant, Frol, as they were riding with dispatches through an abandoned Turkish village. They had to use swords to extricate themselves from the hungry beasts. Bands of Turks would assuredly have better satisfied our imagination, but we accepted the dogs as a substitute. When, however, pressed by our questions, our father told us how he had won the cross of Saint Anne "for gallantry," and the golden sword which he wore, I must confess we felt really disappointed. His story was decidedly too prosaic. The officers of the general staff were lodged in a Turkish village, when it took fire. In a moment the houses were enveloped in flames, and in one of them a child had been left behind. Its mother

uttered despairing cries. Thereupon, Frol, who always accompanied his master, rushed into the flames and saved the child.
The chief commander, who saw the act, at once gave father
the cross for gallantry.

"But, father," we exclaimed, "it was Frol who saved the
child!"

"What of that?" replied he, in the most naïve way. "Was
he not my man? It is all the same."

He also took some part in the campaign of 1831, during the
Polish Revolution, and in Warsaw he made the acquaintance
of, and fell in love with, the youngest daughter of the commander of an army corps, General Sulíma. The marriage was
celebrated with great pomp, in the Lazienki palace; the lieu-
tenant-governor, Count Paskévich, acting as nuptial godfather
on the bridegroom's side. "But your mother," our father used
to add, "brought me no fortune whatever."

This was true. Her father, Nikolái Semiónovich Sulíma, was
not versed in the art of making a career or a fortune. He must
have had in him too much of the blood of those Cossacks of
the Dniéper, who knew how to fight the well-equipped, warlike Poles or armies of the Turks, three times more than themselves, but knew not how to avoid the snares of the Moscow
diplomacy, and, after having fought against the Poles in the
terrible insurrection of 1648, which was the beginning of the
end for the Polish republic, lost all their liberties in falling
under the dominion of the Russian Tsars. One Sulíma was captured by the Poles and tortured to death at Warsaw, but the
other "colonels" of the same stock only fought the more fiercely
on that account, and Poland lost Little Russia. As to our grandfather, during Napoleon I.'s invasion he had cut his way, at
the head of his regiment of cuirassiers, into a French infantry
square bristling with bayonets, and, after having been left for
dead on the battlefield, had recovered with a deep cut in his
head; but he could not become a valet to the favorite of
Alexander I., the omnipotent Arakchéev, and was consequently
sent into a sort of honorary exile, first as a governor-general
of West Siberia, and later of East Siberia. In those times such a
position was considered more lucrative than a gold mine, but
our grandfather returned from Siberia as poor as he went, and
left only modest fortunes to his three sons and three daughters.

When I went to Siberia, in 1862, I often heard his name mentioned with respect. He was driven to despair by the wholesale stealing which went on in those provinces, and which he had no means to repress.

Our mother was undoubtedly a remarkable woman for the times she lived in. Many years after her death, I discovered, in a corner of a store-room of our country-house, a mass of papers covered with her firm but pretty handwriting: diaries in which she wrote with delight of the scenery of Germany, and spoke of her sorrows and her thirst for happiness; books which she had filled with Russian verses, prohibited by censorship,—among them the beautiful historical ballads of Ryléev, the poet, whom Nicholas I. hanged in 1826; other books containing music, French dramas, verses of Lamartine, and Byron's poems that she had copied; and a great number of water-color paintings.

Tall, slim, adorned with a mass of dark chestnut hair, with dark brown eyes and a tiny mouth, she looks quite lifelike in a portrait in oils that was painted *con amore* by a good artist. Always lively and often careless, she was fond of dancing, and the peasant women in our village would tell us how she would admire from a balcony their ring-dances,—slow and full of grace,—and how finally she would herself join in them. She had the nature of an artist. It was at a ball that she caught the cold that produced the inflammation of the lungs which brought her to the grave.

All who knew her loved her. The servants worshiped her memory. It was in her name that Madame Búrman took care of us, and in her name the Russian nurse bestowed upon us her love. While combing our hair, or signing us with the cross in our beds, Uliána would often say, "And your mamma must now look upon you from the skies, and shed tears on seeing you, poor orphans." Our whole childhood is irradiated by her memory. How often, in some dark passage, the hand of a servant would touch Alexander or me with a caress; or a peasant woman, on meeting us in the fields, would ask, "Will you be as good as your mother was? She took compassion on us. You will, surely." "Us" meant, of course, the serfs. I do not know what would have become of us if we had not found in our house, among the serf servants, that atmosphere of love which

children must have around them. We were her children, we
bore likeness to her, and they lavished their care upon us, sometimes in a touching form, as will be seen later on.

Men passionately desire to live after death, but they often
pass away without noticing the fact that the memory of a
really good person always lives. It is impressed upon the next
generation, and is transmitted again to the children. Is not that
an immortality worth striving for?

IV

Two years after the death of our mother our father married
again. He had already cast his eyes upon a nice-looking young
person, who belonged to a wealthy family, when the fates decided another way. One morning, while he was still in his dressing-gown, the servants rushed madly into his room, announcing
the arrival of General Timoféev, the commander of the sixth
army corps, to which our father belonged. This favorite of
Nicholas I. was a terrible man. He would order a soldier to be
flogged almost to death for a mistake made during a parade, or
he would degrade an officer and send him as a private to
Siberia because he had met him in the street with the hooks
of his high, stiff collar unfastened. With Nicholas General
Timoféev's word was all-powerful.

The general, who had never before been in our house, came
to propose to our father to marry his wife's niece, Mademoiselle
Elisabeth Karandinó, one of several daughters of an admiral
of the Black Sea fleet,—a young lady with a classical Greek
profile, said to have been very beautiful. Father accepted, and
his second wedding, like the first, was solemnized with great
pomp.

"You young people understand nothing of this kind of thing,"
he said in conclusion, after having told me the story more than
once, with a very fine humor which I will not attempt to re-
produce. "But do you know what it meant at that time,—the
commander of an army corps? Above all, that one-eyed devil,
as we used to call him, coming himself to propose? Of course
she had no dowry; only a big trunk filled with their ladies'

finery, and that Martha, her one serf, dark as a gypsy, sitting upon it."

I have no recollection whatever of this event. I only remember a big drawing-room in a richly furnished house, and in that room a young lady, attractive, but with a rather too sharp southern look, gamboling with us, and saying, "You see what a jolly mamma you will have;" to which Sásha and I, sulkily looking at her, replied, "Our mamma has flown away to the sky." We regarded so much liveliness with suspicion.

Winter came, and a new life began for us. Our house was sold, and another was bought and furnished completely anew. All that could convey a reminiscence of our mother disappeared,—her portraits, her paintings, her embroideries. In vain Madame Búrman implored to be retained in our house, and promised to devote herself to the baby our stepmother was expecting as to her own child: she was sent away. "Nothing of the Sulímas in my house," she was told. All connection with our uncles and aunts and our grandmother was broken. Uliána was married to Frol, who became a major-domo, while she was made housekeeper; and for our education a richly paid French tutor, M. Poulain, and a miserably paid Russian student, N. P. Smirnóv, were engaged.

Many of the sons of the Moscow nobles were educated at that time by Frenchmen, who represented the débris of Napoleon's Grande Armée. M. Poulain was one of them. He had just finished the education of the youngest son of the novelist Zagóskin, and his pupil, Serge, enjoyed in the Old Equerries' Quarter the reputation of being so well brought up that our father did not hesitate to engage M. Poulain for the considerable sum of six hundred rubles a year.

M. Poulain brought with him his setter, Trésor, his coffeepot Napoléon, and his French textbooks, and he began to rule over us and the serf Matvéi who was attached to our service.

His plan of education was very simple. After having woke us up he attended to his coffee, which he used to take in his room. While we were preparing the morning lessons he made his toilet with minute care: he shampooed his gray hair so as to conceal his growing baldness, put on his tail-coat, sprinkled and washed himself with eau-de-cologne, and then escorted us

downstairs to say good-morning to our parents. We used to
find our father and stepmother at breakfast, and on approaching them we recited in the most official way, "Bonjour, mon
cher papa," and "Bonjour, ma chère maman," and kissed their
hands. M. Poulain made a very complicated and elegant
obeisance in pronouncing the words, "Bonjour, monsieur le
prince," and "Bonjour, madame la princesse," after which the
procession immediately withdrew and retired upstairs. This
ceremony was repeated every morning.

Then our work began. M. Poulain changed his tail-coat for
a dressing-gown, covered his head with a leather cap, and
dropping into an easy-chair said, "Recite the lesson."

We recited it "by heart," from one mark which was made
in the book with the nail to the next mark. M. Poulain had
brought with him the grammar of Noël and Chapsal, memorable to more than one generation of Russian boys and girls;
a book of French dialogues; a history of the world, in one
volume; and a universal geography, also in one volume. We
had to commit to memory the grammar, the dialogues, the
history, and the geography.

The grammar, with its well-known sentences, "What is
grammar?" "The art of speaking and writing correctly," went
all right. But the history book, unfortunately, had a preface,
which contained an enumeration of all the advantages which
can be derived from a knowledge of history. Things went on
smoothly enough with the first sentences. We recited: "The
prince finds in it magnanimous examples for governing his subjects; the military commander learns from it the noble art of
warfare." But the moment we came to law all went wrong.
"The jurisconsult meets in it"—but what the learned lawyer
meets in history we never came to know. That terrible word
"jurisconsult" spoiled all the game. As soon as we reached it
we stopped.

"On your knees, *gros pouff!*" exclaimed Poulain. (That was
for me.) "On your knees, *grand dada!*" (That was for my
brother.) And there we knelt, shedding tears and vainly en-
deavoring to learn all about the jurisconsult.

It cost us many pains, that preface! We were already learning all about the Romans, and used to put our sticks in Uliána's
scales when she was weighing rice, "just like Brennus;" we

jumped from our table and other precipices for the salvation of our country, in imitation of Curtius; but M. Poulain would still from time to time return to the preface, and again put us on our knees for that very same jurisconsult. Was it strange that later on both my brother and I should entertain an undisguised contempt for jurisprudence?

I do not know what would have happened with geography if Monsieur Poulain's book had had a preface. But happily the first twenty pages of the book had been torn away (Serge Zagóskin, I suppose, rendered us that notable service), and so our lessons commenced with the twenty-first page, which began, "of the rivers which water France."

It must be confessed that things did not always end with kneeling. There was in the class-room a birch rod, and Poulain resorted to it when there was no hope of progress with the preface or with some dialogue on virtue and propriety; but one day sister Hélène, who by this time had left the Catherine Institut des Demoiselles, and now occupied a room underneath ours, hearing our cries, rushed, all in tears, into our father's study, and bitterly reproached him with having handed us over to our stepmother, who had abandoned us to "a retired French drummer." "Of course," she cried, "there is no one to take their part, but I cannot see my brothers being treated in this way by a drummer!"

Taken thus unprepared, our father could not make a stand. He began to scold Hélène, but ended by approving her devotion to her brothers. Thereafter the birch rod was reserved for teaching the rules of propriety to the setter, Trésor.

No sooner had M. Poulain discharged himself of his heavy educational duties than he became quite another man,—a lively comrade instead of a gruesome teacher. After lunch he took us out for a walk, and there was no end to his tales: we chattered like birds. Though we never went with him beyond the first pages of syntax, we soon learned, nevertheless, "to speak correctly;" we used to *think* in French; and when he had dictated to us half through a book of mythology, correcting our faults by the book, without ever trying to explain to us why a word must be written in a particular way, we had learned "to write correctly."

After dinner we had our lesson with the Russian teacher, a

student of the faculty of law in the Moscow University. He taught us all "Russian" subjects,—grammar, arithmetic, history, and so on. But in those years serious teaching had not yet begun. In the meantime he dictated to us every day a page of history, and in that practical way we quickly learned to write Russian quite correctly.

Our best time was on Sundays, when all the family, with the exception of us children, went to dine with Madame la Générale Timoféev. It would also happen occasionally that both M. Poulain and N. P. Smirnóv would be allowed to leave the house, and when this occurred we were placed under the care of Uliána. After a hurriedly eaten dinner we hastened to the great hall, to which the younger housemaids soon repaired. All sorts of games were started,—blind man, vulture and chickens, and so on; and then, all of a sudden, Tíkhon, the Jack-of-all-trades, would appear with a violin. Dancing began; not that measured and tiresome dancing, under the direction of a French dancing-master "on india-rubber legs," which made part of our education, but free dancing which was not a lesson, and in which a score of couples turned round any way; and this was only preparatory to the still more animated and rather wild Cossack dance. Tíkhon would then hand the violin to one of the older men, and would begin to perform with his legs such wonderful feats that the doors leading to the hall would soon be filled by the cooks and even the coachmen, who came to see the dance so dear to the Russian heart.

About nine o'clock the big carriage was sent to fetch the family home. Tíkhon, brush in hand, crawled on the floor, to make it shine with its virgin glance, and perfect order was restored in the house. And if, next morning, we two had been submitted to the most severe cross-examination, not a word would have been dropped concerning the previous evening's amusements. We never would have betrayed any one of the servants, nor would they have betrayed us. One Sunday, my brother and I, playing alone in the wide hall, ran against a bracket which supported a costly lamp. The lamp was broken to pieces. Immediately a council was held by the servants. No one scolded us; but it was decided that early next morning Tíkhon should at his risk and peril slip out of the house, and run to the Smiths' Bridge in order to buy another lamp of the same pattern. It cost fifteen rubles,—an enormous sum for the servants; but it was bought, and we never heard a word of reproach about it.

When I think of it now, and all these scenes come back to my memory, I remember that we never heard coarse language in any of the games, nor saw in the dances anything like the kind of dancing which children are now taken to admire in the theaters. In the servants' house, among themselves, they assuredly used coarse expressions; but we were children, —*her* children,—and that protected us from anything of the sort.

In those days children were not bewildered by a profusion of toys, as they are now. We had almost none, and were thus compelled to rely upon our own inventiveness. Besides, we both had early acquired a taste for the theater. The inferior carnival theaters, with the thieving and fighting shows, produced no lasting impression upon us: we ourselves played enough at robbers and soldiers. But the great star of the ballet, Fanny Elssler, came to Moscow, and we saw her. When father took a box in the theater, he always secured one of the best, and paid for it well; but then he insisted that all the members of the family should enjoy it to its full value. Small though I was at that time, Fanny Elssler left upon me the impression of a being so full of grace, so light, and so artistic in all her movements that ever since I have been unable to feel the slightest interest in a dance which belongs more to the domain of gymnastics than to the domain of art.

Of course, the ballet that we saw—Gitana, the Spanish Gypsy—had to be repeated at home; its substance, not the dances. We had a ready-made stage, as the doorway which led from our bedroom into the class-room had a curtain instead of a door. A few chairs put in a half-circle in front of the curtain, with an easy-chair for M. Poulain, became the hall and the imperial lodge, and an audience could easily be mustered with the Russian teacher, Uliána, and a couple of maids from the servants' rooms.

Two scenes of the ballet had to be represented by some means or other: the one where the little Gitana is brought by the gypsies into their camp in a wheelbarrow, and that in which Gitana makes her first appearance on the stage, descending from a hill and crossing a bridge over a brook which reflects her image. The audience burst into frantic applause at this point, and the cheers were evidently called forth—so we thought, at least—by the reflection in the brook.

We found our Gitana in one of the youngest girls in the maid-servants' room. Her rather shabby blue cotton dress was no obstacle to personifying Fanny Elssler. An overturned chair, pushed along by its legs, head downwards, was an acceptable substitute for the wheelbarrow. But the brook! Two chairs and the long ironing-board of Andréi, the tailor, made the bridge, and a piece of blue cotton made the brook. The image in the brook, however, would not appear full size, do what we might with M. Poulain's little shaving-glass. After many unsuccessful endeavors we had to give it up, but we bribed Uliána to behave as if she saw the image, and to applaud loudly at this passage, so that finally we began to believe that perhaps something of it could be seen.

Racine's *Phèdre*, or at least the last act of it, also went off nicely; that is, Sásha recited the melodious verses beautifully,—

A peine nous sortions des portes de Trézène;

and I sat absolutely motionless and unconcerned during the whole length of the tragic monologue intended to apprise me of the death of my son, down to the place where, according to the book, I had to exclaim, "O, dieux!"

But whatsoever we might impersonate, all our performances invariably ended with hell. All candles save one were put out, and this one was placed behind a transparent paper to imitate flames, while my brother and I, concealed from view, howled in the most appalling way as the condemned. Uliána, who did not like to have any allusion to the Evil One made at bedtime, looked horrified; but I ask myself now whether this extremely concrete representation of hell, with a candle and a sheet of paper, did not contribute to free us both at an early age from the fear of eternal fire. Our conception of it was too realistic to resist skepticism.

I must have been very much of a child when I saw the great Moscow actors: Schépkin, Sadóvsky, and Shúmsky, in Gogol's *Revisór* and another comedy; still, I remember not only the salient scenes of the two plays, but even the forms and expressions of these great actors of the realistic school which is now so admirably represented by Duse. I remembered them so well that when I saw the same plays given at St. Petersburg, by actors belonging to the French declamatory school, I found no pleasure in their acting, always comparing them with Schépkin and Sadóvsky, by whom my taste in dramatic art was settled.

This makes me think that parents who wish to develop artistic taste in their children ought to take them occasionally to really well-acted, good plays, instead of feeding them on a profusion of so-called "children's pantomimes."

V

When I was in my eighth year, the next step in my career was taken, in a quite unforeseen way. I do not know exactly on what occasion it happened, but probably it was on the twenty-fifth anniversary of Nicholas I.'s accession, when great festivities were arranged for at Moscow. The imperial family were coming to the old capital, and the Moscow nobility intended to celebrate this event by a fancy-dress ball, in which children were to play an important part. It was agreed that the whole motley crowd of nationalities of which the population of the Russian Empire is composed should be represented at this ball to greet the monarch. Great preparations went on in our house, as well as in all the houses of our neighborhood. Some sort of remarkable Russian costume was made for our stepmother. Our father, being a military man, had to appear, of course, in his uniform; but those of our relatives who were not in the military service were as busy with their Russian, Greek, Caucasian, and Mongolian costumes as the ladies themselves. When the Moscow nobility gives a ball to the imperial family, it must be something extraordinary. As for my brother Alexander and myself, we were considered too young to take part in so important a ceremonial.

And yet, after all, I did take part in it. Our mother was an intimate friend of Madame Nazímova, the wife of the general who was governor of Wílno when the emancipation of the serfs began to be spoken of. Madame Nazímova, who was a very beautiful woman, was expected to be present at the ball with her child, about ten years old, and to wear some wonderfully beautiful costume of a Persian princess, in harmony with which the costume of a young Persian prince, exceedingly rich, with a belt covered with jewels, was made ready for her son. But the boy fell ill just before the ball, and Madame Nazímova thought that one of the children of her best friend would be the best substitute for her own child. Alexander and I were taken to her house to try on the costume. It proved to be too short for Alexander, who was much taller than I, but it fitted me exactly, and therefore it was decided that I should impersonate the Persian prince.

The immense hall of the house of the Moscow nobility was crowded with guests. Each of the children received a standard bearing at its top the arms of one of the sixty provinces of the Russian Empire. I had an eagle floating over a blue sea, which represented, as I learned later on, the arms of the government of Astrakhan, on the Caspian Sea. We were then ranged at the back of the great hall, and slowly marched in two rows toward the raised platform upon which the Emperor and his family stood. As we reached it we marched right and left, and thus stood aligned in one row before the platform. At a given signal all standards were lowered before the Emperor. The apotheosis of autocracy was made most impressive: Nicholas was enchanted. All provinces of the empire worshiped the supreme ruler. Then we children slowly retired to the rear of the hall.

But here some confusion occurred. Chamberlains in their gold-embroidered uniforms were running about, and I was taken out of the ranks; my uncle, Prince Gagárin, dressed as a Tungus (I was dizzy with admiration of his fine leather coat, his bow, and his quiver full of arrows), lifted me up in his arms, and planted me on the imperial platform.

Whether it was because I was the tiniest in the row of boys, or that my round face, framed in curls, looked funny under the high Astrakhan fur bonnet I wore, I know not, but Nicholas wanted to have me on the platform; and there I stood amidst generals and ladies looking down upon me with curiosity. I was told later on that Nicholas I., who was always fond of barrack jokes, took me by the arm, and, leading me to Marie

Alexándrovna (the wife of the heir to the throne), who was then expecting her third child, said in his military way, "That is the sort of boy you must bring me,"—a joke which made her blush deeply. I well remember, at any rate, Nicholas asking me whether I would have sweets; but I replied that I should like to have some of those tiny biscuits which were served with tea (we were never over-fed at home), and he called a waiter and emptied a full tray into my tall bonnet. "I will take them to Sásha," I said to him.

However, the soldier-like brother of Nicholas, Michael, who had the reputation of being a wit, managed to make me cry. "When you are a good boy," he said, "they treat you so," and he passed his big hand over my face downwards; "but when you are naughty, they treat you so," and he passed the hand upwards, rubbing my nose, which already had a marked tendency toward growing in that direction. Tears, which I vainly tried to stop, came into my eyes. The ladies at once took my part, and the good-hearted Marie Alexándrovna took me under her protection. She set me by her side, in a high velvet chair with a gilded back, and our people told me afterward that I very soon put my head in her lap and went to sleep. She did not leave her chair during the whole time the ball was going on.

I remember also that, as we were waiting in the entrance-hall for our carriage, our relatives petted and kissed me, saying, "Pétia, you have been made a page;" but I answered, "I am not a page. I will go home," and was very anxious about my bonnet which contained the pretty little biscuits that I was taking home for Sásha.

I do not know whether Sásha got many of those biscuits, but I recollect what a hug he gave me when he was told about my anxiety concerning the bonnet.

To be inscribed as a candidate for the Corps of Pages was then a great favor, which Nicholas seldom bestowed on the Moscow nobility. My father was delighted, and already dreamed of a brilliant court career for his son. My stepmother, every time she told the story, never failed to add, "It is all because I gave him my blessing before he went to the ball."

Madame Nazímova was delighted, too, and insisted upon having her portrait painted in the costume in which she looked so beautiful, with me standing at her side.

My brother Alexander's fate, also, was decided next year. The jubilee of the Izmáilovsk regiment, to which my father had belonged in his youth, was celebrated about this time at St. Petersburg. One night, while all the household was plunged in deep sleep, a three-horse carriage, ringing with the bells attached to the harnesses, stopped at our gate. A man jumped out of it, loudly shouting, "Open! An ordinance from his Majesty the Emperor."

One can easily imagine the terror which this nocturnal visit spread in our house. My father, trembling, went down to his study. "Court-martial, degradation as a soldier," were words which rang then in the ears of every military man; it was a terrible epoch. But Nicholas simply wanted to have the names of the sons of all the officers who had once belonged to the regiment, in order to send the boys to military schools, if that had not yet been done. A special messenger had been dispatched for that purpose from St. Petersburg to Moscow, and was now calling day and night at the houses of the ex-Izmáilovsk officers.

With a shaking hand my father wrote that his eldest son, Nicholas, was already in the first corps of cadets at Moscow; that his youngest son, Peter, was a candidate for the Corps of Pages; and that there remained only his second son, Alexander, who had not yet entered the military career. A few weeks later came a paper informing father of the "monarch's favor." Alexander was ordered to enter a corps of cadets in Orel, a small provincial town. It cost my father a deal of trouble and a large sum of money to get Alexander sent to a corps of cadets at Moscow. This new "favor" was obtained only in consideration of the fact that our elder brother was in that corps.

And thus, owing to the will of Nicholas I., we had both to receive a military education, though, before we were many years older, we simply hated the military career for its absurdity. But Nicholas was watchful that none of the sons of the nobility should embrace any other profession than the military one, unless they were of infirm health; and so we had all three to be officers, to the great satisfaction of my father.

VI

Wealth was measured in those times by the number of "souls" that a landed proprietor owned. So many "souls" meant so many male serfs: women did not count. My father, who owned nearly twelve hundred souls, in three different provinces, and who had, in addition to his peasants' holdings, large tracts of land which were cultivated by these peasants, was accounted a rich man. He lived up to his reputation, which meant that his house was open to any number of visitors, and that he kept a very large household.

We were a family of eight, occasionally of ten or twelve; but fifty servants at Moscow, and half as many more in the country, were considered not one too many. Four coachmen to attend a dozen horses, three cooks for the masters and two more for the servants, a dozen men to wait upon us at dinnertime (one man, plate in hand, standing behind each person seated at the table), and girls innumerable in the maid-servants' room,—how could any one do with less than this?

Besides, the ambition of every landed proprietor was that everything required for his household should be made at home, by his own men.

"How nicely your piano is always tuned! I suppose Herr Schimmel must be your tuner?" perhaps a visitor would remark.

To be able to answer, "I have my own piano-tuner," was in those times the correct thing.

"What beautiful pastry!" the guests would exclaim, when a work of art, composed of ices and pastry, appeared toward the end of the dinner. "Confess, prince, that it comes from Tremblé" (the fashionable pastry-cook).

"It is made by my own confectioner, a pupil of Tremblé, whom I have allowed to show what he can do," was a reply which elicited general admiration.

To have embroideries, harnesses, furniture,—in fact, everything,—made by one's own men was the ideal of the rich and respected landed proprietor. As soon as the children of the servants attained the age of ten, they were sent as apprentices

to the fashionable shops, where they were obliged to spend
five or seven years chiefly in sweeping, in receiving an incredible number of thrashings, and in running about town on er-
rands of all sorts. I must own that few of them became masters
of their respective arts. The tailors and shoemakers were found
only skillful enough to make clothes or shoes for the servants,
and when a really good pastry was required for a dinner-party
it was ordered at Tremblé's, while our own confectioner was
beating the drum in the band.

That band was another of my father's ambitions, and almost
every one of his male servants, in addition to other accomplish-
ments, was a bass-viol or a clarinet in the band. Makár, the
piano-tuner, alias under-butler, was also a flutist; Andréi, the
tailor, played the French horn; the confectioner was first put
to beat the drum, but he misused his instrument to such a
deafening degree that a tremendous trumpet was bought for
him, in the hope that his lungs would not have the power to
make the same noise as his hands; when, however, this last
hope had to be abandoned, he was sent to be a soldier. As
to "spotted Tíkhon," in addition to his numerous functions in
the household as lamp-cleaner, floor-polisher, and footman, he
rendered himself useful in the band,—to-day as a trombone,
to-morrow as a bassoon, and occasionally as second violin.

The two first violins were the only exceptions to the rule:
they were "violins," and nothing else. My father had bought
them, with their large families, for a handsome sum of money,
from his sisters (he never bought serfs from nor sold them to
strangers). In the evenings when he was not at his club, or
when there was a dinner or an evening party at our house, the
band of twelve to fifteen musicians was summoned. They
played very nicely, and were in great demand for dancing-
parties in the neighborhood; still more when we were in the
country. This was, of course, a constant source of gratification
to my father, whose permission had to be asked to get the
assistance of his band.

Nothing, indeed, gave him more pleasure than to be asked
for help, either in the way mentioned or in any other: for instance, to obtain free education for a boy, or to save somebody
from a punishment inflicted upon him by a law court. Although he was liable to fall into fits of rage, he was undoubt-

edly possessed of a natural instinct toward leniency, and when his patronage was requested he would write scores of letters in all possible directions, to all sorts of persons of high standing, in favor of his protégé. At such times, his mail, which was always heavy, would be swollen by half a dozen special letters, written in a most original, semi-official, and semi-humorous style; each of them sealed, of course, with his arms, in a big square envelope, which rattled like a baby-rattle on account of the quantity of sand it contained,—the use of blotting-paper being then unknown. The more difficult the case, the more energy he would display, until he secured the favor he asked for his protégé, whom in many cases he never saw.

My father liked to have plenty of guests in his house. Our dinner-hour was four, and at seven the family gathered round the *samovar* (tea-urn) for tea. Every one belonging to our circle could drop in at that hour, and from the time my sister Hélène was again with us there was no lack of visitors, old and young, who took advantage of the privilege. When the windows facing the street showed bright light inside, that was enough to let people know that the family was at home and friends would be welcome.

Nearly every night we had visitors. The green tables were opened in the hall for the card-players, while the ladies and the young people stayed in the reception-room or around Hélène's piano. When the ladies had gone, card-playing continued sometimes till the small hours of the morning, and considerable sums of money changed hands among the players. Father invariably lost. But the real danger for him was not at home: it was at the English Club, where the stakes were much higher than in private houses, and especially when he was induced to join a party of "very respectable" gentlemen, in one of the "most respectable" houses of the Old Equerries' Quarter, where gambling went on all night. On an occasion of this kind his losses were sure to be heavy.

Dancing-parties were not infrequent, to say nothing of a couple of obligatory balls every winter. Father's way, in such cases, was to have everything done in a good style, whatever the expense. But at the same time such niggardliness was practiced in our house in daily life that if I were to recount it, I should be accused of exaggeration. It is said of a family of pre-

tenders to the throne of France, renowned for their truly regal
hunting-parties, that in their every-day life even the tallow
candles are minutely counted. The same sort of miserly economy ruled in our house with regard to everything; so much so
that when we, the children of the house, grew up, we detested
all saving and counting. However, in the Old Equerries' Quarter such a mode of life only raised my father in public esteem.
"The old prince," it was said, "seems to be sharp over money
at home; but he knows how a nobleman ought to live."

In our quiet and clean lanes that was the kind of life which
was most in respect. One of our neighbors, General D——, kept
his house up in very grand style; and yet the most comical
scenes took place every morning between him and his cook.
Breakfast over, the old general, smoking his pipe, would himself order the dinner.

"Well, my boy," he would say to the cook, who appeared
in snow-white attire, "to-day we shall not be many; only a
couple of guests. You will make us a soup, you know, with
some spring delicacies,—green peas, French beans, and so on.
You have not given us any as yet, and madam, you know,
likes a good French spring soup."

"Yes, sir."

"Then, anything you like as an entrée."

"Yes, sir."

"Of course, asparagus is not yet in season, but I saw yesterday such nice bundles of it in the shops."

"Yes, sir; eight shillings the bundle."

"Quite right! Then, we are sick of your roasted chickens and
turkeys; you ought to get something for a change."

"Some venison, sir?"

"Yes, yes; anything for a change."

And when the six courses of the dinner had been decided
on, the old general would ask, "Now, how much shall I give
you for to-day's expenses? Six shillings will do, I suppose?"

"One pound, sir."

"What nonsense, my boy! Here are six shillings; I assure you
that's quite enough."

"Eight shillings for asparagus, five for the vegetables."

"Now, look here, my dear boy, be reasonable. I'll go as high
as seven-and-six, and you must be economical."

And the bargaining would go on thus for half an hour, until the two would agree upon fourteen shillings and sixpence, with the understanding that the morrow's dinner should not cost more than three shillings. Whereupon the general, quite happy at having made such a good bargain, would take his sledge, make a round of the fashionable shops, and return quite radiant, bringing for his wife a bottle of exquisite perfume, for which he had paid a fancy price in a French shop, and announcing to his only daughter that a new velvet mantle— "something very simple" and very costly—would be sent for her to try on that afternoon.

All our relatives, who were numerous on my father's side, lived exactly in the same way; and if a new spirit occasionally made its appearance, it usually took the form of some religious passion. Thus, a Prince Gagárin joined the Jesuit order, again to the scandal of "all Moscow;" another young prince entered a monastery, while several older ladies became fanatic devotees.

There was a single exception. One of our nearest relatives, Prince Drútskoy, had spent his youth at St. Petersburg as an officer of the guard. He took no interest in keeping his own tailors and cabinet-makers, for his house was furnished in a grand modern style, and his wearing apparel was all made in the best St. Petersburg shops. Gambling was not his propensity, —he played cards only when in company with ladies; but his weak point was his dinner-table, upon which he spent incredible sums of money.

Lent and Easter were his chief epochs of extravagance. When the Great Lent came, and it would not have been proper to eat meat, cream, or butter, he seized the opportunity to invent all sorts of delicacies in the way of fish. The best shops of the two capitals were ransacked for that purpose; special emissaries were dispatched from his estate to the mouth of the Vólga, to bring back on post-horses (there was no railway at that time) a sturgeon of great size or some extraordinarily cured fish. And when Easter came, there was no end to his inventions.

Easter, in Russia, is the most venerated and also the gayest of the yearly festivals. It is the festival of spring. The immense heaps of snow which have been lying during the winter along the streets rapidly thaw, and roaring streams run down the streets; not like a thief who creeps in by insensible degrees, but frankly and openly spring comes,—every day bringing with it a change in the state of the snow and the progress of the buds on the trees; the night frosts only keep the thaw within reasonable bounds. The last week of the Great Lent, Passion Week, was kept in Moscow, in my childhood, with extreme solemnity; it was a time of general mourning, and crowds of people went to the churches to listen to the impressive reading of those passages of the Gospels which relate the sufferings of the Christ. Not only were meat, eggs, and butter not eaten, but even fish was refused; some of the most rigorous taking no food at all on Good Friday. The more striking was the contrast when Easter came.

On Saturday every one attended the night service, which began in a mournful way. Then, suddenly, at midnight, the resurrection news was announced. All the churches were at once illuminated, and gay peals of bells resounded from hundreds of bell-towers. General rejoicing began. All the people kissed one another thrice on the cheeks, repeating the resurrection words, and the churches, now flooded with light, shone with the gay toilettes of the ladies. The poorest woman had a new dress; if she had only one new dress a year, she would get it for that night.

At the same time, Easter was, and is still, the signal for a real debauch in eating. Special Easter cream cheeses (*páskha*) and Easter bread (*kúlích*) are prepared; and every one, no matter how poor he or she may be, must have be it only a small páskha and a small kúlích, with at least one egg painted red, to be consecrated in the church, and to be used afterward to break the Lent. With most old Russians, eating began at night, after a short Easter mass, immediately after the consecrated food had been brought from church; but in the houses of the nobility the ceremony was postponed till Sunday morning, when a table was covered with all sorts of viands, cheeses and pastry, and all the servants came to exchange with their masters three kisses and a red-painted egg. Throughout Easter week a table spread with Easter food stood in the great hall, and every visitor was invited to partake.

On this occasion Prince Drútskoy surpassed himself.

Whether he was at St. Petersburg or at Moscow, messengers brought to his house, from his estate, a specially prepared cream cheese for the páskha, and his cook managed to make out of it a piece of artistic confectionery. Other messengers were dispatched to the province of Nóvgorod to get a bear's ham, which was cured for the prince's Easter table. And while the princess, with her two daughters, visited the most austere monasteries, in which the night service would last three or four hours in succession, and spent all Passion Week in the most mournful condition of mind, eating only a piece of dry bread between the visits she paid to Russian, Roman, and Protestant preachers, her husband made every morning the tour of the well-known Milútin shops at St. Petersburg, where all possible delicacies are brought from the ends of the earth. There he used to select the most extravagant dainties for his Easter table. Hundreds of visitors came to his house, and were asked "just to taste" this or that extraordinary thing.

The end of it was that the prince managed literally to eat up a considerable fortune. His richly furnished house and beautiful estate were sold, and when he and his wife were old they had nothing left, not even a home, and were compelled to live with their children.

No wonder that when the emancipation of the serfs came, nearly all these families of the Old Equerries' Quarter were ruined. But I must not anticipate events.

VII

To maintain such numbers of servants as were kept in our house would have been simply ruinous, if all provisions had to be bought at Moscow; but in those times of serfdom things were managed very simply. When winter came, father sat at his table and wrote the following:—

"To the manager of my estate, Nikólskoe, situated in the government of Kalúga, district of Meschóvsk, on the river Siréna, from the Prince Alexéi Petróvich Kropótkin, Colonel and Commander of various orders.

"On receipt of this, and as soon as winter communication is established, thou art ordered to send to my house, situated in the city of Moscow, twenty-five peasant-sledges, drawn by two horses each, one horse from each house, and one sledge and one man from each second house, and to load them with [so many] quarters of oats, [so many] of wheat, and [so many] of rye, as also with all the poultry and geese and ducks, well frozen, which have to be killed this winter, well packed and accompanied by a complete list, under the supervision of a well-chosen man;" and so it went on for a couple of pages, till the next full stop was reached. After this there followed an enumeration of the penalties which would be inflicted in case the provisions should not reach the house situated in such a street, number so and so, in due time and in good condition.

Some time before Christmas the twenty-five peasant-sledges really entered our gates, and covered the surface of the wide yard.

"Frol!" shouted my father, as soon as the report of this great event reached him. "Kiriúshka! Yegórka! Where are they? Everything will be stolen! Frol, go and receive the oats! Uliána, go and receive the poultry! Kiriúshka, call the princess!"

All the household was in commotion, the servants running wildly in every direction, from the hall to the yard, and from the yard to the hall, but chiefly to the maid-servants' room, to communicate there the Nikólskoe news: "Pásha is going to marry after Christmas. Aunt Anna has surrendered her soul to God," and so on. Letters had also come from the country, and very soon one of the maids would steal upstairs into my room.

"Are you alone? The teacher is not in?"

"No, he is at the university."

"Well, then, be kind and read me this letter from mother."

And I would read to her the naïve letter, which always began with the words, "Father and mother send you their blessings for ages not to be broken." After this came the news: "Aunt Eupraxie lies ill, all her bones aching; and your cousin is not yet married, but hopes to be after Easter; and Aunt Stepanída's cow died on All Saints' day." Following the news came the greetings, two pages of them: "Brother Paul sends you his greetings, and the sisters Mary and Dária send their greetings, and then Uncle Dmítri sends his many greetings," and so on. However, notwithstanding the monotony of the enumeration, each name awakened some remarks: "Then she

is still alive, poor soul, if she sends her greetings; it is nine years
since she has lain motionless." Or, "Oh, he has not forgotten
me; he must be back, then, for Christmas; such a nice boy.
You will write me a letter, won't you? and I must not forget
him then." I promised, of course, and when the time came I
wrote a letter in exactly the same style.

When the sledges had been unloaded, the hall filled with
peasants. They had put on their best coats over their sheepskins, and waited until father should call them into his room
to have a talk about the snow and the prospects of the next
crops. They hardly dared to walk in their heavy boots on the
polished floor. A few ventured to sit down on the edge of an
oak bench; they emphatically refused to make use of chairs.
So they waited for hours, looking with alarm upon every one
who entered father's room or issued from it.

Some time later on, usually next morning, one of the servants would run slyly upstairs to the class-room.

"Are you alone?"

"Yes."

"Then go quickly to the hall. The peasants want to see you;
something from your nurse."

When I went down to the hall, one of the peasants would
give me a little bundle containing perhaps a few rye cakes,
half a dozen hard-boiled eggs, and some apples, tied in a
motley colored cotton kerchief. "Take that: it is your nurse,
Vasilísa, who sends it to you. Look if the apples are not frozen.
I hope not: I kept them all the journey on my breast. Such a
fearful frost we had." And the broad, bearded face, covered
with frost-bites, would smile radiantly, showing two rows of
beautiful white teeth from beneath quite a forest of hair.

"And this is for your brother, from his nurse Anna," another
peasant would say, handing me a similar bundle. "'Poor boy,'
she says, 'he can never have enough at school.'"

Blushing and not knowing what to say, I would murmur at
last, "Tell Vasilísa that I kiss her, and Anna too, for my
brother." At which all faces would become still more radiant.

"Yes, I will, to be sure."

Then Kiríla, who kept watch at father's door, would whisper
suddenly, "Run quickly upstairs; your father may come out in
a moment. Don't forget the kerchief; they want to take it back."

As I carefully folded the worn kerchief, I most passionately desired to send Vasilísa something. But I had nothing to send, not even a toy, and we never had pocket money.

Our best time, of course, was in the country. As soon as Easter and Whitsuntide had passed, all our thoughts were directed toward Nikólskoe. However, time went on,—the lilacs must be past blooming at Nikólskoe,—and father had still thousands of affairs to keep him in town. At last, five or six peasant-carts entered our yard: they came to take all sorts of things which had to be sent to the country-house. The great old coach and the other coaches in which we were going to make the journey were taken out and inspected once more. The boxes began to be packed. Our lessons made slow progress; at every moment we interrupted our teachers, asking whether this or that book should be taken with us, and long before all others we began packing our books, our slates, and the toys that we ourselves had made.

Everything was ready: the peasant-carts stood heavily loaded with furniture for the country-house, boxes containing the kitchen utensils, and almost countless empty glass jars which were to be brought back in the autumn filled with all kinds of preserves. The peasants waited every morning for hours in the hall; but the order for leaving did not come. Father continued to write all the morning in his room, and disappeared at night. Finally, our stepmother interfered, her maid having ventured to report that the peasants were very anxious to return, as haymaking was near.

Next afternoon, Frol, the major-domo, and Michael Aléev, the first violin, were called into father's room. A sack containing the "food money"—that is, a few coppers a day—for each of the forty or fifty souls who were to accompany the household to Nikólskoe, was handed to Frol, with a list. All were enumerated in that list: the band in full; then the cooks and the under-cooks, the laundresses, the under-laundress who was blessed with a family of six mites, "Polka Squinting," "Domna the Big One," "Domna the Small One," and the rest of them.

The first violin received an "order of march." I knew it well, because father, seeing that he never would be ready, had called me to copy it into the book in which he used to copy all "out-going papers:"—

"To my house servant, Michael Aléev, from Prince Alexéi Petróvich Kropótkin, Colonel and Commander.

"Thou art ordered, on May 29th, at six A. M., to march out with my loads, from the city of Moscow, for my estate, situated in the government of Kalúga, district of Meschóvsk, on the river Siréna, representing a distance of one hundred and sixty miles from this house; to look after the good conduct of the men entrusted to thee, and if any one of them proves to be guilty of misconduct or of drunkenness or of insubordination, to bring the said man before the commander of the garrison detachment of the separate corps of the interior garrisons, with the inclosed circular letter, and to ask that he may be punished by flogging [the first violin knew who was meant], as an example to the others.

"Thou art ordered, moreover, to look especially after the integrity of the goods entrusted to thy care, and to march according to the following order: First day, stop at village So-and-So, to feed the horses; second day, spend the night at the town of Podólsk;" and so on for all the seven or eight days that the journey would last.

Next day, at ten instead of at six,—punctuality is not a Russian virtue ("Thank God, we are not Germans," true Russians used to say),—the carts left the house. The servants had to make the journey on foot; only the children were accommodated with a seat in a bath-tub or basket, on the top of a loaded cart, and some of the women might find an occasional resting-place on the rim of a cart. The others had to walk all the hundred and sixty miles. As long as they were marching through Moscow, discipline was maintained: it was peremptorily forbidden to wear top-boots, or to pass a belt over the coat. But when they were on the road, and we overtook them a couple of days later, and especially when it was known that father would stay a few days longer at Moscow, the men and the women—dressed in all sorts of impossible coats, belted with cotton handkerchiefs, burned by the sun or dripping under the rain, and helping themselves along with sticks cut in the woods —certainly looked more like a wandering band of gypsies than the household of a wealthy landowner. Similar peregrinations were made by every household in those times, and when we saw a file of servants marching along one of our streets, we at once knew that the Apúkhtins or the Priánishnikovs were migrating.

The carts were gone, yet the family did not move. All of us were sick of waiting; but father still continued to write interminable orders to the managers of his estates, and I copied them diligently into the big "outgoing book." At last the order to start was given. We were called downstairs. My father read aloud the order of march, addressed to "the Princess Kropótkin, wife of Prince Alexéi Petróvich Kropótkin, Colonel and Commander," in which the halting-places during the five days' journey were duly enumerated. True, the order was written for May 30, and the departure was fixed for nine A. M., though May was gone, and the departure took place in the afternoon: this upset all calculations. But, as is usual in military marching-orders, this circumstance had been foreseen, and was provided for in the following paragraph:—

"If, however, contrary to expectation, the departure of your highness does not take place at the said day and hour, you are requested to act according to the best of your understanding, in order to bring the said journey to its best issue."

Then, all present, the family and the servants, sat down for a moment, signed themselves with the cross, and bade my father good-by. "I entreat you, Alexis, don't go to the club," our stepmother whispered to him. The great coach, drawn by four horses, with a postilion, stood at the door, with its little folding ladder to facilitate climbing in; the other coaches also were there. Our seats were enumerated in the marching-orders, but our stepmother had to exercise "the best of her understanding" even at that early stage of the proceedings, and we started to the great satisfaction of all.

The journey was an inexhaustible source of enjoyment for us children. The stages were short, and we stopped twice a day to feed the horses. As the ladies screamed at the slightest declivity of the road, it was found more convenient to alight each time the road went up or down hill, which it did continually, and we took advantage of this to have a peep into the woods by the roadside, or a run along some crystal brook. The beautifully kept highroad from Moscow to Warsaw, which we followed for some distance, was covered, moreover, with a variety of interesting objects: files of loaded carts, groups of pilgrims, and all sorts of people. Twice a day we stopped in big, animated villages, and after a good deal of bargaining about the prices to be charged for hay and oats, as well as for the samovárs, we dismounted at the gates of an inn. Cook Andréi bought a chicken and made the soup, while we ran in the meantime to the next wood, or examined the yard of the great inn.

At Máloiaroslávetz, where a battle was fought in 1812, when the Russian army vainly attempted to stop Napoleon in his retreat from Moscow, we usually spent the night. M. Poulain, who had been wounded in the Spanish campaign, knew, or pretended to know, everything about the battle at Máloiaroslávetz. He took us to the battlefield, and explained how the Russians tried to check Napoleon's advance, and how the Grande Armée crushed them and made its way through the Russian lines. He explained it as well as if he himself had taken part in the battle. Here the Cossacks attempted *un mouvement tournant,* but Davout, or some other marshal, routed them and pursued them just beyond these hills on the right. There the left wing of Napoleon crushed the Russian infantry, and here Napoleon himself, at the head of the Old Guard, charged Kutúzov's center, and covered himself and his Guard with undying glory.

We once took the old Kalúga route, and stopped at Tarútino; but here Poulain was much less eloquent. For it was at this place that Napoleon, who intended to retreat by a southern route, was compelled, after a bloody battle, to abandon that plan, and was forced to follow the Smolénsk route, which his army had laid waste during its march on Moscow. But still —so it appeared in Poulain's narrative—Napoleon was deceived by his marshals; otherwise he would have marched straight upon Kíev and Odéssa, and his eagles would have floated over the Black Sea.

Beyond Kalúga we had to cross for a stretch of five miles a beautiful pine forest, which remains connected in my memory with some of the happiest reminiscences of my childhood. The sand in that forest was as deep as in an African desert, and we went all the way on foot, while the horses, stopping every moment, slowly dragged the carriages in the sand. When I was in my teens, it was my delight to leave the family behind, and to walk the whole distance by myself. Immense red pines, centuries old, rose on every side, and not a sound reached the ear except the voices of the lofty trees. In a small ravine a fresh crystal spring murmured, and a passer-by had left in it, for the use of those who should come after him, a small funnel-shaped ladle, made of birch bark, with a split stick for a handle. Noiselessly a squirrel ran up a tree, and the underwood was as full of mysteries as were the trees. In that forest my first love of nature and my first dim perception of its incessant life were born.

Beyond the forest, and past the ferry which took us over the Ugrá, we left the highroad and entered narrow country lanes, where green ears of rye bent toward the coach, and the horses managed to bite mouthfuls of grass on either side of the way, as they ran, closely pressed to one another in the narrow, trenchlike road. At last we caught sight of the willows which marked the approach to our village, and all of a sudden we saw the elegant pale yellow bell-tower of the Nikólskoe church.

For the quiet life of the landlords of those times Nikólskoe was admirably suited. There was nothing in it of the luxury which is seen in richer estates; but an artistic hand was visible in the planning of the buildings and gardens, and in the general arrangement of things. Besides the main house, which father had recently built, there were, round a spacious and well-kept yard, several smaller houses, which, while they gave a greater degree of independence to their inhabitants, did not destroy the close intercourse of the family life. An immense "upper garden" was devoted to fruit trees, and through it the church was reached; the southern slope of the land, which led to the river, was entirely given up to a pleasure garden, where flower-beds were intermingled with alleys of lime-trees, lilacs, and acacias. From the balcony of the main house there was a beautiful view of the river, with the ruins of an old earthen fortress where the Russians offered a stubborn resistance during the Mongol invasion, and further on a great area of yellow grain-fields bordered on the horizon by woods.

In the early years of my childhood we occupied with

M. Poulain one of the separate houses entirely by ourselves; and after his method of education was softened by the intervention of our sister Hélène, we were on the best possible terms with him. Father was invariably absent from home in the summer, which he spent in military inspections, and our stepmother did not pay much attention to us, especially after her own child, Pauline, was born. We were thus always with M. Poulain, who thoroughly enjoyed the stay in the country, and let us enjoy it. The woods; the walks along the river; the climbing over the hills to the old fortress, which Poulain made alive for us as he told how it was defended by the Russians, and how it was captured by the Tartars; the little adventures, in one of which Poulain became our hero by saving Alexander from drowning; an occasional encounter with wolves,—there was no end of new and delightful impressions.

Large parties were organized, also, in which all the family took part, sometimes picking mushrooms in the woods, and afterward having tea in the midst of the forest, where a man a hundred years old lived alone with his little grandson, taking care of bees. At other times we went to one of father's villages where a big pond had been dug, in which golden carp were caught by the thousand,—part of them being taken for the landlord and the remainder being distributed among all the peasants. My former nurse lived in that village. Her family was one of the poorest; besides her husband, she had only a small boy to help her, and a girl, my foster-sister, who became later on a preacher and a "virgin" in the Nonconformist sect to which they belonged. There was no bound to her joy when I came to see her. Cream, eggs, apples, and honey were all that she could offer; but the way in which she offered them, in bright wooden plates, after having covered the table with a fine snow-white linen tablecloth of her own make (with the Russian Nonconformists absolute cleanliness is a matter of religion), and the fond words with which she addressed me, treating me as her own son, left the warmest feelings in my heart. I must say the same of the nurses of my elder brothers, Nicholas and Alexander, who belonged to prominent families of two other Nonconformist sects in Nikólskoe. Few know what treasuries of goodness can be found in the hearts of Russian peasants, even after centuries of the most cruel oppression, which might well have embittered them.

On stormy days M. Poulain had an abundance of tales to tell us, especially about the campaign in Spain. Over and over again we induced him to tell us how he was wounded in a battle, and every time he came to the point when he felt warm blood streaming into his boot, we jumped to kiss him and gave him all sorts of pet names.

Everything seemed to prepare us for the military career: the predilection of our father (the only toys that I remember his having bought for us were a rifle and a real sentry-box); the war tales of M. Poulain; nay, even the library which we had at our disposal. This library, which had once belonged to General Repnínsky, our mother's grandfather, a learned military man of the eighteenth century, consisted exclusively of books on military warfare, adorned with rich plates and beautifully bound in leather. It was our chief recreation, on wet days, to look over the plates of these books, representing the weapons of warfare since the times of the Hebrews, and giving plans of all the battles that had been fought since Alexander of Macedonia. These heavy books also offered excellent material for building out of them strong fortresses which would stand for some time the blows of a battering-ram, and the projectiles of an Archimedean catapult (which, however, persisted in sending stones into the windows, and was soon prohibited). Yet neither Alexander nor I became a military man. The literature of the sixties wiped out the teachings of our childhood.

M. Poulain's opinions about revolutions were those of the Orleanist *Illustration Française*, of which he received back numbers, and of which we knew all the woodcuts. For a long time I could not imagine a revolution otherwise than in the shape of Death riding on a horse, the red flag in one hand and a scythe in the other, mowing down men right and left. So it was pictured in the *Illustration*. But I now think that M. Poulain's dislike was limited to the uprising of 1848, for one of his tales about the Revolution of 1789 deeply impressed my mind.

The title of prince was used in our house with and without occasion. M. Poulain must have been shocked by it, for he began once to tell us what he knew of the great Revolution. I cannot now recall what he said, but one thing I remember, namely, that Count Mirabeau and other nobles one day renounced their titles, and that Count Mirabeau, to show his contempt for aristocratic pretensions, opened a shop decorated with a signboard which bore the inscription, "Mirabeau, tailor." (I tell the story as I had it from M. Poulain.) For a long time after that I worried myself thinking what trade I should take up so as to write, "Kropótkin, such and such a handicraft man." Later on, my Russian teacher, Nikolái Pávlovich Smirnóv, and the general republican tone of Russian literature influenced me in the same way; and when I began to write novels—that is, in my twelfth year—I adopted the signature P. Kropótkin, which I never have departed from, notwithstanding the remonstrances of my chiefs when I was in the military service.

VIII

In the autumn of 1852 my brother Alexander was sent to the corps of cadets, and from that time we saw each other only during the holidays and occasionally on Sundays. The corps of cadets was five miles from our house, and although we had a dozen horses, it always happened that when the time came to send a sledge to the corps there was no horse free for that purpose. My eldest brother, Nicholas, came home very seldom. The relative freedom which Alexander found at school, and especially the influence of two of his teachers in literature, developed his intellect rapidly, and later on I shall have ample occasion to speak of the beneficial influence that he exercised upon my own development. It is a great privilege to have had a loving, intelligent elder brother.

In the meantime I remained at home. I had to wait till my turn to enter the Corps of Pages should come, and that did not happen until I was nearly fifteen years of age. M. Poulain was dismissed, and a German tutor was engaged instead. He was one of those idealistic men who are not uncommon among Germans, but I remember him chiefly on account of the enthusiastic way in which he used to recite Schiller's poetry, accompanying it by a most naïve kind of acting that delighted me. He stayed with us only one winter.

The next winter I was sent to attend the classes at a Moscow gymnasium; and finally I remained with our Russian teacher, Smirnóv. We soon became friends, especially after my father took both of us for a journey to his Riazán estate. During this journey we indulged in all sorts of fun, and we used to invent humorous stories in connection with the men and the things that we saw; while the impression produced upon me by the hilly tracts we crossed added some new and fine touches to my growing love of nature. Under the impulse given me by Smirnóv, my literary tastes also began to grow, and during the years from 1854 to 1857 I had full opportunity to develop them. My teacher, who had by this time finished his studies at the university, obtained a small clerkship in a law court, and spent his mornings there. I was thus left to myself till dinner-time, and after having prepared my lessons and taken a walk, I had plenty of time to read, and especially to write. In the autumn, when my teacher returned to his office at Moscow, while we remained in the country, I was left again to myself, and though in continual intercourse with the family, and spending a good deal of time in playing with my little sister Pauline, I could in fact dispose of my time as I liked for reading and writing.

Serfdom was then in the last years of its existence. It is recent history,—it seems to be only of yesterday; and yet, even in Russia, few realize what serfdom was in reality. There is a dim conception that the conditions which it created were very bad; but those conditions, as they affected human beings bodily and mentally, are not generally understood. It is amazing, indeed, to see how quickly an institution and its social consequences are forgotten when the institution has ceased to exist, and with what rapidity men and things change. I will try to recall the conditions of serfdom by telling, not what I heard, but what I saw.

Uliána, the housekeeper, stands in the passage leading to father's room, and crosses herself; she dares neither to advance nor to retreat. At last, after having recited a prayer, she enters the room, and reports, in a hardly audible voice, that the store of tea is nearly at an end, that there are only twenty pounds of sugar left, and that the other provisions will soon be exhausted.

"Thieves, robbers!" shouts my father. "And you, you are in league with them!" His voice thunders throughout the house. Our stepmother leaves Uliána to face the storm. But father cries, "Frol, call the princess! Where is she?" And when she enters, he receives her with the same reproaches.

"You also are in league with this progeny of Ham; you are standing up for them;" and so on, for half an hour or more.

Then he commences to verify the accounts. At the same time, he thinks about the hay. Frol is sent to weigh what is left of that, and our stepmother is sent to be present during the weighing, while father calculates how much of it ought to be in the barn. A considerable quantity of hay appears to be missing, and Uliána cannot account for several pounds of such and such provisions. Father's voice becomes more and more menacing; Uliána is trembling; but it is the coachman who now enters the room, and is stormed at by his master. Father springs at him, strikes him, but he keeps repeating, "Your highness must have made a mistake."

Father repeats his calculations, and this time it appears that there is more hay in the barn than there ought to be. The shouting continues; he now reproaches the coachman with not having given the horses their daily rations in full; but the coachman calls on all the saints to witness that he gave the animals their due, and Frol invokes the Virgin to confirm the coachman's appeal.

But father will not be appeased. He calls in Makár, the piano-tuner and sub-butler, and reminds him of all his recent sins. He was drunk last week, and must have been drunk yesterday, for he broke half a dozen plates. In fact, the breaking of these plates was the real cause of all the disturbance: our stepmother had reported the fact to father in the morning, and that was why Uliána was received with more scolding than was usually the case, why the verification of the hay was undertaken, and why father now continues to shout that "this progeny of Ham" deserve all the punishments on earth.

Of a sudden there is a lull in the storm. My father takes his seat at the table and writes a note. "Take Makár with this note to the police station, and let a hundred lashes with the birch rod be given to him."

Terror and absolute muteness reign in the house.

The clock strikes four, and we all go down to dinner; but no one has any appetite, and the soup remains in the plates untouched. We are ten ˙at table, and behind each of us a violinist or a trombone-player stands, with a clean plate in his left hand; but Makár is not among them.

"Where is Makár?" our stepmother asks. "Call him in."

Makár does not appear, and the order is repeated. He enters at last, pale, with a distorted face, ashamed, his eyes cast down. Father looks into his plate, while our stepmother, seeing that no one has touched the soup, tries to encourage us.

"Don't you find, children," she says, "that the soup is delicious?"

Tears suffocate me, and immediately after dinner is over I run out, catch Makár in a dark passage, and try to kiss his hand; but he tears it away, and says, either as a reproach or as a question, "Let me alone; you, too, when you are grown up, will you not be just the same?"

"No, no, never!"

Yet father was not among the worst of landowners. On the contrary, the servants and the peasants considered him one of the best. What we saw in our house was going on everywhere, often in much more cruel forms. The flogging of the serfs was a regular part of the duties of the police and of the fire brigade.

A landowner once made the remark to another, "Why is it that the number of souls on your estate increases so slowly? You probably do not look after their marriages."

A few days later the general returned to his estate. He had a list of all the inhabitants of his village brought him, and picked out from it the names of the boys who had attained the age of eighteen, and the girls just past sixteen,—these are the legal ages for marriage in Russia. Then he wrote, "John to marry Anna, Paul to marry Paráshka," and so on with five couples. "The five weddings," he added, "must take place in ten days, the next Sunday but one."

A general cry of despair rose from the village. Women, young and old, wept in every house. Anna had hoped to marry Gregory; Paul's parents had already had a talk with the

Fedótovs about their girl, who would soon be of age. Moreover, it was the season for ploughing, not for weddings; and what wedding can be prepared in ten days? Dozens of peasants came to see the landowner; peasant women stood in groups at the back entrance of the estate, with pieces of fine linen for the landowner's spouse, to secure her intervention. All in vain. The master had said that the weddings should take place at such a date, and so it must be.

At the appointed time, the nuptial processions, in this case more like burial processions, went to the church. The women cried with loud voices, as they are wont to cry during burials. One of the house valets was sent to the church, to report to the master as soon as the wedding ceremonies were over; but soon he came running back, cap in hand, pale and distressed.

"Paráshka," he said, "makes a stand; she refuses to be married to Paul. Father" (that is, the priest) "asked her, 'Do you agree?' but she replied in a loud voice, 'No, I don't.' "

The landowner grew furious. "Go and tell that long-maned drunkard" (meaning the priest; the Russian clergy wear their hair long) "that if Paráshka is not married at once, I will report him as a drunkard to the archbishop. How dares he, clerical dirt, disobey me? Tell him he shall be sent to rot in a monastery, and I shall exile Paráshka's family to the steppes."

The valet transmitted the message. Paráshka's relatives and the priest surrounded the girl; her mother, weeping, fell on her knees before her, entreating her not to ruin the whole family. The girl continued to say "I won't," but in a weaker and weaker voice, then in a whisper, until at last she stood silent. The nuptial crown was put on her head; she made no resistance, and the valet ran full speed to the mansion to announce, "They are married."

Half an hour later, the small bells of the nuptial processions resounded at the gate of the mansion. The five couples alighted from the cars, crossed the yard, and entered the hall. The landlord received them, offering them glasses of wine, while the parents, standing behind the crying daughters, ordered them to bow to the earth before their lord.

Marriages by order were so common that amongst our servants, each time a young couple foresaw that they might be ordered to marry, although they had no mutual inclination for each other, they took the precaution of standing together as godfather and godmother at the christening of a child in one of the peasant families. This rendered marriage impossible, according to Russian Church law. The stratagem was usually successful, but once it ended in a tragedy. Andréi, the tailor, fell in love with a girl belonging to one of our neighbors. He hoped that my father would permit him to go free, as a tailor, in exchange for a certain yearly payment, and that by working hard at his trade he could manage to lay aside some money and to buy freedom for the girl. Otherwise, in marrying one of my father's serfs she would have become the serf of her husband's master. However, as Andréi and one of the maids of our household foresaw that they might be ordered to marry, they agreed to unite as god-parents in the christening of a child. What they had feared happened: one day they were called to the master, and the dreaded order was given.

"We are always obedient to your will," they replied, "but a few weeks ago we acted as godfather and godmother at a christening." Andréi also explained his wishes and intentions. The result was that he was sent to the recruiting board to become a soldier.

Under Nicholas I. there was no obligatory military service for all, such as now exists. Nobles and merchants were exempt, and when a new levy of recruits was ordered, the landowners had to supply a certain number of men from their serfs. As a rule, the peasants, within their village communities, kept a roll amongst themselves; but the house servants were entirely at the mercy of their lord, and if he was dissatisfied with one of them, he sent him to the recruiting board and took a recruit acquittance, which had a considerable money value, as it could be sold to any one whose turn it was to become a soldier.

Military service in those times was terrible. A man was required to serve twenty-five years under the colors, and the life of a soldier was hard in the extreme. To become a soldier meant to be torn away forever from one's native village and surroundings, and to be at the mercy of officers like Timoféev, whom I have already mentioned. Blows from the officers, flogging with birch rods and with sticks, for the slightest fault, were normal affairs. The cruelty that was displayed surpasses all imagination. Even in the corps of cadets, where only noble-

men's sons were educated, a thousand blows with birch rods
were sometimes administered, in the presence of all the corps,
for a cigarette,—the doctor standing by the tortured boy, and
ordering the punishment to end only when he ascertained that
the pulse was about to stop beating. The bleeding victim was
carried away unconscious to the hospital. The commander of
the military schools, the Grand Duke Michael, would quickly
have removed the director of a corps who had not had one or
two such cases every year. "No discipline," he would have said.

With common soldiers it was far worse. When one of them
appeared before a court-martial, the sentence was that a thousand men should be placed in two ranks facing each other,
every soldier armed with a stick of the thickness of the little
finger (these sticks were known under their German name
of *Spitzruthen*), and that the condemned man should be
dragged three, four, five, and seven times between these two
rows, each soldier administering a blow. Sergeants followed
to see that full force was used. After one or two thousand blows
had been given, the victim, spitting blood, was taken to the
hospital and attended to, in order that the punishment might
be finished as soon as he had more or less recovered from the
effects of the first part of it. If he died under the torture, the
execution of the sentence was completed upon the corpse.
Nicholas I. and his brother Michael were pitiless; no remit-
tance of the punishment was ever possible. "I will send you
through the ranks; you shall be skinned under the sticks," were
threats which made part of the current language.

A gloomy terror used to spread through our house when it
became known that one of the servants was to be sent to the
recruiting board. The man was chained and placed under
guard in the office, to prevent suicide. A peasant-cart was
brought to the office door, and the doomed man was taken out
between two watchmen. All the servants surrounded him. He
made a deep bow, asking every one to pardon him his willing
or unwilling offenses. If his father and mother lived in our
village, they came to see him off. He bowed to the ground
before them, and his mother and his other female relatives began loudly to sing out their lamentations,—a sort of half-song
and half-recitative: "To whom do you abandon us? Who will
take care of you in the strange lands? Who will protect you

from cruel men?"—exactly in the same way in which they sang their lamentations at a burial, and with the same words.

Thus Andréi had now to face for twenty-five years the terrible fate of a soldier: all his schemes of happiness had come to a violent end.

The fate of one of the maids, Pauline, or Pólia, as she used to be called, was even more tragical. She had been apprenticed to make fine embroidery, and was an artist at the work. At Nikólskoe her embroidery frame stood in sister Hélène's room, and she often took part in the conversations that went on between our sister and a sister of our stepmother who stayed with Hélène. Altogether, by her behavior and talk Pólia was more like an educated young person than a housemaid.

A misfortune befell her: she realized that she would soon be a mother. She told all to our stepmother, who burst into reproaches: "I will not have that creature in my house any longer! I will not permit such a shame in my house! oh, the shameless creature!" and so on. The tears of Hélène made no difference. Pólia had her hair cut short, and was exiled to the dairy; but as she was just embroidering an extraordinary skirt, she had to finish it at the dairy, in a dirty cottage, at a microscopical window. She finished it, and made many more fine embroideries, all in the hope of obtaining her pardon. But pardon did not come.

The father of her child, a servant of one of our neighbors, implored permission to marry her; but as he had no money to offer, his request was refused. Pólia's "too gentlewoman-like manners" were taken as an offense, and a most bitter fate was kept in reserve for her. There was in our household a man employed as a postilion, on account of his small size; he went under the name of "bandy-legged Fílka." In his boyhood a horse had kicked him terribly, and he did not grow. His legs were crooked, his feet were turned inward, his nose was broken and turned to one side, his jaw was deformed. To this monster it was decided to marry Pólia,—and she was married by force. The couple were sent to become peasants at my father's estate in Riazán.

Human feelings were not recognized, not even suspected, in serfs, and when Turgénev published his little story *Mumú*, and

Grigoróvich began to issue his thrilling novels, in which he made his readers weep over the misfortunes of the serfs, it was to a great number of persons a startling revelation. "They love just as we do; is it possible?" exclaimed the sentimental ladies who could not read a French novel without shedding tears over the troubles of the noble heroes and heroines.

The education which the owners occasionally gave to some of their serfs was only another source of misfortune for the latter. My father once picked out in a peasant house a clever boy, and sent him to be educated as a doctor's assistant. The boy was diligent, and after a few years' apprenticeship made a decided success. When he returned home, my father bought all that was required for a well-equipped dispensary, which was arranged very nicely in one of the side houses of Nikólskoe. In summer time, Sásha the Doctor—that was the familiar name under which this young man went in the household—was busy gathering and preparing all sorts of medical herbs, and in a short time he became most popular in the region round Nikólskoe. The sick people among the peasants came from the neighboring villages, and my father was proud of the success of his dispensary. But this condition of things did not last. One winter, my father came to Nikólskoe, stayed there for a few days, and left. That night Sásha the Doctor shot himself,—by accident, it was reported; but there was a love-story at the bottom of it. He was in love with a girl whom he could not marry, as she belonged to another landowner.

The case of another young man, Gerásim Kruglóv, whom my father educated at the Moscow Agricultural Institute, was almost equally sad. He passed his examinations most brilliantly, getting a gold medal, and the director of the Institute made all possible endeavors to induce my father to give him freedom and to let him go to the university,—serfs not being allowed to enter there. "He is sure to become a remarkable man," the director said, "perhaps one of the glories of Russia, and it will be an honor for you to have recognized his capacities and to have given such a man to Russian science."

"I need him for my own estate," my father replied to the many applications made on the young man's behalf. In reality, with the primitive methods of agriculture which were then in use, and from which my father would never have departed, Gerásim Krugióv was absolutely useless. He made a survey of the estate, but when that was done he was ordered to sit in the servants' room and to stand with a plate at dinner-time. Of course Gerásim resented it very much; his dreams carried him to the university, to scientific work. His looks betrayed his discontent, and our stepmother seemed to find an especial pleasure in offending him at every opportunity. One day in the autumn, a rush of wind having opened the entrance gate, she called out to him, "Garáska, go and shut the gate."

That was the last drop. He answered, "You have a porter for that," and went his way.

My stepmother ran into father's room, crying, "Your servants insult me in your house!"

Immediately Gerásim was put under arrest and chained, to be sent away as a soldier. The parting of his old father and mother with him was one of the most heart-rending scenes I ever saw.

This time, however, fate took its revenge. Nicholas I. died, and military service became more tolerable. Gerásim's great ability was soon remarked, and in a few years he was one of the chief clerks, and the real working force in one of the departments of the ministry of war. Meanwhile, my father, who was absolutely honest, and, at a time when almost every one was receiving bribes and making fortunes, had never let himself be bribed, departed once from the strict rules of the service, in order to oblige the commander of the corps to which he belonged, and consented to allow an irregularity of some kind. It nearly cost him his promotion to the rank of general; the only object of his thirty-five years' service in the army seemed on the point of being lost. My stepmother went to St. Petersburg to remove the difficulty, and one day, after many applications, she was told that the only way to obtain what she wanted was to address herself to a particular clerk in a certain department of the ministry. Although he was a mere clerk, he was the real head of his superiors, and could do everything. This man's name was—Gerásim Ivánovich Krugióv!

"Imagine, our Garáska!" she said to me afterward. "I always knew that he had great capacity. I went to see him, and spoke to him about this affair, and he said, 'I have nothing against the old prince, and I will do all I can for him.'"

Gerásim kept his word: he made a favorable report, and my father got his promotion. At last he could put on the long-coveted red trousers and the red-lined overcoat, and could wear the plumage on his helmet.

These were things which I myself saw in my childhood. If, however, I were to relate what I heard of in those years, it would be a much more gruesome narrative: stories of men and women torn from their families and their villages, and sold, or lost in gambling, or exchanged for a couple of hunting dogs, and then transported to some remote part of Russia for the sake of creating a new estate; of children taken from their parents and sold to cruel or dissolute masters; of flogging "in the stables," which occurred every day with unheard-of cruelty; of a girl who found her only salvation in drowning herself; of an old man who had grown gray-haired in his master's service, and at last hanged himself under his master's window; and of revolts of serfs, which were suppressed by Nicholas I.'s generals by flogging to death each tenth or fifth man taken out of the ranks, and by laying waste the village, whose inhabitants, after a military execution, went begging for bread in the neighboring provinces. As to the poverty which I saw during our journeys in certain villages, especially in those which belonged to the imperial family, no words would be adequate to describe the misery to readers who have not seen it.

To become free was the constant dream of the serfs,—a dream not easily realized, for a heavy sum of money was required to induce a landowner to part with a serf.

"Do you know," my father said to me, once, "that your mother appeared to me after her death? You young people do not believe in these things, but it was so. I sat one night very late in this chair, at my writing-table, and slumbered, when I saw her enter from behind, all in white, quite pale, and with her eyes gleaming. When she was dying she begged me to promise that I would give liberty to her maid, Másha, and I did promise; but then, what with one thing and another, nearly a whole year passed without my having fulfilled my intention. Then she appeared, and said to me in a low voice, 'Alexis, you promised me to give liberty to Másha; have you forgotten it?' I was quite terrified; I jumped out of my chair, but she had vanished. I called the servants, but no one had seen anything. Next morning I went to her grave and had a litany sung, and immediately gave liberty to Másha."

When my father died, Másha came to his burial, and I spoke to her. She was married, and quite happy in her family life. My brother Alexander, in his jocose way, told her what my father had said, and we asked her what she knew of it.

"These things," she replied, "happened a long time ago, so I may tell you the truth. I saw that your father had quite forgotten his promise, so I dressed up in white and spoke like your mother. I recalled the promise he had made to her,—you won't bear a grudge against me, will you?"

"Of course not!"

Ten or twelve years after the scenes described in the early part of this chapter, I sat one night in my father's room, and we talked of things past. Serfdom had been abolished, and my father complained of the new conditions, though not very severely; he had accepted them without much grumbling.

"You must agree, father," I said, "that you often punished your servants cruelly, and even without reason."

"With the people," he replied, "it was impossible to do otherwise;" and, leaning back in his easy-chair, he remained plunged in thought. "But what I did was nothing worth speaking of," he said, after a long pause. "Take that same Sáblev: he looks so soft, and talks in such a thin voice; but he was really terrible with his serfs. How many times they plotted to kill him! I, at least, never took advantage of my maids, whereas that old devil T—— went on in such a way that the peasant women were going to inflict a terrible punishment upon him. . . . Good-by, *bonne nuit!*"

IX

I well remember the Crimean war. At Moscow it affected people but little. Of course, in every house lint and bandages for the wounded were made at evening parties: not much of it, however, reached the Russian armies, immense quantities being stolen and sold to the armies of the enemy. My sister Hélène and other young ladies sang patriotic songs, but the general tone of life in society was hardly influenced by the great struggle that was going on. In the country, on the contrary, the war caused terrible gloominess. The levies of recruits followed one another rapidly, and we continually heard the peasant women singing their funereal songs. The Russian people look upon war as a calamity which is being sent upon them by Providence, and they accepted this war with a solemnity that contrasted strangely with the levity I saw elsewhere under similar circumstances. Young though I was, I realized that feeling of solemn resignation which pervaded our villages.

My brother Nicholas was smitten like many others by the war fever, and before he had ended his course at the corps he joined the army in the Caucasus. I never saw him again.

In the autumn of 1854 our family was increased by the arrival of two sisters of our stepmother. They had had their own house and some vineyards at Sebastopol, but now they were homeless, and came to stay with us. When the allies landed in the Crimea, the inhabitants of Sebastopol were told that they need not be afraid, and had only to stay where they were; but after the defeat at the Alma, they were ordered to leave with all haste, as the city would be invested within a few days. There were few conveyances, and there was no way of moving along the roads in face of the troops which were marching southward. To hire a cart was almost impossible, and the ladies, having abandoned all they had on the road, had a very hard time of it before they reached Moscow.

I soon made friends with the younger of the two sisters, a lady of about thirty, who used to smoke one cigarette after another, and to tell me of all the horrors of their journey. She spoke with tears in her eyes of the beautiful battle-ships which had to be sunk at the entrance of the harbor of Sebastopol, and she could not understand how the Russians would be able to defend Sebastopol from the land; there was no wall even worth speaking of.

I was in my thirteenth year when Nicholas I. died. It was late in the afternoon, the 18th of February (2d of March),

that the policemen distributed in all the houses of Moscow a
bulletin announcing the illness of the Tsar, and inviting the
inhabitants to pray in the churches for his recovery. At that
time he was already dead, and the authorities knew it, as
there was telegraphic communication between Moscow and
St. Petersburg; but not a word having been previously uttered
about his illness, they thought that the people must be gradually prepared for the announcement of his death. We all went
to church and prayed most piously.

Next day, Saturday, the same thing was done, and even on
Sunday morning bulletins about the Tsar's health were distributed. The news of the death of Nicholas reached us only
about midday, through some servants who had been to the
market. A real terror reigned in our house and in the houses of
our relatives, as the information spread. It was said that the
people in the market behaved in a strange way, showing no
regret, but indulging in dangerous talk. Full-grown people
spoke in whispers, and our stepmother kept repeating, "Don't
talk before the men;" while the servants whispered among
themselves, probably about the coming "freedom." The nobles
expected at every moment a revolt of the serfs,—a new uprising of Pugachóv.

At St. Petersburg, in the meantime, men of the educated
classes, as they communicated to one another the news, embraced in the streets. Every one felt that the end of the war
and the end of the terrible conditions which prevailed under
the "iron despot" were near at hand. Poisoning was talked
about, the more so as the Tsar's body decomposed very
rapidly, but the true reason only gradually leaked out: a too
strong dose of an invigorating medicine that Nicholas had
taken.

In the country, during the summer of 1855, the heroic
struggle which was going on in Sebastopol for every yard of
ground and every bit of its dismantled bastions was followed
with a solemn interest. A messenger was sent regularly twice
a week from our house to the district town to get the papers;
and on his return, even before he had dismounted, the papers
were taken from his hands and opened. Hélène or I read them
aloud to the family, and the news was at once transmitted
to the servants' room, and thence to the kitchen, the office, the

priest's house, and the houses of the peasants. The reports which came of the last days of Sebastopol, of the awful bombardment, and finally of the evacuation of the town by our troops were received with tears. In every country-house round about, the loss of Sebastopol was mourned over with as much grief as the loss of a near relative would have been, although every one understood that now the terrible war would soon come to an end.

X

It was in August, 1857, when I was nearly fifteen, that my turn came to enter the Corps of Pages, and I was taken to St. Petersburg. When I left home I was still a child; but human character is usually settled in a definite way at an earlier age than is generally supposed, and it is evident to me that under my childish appearance I was then very much what I was to be later on. My tastes, my inclinations, were already determined.

The first impulse to my intellectual development was given, as I have said, by my Russian teacher. It is an excellent habit in Russian families—a habit now, unhappily, on the decline—to have in the house a student who aids the boys and the girls with their lessons, even when they are at a gymnasium. For a better assimilation of what they learn at school, and for a widening of their conceptions about what they learn, his aid is invaluable. Moreover, he introduces an intellectual element into the family, and becomes an elder brother to the young people,—often something better than an elder brother, because the student has a certain responsibility for the progress of his pupils; and as the methods of teaching change rapidly, from one generation to another, he can assist his pupils much better than the best educated parents could.

Nikolái Pávlovich Smirnóv had literary tastes. At that time, under the wild censorship of Nicholas I., many quite inoffensive works by our best writers could not be published; others were so mutilated as to deprive some passages in them of any meaning. In the genial comedy by Griboédov, *Misfortune from Intelligence*, which ranks with the best comedies of Molière,

Colonel Skalozúb had to be named "Mr. Skalozúb," to the detriment of the sense and even of the verses; for the representation of a colonel in a comical light would have been considered an insult to the army. Of so innocent a book as Gógol's *Dead Souls* the second part was not allowed to appear, nor the first part to be reprinted, although it had long been out of print. Numerous verses of Púshkin, Lérmontov, A. K. Tolstóy, Ryléev, and other poets were not permitted to see the light; to say nothing of such verses as had any political meaning or contained a criticism of the prevailing conditions. All these circulated in manuscript, and Smirnóv used to copy whole books of Gógol and Púshkin for himself and his friends, a task in which I occasionally helped him. As a true child of Moscow he was also imbued with the deepest veneration for those of our writers who lived in Moscow,—some of them in the Old Equerries' Quarter. He pointed out to me with respect the house of the Countess Saliàs (Eugénie Tour), who was our near neighbor, while the house of the noted exile Alexander Hérzen always was associated with a certain mysterious feeling of respect and awe. The house where Gógol lived was for us an object of deep respect, and though I was not nine when he died (in 1851), and had read none of his works, I remember well the sadness his death produced at Moscow. Turgénev well expressed that feeling in a note, for which Nicholas I. ordered him to be put under arrest and sent into exile to his estate.

Púshkin's great poem, *Eugene Onégin,* made but little impression upon me, and I still admire the marvelous simplicity and beauty of his style in that poem more than its contents. But Gógol's works, which I read when I was eleven or twelve, had a powerful effect on my mind, and my first literary essays were in imitation of his humorous manner. An historical novel by Zagóskin, *Iury Miloslávsky,* about the times of the great uprising of 1612, Púshkin's *The Captain's Daughter,* dealing with the Pugachóv uprising, and Dumas's *Queen Marguerite* awakened in me a lasting interest in history. As to other French novels, I have only begun to read them since Daudet and Zola came to the front. Nekrásov's poetry was my favorite from early years; I knew many of his verses by heart.

Nikolái Pávlovich early began to make me write, and with his aid I wrote a long *History of a Sixpence,* for which we invented all sorts of characters, into whose possession the six-pence fell. My brother Alexander had at that time a much more poetical turn of mind. He wrote most romantic stories, and began early to make verses, which he did with wonderful facility and in a most musical and easy style. If his mind had not subsequently been taken up by natural history and philosophical studies, he undoubtedly would have become a poet of mark. In those years his favorite resort for finding poetical inspiration was the gently sloping roof underneath our window. This aroused in me a constant desire to tease him. "There is the poet sitting under the chimney-pot, trying to write his verses," I used to say; and the teasing ended in a fierce scrimmage, which brought our sister Hélène to a state of despair. But Alexander was so devoid of revengefulness that peace was soon concluded, and we loved each other immensely. Among boys, scrimmage and love seem to go hand in hand.

I had even then taken to journalism. In my twelfth year I began to edit a daily journal. Paper was not to be had at will in our house, and my journal was in 32° only. As the Crimean war had not yet broken out, and the only newspaper which my father used to receive was the *Gazette of the Moscow Police,* I had not a great choice of models. As a result my own Gazette consisted merely of short paragraphs announcing the news of the day: as, "Went out to the woods. N. P. Smirnóv shot two thrushes," and so on.

This soon ceased to satisfy me, and in 1855 I started a monthly review, which contained Alexander's verses, my novelettes, and some sort of "varieties." The material existence of this review was fully guaranteed, for it had plenty of subscribers; that is, the editor himself and Smirnóv, who regularly paid his subscription, of so many sheets of paper, even after he had left our house. In return, I accurately wrote out for my faithful subscriber a second copy.

When Smirnóv left us, and a student of medicine, N. M. Pávlov, took his place, the latter helped me in my editorial duties. He obtained for the review a poem by one of his friends, and—still more important—the introductory lecture on physical geography by one of the Moscow professors. Of course this had not been printed before: a reproduction would never have found its way into the review.

Alexander, I need not say, took a lively interest in the paper, and its renown soon reached the corps of cadets. Some young writers on the way to fame undertook the publication of a rival. The matter was serious: in poems and novels we could hold our own; but they had a "critic," and a "critic" who writes, in connection with the characters of some new novel, all sorts of things about the conditions of life, and touches upon a thousand questions which could not be touched upon anywhere else, makes the soul of a Russian review. They had a critic, and we had none! He wrote an article for the first number, and his article was shown to my brother. It was rather pretentious and weak. Alexander at once wrote an anti-criticism, ridiculing and demolishing the critic in a violent manner. There was great consternation in the rival camp when they learned that this anti-criticism would appear in our next issue; they gave up publishing their paper, their best writers joined our staff, and we triumphantly announced the future "exclusive collaboration" of so many distinguished writers.

In August, 1857, the review had to be suspended, after nearly two years' existence. New surroundings and a quite new life were before me. I went away from home with regret, the more so because the whole distance between Moscow and St. Petersburg would be between me and Alexander, and I already considered it a misfortune that I had to enter a military school.

❋ ❋ ❋ ❋ ❋ ❋ ❋ ❋ ❋ ❋ ❋ ❋ ❋ ❋ ❋ ❋

PART TWO

THE CORPS OF PAGES

I

The long-cherished ambition of my father was thus realized. There was a vacancy in the Corps of Pages which I could fill before I had got beyond the age to which admission was limited, and I was taken to St. Petersburg and entered the school. Only a hundred and fifty boys—mostly children of the nobility belonging to the court—received education in this privileged corps, which combined the character of a military school endowed with special rights and of a court institution attached to the imperial household. After a stay of four or five years in the Corps of Pages, those who had passed the final examinations were received as officers in any regiment of the guard or of the army they chose, irrespective of the number of vacancies in that regiment; and each year the first sixteen pupils of the highest form were nominated *pages de chambre;* that is, they were personally attached to the several members of the imperial family,—the emperor, the empress, the grand duchesses, and the grand dukes. That was considered, of course, a great honor; and, moreover, the young men upon whom this honor was bestowed became known at the court, and had afterward every chance of being nominated aides-de-camp of the emperor or of one of the grand dukes, and consequently had every facility for making a brilliant career in the service of the state. Fathers and mothers of families connected with the court took due care, therefore, that their boys should not miss entering the Corps of Pages, even though entrance had to be secured at the expense of other candidates who never saw a vacancy opening for them. Now that I was in the select corps my father could give free play to his ambitious dreams.

The corps was divided into five forms, of which the highest

was the first, and the lowest the fifth, and the intention was
that I should enter the fourth form. However, as it appeared
at the examinations that I was not sufficiently familiar with
decimal fractions, and as the fourth form contained that year
over forty pupils, while only twenty had been mustered for
the fifth form, I was enrolled in the latter.

I felt extremely vexed at this decision. It was with reluctance
that I entered a military school, and now I should have to stay
in it five years instead of four. What should I do in the fifth
form, when I knew already all that would be taught in it?
With tears in my eyes I spoke of it to the inspector (the head
of the educational department), but he answered me with a
joke. "You know," he remarked, "what Cæsar said,—better
to be the first in a village than the second in Rome." To which
I warmly replied that I should prefer to be the very last, if
only I could leave the military school as soon as possible.
"Perhaps, after some time, you will like the school," he remarked, and from that day he became friendly to me.

To the teacher of arithmetic, who also tried to console me,
I gave my word of honor that I would never cast a glance
into his textbook; "and nevertheless you will have to give me
the highest marks." I kept my word; but thinking now of this
scene, I fancy that the pupil was not of a very docile disposition.

And yet, as I look back upon that remote past, I cannot but
feel grateful for having been put in the lower form. Having
only to repeat during the first year what I already knew, I got
into the habit of learning my lessons by merely listening to
what the teachers said in the class-room; and, the lessons over,
I had plenty of time to read and to write to my heart's content.
I never prepared for the examinations, and used to spend the
time which was allowed for that in reading aloud, to a few
friends, dramas of Shakespeare or of Ostróvsky. When I
reached the higher "special" forms, I was also better prepared
to master the variety of subjects we had to study. Besides, I
spent more than half of the first winter in the hospital. Like
all children who are not born at St. Petersburg, I had to pay
a heavy tribute to "the capital on the swamps of Finland,"
in the shape of several attacks of local cholera, and finally one
of typhoid fever.

When I entered the Corps of Pages, its inner life was undergoing a profound change. All Russia awakened at that time from the heavy slumber and the terrible nightmare of Nicholas I.'s reign. Our school also felt the effects of that revival. I do not know, in fact, what would have become of me, had I entered the Corps of Pages one or two years sooner. Either my will would have been totally broken, or I should have been excluded from the school with no one knows what consequences. Happily, the transition period was already in full sway in the year 1857.

The director of the corps was an excellent old man, General Zheltúkhin. But he was the nominal head only. The real master of the school was "the Colonel,"—Colonel Girardot, a Frenchman in the Russian service. People said he was a Jesuit, and so he was, I believe. His ways, at any rate, were thoroughly imbued with the teachings of Loyola, and his educational methods were those of the French Jesuit colleges.

Imagine a short, extremely thin man, with dark, piercing, and furtive eyes, wearing short clipped mustaches, which gave him the expression of a cat; very quiet and firm; not remarkably intelligent, but exceedingly cunning; a despot at the bottom of his heart, who was capable of hating—intensely hating —the boy who would not fall under his fascination, and of expressing that hatred, not by silly persecutions, but unceasingly, by his general behavior,—by an occasionally dropped word, a gesture, a smile, an interjection. His walk was more like gliding along, and the exploring glances he used to cast round without turning his head completed the illusion. A stamp of cold dryness was impressed on his lips, even when he tried to look well disposed, and that expression became still more harsh when his mouth was contorted by a smile of discontent or of contempt. With all this there was nothing of a commander in him; you would rather think, at first sight, of a benevolent father who talks to his children as if they were full-grown people. And yet, you soon felt that every one and everything had to bend before his will. Woe to the boy who would not feel happy or unhappy according to the degree of good disposition shown toward him by the Colonel.

The words "the Colonel" were continually on all lips. Other officers went by their nicknames, but no one dared to give a nickname to Girardot. A sort of mystery hung about him, as if he were omniscient and everywhere present. True, he spent all the day and part of the night in the school. Even when we were in the classes he prowled about, visiting our drawers, which he opened with his own keys. As to the night, he gave a good portion of it to the task of inscribing in small books,—of which he had quite a library,—in separate columns, by special signs and in inks of different colors, all the faults and virtues of each boy.

Play, jokes, and conversation stopped when we saw him slowly moving along through our spacious rooms, hand in hand with one of his favorites, balancing his body forward and backward; smiling at one boy, keenly looking into the eyes of another, casting an indifferent glance upon a third, and giving a slight contortion to his lip as he passed a fourth: and from these looks every one knew that he liked the first boy, that to the second he was indifferent, that he intentionally did not notice the third, and that he disliked the fourth. This dislike was enough to terrify most of his victims,—the more so as no reason could be given for it. Impressionable boys had been brought to despair by that mute, unceasingly displayed aversion and those suspicious looks; in others the result had been a total annihilation of will, as one of the Tolstóys—Theodor, also a pupil of Girardot—has shown in an autobiographic novel, *The Diseases of the Will.*

The inner life of the corps was miserable under the rule of the Colonel. In all boarding-schools the newly entered boys are subjected to petty persecutions. The "greenhorns" are put in this way to a test. What are they worth? Are they not going to turn "sneaks"? And then the "old hands" like to show to newcomers the superiority of an established brotherhood. So it is in all schools and in prisons. But under Girardot's rule these persecutions took on a harsher aspect, and they came, not from the comrades of the same form, but from the first form,—the pages de chambre, who were noncommissioned officers, and whom Girardot had placed in a quite exceptional, superior position. His system was to give them carte blanche; to pretend that he did not know even the horrors they were enacting; and to maintain through them a severe discipline.

To answer a blow received from a page de chambre would have meant, in the times of Nicholas I., to be sent to a battalion of soldiers' sons, if the fact became public; and to revolt in any way against the mere caprice of a page de chambre meant that the twenty youths of the first form, armed with their heavy oak rulers, would assemble in a room, and, with Girardot's tacit approval, administer a severe beating to the boy who had shown such a spirit of insubordination.

Accordingly, the first form did what they liked; and not further back than the preceding winter one of their favorite games had been to assemble the "greenhorns" at night in a room, in their night-shirts, and to make them run round, like horses in a circus, while the pages de chambre, armed with thick india-rubber whips, standing some in the center and the others on the outside, pitilessly whipped the boys. As a rule the "circus" ended in an Oriental fashion, in an abominable way. The moral conceptions which prevailed at that time, and the foul talk which went on in the school concerning what occurred at night after circus, were such that the least said about them the better.

The Colonel knew all this. He had a perfectly organized system of espionage, and nothing escaped his knowledge. But so long as he was not known to know it, all was right. To shut his eyes to what was done by the first form was the foundation of his system of maintaining discipline.

However, a new spirit was awakened in the school, and only a few months before I entered it a revolution had taken place. That year the third form was different from what it had hitherto been. It contained a number of young men who really studied and read a good deal; some of them became, later, men of mark. My first acquaintance with one of them—let me call him von Schauff—was when he was reading Kant's *Critique of Pure Reason*. Besides, they had amongst them some of the strongest youths of the school. The tallest member of the corps was in that form, as also a very strong young man, Kóshtov, a great friend of von Schauff. The third form did not bear the yoke of the pages de chambre with the same docility as their predecessors; they were disgusted with what was going on; and in consequence of an incident, which I prefer not to describe, a fight took place between the third and the first form, with the result that the pages de chambre got a very severe thrashing from their subordinates. Girardot hushed up the affair, but the authority of the first form was broken down. The india-rubber whips remained, but were never again brought into use. The circuses and the like became things of the past.

That much was won; but the lowest form, the fifth, composed almost entirely of very young boys who had just entered the school, had still to obey the petty caprices of the pages de chambre. We had a beautiful garden, filled with old trees, but the boys of the fifth form could enjoy it little: they were forced to run a roundabout, while the pages de chambre sat in it and chattered, or to send back the balls when these gentlemen played ninepins. A couple of days after I had entered the school, seeing how things stood in the garden, I did not go there, but remained upstairs. I was reading, when a page de chambre, with carroty hair and a face covered with freckles, came upon me, and ordered me to go at once to the garden to run the roundabout.

"I shan't; don't you see I am reading?" was my reply.

Anger disfigured his never too pleasant face. He was ready to jump upon me. I took the defensive. He tried to give me blows on the face with his cap. I fenced as best I could. Then he flung his cap on the floor.

"Pick it up."

"Pick it up yourself."

Such an act of disobedience was unheard of in the school. Why he did not beat me unmercifully on the spot I do not know. He was much older and stronger than I was.

Next day and the following days I received similar commands, but obstinately remained upstairs. Then began the most exasperating petty persecutions at every step,—enough to drive a boy to desperation. Happily, I was always of a jovial disposition, and answered them with jokes, or took little heed of them.

Moreover, it all soon came to an end. The weather turned rainy, and we spent most of our time indoors. In the garden the first form smoked freely enough, but when we were indoors the smoking club was "the tower." It was kept beautifully clean, and a fire was always burning there. The pages de

chambre severely punished any of the other boys whom they
caught smoking, but they themselves sat continually at the
fireside chattering and enjoying cigarettes. Their favorite
smoking time was after ten o'clock at night, when all were
supposed to have gone to bed; they kept up their club till
half past eleven, and, to protect themselves from an unexpected
interruption by Girardot, they ordered us to be on the watch.
The small boys of the fifth form were taken out of their beds
in turn, two at a time, and they had to loiter about the
staircase till half past eleven, to give notice of the approach
of the Colonel.

We decided to put an end to these night watches. Long
were the discussions, and the higher forms were consulted as
to what was to be done. At last the decision came: "Refuse,
all of you, to keep the watch; and when they begin to beat
you, which they are sure to do, go, as many of you as can, in
a block, and call in Girardot. He knows it all, but then he
will be bound to stop it." The question whether that would
not be "reporting" was settled in the negative by experts in
matters of honor: the pages de chambre did not behave toward
the others like comrades.

The turn to watch fell that night to a Shakhovskóy, an
old hand, and to Selánov, a newcomer, an extremely timid boy,
who even spoke in a girlish voice. Shakhovskóy was called
upon first, but refused to go, and was left alone. Then two
pages de chambre went to the timid Selánov, who was in bed;
as he refused to obey, they began to flog him brutally with
heavy leather braces. Shakhovskóy woke up several comrades
who were near at hand, and they all ran to find Girardot.

I was also in bed when the two came upon me, ordering me
to take the watch. I refused. Thereupon, seizing two pairs of
braces,—we always used to put our clothes in perfect order on
a bench by the bedside, braces uppermost, and the necktie
across them,—they began to flog me. Sitting up in bed, I fenced
with my hands, and had already received several heavy blows,
when a command resounded,—"The first form to the Colonel!"
The fierce fighters became tame at once, and hurriedly put
my things in order.

"Don't say a word," they whispered.

"The necktie across, in good order," I said to them, while my shoulders and arms burned from the blows.

What Girardot's talk with the first form was we did not know; but next day, as we stood in the ranks before marching downstairs to the dining-room, he addressed us in a minor key, saying how sad it was that pages de chambre should have fallen upon a boy who was right in his refusal. And upon whom? A newcomer, and so timid a boy as Selánov was. The whole school was disgusted at this Jesuitic speech.

No need to say that that was the end of the watch-keeping, and that it gave a final blow to the worrying of the newcomers: it has never been renewed.

It surely was also a blow to Girardot's authority, and he resented it very much. He regarded our form, and me especially, with great dislike (the roundabout affair had been reported to him), and he manifested it at every opportunity. During the first winter, I was a frequent inmate of the hospital. After suffering from typhoid fever, during which the director and the doctor bestowed on me a really parental care, I had very bad and persistently recurring gastric attacks. Girardot, as he made his daily rounds of the hospital, seeing me so often there, began to say to me every morning, half jokingly, in French, "Here is a young man who is as healthy as the New Bridge, and loiters in the hospital." Once or twice I replied jestingly, but at last, seeing malice in this constant repetition, I lost patience and grew very angry.

"How dare you say that?" I exclaimed. "I shall ask the doctor to forbid your entering this room," and so on.

Girardot recoiled two steps; his dark eyes glittered, his thin lip became still thinner. At last he said, "I have offended you, have I? Well, we have in the hall two artillery guns: shall we have a duel?"

"I don't make jokes, and I tell you that I shall bear no more of your insinuations," I continued.

He did not repeat his joke, but regarded me with even more dislike than before.

Every one spoke of Girardot's dislike for me; but I paid no attention to it, and probably increased it by my indifference. For full eighteen months he refused to give me the epaulets, which were usually given to newly entered boys after one or two months' stay at the school, when they had learned some of the rudiments of military drill; but I felt quite happy without that military decoration. At last, an officer—the best teacher of drill in the school, a man simply enamored of drill—volunteered to teach me; and when he saw me performing all the tricks to his entire satisfaction, he undertook to introduce me to Girardot. The Colonel refused again, twice in succession, so that the officer took it as a personal offense; and when the director of the corps once asked him why I had no epaulets yet, he bluntly answered, "The boy is all right; it is the Colonel who does not want him;" whereupon, probably after a remark of the director, Girardot himself asked to examine me again, and gave me the epaulets that very day.

But the Colonel's influence was rapidly vanishing. The whole character of the school was changing. For twenty years Girardot had realized his ideal, which was to have the boys nicely combed, curled, and girlish looking, and to send to the court pages as refined as courtiers of Louis XIV. Whether they learned or not, he cared little; his favorites were those whose clothes-baskets were best filled with all sorts of nail-brushes and scent bottles, whose "private" uniform (which could be put on when we went home on Sundays) was of the best make, and who knew how to make the most elegant *salut oblique*. Formerly, when Girardot had held rehearsals of court ceremonies, wrapping up a page in a striped red cotton cover taken from one of our beds, in order that he might represent the Empress at a *baisemain*, the boys almost religiously approached the imaginary Empress, seriously performed the ceremony of kissing the hand, and retired with a most elegant oblique bow; but now, though they were very elegant at court, they would perform at the rehearsals such bearlike bows that all roared with laughter, while Girardot was simply raging. Formerly, the younger boys who had been taken to a court levee, and had been curled for that purpose, used to keep their curls as long as they would last; now, on returning from the palace, they hurried to put their heads under the cold-water tap, to get rid of the curls. An effeminate appearance was laughed at. To be sent to a levee, to stand there as a decoration, was now considered a drudgery rather than a favor.

And when the small boys who were occasionally taken to the palace to play with the little grand dukes remarked that one of the latter used, in some game, to make a hard whip out of his handkerchief, and use it freely, one of our boys did the same, and so whipped the grand duke that he cried. Girardot was terrified, while the old Sebastopol admiral who was tutor of the grand duke only praised our boy.

A new spirit, studious and serious, developed in the corps, as in all other schools. In former years, the pages, being sure that in one way or another they would get the necessary marks for being promoted officers of the guard, spent the first years in the school hardly learning at all, and only began to study more or less in the last two forms; now the lower forms learned very well. The moral tone also became quite different from what it was a few years before. Oriental amusements were looked upon with disgust, and an attempt or two to revert to old manners resulted in scandals which reached the St. Petersburg drawing-rooms. Girardot was dismissed. He was only allowed to retain his bachelor apartment in the building of the corps, and we often saw him afterward, wrapped in his long military cloak, pacing along, plunged in reflections,—sad, I suppose, because he could not but condemn the new spirit which rapidly developed in the Corps of Pages.

II

All over Russia people were talking of education. As soon as peace had been concluded at Paris, and the severity of censorship had been slightly relaxed, educational matters began to be eagerly discussed. The ignorance of the masses of the people, the obstacles that had hitherto been put in the way of those who wanted to learn, the absence of schools in the country, the obsolete methods of teaching, and the remedies for these evils became favorite themes of discussion in educated circles, in the press, and even in the drawing-rooms of the aristocracy. The first high schools for girls had been opened in 1857, on an excellent plan and with a splendid teaching staff. As by magic a number of men and women came to the front, who have not only devoted their lives to education, but have proved to be remarkable practical pedagogists: their writings would occupy a place of honor in every civilized literature, if they were known abroad.

The Corps of Pages also felt the effect of that revival. Apart from a few exceptions, the general tendency of the three younger forms was to study. The head of the educational department, the inspector, Winkler, who was a well-educated colonel of artillery, a good mathematician, and a man of progressive opinions, hit upon an excellent plan for stimulating that spirit. Instead of the indifferent teachers who formerly used to teach in the lower forms, he endeavored to secure the best ones. In his opinion, no professor was too good to teach the very beginnings of a subject to the youngest boys. Thus, to teach the elements of algebra in the fourth form he invited a first-rate mathematician and a born teacher, Captain Sukhónin, and the form took at once to mathematics. By the way, it so happened that this captain was a tutor of the heir of the throne (Nikolái Alexándrovich, who died at the age of twenty-two), and the heir apparent was brought once a week to the Corps of Pages to be present at the algebra lessons of Captain Sukhónin. Empress Marie Alexándrovna, who was an educated woman, thought that perhaps the contact with studious boys would stimulate her son to learning. He sat amongst us, and had to answer questions like all the others. But he managed mostly, while the teacher spoke, to make drawings very nicely, or to whisper all sorts of droll things to his neighbors. He was good-natured and very gentle in his behavior, but superficial in learning, and still more so in his affections.

For the fifth form the inspector secured two remarkable men. He entered our class-room one day, quite radiant, and told us that we should have a rare chance. Professor Klasóvsky, a great classical scholar and expert in Russian literature, had consented to teach us Russian grammar, and would take us through all the five forms in succession, shifting with us every year to the next form. Another university professor, Herr Becker, librarian of the imperial (national) library, would do the same in German. Professor Klasóvsky, he added, was in weak health that winter, but the inspector was sure that we would be very quiet in his class. The chance of having such a teacher was too good to be lost.

He had thought aright. We became very proud of having university professors for teachers, and although there came voices from the Kamchátka (in Russia, the back benches of each class bear the name of that remote and uncivilized peninsula) to the effect that "the sausage-maker"—that is, the German—must be kept by all means in obedience, public opinion in our form was decidedly in favor of the professors.

"The sausage-maker" won our respect at once. A tall man, with an immense forehead and very kind, intelligent eyes, not devoid of a touch of humor, came into our class, and told us in quite good Russian that he intended to divide our form into three sections. The first section would be composed of Germans, who already knew the language, and from whom he would require more serious work; to the second section he would teach grammar, and later on German literature, in accordance with the established programs; and the third section, he concluded with a charming smile, would be the Kamchátka. "From you," he said, "I shall only require that at each lesson you copy four lines which I will choose for you from a book. The four lines copied, you can do what you like; only do not hinder the rest. And I promise you that in five years you will learn something of German and German literature. Now, who joins the Germans? You, Stackelberg? You, Lamsdorf? Perhaps some one of the Russians? And who joins the Kamchátka?" Five or six boys, who knew not a word of German, took residence in the peninsula. They most conscientiously copied their four lines,—a dozen or a score of lines in the higher forms,—and Becker chose the lines so well, and bestowed so much attention upon the boys, that by the end of the five years they really knew something of the language and its literature.

I joined the Germans. My brother Alexander insisted so much in his letters upon my acquiring German, which possesses so rich a literature and into which every book of value is translated, that I set myself assiduously to learn it. I translated and studied most thoroughly one page of a rather difficult poetical description of a thunderstorm; I learned by heart, as the professor had advised me, the conjugations, the adverbs,

and the prepositions, and began to read. A splendid method
it is for learning languages. Becker advised me, moreover, to
subscribe to a cheap illustrated weekly, and its illustrations
and short stories were a continual inducement to read a few
lines or a column. I soon mastered the language.

Toward the end of the winter I asked Herr Becker to lend
me a copy of Goethe's *Faust*. I had read it in a Russian
translation; I had also read Turgénev's beautiful novel,
Faust; and I now longed to read the great work in the original.
"You will understand nothing in it; it is too philosophical,"
Becker said, with his gentle smile; but he brought me, nevertheless, a little square book, with the pages yellowed by age,
containing the immortal drama. He little knew the unfathomable joy that that small square book gave me. I drank in the
sense and the music of every line of it, beginning with the
very first verses of the ideally beautiful dedication, and soon
knew full pages by heart. Faust's monologue in the forest, and
especially the lines in which he speaks of his understanding
of nature,—

> "Thou
> Not only cold, amazed acquaintance yield'st,
> But grantest that in her profoundest breast
> I gaze, as in the bosom of a friend,"—

simply put me in ecstasy, and till now it has retained its
power over me. Every verse gradually became a dear friend.
And then, is there a higher æsthetic delight than to read
poetry in a language which one does not yet quite thoroughly
understand? The whole is veiled with a sort of slight haze,
which admirably suits poetry. Words, the trivial meanings of
which, when one knows the language colloquially, sometimes
interfere with the poetical image they are intended to convey,
retain but their subtle, elevated sense; while the music of the
poetry is only the more strongly impressed upon the ear.

Professor Klasóvsky's first lesson was a revelation to us. He
was a small man, about fifty years of age, very rapid in his
movements, with bright, intelligent eyes and a slightly sarcastic
expression, and the high forehead of a poet. When he came in
for his first lesson, he said in a low voice that, suffering from a

protracted illness, he could not speak loud enough, and asked us, therefore, to sit closer to him. He placed his chair near the first row of tables, and we clustered round him like a swarm of bees.

He was to teach us Russian grammar; but, instead of the dull grammar lesson, we heard something quite different from what we expected. It was grammar; but here came in a comparison of an old Russian folk-lore expression with a line from Homer or from the Sanskrit Mahabharata, the beauty of which was rendered in Russian words; there, a verse from Schiller was introduced, and was followed by a sarcastic remark about some modern society prejudice; then solid grammar again, and then some wide poetical or philosophical generalization.

Of course, there was much in it that we did not understand, or of which we missed the deeper sense. But do not the bewitching powers of all studies lie in that they continually open up to us new, unsuspected horizons, not yet understood, which entice us to proceed further and further in the penetration of what appears at first sight only in vague outline? Some with their hands placed on one another's shoulders, some leaning across the tables of the first row, others standing close behind Klasóvsky, our eyes glittering, we all hung on his lips. As toward the end of the hour, his voice fell, the more breathlessly we listened. The inspector opened the door of the classroom, to see how we behaved with our new teacher; but on seeing that motionless swarm he retired on tiptoe. Even Daúrov, a restless spirit, stared at Klasóvsky as if to say, "That is the sort of man you are?" Even von Kleinau, a hopelessly obtuse Circassian with a German name, sat motionless. In most of the others something good and elevated simmered at the bottom of their hearts, as if a vision of an unsuspected world was opening before them. Upon me Klasóvsky had an immense influence, which only grew with years. Winkler's prophecy, that, after all, I might like the school, was fulfilled.

In Western Europe, and probably in America, this type of teacher seems not to be generally known, but in Russia there is not a man or woman of mark, in literature or in political life, who does not owe the first impulse toward a higher development to his or her teacher of literature. Every school in the world ought to have such a teacher. Each teacher in a school has his own subject, and there is no link between the different subjects. Only the teacher of literature, guided by the general outlines of the program, but left free to treat it as he likes, can bind together the separate historical and humanitarian sciences, unify them by a broad philosophical and humane conception, and awaken higher ideas and inspirations in the brains and hearts of the young people. In Russia, that necessary task falls quite naturally upon the teacher of Russian literature. As he speaks of the development of the language, of the contents of the early epic poetry, of popular songs and music, and, later on, of modern fiction, of the scientific, political, and philosophical literature of his own country, and the divers æsthetical, political, and philosophical currents it has reflected, he is bound to introduce that generalized conception of the development of human mind which lies beyond the scope of each of the subjects that are taught separately.

The same thing ought to be done for the natural sciences as well. It is not enough to teach physics and chemistry, astronomy and meteorology, zoölogy and botany. The philosophy of all the natural sciences—a general view of nature as a whole, something on the lines of the first volume of Humboldt's *Cosmos*—must be conveyed to the pupils and the students, whatsoever may be the extension given to the study of the natural sciences in the school. The philosophy and the poetry of nature, the methods of all the exact sciences, and an inspired conception of the life of nature must make part of education. Perhaps the teacher of geography might provisionally assume this function; but then we should require quite a different set of teachers of this subject, and a different set of professors of geography in the universities would be needed. What is now taught under this name is anything you like, but it is not geography.

Another teacher conquered our rather uproarious form in a quite different manner. It was the teacher of writing, the last one of the teaching staff. If the "heathen"—that is, the German and the French teachers—were regarded with little respect, the teacher of writing, Ebert, who was a German Jew, was a real martyr. To be insolent with him was a sort of *chic* amongst the pages. His poverty alone must have been the reason why he kept to his lesson in our corps. The old hands, who had stayed for two or three years in the fifth form without moving higher up, treated him very badly; but by some means or other he had made an agreement with them: "One frolic during each lesson, but no more,"—an agreement which, I am afraid, was not always honestly kept on our side.

One day, one of the residents of the remote peninsula soaked the blackboard sponge with ink and chalk and flung it at the calegraphy martyr. "Get it, Ebert!" he shouted, with a stupid smile. The sponge touched Ebert's shoulder, the grimy ink spirted into his face and down on to his white shirt.

We were sure that this time Ebert would leave the room and report the fact to the inspector. But he only exclaimed, as he took out his cotton handkerchief and wiped his face, "Gentlemen, one frolic,—no more to-day!" "The shirt is spoiled," he added, in a subdued voice, and continued to correct some one's book.

We looked stupefied and ashamed. Why, instead of reporting, he had thought at once of the agreement! The feeling of the class turned in his favor. "What you have done is stupid," we reproached our comrade. "He is a poor man, and you have spoiled his shirt! Shame!" somebody cried.

The culprit went at once to make excuses. "One must learn, learn, sir," was all that Ebert said in reply, with sadness in his voice.

All became silent after that, and at the next lesson, as if we had settled it beforehand, most of us wrote in our best possible handwriting, and took our books to Ebert, asking him to correct them. He was radiant; he felt happy that day.

This fact deeply impressed me, and was never wiped out from my memory. To this day I feel grateful to that remarkable man for his lesson.

With our teacher of drawing, who was named Ganz, we never arrived at living on good terms. He continually reported those who played in his class. This, in our opinion, he had no right to do, because he was only a teacher of drawing, but especially because he was not an honest man. In the class he paid little attention to most of us, and spent his time in improving the drawings of those who took private lessons from him, or paid him in order to show at the examinations a good drawing and to get a good mark for it. Against those comrades who did so we had no grudge. On the contrary, we thought it quite right that those who had no capacity for mathematics or no memory for geography, and had but poor marks in these subjects, should improve their total of marks by ordering from a draughtsman a drawing or a topographical map for which they would get "a full twelve." Only for the first two pupils of the form it would not have been fair to resort to such means, while the remainder could do it with untroubled consciences. But the teacher had no business to make drawings to order; and if he chose to act in this way, he ought to bear with resignation the noise and the tricks of his pupils. Instead of this, no lesson passed without his lodging complaints, and each time he grew more arrogant.

As soon as we were moved to the fourth form, and felt ourselves naturalized citizens of the corps, we decided to tighten the bridle upon him. "It is your own fault," our elder comrades told us, "that he takes such airs with you; *we* used to keep him in obedience." So we decided to bring him into subjection.

One day, two excellent comrades of our form approached Ganz with cigarettes in their mouths, and asked him to oblige them with a light. Of course, that was only meant for a joke,— no one ever thought of smoking in the class-rooms,—and, according to our rules of propriety, Ganz had merely to send the two boys away; but he inscribed them in the journal, and they were severely punished. That was the last drop. We decided to give him a "benefit night." That meant that one day all the form, provided with rulers borrowed from the upper forms, would start an outrageous noise by striking the rulers against the tables, and send the teacher out of the class. However, the plot offered many difficulties. We had in our form a lot of "goody" boys who would promise to join in the demonstration, but at the last moment would grow nervous and draw back, and then the teacher would name the others. In such enterprises unanimity is the first requisite, because the punishment, whatsoever it may be, is always lighter when it falls on the whole class instead of on a few.

The difficulties were overcome with a truly Machiavellian

craft. At a given signal all were to turn their backs to Ganz, and then, with the rulers laid in readiness on the desks of the next row, they would produce the required noise. In this way the goody boys would not feel terrified at Ganz's staring at them. But the signal? Whistling, as in robbers' tales, shouting, or even sneezing would not do: Ganz would be capable of naming any one of us as having whistled or sneezed. The signal must be a silent one. One of us, who drew nicely, would take his drawing to show it to Ganz, and the moment he returned and took his seat,—that was to be the time!

All went on admirably. Nesádov took up his drawing, and Ganz corrected it in a few minutes, which seemed to us an eternity. He returned at last to his seat; he stopped for a moment, looking at us; he sat down. . . . All the form turned suddenly on their seats, and the rulers rattled merrily within the desks, while some of us shouted amidst the noise, "Ganz out! Down with him!" The noise was deafening; all the forms knew that Ganz had got his benefit night. He stood there, murmuring something, and finally went out. An officer ran in,— the noise continued; then the sub-inspector dashed in, and after him the inspector. The noise stopped at once. Scolding began.

"The elder under arrest at once!" the inspector commanded; and I, who was the first in the form, and consequently the elder, was marched to the black cell. That spared me seeing what followed. The director came; Ganz was asked to name the ringleaders, but he could name nobody. "They all turned their backs to me, and began the noise," was his reply. Thereupon the form was taken downstairs, and although flogging had been completely abandoned in our school, this time the two who had been reported because they asked for a light were flogged with the birch rod, under the pretext that the benefit night was a revenge for their punishment.

I learned this ten days later, when I was allowed to return to the class. My name, which had been inscribed on the red board in the class, was wiped off. To this I was indifferent; but I must confess that the ten days in the cell, without books, seemed to me rather long, so that I composed (in horrible verses) a poem, in which the deeds of the fourth form were duly glorified.

Of course, our form became now the heroes of the school.
For a month or so we had to tell and retell all about the affair
to the other forms, and received congratulations for having
managed it with such unanimity that nobody was caught separately. And then came the Sundays—all the Sundays down
to Christmas—that the form had to remain at the school, not
being allowed to go home. Being all kept together, we managed
to make those Sundays very gay. The mammas of the goody
boys brought them heaps of sweets; those who had some
money spent it in buying mountains of pastry,—substantial
before dinner, and sweet after it; while in the evenings the
friends from the other forms smuggled in quantities of fruit
for the brave fourth form.

Ganz gave up inscribing any one; but drawing was totally
lost for us. No one wanted to learn drawing from that mer-
cenary man.

III

My brother Alexander was at that time at Moscow, in a corps
of cadets, and we maintained a lively correspondence. As long
as I stayed at home this was impossible, because our father
considered it his prerogative to read all letters addressed to
our house, and he would soon have put an end to any but
a commonplace correspondence. Now we were free to discuss
in our letters whatever we liked. The only difficulty was to get
money for stamps; but we soon learned to write in such fine
characters that we could convey an incredible amount of matter in each letter. Alexander, whose handwriting was beautiful, contrived to get four printed pages on one single page of
note-paper, and his microscopic lines were as legible as the
best small type print. It is a pity that these letters, which he
kept as precious relics, have disappeared. The state police, during one of their raids, robbed him even of these treasures.[5]

Our first letters were mostly about the little details of my
new surroundings, but our correspondence soon took a more
serious character. My brother could not write about trifles.
Even in society he became animated only when some serious
discussion was engaged in, and he complained of feeling "a

dull pain in the brain"—a physical pain, as he used to say—
when he was with people who cared only for small talk. He
was very much in advance of me in his intellectual development, and he urged me forward, raising new scientific and
philosophical questions one after another, and advising me
what to read or to study. What a happiness it was for me to
have such a brother!—a brother who, moreover, loved me passionately. To him I owe the best part of my development.

Sometimes he would advise me to read poetry, and would
send me in his letters quantities of verses and whole poems,
which he wrote from memory. "Read poetry," he wrote:
"poetry makes men better." How often, in my later life, I realized the truth of this remark of his! Read poetry: it makes
men better. He himself was a poet, and had a wonderful
facility for writing most musical verses; indeed, I think
it a great pity that he abandoned poetry. But the reaction
against art, which arose among the Russian youth in the early
sixties, and which Turgénev has depicted in Bazárov (*Fathers
and Sons*), induced him to look upon his verses with contempt, and to plunge headlong into the natural sciences. I
must say, however, that my favorite poet was none of those
whom his poetical gift, his musical ear, and his philosophical
turn of mind made him like best. His favorite Russian poet was
Venevítinov, while mine was Nekrásov, whose verses were very
often unmusical, but appealed most to my heart by their
sympathy for "the downtrodden and ill-treated."

"One must have a set purpose in his life," he wrote me once.
"Without an aim, without a purpose, life is not life." And he
advised me to get a purpose in my life worth living for. I was
too young then to find one; but something undetermined,
vague, "good" altogether, already rose under that appeal, even
though I could not say what that "good" would be.

Our father gave us very little spending money, and I never
had any to buy a single book; but if Alexander got a few
rubles from some aunt, he never spent a penny of it for pleasure, but bought a book and sent it to me. He objected, though,
to indiscriminate reading. "One must have some question," he
wrote, "addressed to the book one is going to read." However,
I did not then appreciate this remark, and cannot think now
without amazement of the number of books, often of a quite

special character, which I read in all branches, but particularly in the domain of history. I did not waste my time upon French novels, since Alexander, years before, had characterized them in one blunt sentence: "They are stupid and full of bad language."

The great questions concerning the conception we should form of the universe—our *Weltanschauung*, as the Germans say—were, of course, the dominant subjects in our correspondence. In our childhood we had never been religious. We were taken to church; but in a Russian church, in a small parish or in a village, the solemn attitude of the people is far more impressive than the mass itself. Of all that I ever had heard in church only two things had impressed me: the twelve passages from the Gospels, relative to the sufferings of the Christ, which are read in Russia at the night service on the eve of Good Friday, and the short prayer condemning the spirit of domination, which is recited during the Great Lent, and is really beautiful by reason of its simple, unpretentious words and feeling. Púshkin has rendered it into Russian verse.

Later on, at St. Petersburg, I went several times to a Roman Catholic church, but the theatrical character of the service and the absence of real feeling in it shocked me, the more so when I saw there with what simple faith some retired Polish soldier or a peasant woman would pray in a remote corner. I also went to a Protestant church; but coming out of it I caught myself murmuring Goethe's words:—

> "But you will never link hearts together
> Unless the linking springs from your own heart."

Alexander, in the meantime, had embraced with his usual passion the Lutheran faith. He had read Michelet's book on Servetus, and had worked out for himself a religion on the lines of that great fighter. He studied with enthusiasm the Augsburg declaration, which he copied out and sent me, and our letters now became full of discussions about grace, and of texts from the apostles Paul and James. I followed my brother, but theological discussions did not deeply interest me. Since I had recovered from the typhoid fever I had taken to quite different reading.

Our sister Hélène, who was now married, was at St. Peters-

burg, and every Saturday night I went to visit her. Her husband
had a good library, in which the French philosophers of the
last century and the modern French historians were well represented, and I plunged into them. Such books were prohibited
in Russia, and evidently could not be taken to school; so I
spent most of the night, every Saturday, in reading the works
of the encyclopædists, the philosophical dictionary of Voltaire,
the writings of the Stoics, especially Marcus Aurelius, and so
on. The infinite immensity of the universe, the greatness of
nature, its poetry, its ever throbbing life, impressed me more
and more; and that never ceasing life and its harmonies gave
me the ecstasy of admiration which the young soul thirsts for,
while my favorite poets supplied me with an expression in
words of that awakening love of mankind and faith in its
progress which make the best part of youth and impress man
for a life.

Alexander, by this time, had gradually come to a Kantian
agnosticism, and the "relativity of perceptions," "perceptions in
time and space, and time only," and so on, filled pages and
pages in our letters, the writing of which became more and
more microscopical as the subjects under discussion grew in
importance. But neither then nor later on, when we used to
spend hours and hours in discussing Kant's philosophy, could
my brother convert me to become a disciple of the Königsberg
philosopher.

Natural sciences—that is, mathematics, physics, and astronomy—were my chief studies. In the year 1858, before Darwin
had brought out his immortal work, a professor of zoölogy at
the Moscow University, Roulier, published three lectures on
transformism, and my brother took up at once his ideas concerning the variability of species. He was not satisfied, however, with approximate proofs only, and began to study a number of special books on heredity and the like; communicating
to me in his letters the main facts, as well as his ideas and his
doubts. The appearance of *The Origin of Species* did not
settle his doubts on several special points, but only raised new
questions and gave him the impulse for further studies. We
afterward discussed—and that discussion lasted for many years
—various questions relative to the origin of variations, their
chances of being transmitted and being accentuated; in short,

those questions which have been raised quite lately in the
Weismann-Spencer controversy, in Galton's researches, and in
the works of the modern Neo-Lamarckians. Owing to his
philosophical and critical mind, Alexander had noticed at once
the fundamental importance of these questions for the theory
of variability of species, even though they were so often over-
looked then by many naturalists.

I must also mention a temporary excursion into the domain
of political economy. In the years 1858 and 1859 every one in
Russia talked of political economy; lectures on free trade and
protective duties attracted crowds of people, and my brother,
who was not yet absorbed by the variability of species, took a
lively though temporary interest in economical matters, sending me for reading the *Political Economy* of Jean Baptiste Say.
I read a few chapters only: tariffs and banking operations did
not interest me in the least; but Alexander took up these matters so passionately that he even wrote letters to our stepmother, trying to interest her in the intricacies of the customs
duties. Later on, in Siberia, as we were re-reading some of the
letters of that period, we laughed like children when we fell
upon one of his epistles in which he complained of our stepmother's incapacity to be moved even by such burning questions, and raged against a greengrocer whom he had caught
in the street, and who, "would you believe it," he wrote with
signs of exclamation, "although he was a tradesman, affected
a pig-headed indifference to tariff questions!"

Every summer about one half of the pages were taken to a
camp at Peterhof. The lower forms, however, were dispensed
from joining the camp, and I spent the first two summers at
Nikólskoe. To leave the school, to take the train to Moscow,
and there to meet Alexander was such a happy prospect that
I used to count the days that had to pass till that glorious one
should arrive. But on one occasion a great disappointment
awaited me at Moscow. Alexander had not passed his examinations, and was left for another year in the same form. He was,
in fact, too young to enter the special classes; but our father
was very angry with him, nevertheless, and would not permit
us to see each other. I felt very sad. We were not children any
more, and had so much to say to each other. I tried to obtain

permission to go to our aunt Sulíma, at whose house I might meet Alexander, but it was absolutely refused. After our father remarried we were never allowed to see our mother's relations.

That spring our Moscow house was full of guests. Every night the reception-rooms were flooded with lights, the band played, the confectioner was busy making ices and pastry, and card-playing went on in the great hall till a late hour. I strolled aimlessly about in the brilliantly illuminated rooms, and felt unhappy.

One night, after ten, a servant beckoned me, telling me to come out to the entrance hall. I went. "Come to the coachmen's house," the old major-domo Frol whispered to me. "Alexander Alexéevich is here."

I dashed across the yard, up the flight of steps leading to the coachmen's house, and into a wide, half-dark room, where, at the immense dining-table of the servants, I saw Alexander.

"Sásha, dear, how did you come?" and in a moment we rushed into each other's arms, hugging each other and unable to speak from emotion.

"Hush, hush! they may overhear you," said the servants' cook, Praskóvia, wiping away her tears with her apron. "Poor orphans! If your mother were only alive"—

Old Frol stood, his head deeply bent, his eyes also twinkling. "Look here, Pétia, not a word to any one; to no one," he said, while Praskóvia placed on the table an earthenware jar full of porridge for Alexander.

He, glowing with health, in his cadet uniform, already had begun to talk about all sorts of matters, while he rapidly emptied the porridge pot. I could hardly make him tell me how he came there at such a late hour. We lived then near the Smolénsky boulevard, within a stone's throw of the house where our mother died, and the corps of cadets was at the opposite outskirts of Moscow, full five miles away.

He had made a doll out of bedclothes, and had put it in his bed, under the blankets; then he went to the tower, descended from a window, came out unnoticed, and walked the whole distance.

"Were you not afraid at night, in the deserted fields round your corps?" I asked.

"What had I to fear? Only lots of dogs were upon me; I had teased them myself. To-morrow I shall take my sword with me."

The coachmen and other servants came in and out; they sighed as they looked at us, and took seats at a distance, along the walls, exchanging words in a subdued tone, so as not to disturb us; while we two, in each other's arms, sat there till midnight, talking about nebulæ and Laplace's hypothesis, the structure of matter, the struggles of the papacy under Boniface VIII. with the imperial power, and so on.

From time to time one of the servants would hurriedly run in, saying, "Pétinka, go and show thyself in the hall; they are moving about and may ask for thee."

I implored Sásha not to come next night; but he came, nevertheless,—not without having had a scrimmage with the dogs, against whom he had taken his sword. I responded with feverish haste, when, earlier than the day before, I was called once more to the coachmen's house. Alexander had made part of the journey in a cab. The previous night, one of the servants had brought him what he had got from the card-players and asked him to take it. He took some small coin to hire a cab, and so he came earlier than on his first visit.

He intended to come next night, too, but for some reason it would have been dangerous for the servants, and we decided to part till the autumn. A short "official" note made me understand next day that his nocturnal escapades had passed unnoticed. How terrible would have been the punishment, if they had been discovered! It is awful to think of it: flogging before the corps till he was carried away unconscious on a sheet, and then degradation to a soldiers' sons' battalion,—anything was possible, in those times.

What our servants would have suffered for hiding us, if information of the affair had reached our father's ears, would have been equally terrible; but they knew how to keep secrets, and not to betray one another. They all knew of the visits of Alexander, but none of them whispered a word to any one of the family. They and I were the only ones in the house who ever knew anything about it.

IV

That same year I made my start as an investigator of popular
life. This work brought me one step nearer to our peasants,
making me see them under a new light; later, it also helped
me a great deal in Siberia.

Every year, in July, on the day of "The Holy Virgin of
Kazan," which was the fête of our church, a pretty large fair
was held in Nikólskoe. Tradesmen came from all the neighboring towns, and many thousands of peasants flocked from thirty
miles round to our village, which for a couple of days had a
most animated aspect. A remarkable description of the village
fairs of South Russia had been published that year by the
Slavophile Aksákov, and my brother, who was then at the
height of his politico-economical enthusiasm, advised me to
make a statistical description of our fair, and to determine
the returns of goods brought in and sold. I followed his advice,
and to my great amazement I really succeeded: my estimate
of returns, so far as I can judge now, was not more unreliable
than many similar estimates in books of statistics.

Our fair lasted only a little more than twenty-four hours. On
the eve of the fête the great open space given to the fair was
full of life and animation. Long rows of stalls, to be used for
the sale of cottons, ribbons, and all sorts of peasant women's
attire, were hurriedly built. The restaurant, a substantial stone
building, was furnished with tables, chairs, and benches, and
its floor was strewn over with bright yellow sand. Three wine
shops were erected, and freshly cut brooms, planted on high
poles, rose high in the air, to attract the peasants from a distance. Rows and rows of smaller stalls, for the sale of crockery,
boots, stoneware, gingerbread, and all sorts of small things,
rose as if by a magic wand, while in a special corner of the
fair-ground holes were dug to receive immense cauldrons, in
which bushels of millet and sarrazin and whole sheep were
boiled, for supplying the thousands of visitors with hot *shchi*
and *kásha* (soup and porridge). In the afternoon, the four
roads leading to the fair were blocked by hundreds of peasant-

carts, and heaps of pottery, casks filled with tar, corn, and cattle were exhibited along the roadsides.

The night service on the eve of the fête was performed in our church with great solemnity. Half a dozen priests and deacons, from the neighboring villages, took part in it, and their chanters, reinforced by young tradespeople, sang in the choirs such ritornellos as could usually be heard only at the bishop's in Kalúga. The church was crowded; all prayed fervently. The tradespeople vied with one another in the number and sizes of the wax candles which they lighted before the ikons, as offerings to the local saints for the success of their trade, and the crowd being so great as not to allow the last comers to reach the altar, candles of all sizes—thick and thin, white and yellow, according to the offerer's wealth—were handed from the back of the church through the crowd, with whispers: "To the Holy Virgin of Kazan, our Protector;" "To Nicholas the Favorite;" "To Frol and Laur" (the horse saints, —that was from those who had horses to sell); or simply to "The Saints," without further specification.

Immediately after the night service was over, the "forefair" began, and I had now to plunge headlong into my work of asking hundreds of people what was the value of the goods they had brought in. To my great astonishment I got on admirably. Of course, I was myself asked questions: "Why do you do this?" "Is it not for the old prince, who intends increasing the market dues?" But the assurance that the "old prince" knew and would know nothing of it (he would have thought it a disgraceful occupation) settled all doubts at once. I soon caught the proper way of asking questions, and after I had taken half a dozen cups of tea, in the restaurant, with some tradespeople (oh, horror, if my father had learned that!), all went on very well. Vasíli Ivánov, the elder of Nikólskoe, a beautiful young peasant, with a fine intelligent face and a silky fair beard, took an interest in my work. "Well, if thou wantest it for thy learning, get at it; thou wilt tell us later on what thou hast found out," was his conclusion, and he told some of the people that it was "all right."

In short, the imports were determined very nicely. But next day the sales offered certain difficulties, chiefly with the dry-goods merchants, who did not themselves yet know how much they had sold. On the day of the fête the young peasant women simply stormed the shops; each of them, having sold some linen of her own make, was now buying some cotton print and a bright kerchief for herself, a colored handkerchief for her husband, perhaps some lace, a ribbon or two, and a number of small gifts for grandmother, grandfather, and the children who had remained at home. As to the peasants who sold crockery, or ginger cakes, or cattle, or hemp, they at once determined their sales, especially the old women. "Good sale, grandmother?" I would ask. "No need to complain, my son. Why should I anger God! Nearly all is sold." And out of their small items tens of thousands of rubles grew in my notebook. One point only remained unsettled. A wide space was given up to many hundreds of peasant women who stood in the burning sun, each with her piece of hand-woven linen, sometimes exquisitely fine, which she had brought for sale. Scores of buyers, with gypsy faces and shark-like looks, moved about in the crowd, buying. Only rough estimates of these sales could be made.

I made no reflections at that time about this new experience of mine; I was simply happy to see that it was not a failure. But the serious good sense and sound judgment of the Russian peasants which I witnessed during this couple of days left upon me a lasting impression. Later, when we were spreading socialist doctrines amongst the peasants, I could not but wonder why some of my friends, who had received a seemingly far more democratic education than myself, did not know how to talk to the peasants or to the factory workers from the country. They tried to imitate the "peasants' talk" by introducing a profusion of so-called "popular phrases," but they only rendered themselves the more incomprehensible.

Nothing of the sort is needed, either in talking to peasants or in writing for them. The Great Russian peasant perfectly well understands the educated man's talk, provided it is not stuffed with words taken from foreign languages. What the peasant does not understand is abstract notions when they are not illustrated by concrete examples. But my experience is that when you speak to the Russian peasant plainly, and start from concrete facts,—and the same is true with regard to village folk of all nationalities,—there is no generalization from the whole world of science, social or natural, which cannot be conveyed to a man of average intelligence, if you yourself understand it concretely. The chief difference between the educated and the uneducated man is, I should say, that the latter is not able to follow a chain of conclusions. He grasps the first of them, and maybe the second, but he gets tired at the third, if he does not see what you are driving at. But how often do we meet the same difficulty in educated people.

One more impression I gathered from that work of my boyhood, an impression which I did not formulate till afterward, and which will probably astonish many a reader. It is the spirit of equality which is highly developed in the Russian peasant, and in fact in the rural population everywhere. The Russian peasant is capable of much servile obedience to the landlord and the police officer; he will bend before their will in a servile manner; but he does not consider them superior men, and if the next moment that same landlord or officer talks to the same peasant about hay or ducks, the latter will reply to him as an equal to an equal. I never saw in a Russian peasant that servility, grown to be a second nature, with which a small functionary talks to one of high rank, or a valet to his master. The peasant too easily submits to force, but he does not worship it.

I returned that summer from Nikólskoe to Moscow in a new fashion. There being then no railway between Kalúga and Moscow, there was a man, Buck by name, who kept some sort of carriages running between the two towns. Our people never thought of traveling in these carriages: they had their own horses and conveyances; but when my father, in order to save my stepmother a double journey, proposed to me, half in joke, that I should travel alone in that way, I accepted his offer with delight.

A tradesman's wife, old and very stout, and myself on the back seats, and a tradesman or artisan on the front seat, were the only occupants of the carriage. I found the journey very pleasant,—first of all because I was traveling by myself (I was not yet sixteen), and next because the old lady, who had brought with her for a three days' journey a colossal hamper full of provisions, treated me to all sorts of home-made

delicacies. The surroundings during that journey were delightful. One evening especially is still vivid in my memory. We
came to one of the great villages and stopped at an inn. The
old lady ordered a samovár for herself, while I went out into
the street, walking about anywhere. A small "white inn," at
which only food is served, but no drinks, attracted my attention, and I went in. Numbers of peasants sat round the small
tables, which were covered with white napkins, and enjoyed
their tea. I followed their example.

Everything there was new to me. It was a village of "Crown
peasants," that is, peasants who had not been serfs, and enjoyed a relative well-being, probably owing to the weaving of
linen, which they carried on as a home industry. Slow, serious
conversations, with occasional laughter, were going on at the
tables, and after the usual introductory questions, I soon found
myself engaged in a conversation with a dozen peasants about
the crops in our neighborhood, and answering all sorts of inquiries. They wanted to know all about St. Petersburg, and
especially about the rumors concerning the coming abolition of
serfdom. A feeling of simplicity and of natural relations of
equality, as well as of hearty goodwill, which I always felt
afterwards when among peasants or in their houses, pervaded
me at that inn. Nothing extraordinary happened that night,
so that I even ask myself whether the incident is worth mentioning at all; and yet, that warm dark night in the village,
that small inn, that talk with the peasants, and the keen interest they took in hundreds of things lying far beyond their
habitual surroundings, have made a poor "white inn" more
attractive to me ever since than the best restaurant in the
world.

v

Stormy times came now in the life of our corps. When Girardot
was dismissed, his place was taken by one of our officers,
Captain B——. He was rather good-natured than otherwise,
but he had got it into his head that he was not treated by us
with due reverence corresponding to the high position which
he now occupied, and he tried to enforce upon us more respect

and awe towards himself. He began by quarreling over all sorts of petty things with the upper form, and—what was still worse in our opinion—he attempted to destroy our "liberties," the origin of which was lost in "the darkness of time," and which, insignificant in themselves, were perhaps on that very account only the dearer to us.

The result of it was that for several days the school was in an open revolt, which ended in wholesale punishment, and in the exclusion from the corps of two of our favorite pages de chambre.

Then the same captain began to intrude into the class-rooms, where we used to spend one hour in the morning in preparing our lessons, before the classes began. We were considered to be there under our teaching staff, and were happy to have nothing to do with our military officers. We resented that intrusion very much, and one day I loudly expressed our discontent by telling the captain that this was the place of the inspector of the classes, not his. I spent weeks under arrest for that frankness, and perhaps would have been excluded from the school, had it not been that the inspector of the classes, his aide, and even our old director judged that, after all, I had only expressed aloud what they all used to say to themselves.

No sooner were these troubles over, than the death of the Dowager Empress, the widow of Nicholas I., brought a new interruption in our work.

The burial of crowned heads is always so arranged as to produce a deep impression on the crowds. The body of the Empress was brought from Tsárskoe Seló, where she died, to St. Petersburg, and here, followed by the imperial family, all the high dignitaries of the state, and scores of thousands of functionaries and corporations, and preceded by hundreds of clergy and choirs, it was taken from the railway station, through the main thoroughfares, to the fortress, where it had to lie in state for several weeks. A hundred thousand men of the guard were placed along the streets, and thousands of people, dressed in the most gorgeous uniforms, preceded, accompanied, and followed the hearse in a solemn procession. Litanies were sung at every important crossing of the streets, and here the ringing of the bells on the church towers, the voices of the vast choirs, and the sounds of the military bands united in the most impressive way, so as to make people believe that the immense crowds really mourned the loss of the Empress.

As long as the body lay in state in the cathedral of the fortress, the pages, among others, had to keep watch round it, night and day. Three pages de chambre and three maids of honor always stood close by the coffin, which was placed on a high pedestal, while some twenty pages were stationed on the platform, upon which litanies were sung twice every day, in the presence of the Emperor and all his family. Consequently, every week nearly one half of the corps was taken in turns to the fortress, to lodge there. We were relieved every two hours, and in the daytime our service was not difficult; but when we had to rise in the night, to dress in our court uniforms, and then to walk through the dark and gloomy inner courts of the fortress to the cathedral, to the sound of the gloomy chime of the fortress bells, a cold shiver seized me at the thought of the prisoners who were immured somewhere in this Russian Bastille. "Who knows," thought I, "whether in my turn I shall not also have to join them some day."

The burial did not pass without an accident, which might have had serious consequences. An immense canopy had been erected under the dome of the cathedral, over the coffin. A huge gilded crown rose above it, and from this crown an immense purple mantle, lined with ermine, hung towards the four thick pilasters which support the dome of the cathedral. It was impressive, but we boys soon made out that the crown was of gilded cardboard and wood, the mantle of velvet only in its lower part, while higher up it was red cotton, and that the ermine lining was simply cotton flannelette or swansdown, to which tails of black squirrels had been sewn; the escutcheons, which represented the arms of Russia, veiled with black crêpe, were simple cardboard. But the crowds, which were allowed at certain hours of the night to pass by the coffin, and to kiss in a hurry the gold brocade which covered it, surely had no time to closely examine the flannelette ermine or the cardboard escutcheons, and the desired theatrical effect was obtained even by such cheap means.

When a litany is sung in Russia, all people present hold

lighted wax candles, which have to be put out after certain prayers have been read. The imperial family also held such candles, and one day, the young son of the Grand Duke Constantine, seeing that the others put out their wax candles by turning them upside down, did the same. The black gauze which hung behind him from an escutcheon took fire, and in a second the escutcheon and the cotton stuff were ablaze. An immense tongue of fire ran up the heavy folds of the supposed ermine mantle.

The service was stopped. All looks were directed with terror upon the tongue of fire, which went higher and higher toward the cardboard crown and the woodwork that supported the whole structure. Bits of burning stuff began to fall, threatening to set fire to the black gauze veils of the ladies present.

Alexander II. lost his presence of mind for a couple of seconds only, but he recovered immediately, and said in a composed voice: "The coffin must be taken!" The pages de chambre at once covered it with the thick gold brocade, and we all advanced to lift it; but in the meantime the big tongue of flame had broken into a number of smaller ones, which now slowly devoured only the fluffy outside of the cotton stuff and, meeting more and more dust and soot in the upper parts of the structure, gradually died out in its folds.

I cannot say what I looked at most: the creeping fire or the stately slender figures of the three ladies who stood by the coffin, the long trains of their black dresses spreading over the steps which led to the upper platform, and their black lace veils hanging down their shoulders. None of them had made the slightest movement: they stood like three beautiful carved images. Only in the dark eyes of one of them, Mademoiselle Gamaléia, tears glittered like pearls. She was a daughter of South Russia, and was the only really handsome lady amongst the maids of honor at the court.

At the corps everything was upside down. The classes were interrupted; those of us who returned from the fortress were lodged in temporary quarters, and, having nothing to do, spent the whole day in all sorts of frolics. In one of them we managed to open a cupboard which stood in the room, and contained a splendid collection of models of all kinds of animals, for the teaching of natural history. That was its official purpose, but it

was never even so much as shown to us, and now that we got
hold of it we utilized it in our own way. With a human skull,
which was in the collection, we made a ghostly figure where-
with to frighten other comrades and the officers at night. As
to the animals, we placed them in the most ludicrous positions
and groups: monkeys were seen riding on lions, sheep were
playing with leopards, the giraffe danced with the elephant,
and so on. The worst was that a few days later one of the
Prussian princes, who had come to assist at the burial ceremony (it was the one, I think, who became later on the Emperor Frederic), visited our school, and was shown all that
concerned our education. Our director did not fail to boast
of the excellent educational appliances which we had, and
brought his guest to that unfortunate cupboard. When the
German prince caught a glimpse of our zoölogical classification, he drew a long face and quickly turned away. The director looked horrified; he had lost the power of speech, and
only pointed repeatedly with his hand at some sea stars, which
were placed in glass boxes on the walls beside the cupboard.
The suite of the prince tried to look as if they had noticed
nothing, and only threw rapid glances at the cause of so much
disturbance, while we wicked boys made all sorts of faces in
order not to burst with laughter.

VI

The school years of a Russian youth are so different from the
corresponding period in west European schools, that I must
dwell further on my school life. Russian boys, as a rule, while
they are yet at a lyceum or in a military school, take an interest
in a wide circle of social, political, and philosophical matters.
It is true that the Corps of Pages was, of all schools, the least
congenial place for such a development; but in those years of
general revival, broader ideas penetrated even there, and carried some of us away, without, however, preventing us from
taking a very lively part in "benefit nights" and all sorts of
frolics.

While I was in the fourth form I became interested in history, and with the aid of notes made during the lessons, and

helping myself with reading, I wrote quite a course of early mediæval history for my own use. Next year, the struggle between Pope Boniface VIII. and the imperial power attracted my special attention, and now it became my ambition to be admitted to the Imperial Library as a reader, to study that great struggle. That was contrary to the rules of the library, pupils of secondary schools not being admitted; our good Herr Becker, however, smoothed the way out of the difficulty, and I was allowed at last to enter the sanctuary, and to take a seat at one of the readers' small tables, on one of the red velvet sofas which then formed a part of the furniture of the reading-room.

From various textbooks and some books from our own library, I soon got to the sources. Knowing no Latin, I discovered, nevertheless, a rich supply of original sources in Old Teutonic and Old French, and found an immense æsthetic enjoyment in the quaint structure and expressiveness of the Old French in the chronicles. Quite a new structure of society and quite a world of complicated relations opened before me; and from that time I learned to value far more highly the original sources of history than the works of modernized generalizations in which the prejudices of modern politics, or even mere current formulæ, are often substituted for the real life of the period. Nothing gives more impetus to one's intellectual development than some sort of independent research, and these studies of mine afterwards helped me very much.

Unhappily I had to abandon them when we reached the second form (the last but one). The pages had to study during the last two years nearly all that was taught in other military schools in three special forms, and we had a vast amount of work to do for the school. Natural sciences, mathematics, and military sciences necessarily relegated history to the background.

In the second form we began seriously to study physics. We had an excellent teacher, a very intelligent man with a sarcastic turn of mind, who hated learning from memory, and managed to make us *think*, instead of merely learning facts. He was a good mathematician, and taught us physics on a mathematical basis, admirably explaining at the same time the leading ideas of physical research and physical apparatus. Some of his questions were so original and his explanations so good that they engraved themselves forever in my memory.

Our textbook of physics was not bad (most textbooks for the military schools had been written by the best men at the time), but it was rather old, and our teacher, who followed his own system in teaching, began to prepare a short summary of his lessons,—a sort of *aide-mémoire*. However, after a few weeks it so happened that the task of writing this summary fell upon me, and our teacher, acting as a true pedagogist, trusted it entirely to me, only reading the proofs. When we came to the chapters on heat, electricity, and magnetism, they had to be written entirely anew, with more developments, and this I did, thus preparing a nearly complete textbook of physics, which was printed for the use of the school.

In the second form we also began to study chemistry, and in this, too, we had a first-rate teacher,—a passionate lover of the subject, who had himself made valuable original researches. The years 1859–61 were years of a universal revival of taste for the exact sciences. Grove, Clausius, Joule, and Séguin showed that heat and all physical forces are but divers modes of motion; Helmholtz began about that time his epoch-making researches in sound; Tyndall, in his popular lectures, made one touch, so to say, the very atoms and molecules. Gerhardt and Avogadro introduced the theory of substitutions, and Mendeléev, Lothar Meyer, and Newlands discovered the periodical law of elements; Darwin, with his *Origin of Species*, revolutionized all biological sciences; while Karl Vogt and Moleschott, following Claude Bernard, laid the foundations of true psychology in physiology. It was a time of scientific revival, and the current which carried minds toward natural science was irresistible. Numbers of excellent books were published at that time in Russian translations, and I soon understood that whatever one's subsequent studies might be, a thorough knowledge of the natural sciences and familiarity with their methods must lie at the foundation. Five or six of us joined together to get some sort of laboratory for ourselves. With the elementary apparatus recommended for beginners in Stöckhardt's excellent textbook, we started our laboratory in a small bedroom of two of our comrades, the Zasetsky brothers.

Their father, an old admiral in retirement, was delighted to see his sons engaged in so useful a pursuit, and did not object to our coming together on Sundays and during the holidays in that room, by the side of his own study. With Stöckhardt's book as a guide, we systematically made all experiments. I must say that once we nearly set the house on fire, and that more than once we poisoned all the rooms with chlorine and similar stuffs. But the old admiral, when we related the adventure at dinner time, took it very nicely, and told us how he and his comrades also nearly set a house on fire in the far less useful pursuit of punch making; while the mother only said, amidst her paroxysms of coughing: "Of course, if it *is* necessary for your learning to handle such nasty smelling things, then there's nothing to be done!"

After dinner she usually took her seat at the piano, and till late at night we would go on singing duets, trios, and choruses from the operas. Or we would take the score of some Italian or Russian opera and go through it from the beginning to the end,—the mother and her daughter acting as the prima donnas, while we managed more or less successfully to maintain all the other parts. Chemistry and music thus went hand in hand.

Higher mathematics also absorbed a great deal of my time. Several of us had already decided that we should not enter a regiment of the Guard, where all our time would be given to military drill and parades, and we intended to enter, after promotion, one of the military academies,—artillery or engineering. In order to do so we had to prepare in higher geometry, differential calculus, and the beginnings of integral calculus, and we took private lessons for that purpose. At the same time, elementary astronomy being taught to us under the name of mathematical geography, I plunged into astronomical reading, especially during the last year of my stay at school. The never-ceasing life of the universe, which I conceived as *life* and evolution, became for me an inexhaustible source of higher poetical thought, and gradually the sense of Man's oneness with Nature, both animate and inanimate—the Poetry of Nature—became the philosophy of my life.

If the teaching in our school had been limited to the subjects I have mentioned, our time would have been pretty well occupied. But we also had to study in the domain of humanitarian science, history, law,—that is, the main outlines of the Russian code,—and political economy in its essential leading principles, including a course of comparative statistics; and we had to master formidable courses of military science,—tactics, military history (the campaigns of 1812 and 1815 in all their details), artillery and field fortification. Looking back now upon this education, I think that apart from the subjects relating to military warfare, for which more detailed studies in the exact sciences might have been advantageously substituted, the variety of subjects which we were taught was not beyond the capacity of the average youth. Owing to a pretty good knowledge of elementary mathematics and physics, which we gained in the lower forms, most of us managed to do all the work. Some studies were neglected by the majority of us, especially law, as also modern history, for which we had unfortunately an old wreck of a master, who was kept at his post only in order to give him his full old-age pension. Moreover, some latitude was given us in the choice of the subjects we liked best, and while we underwent severe examinations in these chosen subjects, we were treated rather leniently in the remainder. But the chief cause of the relative success which was obtained in the school was that the teaching was rendered as concrete as possible. As soon as we had learned elementary geometry on paper, we relearned it in the field, with poles and the surveyor's chain, and next with the astrolabe, the compass, and the surveyor's table. After such a concrete training, elementary astronomy offered no difficulties, while the surveys themselves were an endless source of enjoyment.

The same system of concrete teaching was applied to fortification. In the winter we solved such problems as, for instance, the following: Having a thousand men and a fortnight at your disposal, build the strongest fortification you can build, to protect that bridge for a retreating army; and we hotly discussed our schemes with the teacher when he criticized them. In the summer we applied our knowledge in the field. To these practical exercises I attribute the ease with which most of us mastered such a variety of scientific subjects at the age of seventeen or eighteen.

With all that, we had plenty of time for amusement and all sorts of frolics. Our best time was when the examinations were over, and we had three or four weeks quite free before going to camp, or when we returned from camp, and had another three weeks free before the beginning of lessons. The few of us who remained then in the school were allowed, during the vacations, to go out just as we liked, always finding bed and food at the school. I worked in the library, or visited the picture galleries of the Hermitage, studying one by one all the best pictures of each school separately; or I went to the different Crown manufactories of playing-cards, cottons, iron, china, and glass which are open to the public. Sometimes we went out rowing on the Nevá, spending the whole night on the river; sometimes in the Gulf of Finland with fishermen,—a melancholy northern night, during which the morning dawn meets the afterglow of the setting sun, and a book can be read in the open air at midnight. For all this we found plenty of time.

After my visits to the manufactories I took a liking to strong and perfect machinery. Seeing how a gigantic paw, coming out of a shanty, grasps a log floating in the Nevá, pulls it inside, and puts it under the saws, which cut it into boards; or how a huge red-hot iron bar is transformed into a rail after it has passed between two cylinders, I understood the poetry of machinery. In our present factories, machinery work is killing for the worker, because he becomes a lifelong servant to a given machine, and never is anything else. But this is a matter of bad organization, and has nothing to do with the machine itself. Overwork and lifelong monotony are equally bad whether the work is done with the hand, with plain tools, or with a machine. But apart from these, I fully understand the pleasure that man can derive from a consciousness of the might of his machine, the intelligent character of its work, the gracefulness of its movements, and the correctness of what it is doing; and I think that William Morris's hatred of machines only proved that the conception of the machine's power and gracefulness was missing in his great poetical genius.

Music also played a very great part in my development. From it I borrowed even greater joy and enthusiasm than from poetry. The Russian opera hardly existed in those times; but the Italian opera, which had a number of first-rate stars in it, was the most popular institution at St. Petersburg. When the prima donna Bosio fell ill, thousands of people, chiefly of the youth, stood till late at night at the door of her hotel to get news of her. She was not beautiful, but seemed so much so when she sang that young men madly in love with her could be counted by the hundred; and when she died, she had a burial such as no one had ever had at St. Petersburg before. All St. Petersburg was then divided into two camps: the admirers of the Italian opera, and those of the French stage, which even then was showing in germ the putrid Offenbachian current that a few years later infected all Europe. Our form was also divided, half and half, between these two camps, and I belonged to the former. We were not permitted to go to the pit or to the balcony, while all the boxes in the Italian opera were always taken months in advance, by subscription, and even transmitted in certain families as an hereditary possession. But we gained admission, on Saturday nights, to the passages in the uppermost gallery, and had to stand there in a Turkish bath atmosphere, while to conceal our showy uniforms we used to wear our black overcoats, lined with wadding and with a fur collar, tightly buttoned in spite of the heat. It is a wonder that none of us got pneumonia in this way, especially as we came out overheated with the ovations which we used to make to our favorite singers, and stood afterwards at the stage door to catch one more glimpse of our favorites, and to cheer them. The Italian opera, in those years, was in some strange way intimately connected with the radical movement, and the revolutionary recitatives in *Wilhelm Tell* and *The Puritans* were always met with stormy applause and vociferations which went straight to the heart of Alexander II.; while in the sixth-story galleries, and in the smoking-room of the opera, and at the stage door the best part of the St. Petersburg youth came together in a common idealist worship of a noble art. All this may seem childish; but many higher ideas and pure inspirations were kindled in us by this worship of our favorite artists.

VII

Every summer we went out camping at Peterhof, with the other military schools of the St. Petersburg district. On the whole, our life there was very pleasant, and certainly it was excellent for our health: we slept in spacious tents, bathed in the sea, and spent a great deal of time during the six weeks in open-air exercise.

In military schools the main purpose of camp life was evidently military drill, which we all disliked very much, but the dullness of which was occasionally relieved by making us take part in manœuvres. One night, as we were going to bed, Alexander II. aroused the whole camp by having the alert sounded. In a few minutes all the camp was alive,—several thousand boys gathering round their colors, and the guns of the artillery school booming in the stillness of the night. All military Peterhof came galloping to the camp, but owing to some misunderstanding the Emperor remained on foot. Orderlies hurried in all directions to get a horse for him, but there was none, and not being a good rider, he would not ride any horse but one of his own. He was very angry, and freely gave vent to his anger. "Imbecile (*durák*), have I only one horse?" I heard him shout to an orderly who reported that his horse was in another camp.

With the coming darkness, the booming of the guns, and the rattling of the cavalry, we boys grew very much excited, and when Alexander ordered a charge, our column charged straight upon him. Tightly packed in the ranks, with lowered bayonets, we must have had a menacing aspect; and I saw the Emperor, who was still on foot, clearing the way for the column in three formidable jumps. I understood then the meaning of a column which marches in serried ranks under the excitement of the music and the march itself. There stood before us the Emperor, our commander, whom we all venerated; but I felt that in this moving mass not one page or cadet would have moved an inch aside or stopped to make room for him. We were the marching column, he was but an obstacle, and the column would have marched over him. "Why should he be in our way?" the pages said afterward. Boys, rifle in hand, are even more terrible in such cases than old soldiers.

Next year, when we took part in the great manœuvres of the St. Petersburg garrison, I saw some of the sidelights of warfare. For two days in succession we did nothing but march up and down in a space of about twenty miles, without having the slightest idea of what was going on round us, or for what purpose we were marched. Cannon boomed now in our neighborhood and now far away; sharp musketry fire was heard somewhere in the hills and the woods; orderlies galloped up and down, bringing an order to advance and next an order to retreat; and we marched, marched, and marched, seeing no sense in all these movements and counter movements. Masses of cavalry had passed along the same road, making it a deep bed of movable sand, and we had to advance and retreat several times over the same ground, till at last our column broke all discipline and became an incoherent mass of pilgrims rather than a military unit. The color guard alone remained in the road; the remainder slowly paced along the sides of the road in the wood. The orders and the supplications of the officers were of no avail.

Suddenly a shout came from behind: "The Emperor is coming! The Emperor!" The officers ran about, begging us to form ranks: nobody listened to them.

The Emperor came, and ordered a retreat once more. "About!" the word of command rang out. "The Emperor is behind us; please turn round," the officers whispered; but the battalion took hardly any notice of the command, and none whatever of the presence of the Emperor. Happily, Alexander II. was no fanatic of militarism, and after having said a few words to cheer us, with a promise of rest, he galloped off.

I understood then how much depends in warfare upon the state of mind of the troops, and how little can be done by mere discipline when more than an average effort is required from the soldiers. What can discipline do when tired troops have to make a supreme effort to reach the field of battle at a given hour! It is absolutely powerless; only enthusiasm and confidence can at such moments induce the soldiers to do "the impossible," and it is the impossible that continually must be accomplished to secure success. How often I recalled to memory that object lesson later on, in Siberia, when we also had to do "the impossible" during our scientific expeditions!

Comparatively little of our time, however, during our stay in the camp was given to military drill and manœuvres. A good deal of it was employed in practical work in surveying and fortification. After a few preliminary exercises we were given a reflecting compass and told, "Go and make a plan of, say, this lake, or those roads, or that part, measuring the angles with the compass and the distances by pacing." Early in the morning, after a hurriedly swallowed breakfast, a boy would fill his capacious military pockets with slices of rye bread, and would go out for four or five hours in the parks, miles away, mapping with his compass and paces the beautiful shady roads, the rivulets, and the lakes. His work was afterward compared with accurate maps, and prizes in optical and drawing instruments, at the boy's choice, were awarded. For me, these surveys were a deep source of enjoyment. The independent work, the isolation under the centuries-old trees, the life of the forest which I could enjoy undisturbed, while there was at the same time the interest in the work,—all these left deep traces on my mind; and when I became an explorer of Siberia, and several of my comrades became explorers of central Asia, these surveys were found to have been an excellent preparation.

Finally, in the last form, parties of four boys were taken every second day to some villages at a considerable distance from the camp, and there they had to make a detailed survey of several square miles, with the aid of the surveyor's table and a telescopic ruler. Officers of the general staff came from time to time to verify their work and to advise them. This life amid the peasants in the villages had the best effect upon the intellectual and moral development of the boys.

At the same time there were exercises in the construction of natural size cross-sections of fortifications. We were taken out by an officer into the open field, and there we had to make the profile of a bastion, or of a complicated bridge head, nailing battens and poles together in exactly the same way as railway engineers do in tracing a railway. When it came to embrasures and barbettes, we had to calculate a great deal in order to obtain the inclinations of the different planes, and after that geometry ceased to be difficult to understand.

We delighted in such work, and once, in town, finding in our garden a heap of clay and gravel, we began to build a real fortification on a reduced scale, with well calculated straight and oblique embrasures and barbettes. All was done very neatly, and our ambition now was to obtain some planks for making the platforms for the guns, and to place upon them the model guns which we had in our class-rooms. But, alas! our trousers wore an alarming aspect. "What are you doing there?" our captain exclaimed. "Look at yourselves! You look like navvies" (that was exactly what we were proud of). "What if the grand duke comes and finds you in such a state!"

"We will show him our fortification and ask him to get us tools and boards for the platforms."

All protests were vain. A dozen workmen were sent next day to cart away our beautiful structure as if it were a mere heap of mud!

I mention this to show how children and youths long for the application of what they learn at school in the abstract, and how stupid are the educators who are unable to see what a powerful aid they could find in this direction for helping their pupils to grasp the real sense of the things they learn. In our school, all was directed towards training us for warfare; we should have worked with the same enthusiasm, however, at laying out a railway, at building a log house, or at cultivating a garden or a field. But all this longing of children and youths for *real* work is wasted simply because our idea of the school is still the mediæval scholasticism, the mediæval monastery!

VIII

The years 1857–61 were years of rich growth in the intellectual forces of Russia. All that had been whispered for the last decade, in the secrecy of friendly meetings, by the generation represented in Russian literature by Turgénev, Tolstóy, Hérzen, Bakúnin, Ogarióv, Kavélin, Dostoévsky, Grigoróvich, Ostróvsky, and Nekrásov, began now to leak out in the press. Censorship was still very rigorous; but what could not be said openly in political articles was smuggled in under the form of novels, humorous sketches, or veiled comments on west European events, and every one read between the lines and understood.

Having no acquaintances at St. Petersburg apart from the school and a narrow circle of relatives, I stood outside the radical movement of those years,—miles, in fact, away from it. And yet, this was, perhaps, the main feature of the movement,—that it had the power to penetrate into so "well meaning" a school as our corps was, and to find an echo in such a circle as that of my Moscow relatives.

I used at that time to spend my Sundays and holidays at the house of my aunt, Princess Drútskaia. Prince Drútskoy thought only of extraordinary lunches and dinners, while his wife and their young daughter led a very gay life. My cousin was a beautiful girl of nineteen, of a most amiable disposition, and nearly all her male cousins were madly in love with her. She, in turn, fell in love with one of them, and wanted to marry him. But to marry a cousin is considered a great sin by the Russian Church, and the old princess tried in vain to obtain a special permission from the high ecclesiastical dignitaries. Now she brought her daughter to St. Petersburg, hoping that she might choose among her many admirers a more suitable husband than her own cousin. It was labor lost, I must add; but their fashionable apartment was full of brilliant young men from the Guards and from the diplomatic service.

Such a house would be the last to be thought of in connection with revolutionary ideas; and yet it was in that house that I made my first acquaintance with the revolutionary literature of the times. The great refugee, Hérzen, had just begun to issue at London his review, *The Polar Star,* which made a commotion in Russia, even in the palace circles, and was widely circulated secretly at St. Petersburg. My cousin got it in some way, and we used to read it together. Her heart revolted against the obstacles which were put in the way of her happiness, and her mind was the more open to the powerful criticisms which the great writer launched against the Russian autocracy and all the rotten system of misgovernment. With a feeling near to worship I used to look on the medallion which was printed on the paper cover of *The Polar Star,* and which represented the noble heads of the five "Decembrists" whom

Nicholas I. had hanged after the rebellion of December 14, 1825,—Bestúzhev, Kakhóvsky, Péstel, Ryléev, and Muraviór-Apóstol.

The beauty of the style of Hérzen,—of whom Turgénev has truly said that he wrote in tears and blood, and that no other Russian had ever so written,—the breadth of his ideas, and his deep love of Russia took possession of me, and I used to read and re-read those pages, even more full of heart than of brain.

In 1859, or early in 1860, I began to edit my first revolutionary paper. At that age, what could I be but a constitutionalist? —and my paper advocated the necessity of a constitution for Russia. I wrote about the foolish expenses of the court, the sums of money which were spent at Nice to keep quite a squadron of the navy in attendance on the Dowager Empress, who died in 1860; I mentioned the misdeeds of the functionaries which I continually heard spoken of, and I urged the necessity of constitutional rule. I wrote three copies of my paper, and slipped them into the desks of three comrades of the higher forms, who, I thought, might be interested in public affairs. I asked my readers to put their remarks behind the Scotch clock in our library.

With a throbbing heart, I went next day to see if there was something for me behind the clock. Two notes were there, indeed. Two comrades wrote that they fully sympathized with my paper, and only advised me not to risk too much. I wrote my second number, still more vigorously insisting upon the necessity of uniting all forces in the name of liberty. But this time there was no reply behind the clock. Instead the two comrades came to me.

"We are sure," they said, "that it is you who edit the paper, and we want to talk about it. We are quite agreed with you, and we are here to say, 'Let us be friends.' Your paper has done its work,—it has brought us together; but there is no need to continue it. In all the school there are only two more who would take any interest in such matters, while if it becomes known that there is a paper of this kind, the consequences will be terrible for all of us. Let us constitute a circle and talk about everything; perhaps we shall put something into the heads of a few others."

This was so sensible that I could only agree, and we sealed

our union by a hearty shaking of hands. From that time we three became firm friends, and used to read a great deal together and discuss all sorts of things.

The abolition of serfdom was the question which then engrossed the attention of all thinking men.

The revolution of 1848 had had its distant echo in the hearts of the Russian peasant folk, and from the year 1850 the insurrections of revolted serfs began to take serious proportions. When the Crimean war broke out, and militia was levied all over Russia, these revolts spread with a violence never before heard of. Several serf-owners were killed by their serfs, and the peasant uprisings became so serious that whole regiments, with artillery, were sent to quell them, whereas in former times small detachments of soldiers would have been sufficient to terrorize the peasants into obedience.

These outbreaks on the one side, and the profound aversion to serfdom which had grown up in the generation which came to the front with the advent of Alexander II. to the throne, rendered the emancipation of the peasants more and more imperative. The Emperor, himself averse to serfdom, and supported, or rather influenced, in his own family by his wife, his brother Constantine, and the Grand Duchess Hélène Pávlovna, took the first steps in that direction. His intention was that the initiative of the reform should come from the nobility, the serf-owners themselves. But in no province of Russia could the nobility be induced to send a petition to the Tsar to that effect. In March, 1856, he himself addressed the Moscow nobility on the necessity of such a step; but a stubborn silence was all their reply to his speech, so that Alexander II., growing quite angry, concluded with those memorable words of Hérzen: "It is better, gentlemen, that it should come from above than to wait till it comes from beneath." Even these words had no effect, and it was to the provinces of Old Poland,—Gródno, Wílno, and Kóvno,—where Napoleon I. had abolished serfdom (on paper) in 1812, that recourse was had. The governor-general of those provinces, Nazímov, managed to obtain the desired address from the Polish nobility. In November, 1857, the famous "rescript" to the governor-general of the Lithuanian provinces, announcing the intention of the Emperor to abolish serfdom, was launched, and we read, with tears in our eyes, the beautiful article of Hérzen, "Thou hast conquered, Galilean," in which the refugees at London declared that they would no more look upon Alexander II. as an enemy, but would support him in the great work of emancipation.

The attitude of the peasants was very remarkable. No sooner had the news spread that the liberation long sighed for was coming than the insurrections nearly stopped. The peasants waited now, and during a journey which Alexander made in Middle Russia they flocked around him as he passed, beseeching him to grant them liberty,—a petition, however, which Alexander received with great repugnance. It is most remarkable—so strong is the force of tradition—that the rumor went among the peasants that it was Napoleon III. who had required of the Tsar, in the treaty of peace, that the peasants should be freed. I frequently heard this rumor; and on the very eve of the emancipation they seemed to doubt that it would be done without pressure from abroad. "Nothing will be done unless Garibaldi comes," was the reply which a peasant made at St. Petersburg to a comrade of mine who talked to him about "freedom coming."

But after these moments of general rejoicing years of incertitude and disquiet followed. Specially appointed committees in the provinces and at St. Petersburg discussed the proposed liberation of the serfs, but the intentions of Alexander II. seemed unsettled. A check was continually put upon the press, in order to prevent it from discussing details. Sinister rumors circulated at St. Petersburg and reached our corps.

There was no lack of young men amongst the nobility who earnestly worked for a frank abolition of the old servitude; but the serfdom party drew closer and closer round the Emperor, and got power over his mind. They whispered into his ears that the day serfdom was abolished the peasants would begin to kill the landlords wholesale, and Russia would witness a new Pugachóv uprising, far more terrible than that of 1773. Alexander, who was a man of weak character, only too readily lent his ear to such predictions. But the huge machine for working out the emancipation law had been set to work. The committees had their sittings; scores of schemes of emancipation, addressed to the Emperor, circulated in manuscript or were printed at London. Hérzen, seconded by Turgénev, who kept him well informed about all that was going on in government circles, discussed in his *Bell* and his *Polar Star* the details of the various schemes, and Chernyshévsky in the *Contemporary* (*Sovreménnik*). The Slavophiles, especially Aksákov and Beliáev, had taken advantage of the first moments of relative freedom allowed the press to give the matter a wide publicity in Russia, and to discuss the features of the emancipation with a thorough understanding of its technical aspects. All intellectual St. Petersburg was with Hérzen, and particularly with Chernyshévsky, and I remember how the officers of the Horse Guards, whom I saw on Sundays, after the church parade, at the home of my cousin (Dmítri Nikoláevich Kropótkin, who was aide-de-camp of that regiment and aide-de-camp of the Emperor), used to side with Chernyshévsky, the leader of the advanced party in the emancipation struggle. The whole disposition of St. Petersburg, in the drawing-rooms and in the street, was such that it was impossible to go back. The liberation of the serfs had to be accomplished; and another important point was won,—the liberated serfs would receive, besides their homesteads, the land that they had hitherto cultivated for themselves.

However, the party of the old nobility was not discouraged. They centered their efforts on obtaining a postponement of the reform, on reducing the size of the allotments, and on imposing upon the emancipated serfs so high a redemption tax for the land that it would render their economical freedom illusory; and in this they fully succeeded. Alexander II. dismissed the real soul of the whole business, Nicholas Miliútin (brother of the minister of war), saying to him, "I am so sorry to part with you, but I must: the nobility describe you as one of the Reds." The first committees, which had worked out the scheme of emancipation, were dismissed, too, and new committees revised the whole work in the interest of the serf-owners; the press was muzzled once more.

Things assumed a very gloomy aspect. The question whether the liberation would take place at all was now asked. I feverishly followed the struggle, and every Sunday, when my comrades returned from their homes, I asked them what their parents said. By the end of 1860 the news became worse and

worse. "The Valúev party has got the upper hand." "They intend to revise the whole work." "The relatives of the Princess
X., a friend of the Tsar, work hard upon him." "The liberation
will be postponed: they fear a revolution."

In January, 1861, slightly better rumors began to circulate,
and it was generally hoped that something would be heard of
the emancipation on the day of the Emperor's accession to the
throne, the 19th of February.

The 19th came, but it brought nothing with it. I was on that
day at the palace. There was no grand levee, only a small one;
and pages of the second form were sent to such levees in order
to get accustomed to the palace ways. It was my turn that
day; and as I was seeing off one of the grand duchesses who
came to the palace to assist at the mass, her husband did not
appear, and I went to fetch him. He was called out of the
Emperor's study, and I told him, in a half jocose way, of the
perplexity of his wife, without having the slightest suspicion
of the important matters that may have been talked of in the
study at that time. Apart from a few of the initiated, no one
in the palace suspected that the manifesto had been signed on
the 19th of February, and was kept back for a fortnight only
because the next Sunday, the 26th, was the beginning of the
carnival week, and it was feared that, owing to the drinking
which goes on in the villages during the carnival, peasant
insurrections might break out. Even the carnival fair, which
used to be held at St. Petersburg on the square near the winter
palace, was removed that year to another square, from fear
of a popular insurrection in the capital. Most terrible instruc-
tions had been issued to the army as to the ways of repressing
peasant uprisings.

A fortnight later, on the last Sunday of the carnival (March
5, or rather March 17, New Style), I was at the corps, having
to take part in the military parade at the riding-school. I was
still in bed, when my soldier servant, Ivánov, dashed in with
the tea tray, exclaiming, "Prince, freedom! The manifesto is
posted on the Gostínoi Dvor" (the shops opposite the corps).

"Did you see it yourself?"

"Yes. People stand round; one reads, the others listen. It *is*
freedom!"

In a couple of minutes I was dressed, and out. A comrade was coming in.

"Kropótkin, freedom!" he shouted. "Here is the manifesto. My uncle learned last night that it would be read at the early mass at the Isaac Cathedral; so we went. There were not many people there; peasants only. The manifesto was read and distributed after the mass. They well understood what it meant. When I came out of the church, two peasants, who stood in the gateway, said to me in such a droll way, 'Well, sir? now—all gone?'" And he mimicked how they had shown him the way out. Years of expectation were in that gesture of sending away the master.

I read and re-read the manifesto. It was written in an elevated style by the old Metropolitan of Moscow, Philarète, but with a useless mixture of Russian and Old Slavonian which obscured the sense. It was liberty; but it was not liberty yet, the peasants having to remain serfs for two years more, till the 19th of February, 1863. Notwithstanding all this, one thing was evident: serfdom was abolished, and the liberated serfs would get the land and their homesteads. They would have to pay for it, but the old stain of slavery was removed. They would be slaves no more; the reaction had *not* got the upper hand.

We went to the parade; and when all the military performances were over, Alexander II., remaining on horseback, loudly called out, "The officers to me!" They gathered round him, and he began, in a loud voice, a speech about the great event of the day.

"The officers . . . the representatives of the nobility in the army"—these scraps of sentences reached our ears—"an end has been put to centuries of injustice . . . I expect sacrifices from the nobility . . . the loyal nobility will gather round the throne" . . . and so on. Enthusiastic hurrahs resounded amongst the officers as he ended.

We ran rather than marched back on our way to the corps, —hurrying to be in time for the Italian opera, of which the last performance in the season was to be given that afternoon; some manifestation was sure to take place then. Our military attire was flung off with great haste, and several of us dashed, light-footed, to the sixth-story gallery. The house was crowded.

During the first entr'acte the smoking-room of the opera filled with excited young men, who all talked to one another, whether acquainted or not. We planned at once to return to the hall, and to sing, with the whole public in a mass choir, the hymn "God Save the Tsar."

However, sounds of music reached our ears, and we all hurried back to the hall. The band of the opera was already playing the hymn, which was drowned immediately in enthusiastic hurrahs coming from all parts of the hall. I saw Bavéri, the conductor of the band, waving his stick, but not a sound could be heard from the powerful band. Then Bavéri stopped, but the hurrahs continued. I saw the stick waved again in the air; I saw the fiddle-bows moving, and musicians blowing the brass instruments, but again the sound of voices overwhelmed the band. Bavéri began conducting the hymn once more, and it was only by the end of that third repetition that isolated sounds of the brass instruments pierced through the clamor of human voices.

The same enthusiasm was in the streets. Crowds of peasants and educated men stood in front of the palace, shouting hurrahs, and the Tsar could not appear without being followed by demonstrative crowds running after his carriage. Hérzen was right when, two years later, as Alexander was drowning the Polish insurrection in blood, and "Muravióv the Hanger" was strangling it on the scaffold, he wrote, "Alexander Nikoláevich, why did you not die on that day? Your name would have been transmitted in history as that of a hero."

Where were the uprisings which had been predicted by the champions of slavery? Conditions more indefinite than those which had been created by the Polozhénie (the emancipation law) could not have been invented. If anything could have provoked revolts, it was precisely the perplexing vagueness of the conditions created by the new law. And yet, except in two places where there were insurrections, and a very few other spots where small disturbances entirely due to misunderstandings and immediately appeased took place, Russia remained quiet,—more quiet than ever. With their usual good sense, the peasants had understood that serfdom was done away with, that "freedom had come," and they accepted the conditions imposed upon them, although these conditions were very heavy.

I was in Nikólskoe in August, 1861, and again in the summer of 1862, and I was struck with the quiet, intelligent way in which the peasants had accepted the new conditions. They knew perfectly well how difficult it would be to pay the redemption tax for the land, which was in reality an indemnity to the nobles in lieu of the obligations of serfdom. But they so much valued the abolition of their personal enslavement that they accepted the ruinous charges—not without murmuring, but as a hard necessity—the moment that personal freedom was obtained. For the first months they kept two holidays a week, saying that it was a sin to work on Friday; but when the summer came they resumed work with even more energy than before.

When I saw our Nikólskoe peasants, fifteen months after the liberation, I could not but admire them. Their inborn good nature and softness remained with them, but all traces of servility had disappeared. They talked to their masters as equals talk to equals, as if they never had stood in different relations. Besides, such men came out from among them as could make a stand for their rights. The Polozhénie was a large and difficult book, which it took me a good deal of time to understand; but when Vasíli Ivánov, the elder of Nikólskoe, came one day to ask me to explain to him some obscurity in it, I saw that he, who was not even a fluent reader, had admirably found his way amongst the intricacies of the chapters and paragraphs of the law.

The "household people"—that is, the servants—came out the worst of all. They got no land, and would hardly have known what to do with it if they had. They got freedom, and nothing besides. In our neighborhood nearly all of them left their masters; none, for example, remained in the household of my father. They went in search of positions elsewhere, and a number of them found employment at once with the merchant class, who were proud of having the coachman of Prince So-and-So, or the cook of General So-and-So. Those who knew a trade found work in the towns: for instance, my father's band remained a band, and made a good living at Kalúga, retaining amiable relations with us. But those who had no trade had hard times before them; and yet, the majority preferred to live anyhow, rather than remain with their old masters.

As to the landlords, while the larger ones made all possible efforts at St. Petersburg to reintroduce the old conditions under one name or another (they succeeded in doing so to some extent under Alexander III.), by far the greater number submitted to the abolition of serfdom as to a sort of necessary calamity. The young generation gave to Russia that remarkable staff of "peace mediators" and justices of the peace who contributed so much to the peaceful issue of the emancipation. As to the old generation, most of them had already discounted the considerable sums of money they were to receive from the peasants for the land which was granted to the liberated serfs, and which was valued much above its market price; they schemed as to how they would squander that money in the restaurants of the capitals, or at the green tables in gambling. And they did squander it, almost all of them, as soon as they got it.

For many landlords, the liberation of the serfs was an excellent money transaction. Thus, land which my father, in anticipation of the emancipation, sold in parcels at the rate of eleven rubles the Russian acre, was now estimated at forty rubles in the peasants' allotments,—that is, three and a half times above its market value,—and this was the rule in all our neighborhood; while in my father's Tambóv estate, on the prairies, the *mir*—that is, the village community—rented all his land for twelve years, at a price which represented twice as much as he used to get from that land by cultivating it with servile labor.

Eleven years after that memorable time I went to the Tambóv estate, which I had inherited from my father. I stayed there for a few weeks, and on the evening of my departure our village priest—an intelligent man of independent opinions, such as one meets occasionally in our southern provinces— went out for a walk round the village. The sunset was glorious; a balmy air came from the prairies. He found a middle-aged peasant—Antón Savéliev—sitting on a small eminence outside the village and reading a book of psalms. The peasant hardly knew how to spell, in Old Slavonic, and often he would read a book from the last page, turning the pages backward; it was the process of reading which he liked most, and then a word would strike him, and its repetition pleased him. He was reading now a psalm of which each verse began with the word "rejoice."

"What are you reading?" he was asked.

"Well, father, I will tell you," was his reply. "Fourteen years ago the old prince came here. It was in the winter. I had just returned home, almost frozen. A snowstorm was raging. I had scarcely begun undressing, when we heard a knock at the window: it was the elder, who was shouting, 'Go to the prince! He wants you!' We all—my wife and our children—were thunderstruck. 'What can he want of you?' my wife cried, in alarm. I signed myself with the cross and went; the snowstorm almost blinded me as I crossed the bridge. Well, it ended all right. The old prince was taking his afternoon sleep, and when he woke up he asked me if I knew plastering work, and only told me, 'Come to-morrow to repair the plaster in that room.' So I went home quite happy, and when I came to the bridge I found my wife standing there. She had stood there all the time in the snowstorm, with the baby in her arms, waiting for me. 'What has happened, Savélich?' she cried. 'Well,' I said, 'no harm; he only asked me to make some repairs.' That, father, was under the old prince. And now, the young prince came here the other day. I went to see him, and found him in the garden, at the tea table, in the shadow of the house; you, father, sat with him, and the elder of the canton, with his mayor's chain upon his breast. 'Will you have tea, Savélich?' he asks me. 'Take a chair. Petr Grigóriev,'—he says that to the old one,—'give us one more chair.' And Petr Grigóriev—you know what a terror for us he was when he was the manager of the old prince—brought the chair, and we all sat round the tea table, talking, and he poured out tea for all of us. Well, now, father, the evening is so beautiful, the balm comes from the prairies, and I sit and read, 'Rejoice! Rejoice!' "

This is what the abolition of serfdom meant for the peasants.

IX

In June, 1861, I was nominated sergeant of the Corps of Pages. Some of our officers, I must say, did not like the idea of it, saying that there would be no "discipline" with me acting as a sergeant; but it could not be helped; it was usually the first pupil of the upper form who was nominated sergeant, and I had been at the top of our form for several years in succession. This appointment was considered very enviable, not only because the sergeant occupied a privileged position in the school and was treated like an officer, but especially because he was also the page de chambre of the Emperor for the time being; and to be personally known to the Emperor was of course considered as a stepping-stone to further distinctions. The most important point to me was, however, that it freed me from all the drudgery of the inner service of the school, which fell on the pages de chambre, and that I should have for my studies a separate room, where I could isolate myself from the bustle of the school. True, there was also an important drawback to it: I had always found it tedious to pace up and down, many times a day, the whole length of our rooms, and used therefore to run the distance full speed, which was severely prohibited; and now I should have to walk very solemnly, with the service-book under my arm, instead of running! A consultation was even held among a few friends of mine upon this serious matter, and it was decided that from time to time I could still find opportunities to take my favorite runs; as to my relations with all the others, it depended upon myself to put them on a new comrade-like footing, and this I did.

The pages de chambre had to be at the palace frequently, in attendance at the great and small levees, the balls, the receptions, the gala dinners, and so on. During Christmas, New Year, and Easter weeks we were summoned to the palace almost every day, and sometimes twice a day. Moreover, in my military capacity of sergeant I had to report to the Emperor every Sunday, at the parade in the riding-school, that "all was well at the company of the Corps of Pages," even when one third of the school was ill of some contagious disease.

"Shall I not report to-day that all is not quite well?" I asked
the colonel on this occasion. "God bless you," was his reply,
"you ought only to say so if there were an insurrection!"

Court life has undoubtedly much that is picturesque about
it. With its elegant refinement of manners,—superficial though
it may be,—its strict etiquette, and its brilliant surroundings,
it is certainly meant to be impressive. A great levee is a fine
pageant, and even the simple reception of a few ladies by the
Empress becomes quite different from a common call, when it
takes place in a richly decorated drawing-room of the palace,—
the guests ushered by chamberlains in gold-embroidered uniforms, the hostess followed by brilliantly dressed pages and a
suite of ladies, and everything conducted with striking solemnity. To be an actor in the court ceremonies, in attendance
upon the chief personages, offered something more than the
mere interest of curiosity for a boy of my age. Besides, I then
looked upon Alexander II. as a sort of hero; a man who attached no importance to the court ceremonies, but who, at
this period of his reign, began his working day at six in the
morning, and was engaged in a hard struggle with a powerful
reactionary party in order to carry through a series of reforms, in which the abolition of serfdom was only the first
step.

But gradually, as I saw more of the spectacular side of court
life, and caught now and then a glimpse of what was going on
behind the scenes, I realized not only the futility of these shows
and the things they were intended to conceal, but also that
these small things so much absorbed the court as to prevent
consideration of matters of far greater importance. The realities
were often lost in the acting. And then from Alexander II. himself slowly faded the aureole with which my imagination had
surrounded him; so that by the end of the year, even if at the
outset I had cherished some illusions as to useful activity in
the spheres nearest to the palace, I should have retained none.

On every important holiday, as also on the birthdays and
name days of the Emperor and Empress, on the coronation
day, and on other similar occasions, a great levee was held
at the palace. Thousands of generals and officers of all ranks,
down to that of captain, as well as the high functionaries of
the civil service, were arranged in lines in the immense halls

of the palace, to bow at the passage of the Emperor and his
family, as they solemnly proceeded to the church. All the members of the imperial family came on those days to the palace,
meeting together in a drawing-room, and merrily chatting till
the moment arrived for putting on the mask of solemnity.
Then the column was formed. The Emperor, giving his hand
to the Empress, opened the march. He was followed by his
page de chambre, and he in turn by the general aide-de-camp,
the aide-de-camp on duty that day, and the minister of the
imperial household; while the Empress, or rather the immense
train of her dress, was attended by her two pages de chambre,
who had to support the train at the turnings and to spread it
out again in all its beauty. The heir apparent, who was a
young man of eighteen, and all the other grand dukes and
duchesses came next, in the order of their right of succession
to the throne,—each of the grand duchesses followed by her
page de chambre; then there was a long procession of the
ladies in attendance, old and young, all wearing the so-called
Russian costume,—that is, an evening dress which was supposed to resemble the costume worn by the women of Old
Russia.

As the procession passed, I could see how each of the eldest
military and civil functionaries, before making his bow, would
try to catch the eye of the Emperor, and if he had his bow
acknowledged by a smiling look of the Tsar, or by a hardly
perceptible nod of the head, or perchance by a word or two,
he would look round upon his neighbors, full of pride, in the
expectation of their congratulations.

From the church the procession returned in the same way,
and then every one hurried back to his own affairs. Apart from
a few devotees and some young ladies, not one in ten present
at these levees regarded them otherwise than as a tedious duty.

Twice or thrice during the winter great balls were given at
the palace, and thousands of people were invited to them.
After the Emperor had opened the dances with a polonaise,
full liberty was left to every one to enjoy the time as he liked.
There was plenty of room in the immense brightly illuminated
halls, where young girls were easily lost to the watchful eyes
of their parents and aunts, and many thoroughly enjoyed the

dances and the supper, during which the young people managed to be left to themselves.

My duties at these balls were rather difficult. Alexander II. did not dance, nor did he sit down, but he moved all the time amongst his guests, his page de chambre having to follow him at a distance, so as to be within easy call, and yet not inconveniently near. This combination of presence with absence was not easy to attain, nor did the Emperor require it: he would have preferred to be left entirely to himself; but such was the tradition, and he had to submit to it. The worst was when he entered a dense crowd of ladies who stood round the circle in which the grand dukes danced, and slowly circulated among them. It was not at all easy to make a way through this living garden, which opened to give passage to the Emperor, but closed in immediately behind him. Instead of dancing themselves, hundreds of ladies and girls stood there, closely packed, each in the expectation that one of the grand dukes would perhaps notice her and invite her to dance a waltz or a polka. Such was the influence of the court upon St. Petersburg society that if one of the grand dukes cast his eye upon a girl, her parents would do all in their power to make their child fall madly in love with the great personage, even though they knew well that no marriage could result from it,—the Russian grand dukes not being allowed to marry "subjects" of the Tsar. The conversations which I once heard in a "respectable" family, connected with the court, after the heir apparent had danced twice or thrice with a girl of seventeen, and the hopes which were expressed by her parents surpassed all that I could possibly have imagined.

Every time that we were at the palace we had lunch or dinner there, and the footmen would whisper to us bits of news from the scandalous chronicle of the place, whether we cared for it or not. They knew everything that was going on in the different palaces,—that was their domain. For truth's sake, I must say that during the year which I speak of, that sort of chronicle was not as rich in events as it became in the seventies. The brothers of the Tsar were only recently married, and his sons were all very young. But the relations of the Emperor himself with the Princess X., whom Turgénev has so admirably

depicted in *Smoke* under the name of Irène, were even more
freely spoken of by the servants than by St. Petersburg society.
One day, however, when we entered the room where we used
to dress, we were told, "The X. has to-day got her dismissal,—
a complete one this time." Half an hour later, we saw the lady
in question coming to assist at mass, with eyes swollen from
weeping, and swallowing her tears during the mass, while the
other ladies managed so to stand at a distance from her as to
put her in evidence. The footmen were already informed about
the incident, and commented upon it in their own way. There
was something truly repulsive in the talk of these men, who
the day before would have crouched down before the same
lady.

The system of espionage which is exercised in the palace,
especially around the Emperor himself, would seem almost incredible to the uninitiated. The following incident will give
some idea of it. A few years later, one of the grand dukes
received a severe lesson from a St. Petersburg gentleman. The
latter had forbidden the grand duke his house, but, returning
home unexpectedly, he found him in his drawing-room, and
rushed upon him with his lifted stick. The young man dashed
down the staircase, and was already jumping into his carriage,
when the pursuer caught him, and dealt him a blow with his
stick. The policeman who stood at the door saw the adventure
and ran to report it to the chief of the police, General Trépov,
who, in his turn, jumped into his carriage and hastened to the
Emperor, to be the first to report the "sad incident." Alexander
II. summoned the grand duke and had a talk with him. A
couple of days later, an old functionary who belonged to the
Third Section of the Emperor's Chancery,—that is, to the state
police,—and who was a friend at the house of one of my
comrades, related the whole conversation. "The Emperor," he
informed us, "was very angry, and said to the grand duke in
conclusion, 'You should know better how to manage your little
affairs.'" He was asked, of course, how he could know anything
about a private conversation, but the reply was very characteristic: "The words and the opinions of his Majesty must
be known to our department. How otherwise could such a
delicate institution as the state police be managed? Be sure

that the Emperor is the most closely watched person in all St. Petersburg."

There was no boasting in these words. Every minister, every governor-general, before entering the Emperor's study with his reports, had a talk with the private valet of the Emperor, to know what was the mood of the master that day; and, according to that mood, he either laid before him some knotty affair, or let it lie at the bottom of his portfolio in hope of a more lucky day. The governor-general of East Siberia, when he came to St. Petersburg, always sent his private aide-de-camp with a handsome gift to the private valet of the Emperor. "There are days," he used to say, "when the Emperor would get into a rage, and order a searching inquest upon every one and myself, if I should lay before him on such a day certain reports; whereas there are other days when all will go off quite smoothly. A precious man that valet is." To know from day to day the frame of mind of the Emperor was a substantial part of the art of retaining a high position,—an art which later on Count Shuválov and General Trépov understood to perfection; also Count Ignátiev, who, I suppose from what I saw of him, possessed that art even without the help of the valet.

At the beginning of my service I felt a great admiration for Alexander II., the liberator of the serfs. Imagination often carries a boy beyond the realities of the moment, and my frame of mind at that time was such that if an attempt had been made in my presence upon the Tsar, I should have covered him with my body. One day, at the beginning of January, 1862, I saw him leave the procession and rapidly walk alone toward the halls where parts of all the regiments of the St. Petersburg garrison were aligned for a parade. This parade usually took place outdoors, but this year, on account of the frost, it was held indoors, and Alexander II., who generally galloped at full speed in front of the troops at the reviews, had now to march in front of the regiments. I knew that my court duties ended as soon as the Emperor appeared in his capacity of military commander of the troops, and that I had to follow him to this spot, but no further. However, on looking round, I saw that he was quite alone. The two aides-de-camp had disappeared, and there was with him not a single man of his suite. "I will not leave him alone!" I said to myself, and followed him.

Whether Alexander II. was in a great hurry that day, or had other reasons to wish that the review should be over as soon as possible, I cannot say, but he dashed in front of the troops, and marched along their rows at such a speed, making such big and rapid steps,—he was very tall,—that I had the greatest difficulty in following him at my most rapid pace, and in places had almost to run in order to keep close behind him. He hurried as if running away from a danger. His excitement communicated itself to me, and every moment I was ready to jump in front of him, regretting only that I had on my ordnance sword and not my own sword, with a Toledo blade, which pierced copper and was a far better weapon. It was only after he had passed in front of the last battalion that he slackened his pace, and, on entering another hall, looked round, to meet my eyes glittering with the excitement of that mad march. The younger aide-de-camp was running at full speed, two halls behind. I was prepared to get a severe scolding, instead of which Alexander II. said to me, perhaps betraying his own inner thoughts: "You here? Brave boy!" and as he slowly walked away, he turned into space that problematic, absent-minded gaze, which I had begun often to notice.

Such was then the frame of my mind. However, various small incidents, as well as the reactionary character which the policy of Alexander II. was decidedly taking, instilled more and more doubts into my heart. Every year, on January 6, a half Christian and half pagan ceremony of sanctifying the waters is performed in Russia. It is also performed at the palace. A pavilion is built on the Nevá River, opposite the palace, and the imperial family, headed by the clergy, proceed from the palace, across the superb quay, to the pavilion, where a Te Deum is sung and the cross is plunged into the water of the river. Thousands of people stand on the quay and on the ice of the Nevá to witness the ceremony from a distance. All have to stand bareheaded during the service. This year, as the frost was rather sharp, an old general had put on a wig, and in the hurry of drawing on his cape, his wig had been dislodged and now lay across his head, without his noticing it. The Grand Duke Constantine, having caught sight of it, laughed the whole time the Te Deum was being sung, with the younger grand dukes, looking in the direction of the unhappy general, who smiled stupidly without knowing why he was the cause of so much hilarity. Constantine finally whispered to the Emperor, who also looked at the general and laughed.

A few minutes later, as the procession once more crossed the quay, on its way back to the palace, an old peasant, bareheaded too, pushed himself through the double hedge of soldiers who lined the path of the procession, and fell on his knees just at the feet of the Emperor, holding out a petition, and crying with tears in his eyes, "Father, defend us!" Ages of oppression of the Russian peasantry was in this exclamation; but Alexander II., who a few minutes before laughed during the church-service at a wig lying the wrong way, now passed by the peasant without taking the slightest notice of him. I was close behind him, and only saw in him a shudder of fear at the sudden appearance of the peasant, after which he went on without deigning even to cast a glance on the human figure at his feet. I looked round. The aides-de-camp were not there; the Grand Duke Constantine, who followed, took no more notice of the peasant than his brother did; there was nobody even to take the petition, so that I took it, although I knew that I should get a scolding for doing so. It was not my business to receive petitions, but I remembered what it must have cost the peasant before he could make his way to the capital, and then through the lines of police and soldiers who surrounded the procession. Like all peasants who hand petitions to the Tsar, he was going to be put under arrest, for no one knows how long.

On the day of the emancipation of the serfs, Alexander II. was worshiped at St. Petersburg; but it is most remarkable that, apart from that moment of general enthusiasm, he had not the love of the city. His brother Nicholas—no one could say why—was at least very popular among the small tradespeople and the cabmen; but neither Alexander II., nor his brother Constantine, the leader of the reform party, nor his third brother, Michael, had won the hearts of any class of people in St. Petersburg. Alexander II. had retained too much of the despotic character of his father, which pierced now and

then through his usually good-natured manners. He easily lost
his temper, and often treated his courtiers in the most con-
temptuous way. He was not what one would describe as a
truly reliable man, either in his policy or in his personal sympathies, and he was vindictive. I doubt whether he was sin-
cerely attached to any one. Some of the men in his nearest
surroundings were of the worst description,—Count Adlerberg,
for instance, who made him pay over and over again his enormous debts, and others renowned for their colossal thefts.
From the beginning of 1862 he commenced to show himself
capable of reviving the worst practices of his father's reign.
It was known that he still wanted to carry through a series of
important reforms in the judicial organization and in the army;
that the terrible corporal punishments were about to be abolished, and that a sort of local self-government, and perhaps a
constitution of some sort, would be granted. But the slightest
disturbance was repressed under his orders with a stern severity: he took each movement as a personal offense, so that at
any moment one might expect from him the most reactionary
measures. The disorders which broke out at the universities of
St. Petersburg, Moscow, and Kazán, in October, 1861, were
repressed with an ever increasing strictness. The University of
St. Petersburg was closed, and although free courses were
opened by most of the professors at the Town Hall, they were
also soon closed, and some of the best professors left the university. Immediately after the abolition of serfdom, a great
movement began for the opening of Sunday schools; they were
opened everywhere by private persons and corporations,—all
the teachers being volunteers,—and the peasants and workers,
old and young, flocked to these schools. Officers, students, even
a few pages, became teachers; and such excellent methods
were worked out that (Russian having a phonetic spelling)
we succeeded in teaching a peasant to read in nine or ten
lessons. But suddenly all Sunday schools, in which the mass of
the peasantry would have learned to read in a few years, without any expenditure by the state, were closed. In Poland,
where a series of patriotic manifestations had begun, the Cossacks were sent out to disperse the crowds with their whips,
and to arrest hundreds of people in the churches with their
usual brutality. Men were shot in the streets of Warsaw by

the end of 1861, and for the suppression of the few peasant insurrections which broke out, the horrible flogging through the double line of soldiers—that favorite punishment of Nicholas I.—was applied. The despot that Alexander II. became in the years 1870–81 was foreshadowed in 1862.

Of all the imperial family, undoubtedly the most sympathetic was the Empress Marie Alexándrovna. She was sincere, and when she said something pleasant, she meant it. The way in which she once thanked me for a little courtesy (it was after her reception of the ambassador of the United States, who had just come to St. Petersburg) deeply impressed me: it was not the way of a lady spoiled by courtesies, as an empress is supposed to be. She certainly was not happy in her home life; nor was she liked by the ladies of the court, who found her too severe, and could not understand why she should take so much to heart the *étourderies* of her husband. It is now known that she played a by no means unimportant part in bringing about the abolition of serfdom. But at that time her influence in this direction seems to have been little known, the Grand Duke Constantine and the Grand Duchess Hélène Pávlovna, who was the main support of Nicholas Miliútin at the court, being considered the two leaders of the reform party in the palace spheres. The Empress was better known for the decisive part she had taken in the creation of girls' gymnasia (high schools), which received from the outset a high standard of organization and a truly democratic character. Her friendly relations with Ushínsky, a great pedagogist, saved him from sharing the fate of all men of mark of that time,—that is, exile.

Being very well educated herself, Marie Alexándrovna did her best to give a good education to her eldest son. The best men in all branches of knowledge were sought as teachers, and she even invited for that purpose Kavélin, although she knew well his friendly relations with Hérzen. When he mentioned to her that friendship, she replied that she had no grudge against Hérzen, except for his violent language about the Empress Dowager.

The heir apparent was extremely handsome,—perhaps, even too femininely handsome. He was not proud in the least, and during the levees he used to chatter in the most comrade-like way with the pages de chambre. (I even remember, at the reception of the diplomatic corps on New Year's Day, trying to make him appreciate the simplicity of the uniform of the ambassador of the United States as compared with the parrot-colored uniforms of the other ambassadors.) However, those who knew him well described him as profoundly egoistic, a man absolutely incapable of contracting an attachment to any one. This feature was prominent in him, even more than it was in his father. As to his education, all the pains taken by his mother were of no avail. In August, 1861, his examinations, which were made in the presence of his father, proved to be a dead failure, and I remember Alexander II., at a parade of which the heir apparent was the commander, and during which he made some mistake, loudly shouting out, so that every one would hear it, "Even that you could not learn!" He died, as is known, at the age of twenty-two, from some disease of the spinal cord.

His brother, Alexander, who became the heir apparent in 1865, and later on was Alexander III., was a decided contrast to Nicholas Alexándrovich. He reminded me so much of Paul I., by his face, his figure, and his contemplation of his own grandeur, that I used to say, "If he ever reigns, he will be another Paul I. in the Gátchina palace, and will have the same end as his great-grandfather had at the hands of his own courtiers." He obstinately refused to learn. It was rumored that Alexander II., having had so many difficulties with his brother Constantine, who was better educated than himself, adopted the policy of concentrating all his attention on the heir apparent, and neglecting the education of his other sons; however, I doubt if such was the case: Alexander Alexándrovich must have been averse to any education from childhood; in fact, his spelling, which I saw in the telegrams he addressed to his bride at Copenhagen, was unimaginably bad. I cannot render here his Russian spelling, but in French he wrote, "*Ecri* à oncle à propos parade . . . les nouvelles sont *mauvaisent*," and so on.

He is said to have improved in his manners toward the end of his life, but in 1870, and also much later, he was a true descendant of Paul I. I knew at St. Petersburg an officer, of Swedish origin (from Finland), who had been sent to the United States to order rifles for the Russian army. On his return he had to report about his mission to Alexander Alexándrovich, who had been appointed to superintend the re-arming of the army. During this interview, the Tsarevich, giving full vent to his violent temper, began to scold the officer, who probably replied with dignity, whereupon the prince fell into a real fit of rage, insulting the officer in bad language. The officer, who belonged to that type of self-respecting but very loyal men who are frequently met with amongst the Swedish nobility in Russia, left at once, and wrote a letter in which he asked the heir apparent to apologize within twenty-four hours, adding that if the apology did not come, he would shoot himself. It was a sort of Japanese duel. Alexander Alexándrovich sent no excuses, and the officer kept his word. I saw him at the house of a warm friend of mine, his intimate friend, when he was expecting every minute to receive the apology. Next morning he was dead. The Tsar was very angry with his son, and ordered him to follow the hearse of the officer to the grave. But even this terrible lesson did not cure the young man of his Románov haughtiness and impetuosity.

❋ ❋ ❋ ❋ ❋ ❋ ❋ ❋ ❋ ❋ ❋ ❋ ❋ ❋ ❋ ❋ ❋

PART THREE

SIBERIA

I

In the middle of May, 1862, a few weeks before our promotion,
I was told one day by the captain to make up the final list of
the regiments which each of us intended to join. We had the
choice of all the regiments of the Guard, which we could enter
with the first officer's grade, and of the Army with the third
grade of lieutenant. I took a list of our form and went the
rounds of my comrades. Every one knew well the regiment he
was going to join, most of them already wearing in the garden
the officer's cap of that regiment.

"Her Majesty's Cuirassiers," "The Body Guard Preobrazhén-
sky," "The Horse Guards," were the replies which I inscribed.

"But you, Kropótkin? The artillery? The Cossacks?" I was
asked on all sides. I could not stand these questions, and at
last, asking a comrade to complete the list, I went to my room
to think once more over my final decision.

That I should not enter a regiment of the Guard, and give
my life to parades and court balls, I had settled long ago. My
dream was to enter the university,—to study, to live the student's life. That meant, of course, to break entirely with my
father, whose ambitions were quite different, and to rely for
my living upon what I might earn by means of lessons. Thousands of Russian students live in that way, and such a life did
not frighten me in the least. But how should I get over the first
steps in that life? In a few weeks I should have to leave the
school, to don my own clothes, to have my own lodging, and I
saw no possibility of providing even the little money which
would be required for the most modest start. Then, failing the
university, I had been often thinking of late that I could enter
the artillery academy. That would free me for two years from

the drudgery of military service, and, besides the military sciences, I could study mathematics and physics. But the wind of reaction was blowing, and the officers in the academies had been treated during the previous winter as if they were schoolboys; in two academies they had revolted, and in one of them they had left in a body.

My thoughts turned more and more toward Siberia. The Amúr region had recently been annexed by Russia; I had read all about that Mississippi of the East, the mountains it pierces, the subtropical vegetation of its tributary, the Usurí, and my thoughts went further,—to the tropical regions which Humboldt had described, and to the great generalizations of Ritter, which I delighted to read. Besides, I reasoned, there is in Siberia an immense field for the application of the great reforms which have been made or are coming: the workers must be few there, and I shall find a field of action to my tastes. The worst was that I should have to separate from my brother Alexander; but he had been compelled to leave the University of Moscow after the last disorders, and in a year or two, I guessed (and guessed rightly), in one way or another we should be together. There remained only the choice of the regiment in the Amúr region. The Usurí attacted me most; but, alas! there was on the Usurí only one regiment of infantry Cossacks. A Cossack not on horseback,—that was too bad for the boy that I still was, and I settled upon "the mounted Cossacks of the Amúr."

This I wrote on the list, to the great consternation of all my comrades. "It is so far," they said, while my friend Daúrov, seizing the Officers' Handbook, read out of it, to the horror of all present: "Uniform, black, with a plain red collar without braids; fur bonnet made of dog's fur or any other fur; trousers, gray."

"Only look at that uniform!" he exclaimed. "Bother the cap! —you can wear one of wolf or bear fur; but think only of the trousers! Gray, like a soldier of the Train!" The consternation reached its climax after that reading.

I joked as best I could, and took the list to the captain.

"Kropótkin must always have his joke!" he cried. "Did I not tell you that the list must be sent to the grand duke to-day?"

Astonishment and pity were depicted on his face when I told him that the list really stated my intention.

However, next day, my resolution almost gave way when I saw how Klasóvsky took my decision. He had hoped to see me in the university, and had given me lessons in Latin and Greek for that purpose; and I did not dare to tell him what really prevented me from entering the university: I knew that if I told him the truth, he would offer to share with me the little that he had.

Then my father telegraphed to the director that he forbade my going to Siberia; and the matter was reported to the grand duke, who was the chief of the military schools. I was called before his assistant, and talked about the vegetation of the Amúr and like things, because I had strong reasons for believing that if I said I wanted to go to the university, and could not afford it, a bursary would be offered to me by some one of the imperial family,—an offer which by all means I wished to avoid.

It is impossible to say how all this would have ended, but an event of much importance—the great fire at St. Petersburg—brought about in an indirect way a solution of my difficulties.

On the Monday after Trinity—the day of the Holy Ghost, which was that year on May 26, Old Style—a terrible fire broke out in the so-called Apráxin Dvor. The Apráxin Dvor was an immense space, more than half a mile square, which was entirely covered with small shops,—mere shanties of wood,—where all sorts of second- and thirdhand goods were sold. Old furniture and bedding, secondhand dresses and books, poured in from every quarter of the city, and were stored in the small shanties, in the passages between them, and even on their roofs. This accumulation of inflammable materials had at its back the Ministry of the Interior and its archives, where all the documents concerning the liberation of the serfs were kept; and in the front of it, which was lined by a row of shops built of stone, was the state Bank. A narrow lane, also bordered with stone shops, separated the Apráxin Dvor from a wing of the Corps of Pages, which was occupied by grocery and oil shops in its lower story, and had the apartments of the officers in its upper story. Almost opposite the Ministry of the Interior, on the other side of a canal, there were extensive timber yards. This labyrinth of small shanties and the timber yards opposite took fire almost at the same moment, at four o'clock in the afternoon.

If there had been wind on that day, half the city would have perished in the flames, including the Bank, several Ministries, the Gostínoi Dvor (another great block of shops on the Nevsky Prospekt), the Corps of Pages, and the National Library.

I was that afternoon at the Corps, dining at the house of one of our officers, and we dashed to the spot as soon as we saw from the windows the first clouds of smoke rising in our immediate neighborhood. The sight was terrific. Like an immense snake, rattling and whistling, the fire threw itself in all directions, right and left, enveloped the shanties, and suddenly rose in a huge column, darting out its whistling tongues to lick up more shanties with their contents. Whirlwinds of smoke and fire were formed; and when the whirls of burning feathers from the bedding shops began to sweep about the space, it became impossible to remain any longer inside the burning market. The whole had to be abandoned.

The authorities had entirely lost their heads. There was not, at that time, a single steam fire engine in St. Petersburg, and it was workmen who suggested bringing one from the iron works of Kólpino, situated twenty miles by rail from the capital. When the engine reached the railway station, it was the people who dragged it to the conflagration. Of its four lines of hose, one was damaged by an unknown hand, and the other three were directed upon the Ministry of the Interior.

The grand dukes came to the spot and went away again. Late in the evening, when the Bank was out of danger, the Emperor also made his appearance, and said, what every one knew already, that the Corps of Pages was now the key of the battle, and must be saved by all means. It was evident that if the Corps had taken fire, the National Library and half of the Nevsky Prospekt would have gone.

It was the crowd, the people, who did everything to prevent the fire from spreading further and further. There was a moment when the Bank was seriously menaced. The goods cleared from the shops opposite were thrown into the Sadóvaia

street, and lay in great heaps upon the walls of the left wing
of the Bank. The articles which covered the street itself continually took fire, but the people, roasting there in an almost
unbearable heat, prevented the flames from being communicated to the piles of goods on the other side. They swore at all
the authorities, seeing that there was not a pump on the spot.
"What are they all doing at the Ministry of the Interior, when
the Bank and the Foundlings' House are going to take fire?
They have all lost their heads!" "Where is the chief of police
that he cannot send a fire brigade to the Bank?" they said. I
knew the chief, General Annenkov, personally, as I had met
him once or twice at our sub-inspector's house, where he came
with his brother, the well-known literary critic, and I volunteered to find him. I found him, indeed, walking aimlessly in
a street; and when I reported to him the state of affairs, incredible though it may seem, it was to me, a boy, that he gave
the order to move one of the fire brigades from the Ministry to
the Bank. I exclaimed, of course, that the men would never
listen to me, and I asked for a written order; but General
Annenkov had not, or pretended not to have, a scrap of paper,
so that I requested one of our officers, L. L. Gosse, to come
with me to transmit the order. We at last prevailed upon the
captain of one fire brigade—who swore at all the world and at
his chiefs—to move his men to the Bank.

The Ministry itself was not on fire; it was the archives which
were burning, and many boys, chiefly cadets and pages, together with a number of clerks, carried bundles of papers out
of the burning building and loaded them into cabs. Often a
bundle would fall out, and the wind, taking possession of its
leaves, would strew them about the square. Through the
smoke a sinister fire could be seen raging in the timber yards
on the other side of the canal.

The narrow lane which separated the Corps of Pages from
the Apráxin Dvor was in a deplorable state. The shops which
lined it were full of brimstone, oil, turpentine, and the like, and
immense tongues of fire of many hues, thrown out by explosions, licked the roofs of the wing of the Corps, which bordered
the lane on its other side. The windows and the pilasters under
the roof began already to smoulder, while the pages and some
cadets, after having cleared the lodgings, pumped water

through a small fire engine, which received at long intervals scanty supplies from old-fashioned barrels which had to be filled with ladles. A couple of firemen who stood on the hot roof continually shouted out, "Water! Water!" in tones which were simply heart-rending. I could not stand these cries, and I rushed into the Sadóvaia street, where by sheer force I compelled the driver of one of the barrels belonging to a police fire-brigade to enter our yard, and to supply our pump with water. But when I attempted to do the same once more, I met with an absolute refusal from the driver. "I shall be court-martialed," he said, "if I obey you." On all sides my comrades urged me, "Go and find somebody,—the chief of the police, the grand duke, any one,—and tell them that without water we shall have to abandon the Corps to the fire." "Ought we not to report to our director?" somebody would remark. "Bother the whole lot! you won't find them with a lantern. Go and do it yourself."

I went once more in search of General Annenkov, and was at last told that he must be in the yard of the Bank. Several officers stood there around a general in whom I recognized the governor-general of St. Petersburg, Prince Suvórov. The gate, however, was locked, and a Bank official who stood at it refused to let me in. I insisted, menaced, and finally was admitted. Then I went straight to Prince Suvórov, who was writing a note on the shoulder of his aide-de-camp.

When I reported to him the state of affairs, his first question was, "Who has sent you?" "Nobody—the comrades," was my reply. "So you say the Corps will soon be on fire?" "Yes." He started at once, and, seizing in the street an empty hatbox, covered his head with it, and ran full speed to the lane. Empty barrels, straw, wooden boxes, and the like covered the lane, between the flames of the oil shops on the one side and the buildings of our Corps, of which the window frames and the pilasters were smouldering, on the other side. Prince Suvórov acted resolutely. "There is a company of soldiers in your garden," he said to me: "take a detachment and clear that lane—at once. A hose from the steam engine will be brought here immediately. Keep it playing. I trust it to you personally."

It was not easy to move the soldiers out of our garden. They had cleared the barrels and boxes of their contents, and with their pockets full of coffee, and with conical lumps of sugar concealed in their *képis*, they were enjoying the warm night under the trees, cracking nuts. No one cared to move till an officer interfered. The lane was cleared, and the pump kept going. The comrades were delighted, and every twenty minutes we relieved the men who directed the jet of water, standing by their side in a terrible scorching heat.

About three or four in the morning it was evident that bounds had been put to the fire; the danger of its spreading to the Corps was over, and after having quenched our thirst with half a dozen glasses of tea, in a small "white inn" which happened to be open, we fell, half dead from fatigue, on the first bed that we found unoccupied in the hospital of the Corps.

Next morning I woke up early and went to see the site of the conflagration. On my return to the Corps I met the Grand Duke Michael, whom I accompanied, as was my duty, on his round. The pages, with their faces quite black from the smoke, with swollen eyes and inflamed lids, some of them with their hair burned, raised their heads from the pillows. It was hard to recognize them. They were proud, though, of feeling that they had not been merely "white hands," and had worked as hard as any one else.

This visit of the grand duke settled my difficulties. He asked me why I conceived that fancy of going to the Amúr,—whether I had friends there, whether the governor-general knew me; and learning that I had no relatives in Siberia, and knew nobody there, he exclaimed, "But how are you going, then? They may send you to a lonely Cossack village. What will you do there? I had better write about you to the governor-general, to recommend you."

After such an offer I was sure that my father's objections would be removed,—and so it proved. I was free to go to Siberia.

This great conflagration became a turning-point not only in the policy of Alexander II., but also in the history of Russia for that part of the century. That it was not a mere accident was self-evident. Trinity and the day of the Holy Ghost are great holidays in Russia, and there was nobody inside the market except a few watchmen; besides, the Apráxin market and the timber yards took fire at the same time, and the conflagration at St. Petersburg was followed by similar disasters in several provincial towns. The fire was lit by somebody, but by whom? This question remains unanswered to the present time.

Katkóv, the ex-Whig, who was inspired with personal hatred of Hérzen, and especially of Bakúnin, with whom he had once to fight a duel, on the very day after the fire accused the Poles and the Russian revolutionists of being the cause of it; and that opinion prevailed at St. Petersburg and at Moscow.

Poland was preparing then for the revolution which broke out in the following January, and the secret revolutionary government had concluded an alliance with the London refugees; it had its men in the very heart of the St. Petersburg administration. Only a short time after the conflagration occurred, the lord lieutenant of Poland, Count Lüders, was shot at by a Russian officer; and when the Grand Duke Constantine was nominated in his place (with the intention, it was said, of making Poland a separate kingdom for Constantine), he also was immediately shot at, on June 26. Similar attempts were made in August against the Marquis Wielepólsky, the Polish leader of the pro-Russian Union party. Napoleon III. maintained among the Poles the hope of an armed intervention in favor of their independence. In such conditions, judging from the ordinary narrow military standpoint, to destroy the Bank of Russia and several Ministries, and to spread a panic in the capital, might have been considered a good plan of warfare; but there never was the slightest scrap of evidence forthcoming to support this hypothesis.

On the other side, the advanced parties in Russia saw that no hope could any longer be placed in Alexander's reformatory initiative: he was clearly drifting into the reactionary camp. To men of forethought it was evident that the liberation of the serfs, under the conditions of redemption which were imposed upon them, meant their certain ruin, and revolutionary proclamations were issued in May, at St. Petersburg, calling the people and the army to a general revolt, while the educated classes were asked to insist upon the necessity of a national convention. Under such circumstances, to disorganize the machine of the government might have entered into the plans of some revolutionists.

Finally, the indefinite character of the emancipation had

produced a great deal of fermentation among the peasants, who constitute a considerable part of the population in all Russian cities; and through all the history of Russia, every time such a fermentation has begun, it has resulted in anonymous letters foretelling fires, and eventually in incendiarism.

It was possible that the idea of setting the Apráxin market on fire might occur to isolated men in the revolutionary camp, but neither the most searching inquiries nor the wholesale arrests which began all over Russia and Poland immediately after the fire revealed the slightest indication that such was really the case. If anything of the sort had been found, the reactionary party would have made capital out of it. Many reminiscences and volumes of correspondence from those times have since been published, but they contain no hint whatever in support of this suspicion.

On the contrary, when similar conflagrations broke out in several towns on the Vólga, and especially at Sarátov, and when Zhdánov, a member of the Senate, was sent by the Tsar to make a searching inquiry, he returned with the firm conviction that the conflagration at Sarátov was the work of the reactionary party. There was among that party a general belief that it would be possible to induce Alexander II. to postpone the final abolition of serfdom, which was to take place on February 19, 1863. They knew the weakness of his character, and immediately after the great fire at St. Petersburg, they began a violent campaign for postponement, and for the revision of the emancipation law in its practical applications. It was rumored in well-informed legal circles that Senator Zhdánov was in fact returning with positive proofs of the culpability of the reactionaries at Sarátov; but he died on his way back, his portfolio disappeared, and it has never been found.

Be it as it may, the Apráxin fire had the most deplorable consequences. After it Alexander II. surrendered to the reactionaries, and—what was still worse—the public opinion of that part of society at St. Petersburg, and especially at Moscow, which carried most weight with the government suddenly threw off its liberal garb, and turned against not only the more advanced section of the reform party, but even against its moderate wing. A few days after the conflagration, I went on Sunday to see my cousin, the aide-de-camp of the Emperor, in whose apartment I had often seen the Horse Guard officers in sympathy with Chernyshévsky; my cousin himself had been up till then an assiduous reader of *The Contemporary* (the organ of the advanced reform party). Now he brought several numbers of *The Contemporary*, and, putting them on the table I was sitting at, said to me, "Well, now, after *this* I will have no more of that incendiary stuff; enough of it,"—and these words expressed the opinion of "all St. Petersburg." It became improper to talk of reforms. The whole atmosphere was laden with a reactionary spirit. *The Contemporary* and other similar reviews were suppressed; the Sunday schools were prohibited under any form; wholesale arrests began. The capital was placed under a state of siege.

A fortnight later, on June 13 (25), the time which we pages and cadets had so long looked for came at last. The Emperor gave us a sort of military examination in all kinds of evolutions, —during which we commanded the companies, and I paraded on a horse before the battalion,—and we were promoted to be officers.

When the parade was over, Alexander II. loudly called out, "The promoted officers to me!" and we gathered round him. He remained on horseback.

Here I saw him in a quite new light. The man who the next year appeared in the rôle of a bloodthirsty and vindictive suppressor of the insurrection in Poland rose now, full size, before my eyes, in the speech he addressed to us.

He began in a quiet tone. "I congratulate you: you are officers." He spoke about military duty and loyalty as they are usually spoken of on such occasions. "But if any one of you," he went on, distinctly shouting out every word, his face suddenly contorted with anger,—"but if any one of you—which God preserve you from—should under any circumstances prove disloyal to the Tsar, the throne, and the fatherland, take heed of what I say,—he will be treated with all the se-veri-ty of the laws, without the slightest com-mi-se-ra-tion!"

His voice failed; his face was peevish, full of that expression of blind rage which I saw in my childhood on the faces of landlords when they threatened their serfs "to skin them under the rods." He violently spurred his horse, and rode out of our circle. Next morning, the 14th of June, by his orders, three officers were shot at Módlin in Poland, and one soldier, Szur by name, was killed under the rods.

"Reaction, full speed backwards," I said to myself, as we made our way back to the Corps.

I saw Alexander II. once more before leaving St. Petersburg. Some days after our promotion, all the newly appointed officers were at the palace, to be presented to him. My more than modest uniform, with its prominent gray trousers, attracted universal attention, and every moment I had to satisfy the curiosity of officers of all ranks, who came to ask me what was the uniform that I wore. The Amúr Cossacks being then the youngest regiment of the Russian army, I stood somewhere near the end of the hundreds of officers who were present. Alexander II. found me, and asked, "So you go to Siberia? Did your father consent to it, after all?" I answered in the affirmative. "Are you not afraid to go so far?" I warmly replied, "No, I want to work. There must be so much to do in Siberia to apply the great reforms which are going to be made." He looked straight at me; he became pensive; at last he said, "Well, go; one can be useful everywhere;" and his face took on such an expression of fatigue, such a character of complete surrender, that I thought at once, "He is a used-up man; he is going to give it all up."

St. Petersburg had assumed a gloomy aspect. Soldiers marched in the streets, Cossack patrols rode round the palace, the fortress was filled with prisoners. Wherever I went I saw the same thing,—the triumph of the reaction. I left St. Petersburg without regret.

I went every day to the Cossack administration to ask them to make haste and deliver me my papers, and as soon as they were ready, I hurried to Moscow to join my brother Alexander.

II

The five years that I spent in Siberia were for me a genuine education in life and human character. I was brought into contact with men of all descriptions: the best and the worst; those

who stood at the top of society and those who vegetated at
the very bottom,—the tramps and the so-called incorrigible
criminals. I had ample opportunities to watch the ways and
habits of the peasants in their daily life, and still more opportunities to appreciate how little the state administration could
give to them, even if it was animated by the very best intentions. Finally, my extensive journeys, during which I traveled
over fifty thousand miles in carts, on board steamers, in boats,
but chiefly on horseback, had a wonderful effect in strengthen-
ing my health. They also taught me how little man really needs
as soon as he comes out of the enchanted circle of conventional
civilization. With a few pounds of bread and a few ounces of
tea in a leather bag, a kettle and a hatchet hanging at the side
of the saddle, and under the saddle a blanket, to be spread at
the camp-fire upon a bed of freshly cut spruce twigs, a man
feels wonderfully independent, even amidst unknown mountains thickly clothed with woods, or capped with snow. A book
might be written about this part of my life, but I must rapidly
glide over it here, there being so much more to say about the
later periods.

Siberia is not the frozen land buried in snow and peopled
with exiles only, that it is imagined to be, even by many Russians. In its southern parts it is as rich in natural productions
as are the southern parts of Canada, which it resembles so
much in its physical aspects; and beside half a million of natives, it has a population of more than four millions of Russians. The southern parts of West Siberia are as thoroughly
Russian as the provinces to the north of Moscow. In 1862 the
upper administration of Siberia was far more enlightened and
far better all round than that of any province of Russia proper.
For several years the post of governor-general of East Siberia
had been occupied by a remarkable personage, Count N. N.
Muravióv, who annexed the Amúr region to Russia. He was
very intelligent, very active, extremely amiable, and desirous
to work for the good of the country. Like all men of action of
the governmental school, he was a despot at the bottom of his
heart; but he held advanced opinions, and a democratic republic would not have quite satisfied him. He had succeeded
to a great extent in getting rid of the old staff of civil service
officials, who considered Siberia a camp to be plundered, and

he had gathered around him a number of young officials, quite honest, and many of them animated by the same excellent intentions as himself. In his own study, the young officers, with the exile Bakúnin among them (he escaped from Siberia in the autumn of 1861), discussed the chances of creating the United States of Siberia, federated across the Pacific Ocean with the United States of America.

When I came to Irkútsk, the capital of East Siberia, the wave of reaction which I saw rising at St. Petersburg had not yet reached these distant dominions. I was very well received by the young governor-general, Korsákov, who had just succeeded Muravióv, and he told me that he was delighted to have about him men of liberal opinions. As to the commander of the general staff, Kúkel,—a young general not yet thirty-five years old, whose personal aide-de-camp I became,—he at once took me to a room in his house, where I found, together with the best Russian reviews, complete collections of the London revolutionary editions of Hérzen. We were soon warm friends.

General Kúkel temporarily occupied at that time the post of governor of Transbaikália, and a few weeks later we crossed the beautiful Lake Baikál and went further east, to the little town of Chitá, the capital of the province. There I had to give myself, heart and soul, without loss of time, to the great reforms which were then under discussion. The St. Petersburg ministries had applied to the local authorities, asking them to work out schemes of complete reform in the administration of the provinces, the organization of the police, the tribunals, the prisons, the system of exile, the self-government of the townships,—all on broadly liberal bases laid down by the Emperor in his manifestoes.

Kúkel, supported by an intelligent and practical man, Colonel Pedashénko, and a couple of well-meaning civil service officials, worked all day long, and often a good deal of the night. I became the secretary of two committees,—for the reform of the prisons and the whole system of exile, and for preparing a scheme of municipal self-government,—and I set to work with all the enthusiasm of a youth of nineteen years. I read much about the historical development of these institutions in Russia and their present condition abroad, excellent works and papers dealing with these subjects having been published by the ministries of the interior and of justice; but what we did in Transbaikália was by no means merely theoretical. I discussed first the general outlines, and subsequently every point of detail, with practical men, well acquainted with the real needs and the local possibilities; and for that purpose I met a considerable number of men both in town and in the province. Then the conclusions we arrived at were re-discussed with Kúkel and Pedashénko; and when I had put the results into a preliminary shape, every point was again very thoroughly thrashed out in the committees. One of these committees, for preparing the municipal government scheme, was composed of citizens of Chitá, elected by all the population, as freely as they might have been elected in the United States. In short, our work was very serious; and even now, looking back at it through the perspective of so many years, I can say in full confidence that if municipal self-government had been granted then, in the modest shape which we gave to it, the towns of Siberia would be very different from what they are. But nothing came of it all, as will presently be seen.

There was no lack of other incidental occupations. Money had to be found for the support of charitable institutions; an economic description of the province had to be written in connection with a local agricultural exhibition; or some serious inquiry had to be made. "It is a great epoch we live in; work, my dear friend; remember that you are the secretary of all existing and future committees," Kúkel would sometimes say to me,—and I worked with doubled energy.

An example or two will show with what results. There was in our province a "district chief"—that is, a police officer invested with very wide and indeterminate rights—who was simply a disgrace. He robbed the peasants and flogged them right and left,—even women, which was against the law; and when a criminal affair fell into his hands, it might lie there for months, men being kept in the meantime in prison till they gave him a bribe. Kúkel would have dismissed this man long before, but the governor-general did not like the idea of it, because he had strong protectors at St. Petersburg. After much hesitation, it was decided at last that I should go to make an investigation on the spot, and collect evidence against the man.

This was not by any means easy, because the peasants, terrorized by him, and well knowing an old Russian saying, "God is far away, while your chief is your next-door neighbor," did not dare to testify. Even the woman he had flogged was afraid at first to make a written statement. It was only after I had stayed a fortnight with the peasants, and had won their confidence, that the misdeeds of their chief could be brought to light. I collected crushing evidence, and the district chief was dismissed. We congratulated ourselves on having got rid of such a pest. What was, however, our astonishment when, a few months later, we learned that this same man had been nominated to a higher post in Kamchátka! There he could plunder the natives free of any control, and so he did. A few years later he returned to St. Petersburg a rich man. The articles he occasionally contributes now to the reactionary press are, as one might expect, full of high "patriotic" spirit.

The wave of reaction, as I have already said, had not then reached Siberia, and the political exiles continued to be treated with all possible leniency, as in Muraviór's time. When, in 1861, the poet Mikháilov was condemned to hard labor for a revolutionary proclamation which he had issued, and was sent to Siberia, the governor of the first Siberian town on his way, Tobólsk, gave a dinner in his honor, in which all the officials took part. In Transbaikália he was not kept at hard labor, but was allowed officially to stay in the hospital prison of a small mining village. His health being very poor,—he was dying from consumption, and did actually die a few months later,—General Kúkel gave him permission to stay in the house of his brother, a mining engineer, who had rented a gold mine from the Crown on his own account. Unofficially that was well known all over Siberia. But one day we learned from Irkútsk that, in consequence of a secret denunciation, the general of the gendarmes (state police) was on his way to Chitá, to make a strict inquiry into the affair. An aide-de-camp of the governor-general brought us the news. I was dispatched in great haste to warn Mikháilov, and to tell him that he must return at once to the hospital prison, while the general of the gendarmes was kept at Chitá. As that gentleman found himself every night the winner of considerable sums of money at the green table in Kúkel's house, he soon decided not to exchange this pleasant pastime for a long journey to the mines in a temperature which was then a dozen degrees below the freezing-point of mercury, and eventually went back to Irkútsk, quite satisfied with his lucrative mission.

The storm, however, was coming nearer and nearer, and it swept everything before it soon after the insurrection broke out in Poland.

III

In January, 1863, Poland rose against Russian rule. Insurrectionary bands were formed, and a war began which lasted for full eighteen months. The London refugees had implored the Polish revolutionary committees to postpone the movement. They foresaw that it would be crushed, and would put an end to the reform period in Russia. But it could not be helped. The repression of the nationalist manifestations which took place at Warsaw in 1861, and the cruel, quite unprovoked executions which followed, exasperated the Poles. The die was cast.

Never before had the Polish cause so many sympathizers in Russia as at that time. I do not speak of the revolutionists; but even among the more moderate elements of Russian society it was thought, and was openly said, that it would be a benefit for Russia to have in Poland a friendly neighbor instead of a hostile subject. Poland will never lose her national character, it is too strongly developed; she has, and will have, her own literature, her own art and industry. Russia can keep her in servitude only by means of sheer force and oppression,—a condition of things which has hitherto favored, and necessarily will favor, oppression in Russia herself. Even the peaceful Slavophiles were of that opinion; and while I was at school, St. Petersburg society greeted with full approval the "dream" which the Slavophile Iván Aksákov had the courage to print in his paper, *The Day*. His dream was that the Russian troops had evacuated Poland, and he discussed the excellent results which would follow.

When the revolution of 1863 broke out, several Russian officers refused to march against the Poles, while others openly took their part, and died either on the scaffold or on the battle-field. Funds for the insurrection were collected all over Russia, —quite openly in Siberia,—and in the Russian universities the students equipped those of their comrades who were going to join the revolutionists.

Then, amidst this effervescence, the news spread over Russia that, during the night of January 10, bands of insurgents had fallen upon the soldiers who were cantoned in the villages, and had murdered them in their beds, although on the very eve of that day the relations of the troops with the Poles seemed to be quite friendly. There was some exaggeration in the report, but unfortunately there was also truth in it, and the impression it produced in Russia was most disastrous. The old antipathies between the two nations, so akin in their origins, but so differ-ent in their national characters, woke once more.

Gradually the bad feeling faded away to some extent. The gallant fight of the always brave sons of Poland, and the in-domitable energy with which they resisted a formidable army, won sympathy for that heroic nation. But it became known that the Polish revolutionary committee, in its demand for the reëstablishment of Poland with its old frontiers, included the Little Russian or Ukraínian provinces, the Greek Orthodox population of which hated its Polish rulers, and more than once in the course of the last three centuries had slaughtered them wholesale. Moreover, Napoleon III. began to menace Russia with a new war,—a vain menace, which did more harm to the Poles than all other things put together. And finally, the radical elements of Russia saw with regret that now the purely na-tionalist elements of Poland had got the upper hand, the revo-lutionary government did not care in the least to grant the land to the serfs,—a blunder of which the Russian government did not fail to take advantage, in order to appear in the position of protector of the peasants against their Polish landlords.

When the revolution broke out in Poland, it was generally believed in Russia that it would take a democratic, republican turn; and that the liberation of the serfs on a broad democratic basis would be the first thing which a revolutionary govern-ment, fighting for the independence of the country, would accomplish.

The emancipation law, as it had been enacted at St. Petersburg in 1861, provided ample opportunity for such a course of action. The personal obligations of the serfs to their owners came to an end only on the 19th of February, 1863. Then, a very slow process had to be gone through in order to obtain a sort of agreement between the landlords and the serfs as to the size and the location of the land allotments which were to be given to the liberated serfs. The yearly payments for these allotments (disproportionally high) were fixed by law at so much per acre; but the peasants had also to pay an additional sum for their homesteads, and of this sum the maximum only had been fixed by the statute,—it having been thought that the landlords might be induced to forego that additional payment, or to be satisfied with only a part of it. As to the so-called "redemption" of the land,—in which case the government undertook to pay the landlord its full value in state bonds, and the peasants, receiving the land, had to pay in return, for forty-nine years, six per cent on that sum as interest and annuities,—not only were these payments extravagant and ruinous for the peasants, but no time was fixed for the redemption. It was left to the will of the landlord, and in an immense number of cases the redemption arrangements had not even been entered upon, twenty years after the emancipation.

Under such conditions a revolutionary government had ample opportunity for immensely improving upon the Russian law. It was bound to accomplish an act of justice towards the serfs—whose condition in Poland was as bad as, and often worse than in Russia itself—by granting them better and more definite terms of emancipation. But nothing of the sort was done. The purely nationalist party and the aristocratic party having obtained the upper hand in the movement, this fundamentally important matter was left out of sight. This made it easy for the Russian government to win the peasants to its side.

Full advantage was taken of this mistake when Nicholas Miliútin was sent to Poland by Alexander II. with the mission of liberating the peasants in the way he intended doing it in Russia,—whether the landlords were ruined in consequence or not. "Go to Poland; apply there your Red program against the Polish landlords," said Alexander II. to him; and Miliútin, together with Prince Cherkássky and many others, really did their best to take the land from the landlords and give good-sized allotments to the peasants.

I once met one of the Russian functionaries who went to Poland under Miliútin and Prince Cherkássky. "We had full liberty," he said to me, "to turn over the land to the peasants. My usual plan was to go and to convoke the peasants' assembly. 'Tell me first,' I would say, 'what land do you hold at this moment?' They would point it out to me. 'Is this all the land you ever held?' I would then ask. 'Surely not,' they would reply with one voice. 'Years ago these meadows were ours; this wood was once in our possession; these fields, too,' they would say. I would let them go on talking all over and then would ask: 'Now, which of you can certify under oath that this land or that land has ever been held by you?' Of course there would be nobody forthcoming,—it was all too long ago. At last, some old man would be thrust out from the crowd, the rest saying: 'He knows all about it; he can swear to it.' The old man would begin a long story about what he knew in his youth, or had heard from his father, but I would cut the story short. . . . 'State on oath what you know to have been held by the *gmína* (the village community), and the land is yours.' And as soon as he took the oath—one could trust that oath implicitly—I wrote out the papers and declared to the assembly: 'Now, this land is yours. You stand no longer under any obligations whatever to your late masters: you are simply their neighbors; all you will have to do is to pay the redemption tax, so much every year, to the government. Your homesteads go with the land: you get them free.'"

One can imagine the effect which such a policy had upon the peasants. A cousin of mine, Petr Nikoláevich Kropótkin, a brother of the aide-de-camp whom I have mentioned, was in Poland or in Lithuania with his regiment of uhlans of the guard. The revolution was so serious that even the regiments of the guard had been sent from St. Petersburg against it, and it is now known that when Michael Muravióv was sent to Lithuania and came to take leave of the Empress Marie, she said to him: "Save at least Lithuania for Russia!" Poland was regarded as lost.

"The armed bands of the revolutionists held the country,"

my cousin said to me, "and we were powerless to defeat them, or even to find them. Small bands over and over again attacked our smaller detachments, and as they fought admirably, and knew the country, and found support in the population, they often had the best of the skirmishes. We were thus compelled to march in large columns only. We would cross a region, marching through the woods, without finding any trace of the bands; but when we marched back again, we learned that bands had reappeared in our rear; that they had levied the patriotic tax in the country; and if some peasant had rendered himself useful in any way to our troops, we found him hanged on a tree by the revolutionary bands. So it went on for months, with no chance of improvement, until Miliútin and Cherkássky came and freed the peasants, giving them the land. Then—all was over. The peasants sided with us; they helped us to capture the bands, and the insurrection came to an end."

I often spoke with the Polish exiles in Siberia upon this subject, and some of them understood the mistake that had been made. A revolution, from its very outset, must be an act of justice towards "the downtrodden and the oppressed," not a promise of such reparation later on; otherwise it is sure to fail. Unfortunately, it often happens that the leaders are so much absorbed with mere questions of military tactics that they forget the main thing. For revolutionists not to succeed in proving to the masses that a new era has really begun for them is to insure the certain failure of their cause.

The disastrous consequences for Poland of this revolution are known; they belong to the domain of history. How many thousand men perished in battle, how many hundreds were hanged, and how many scores of thousands were transported to various provinces of Russia and Siberia is not yet fully known. But even the official figures which were printed in Russia a few years ago show that in the Lithuanian provinces alone—not to speak of Poland proper—that terrible man, Michael Muravióv, to whom the Russian government has just erected a monument at Wílno, hanged by his own authority 128 Poles, and transported to Russia and Siberia 9423 men and women. Official lists, also published in Russia, give 18,672 men and women exiled to Siberia from Poland, of whom 10,-

407 were sent to East Siberia. I remember that the governor-general of East Siberia mentioned to me the same number, about 11,000 persons, sent to hard labor or exile in his domains. I saw them there, and witnessed their sufferings. Altogether, something like 60,000 or 70,000 persons, if not more, were torn out of Poland and transported to different provinces of Russia, to the Urals, to Caucasus, and to Siberia.

For Russia the consequences were equally disastrous. The Polish insurrection was the definitive close of the reform period. True, the law of provincial self-government (*Zémstvos*) and the reform of the law courts were promulgated in 1864 and 1866; but both were ready in 1862, and, moreover, at the last moment Alexander II. gave preference to the scheme of self-government which had been prepared by the reactionary party of Valúev, as against the scheme that had been prepared by Nicholas Miliútin; and immediately after the promulgation of both reforms, their importance was reduced, and in some cases destroyed, by the enactment of a number of by-laws.

Worst of all, public opinion itself took a further step backward. The hero of the hour was Katkóv, the leader of the serfdom party, who appeared now as a Russian "patriot," and carried with him most of the St. Petersburg and Moscow society. After that time, those who dared to speak of reforms were at once classed by Katkóv as "traitors to Russia."

The wave of reaction soon reached our remote province. One day in March a paper was brought by a special messenger from Irkútsk. It intimated to General Kúkel that he was at once to leave the post of governor of Transbaikália and go to Irkútsk, waiting there for further orders, and that he was not to reassume the post of commander of the general staff.

Why? What did that mean? There was not a word of explanation. Even the governor-general, a personal friend of Kúkel, had not run the risk of adding a single word to the mysterious order. Did it mean that Kúkel was going to be taken between two gendarmes to St. Petersburg, and immured in that huge stone coffin, the fortress of St. Peter and St. Paul? All was possible. Later on we learned that such was indeed the intention; and so it would have been done but for the energetic intervention of Count Nicholas Muravióv, "the conqueror of

the Amúr," who personally implored the Tsar that Kúkel
should be spared that fate.

Our parting with Kúkel and his charming family was like a
funeral. My heart was very heavy. I not only lost in him a
dear personal friend, but I felt also that this parting was the
burial of a whole epoch, full of long-cherished hopes,—"full of
illusions," as it became the fashion to say.

So it was. A new governor came,—a good-natured, "leave-
me-in-peace" man. With renewed energy, seeing that there
was no time to lose, I completed our plans for the reform of
the system of exile and municipal self-government. The governor made a few objections here and there for formality's sake,
but finally signed the schemes, and they were sent to head-
quarters. But at St. Petersburg reforms were no longer wanted.
There our projects lie buried still, with hundreds of similar
ones from all parts of Russia. A few "improved" prisons, even
more terrible than the old unimproved ones, have been built
in the capitals, to be shown during prison congresses to distinguished foreigners; but the remainder, and the whole system
of exile, were found by George Kennan[6] in 1886 in exactly the
same state in which I left them in 1862. Only now, after thirty-
five years have passed away, the authorities are introducing
the reformed tribunals and a parody of self-government in
Siberia, and committees have been nominated again to inquire
into the system of exile.

When Kennan came back to London from his journey to
Siberia, he managed, on the very next day after his arrival in
London, to hunt up Stepniák, Chaikóvsky, myself, and another
Russian refugee. In the evening we all met at Kennan's room
in a small hotel near Charing Cross. We saw him for the first
time, and having no excess of confidence in enterprising Eng-
lishmen who had previously undertaken to learn all about the
Siberian prisons without even learning a word of Russian, we
began to cross-examine Kennan. To our astonishment, he not
only spoke excellent Russian, but he knew everything worth
knowing about Siberia. One or another of us had been acquainted with the greater proportion of all political exiles in
Siberia, and we besieged Kennan with questions: "Where is
So-and-So? Is he married? Is he happy in his marriage? Does

he still keep fresh in spirit?" We were soon satisfied that Kennan knew all about every one of them.

When this questioning was over, and we were preparing to leave, I asked, "Do you know, Mr. Kennan, if they have built a watchtower for the fire brigade at Chitá?" Stepniák looked at me, as if to reproach me for abusing Kennan's goodwill. Kennan, however, began to laugh, and I soon joined him. And with much laughter we tossed each other questions and answers: "Why, do you know about that?" "And you too?" "Built?" "Yes, double estimates!" and so on, till at last Stepniák interfered, and in his most severely good-natured way objected: "Tell us at least what you are laughing about." Whereupon Kennan told the story of that watchtower which his readers must remember. In 1859 the Chitá people wanted to build a watchtower, and collected the money for it; but their estimates had to be sent to St. Petersburg. So they went to the ministry of the interior; but when they came back, two years later, duly approved, all the prices for timber and work had gone up in that rising young town. This was in 1862, while I was at Chitá. New estimates were made and sent to St. Petersburg, and the story was repeated for full twenty-five years, till at last the Chitá people, losing patience, put in their estimates prices nearly double the real ones. These fantastic estimates were solemnly considered at St. Petersburg, and approved. This is how Chitá got its watchtower.

It has often been said that Alexander II. committed a great fault, and brought about his own ruin, by raising so many hopes which later on he did not satisfy. It is seen from what I have just said—and the story of little Chitá was the story of all Russia—that he did worse than that. It was not merely that he raised hopes. Yielding for a moment to the current of public opinion around him, he induced men all over Russia to set to work, to issue from the domain of mere hopes and dreams, and to touch with the finger the reforms that were required. He made them realize what could be done immediately, and how easy it was to do it; he induced them to sacrifice whatever of their ideals could not be immediately realized, and to demand only what was practically possible at the time. And when they had framed their ideas, and had shaped them into laws which merely required his signature to become realities, then he refused that signature. No reactionist could raise, or ever has raised, his voice to assert that what was left—the unreformed tribunals, the absence of municipal self-government, or the system of exile—was good and was worth maintaining: no one has dared to say that. And yet, owing to the fear of doing anything, all was left as it was; for thirty-five years those who ventured to mention the necessity of a change were treated as "suspects;" and institutions unanimously recognized as bad were permitted to continue in existence only that nothing more might be heard of that abhorred word "reform."

IV

As there was nothing more to be done in the direction of reform, I tried to do what seemed to be possible under the existing circumstances,—only to become convinced of the absolute uselessness of such efforts. In my new capacity of attaché to the governor-general for Cossack affairs, I made, for instance, a most thorough investigation of the economical conditions of the Usurí Cossacks, whose crops used to be lost every year, so that the government had every winter to feed them in order to save them from famine. When I returned from the Usurí with my report, I received congratulations on all sides, I was promoted, I got special rewards. All the measures I recommended were accepted, and special grants of money were given for aiding the emigration of some and for supplying cattle to others, as I had suggested. But the practical realization of the measures went into the hands of some old drunkard, who would squander the money and pitilessly flog the unfortunate Cossacks for the purpose of converting them into good agriculturalists. And thus it went on in all directions, beginning with the Winter Palace at St. Petersburg, and ending with the Usurí and Kamchátka.

The higher administration of Siberia was influenced by excellent intentions, and I can only repeat that, everything considered, it was far better, far more enlightened, and far more interested in the welfare of the country than the administration of any other province of Russia. But it was an administration,—a branch of the tree which had its root at St. Petersburg, and that was quite sufficient to paralyze all its excellent intentions, and to make it interfere with all beginnings of local spontaneous life and progress. Whatever was started for the good of the country by local men was looked at with distrust, and was immediately paralyzed by hosts of difficulties which came, not so much from the bad intentions of men,—men, as a rule, are better than institutions,—but simply because they belonged to a pyramidal, centralized administration. The very fact of its being a government which had its source in a distant capital caused it to look upon everything from the point of view of a functionary of the government who thinks, first of all, about what his superiors will say, and how this or that will appear in the administrative machinery, and not of the interests of the country.

Gradually I turned my energy more and more toward scientific exploration. In 1865 I explored the western Saiáns, where I got a new glimpse into the structure of the Siberian highlands, and came upon another important volcanic region on the Chinese frontier; and finally, next year, I undertook a long journey to discover a direct communication between the gold mines of the Yakútsk province (on the Vitím and the Olókma) and Transbaikália. For several years (1860–64) the members of the Siberian expedition had tried to find such a passage, and had endeavored to cross the series of very wild stony parallel ridges which separate these mines from Transbaikália; but when they reached that region, coming from the south, and saw before them these dreary mountains spreading for hundreds of miles northward, all of them, save one who was killed by natives, returned southward. It was evident that, in order to be successful, the expedition must move from the north to the south,—from the dreary and unknown wilderness to the warmer and populated regions. It also happened that while I was preparing for the expedition, I was shown a map which a native had traced with his knife on a piece of bark. This little map—a splendid example, by the way, of the usefulness of the geometrical sense in the lowest stages of civilization, and one which would consequently interest A. R. Wallace—so struck me by its seeming truth to nature that I fully trusted to it, and began my journey, following the indications of the map. In company with a young and promising naturalist, Poliakóv,

and a topographer, I went first down the Léna to the northern
gold mines. There we equipped our expedition, taking provisions for three months, and started southward. An old Yakút
hunter, who twenty years before had once followed the passage indicated on the Tungus map, undertook to act for us as
guide, and to cross the mountain region,—full 250 miles wide,
—following the river valleys and gorges indicated by the knife
of the Tungus on the birch-bark map. He really accomplished
this wonderful feat, although there was no track of any sort to
follow, and all the valleys that one sees from the top of a mountain pass, all equally filled with woods, seem, to the unprac-
ticed eye, to be absolutely alike.

This time the passage was found. For three months we wandered in the almost totally uninhabited mountain deserts and
over the marshy plateau, till at last we reached our destination,
Chitá. I am told that this passage is now of value for bringing
cattle from the south to the gold mines; as for me, the journey
helped me immensely afterward in finding the key to the structure of the mountains and plateaus of Siberia,—but I am not
writing a book of travel, and must stop.

The years that I spent in Siberia taught me many lessons
which I could hardly have learned elsewhere. I soon realized
the absolute impossibility of doing anything really useful for
the mass of the people by means of the administrative machinery. With this illusion I parted forever. Then I began to
understand not only men and human character, but also the
inner springs of the life of human society. The constructive
work of the unknown masses, which so seldom finds any mention in books, and the importance of that constructive work
in the growth of forms of society, fully appeared before my
eyes. To witness, for instance, the ways in which the communities of Dukhobórs (brothers of those who are now going to
settle in Canada, and who find such a hearty support in the
United States) migrated to the Amúr region, to see the immense advantages which they got from their semi-communistic
brotherly organization, and to realize what a wonderful success their colonization was, amidst all the failures of state colonization, was learning something which cannot be learned
from books. Again, to live with natives, to see at work all the

complex forms of social organization which they have elaborated far away from the influence of any civilization, was, as it were, to store up floods of light which illuminated my subsequent reading. The part which the unknown masses play in the accomplishment of all important historical events, and even in war, became evident to me from direct observation, and I came to hold ideas similar to those which Tolstóy expresses concerning the leaders and the masses in his monumental work, *War and Peace*.

Having been brought up in a serf-owner's family, I entered active life, like all young men of my time, with a great deal of confidence in the necessity of commanding, ordering, scolding, punishing, and the like. But when, at an early stage, I had to manage serious enterprises and to deal with men, and when each mistake would lead at once to heavy consequences, I began to appreciate the difference between acting on the principle of command and discipline and acting on the principle of common understanding. The former works admirably in a military parade, but it is worth nothing where real life is concerned, and the aim can be achieved only through the severe effort of many converging wills. Although I did not then formulate my observations in terms borrowed from party struggles, I may say now that I lost in Siberia whatever faith in state discipline I had cherished before. I was prepared to become an anarchist.

From the age of nineteen to twenty-five I had to work out important schemes of reform, to deal with hundreds of men on the Amúr, to prepare and to make risky expeditions with ridiculously small means, and so on; and if all these things ended more or less successfully, I account for it only by the fact that I soon understood that in serious work commanding and discipline are of little avail. Men of initiative are required everywhere; but once the impulse has been given, the enterprise must be conducted, especially in Russia, not in military fashion, but in a sort of communal way, by means of common understanding. I wish that all framers of plans of state discipline could pass through the school of real life before they begin to frame their state Utopias. We should then hear far less than at present of schemes of military and pyramidal organization of society.

With all that, life in Siberia became less and less attractive to me, although my brother Alexander had joined me in 1864 at Irkútsk, where he commanded a squadron of Cossacks. We were happy to be together; we read a great deal, and discussed all the philosophical, scientific, and sociological questions of the day; but we both longed after intellectual life, and there was none in Siberia. The occasional passage through Irkútsk of Raphael Pumpelly or of Adolph Bastian—the only two men of science who visited our capital during my stay there—was quite an event for both of us. The scientific and especially the political life of Western Europe, of which we heard through the papers, attracted us, and the return to Russia was the subject to which we continually came back in our conversations.

We decided then to leave the military service and to return to Russia. This was not an easy matter, especially as Alexander had married in Siberia; but at last all was arranged, and early in 1867 we were on our way to St. Petersburg.

✷ ✷ ✷ ✷ ✷ ✷ ✷ ✷ ✷ ✷ ✷ ✷ ✷ ✷ ✷ ✷ ✷

PART FOUR

ST. PETERSBURG; FIRST JOURNEY TO WESTERN EUROPE

I

Early in the autumn of 1867 my brother and I, with his family, were settled at St. Petersburg. I entered the university, and sat on the benches among young men, almost boys, much younger than myself. What I so longed for five years before was accomplished,—I could study; and, acting upon the idea that a thorough training in mathematics is the only solid basis for all subsequent work and thought, I joined the physico-mathematical faculty in its mathematical section. My brother entered the military academy for jurisprudence, whilst I entirely gave up military service, to the great dissatisfaction of my father, who hated the very sight of a civilian dress. We both had now to rely entirely upon ourselves.

Study at the university and scientific work absorbed all my time for the next five years. A student of the mathematical faculty has, of course, very much to do, but my previous studies in higher mathematics permitted me to devote part of my time to geography; and, moreover, I had not lost in Siberia the habit of hard work.

The report of my last expedition was in print; but in the meantime a vast problem rose before me. The journeys that I had made in Siberia had convinced me that the mountains which at that time were drawn on the maps of Northern Asia were mostly fantastic, and gave no idea whatever of the structure of the country. The great plateaus which are so prominent a feature of Asia were not even suspected by those who drew the maps. Instead of them, several great ridges, such as, for instance, the eastern portion of the Stanovói, which used to be drawn on the maps as a black worm creeping eastward, had grown up in the topographic bureaus, contrary to the indications and even to the sketches of such explorers as L. Schwartz. These ridges have no existence in nature. The heads of the rivers which flow toward the Arctic Ocean on the one side, and toward the Pacific on the other, lie intermingled on the surface of a vast plateau; they rise in the same marshes. But, in the European topographer's imagination, the highest mountain ridges must run along the chief water-partings, and the topographers had drawn there the highest Alps, of which there is no trace in reality. Many such imaginary mountains were made to intersect the maps of Northern Asia in all directions.

To discover the true leading principles in the disposition of the mountains of Asia—the harmony of mountain formation—now became a question which for years absorbed my attention. For a considerable time the old maps, and still more the generalizations of Alexander von Humboldt, who, after a long study of Chinese sources, had covered Asia with a network of mountains running along the meridians and parallels, hampered me in my researches, until at last I saw that even Humboldt's generalizations, stimulating though they had been, did not agree with the facts.

Beginning, then, with the beginning, in a purely inductive way, I collected all the barometrical observations of previous travelers, and from them calculated hundreds of altitudes; I marked on a large scale map all geological and physical observations that had been made by different travelers,—the facts, not the hypotheses; and I tried to find out what structural lines would answer best to the observed realities. This preparatory work took me more than two years; and then followed months of intense thought, in order to find out what all the bewildering chaos of scattered observations meant, until one day, all of a sudden, the whole became clear and comprehensible, as if it were illuminated with a flash of light. The main structural lines of Asia are *not* north and south, or west and east; they are from the southwest to the northeast,—just as, in the Rocky Mountains and the plateaus of America, the lines are northwest to southeast; only secondary ridges shoot out northwest. Moreover, the mountains of Asia are not bundles of independent ridges, like the Alps, but are subordinated to an immense plateau, an old continent which once pointed toward Behring Strait. High border ridges have towered up along its fringes, and in the course of ages, terraces, formed by later sediments, have emerged from the sea, thus adding on both sides to the width of that primitive backbone of Asia.

There are not many joys in human life equal to the joy of the sudden birth of a generalization, illuminating the mind after a long period of patient research. What has seemed for years so chaotic, so contradictory, and so problematic takes at once its proper position within an harmonious whole. Out of a wild confusion of facts and from behind the fog of guesses, —contradicted almost as soon as they are born,—a stately picture makes its appearance, like an Alpine chain suddenly emerging in all its grandeur from the mists which concealed it the moment before, glittering under the rays of the sun in all its simplicity and variety, in all its mightiness and beauty. And when the generalization is put to a test, by applying it to hundreds of separate facts which had seemed to be hopelessly contradictory the moment before, each of them assumes its due position, increasing the impressiveness of the picture, accentuating some characteristic outline, or adding an unsuspected detail full of meaning. The generalization gains in strength and extent; its foundations grow in width and solidity; while in the distance, through the far-off mist on the horizon, the eye detects the outlines of new and still wider generalizations.

He who has once in his life experienced this joy of scientific creation will never forget it; he will be longing to renew it; and he cannot but feel with pain that this sort of happiness is the lot of so few of us, while so many could also live through it,—on a small or on a grand scale,—if scientific methods and leisure were not limited to a handful of men.

This work I consider my chief contribution to science. My first intention was to produce a bulky volume, in which the new ideas about the mountains and plateaus of Northern Asia should be supported by a detailed examination of each separate region; but in 1873, when I saw that I should soon be arrested, I only prepared a map which embodied my views and wrote an explanatory paper. Both were published by the Geographical Society, under the supervision of my brother, while I was already in the fortress of St. Peter and St. Paul. Petermann, who was then preparing a map of Asia, and knew my preliminary work, adopted my scheme for his map, and it has been accepted since by most cartographers. The map of Asia, as it is now understood, explains, I believe, the main physical features of the great continent, as well as the distribution of its climates, faunas, and floras, and even its history. It reveals, also, as I was able to see during my last journey to America, striking analogies between the structure and the geological growth of the two continents of the northern hemisphere. Very few cartographers could say now whence all these changes in the map of Asia have come; but in science it is better that new ideas should make their way independently of any name attached to them. The errors, which are unavoidable in a first generalization, are easier to rectify.

II

At the same time I worked a great deal for the Russian Geographical Society in my capacity of secretary to its section of physical geography. I was sent out by the Geographical Society for a modest tour in Finland and Sweden, to explore the glacial deposits; and that journey drifted me in a quite different direction.

The Russian Academy of Sciences sent out that summer two of its members—the old geologist General Helmersen and Frederick Schmidt, the indefatigable explorer of Siberia—to study the structure of those long ridges of drift which are known as *åsar* in Sweden and Finland, and as *eskers, kames,* and so on, in the British Isles. The Geographical Society sent me to Finland for the same purpose. We visited, all three, the beautiful ridge of Pungahárju and then separated. I worked hard during the summer. I traveled a great deal in Finland, and crossed over to Sweden, where I spent many happy hours in the company of A. Nordenskjöld. As early as then—1871— he mentioned to me his schemes for reaching the mouths of the Siberian rivers, and even the Behring Strait, by the northern route. Returning to Finland I continued my researches till late in the autumn, and collected a mass of most interesting observations relative to the glaciation of the country. But I also thought a great deal during this journey about social matters, and these thoughts had a decisive influence upon my subsequent development.

All sorts of valuable materials relative to the geography of Russia passed through my hands in the Geographical Society, and the idea gradually came to me of writing an exhaustive physical geography of that immense part of the world. My intention was to give a thorough geographical description of the country, basing it upon the main lines of the surface structure, which I began to disentangle for European Russia; and to sketch, in that description, the different forms of economic life which ought to prevail in different physical regions. Take, for instance, the wide prairies of Southern Russia, so often visited by droughts and failure of crops. These droughts and failures must not be treated as accidental calamities: they are as much a natural feature of that region as its position on a southern slope, its fertility, and the rest; and the whole of the economic life of the southern prairies ought to be organized in prevision of the unavoidable recurrence of periodical droughts. Each region of the Russian Empire ought to be treated in the same scientific way, just as Karl Ritter has treated parts of Asia in his beautiful monographs.

But such a work would have required plenty of time and full freedom for the writer, and I often thought how helpful to this end it would be were I to occupy some day the position of secretary to the Geographical Society. Now, in the autumn of 1871, as I was working in Finland, slowly moving on foot toward the seacoast along the newly built railway, and closely watching the spot where the first unmistakable traces of the former extension of the post-glacial sea would appear, I received a telegram from the Geographical Society: "The council begs you to accept the position of secretary to the Society." At the same time the outgoing secretary strongly urged me to accept the proposal.

My hopes were realized. But in the meantime other thoughts and other longings had pervaded my mind. I seriously thought over the reply, and wired, "Most cordial thanks, but cannot accept."

III

It often happens that men pull in a certain political, social, or familiar harness simply because they never have time to ask themselves whether the position they stand in and the work they accomplish are right; whether their occupations really suit their inner desires and capacities, and give them the satisfaction which every one has the right to expect from his work. Active men are especially liable to find themselves in such a position. Every day brings with it a fresh batch of work, and a man throws himself into his bed late at night without having completed what he had expected to do; then in the morning he hurries to the unfinished task of the previous day. Life goes, and there is no time left to think, no time to consider the direction that one's life is taking. So it was with me.

But now, during my journey in Finland, I had leisure. When I was crossing in a Finnish two-wheeled *karria* some plain which offered no interest to the geologist, or when I was walking, hammer on shoulder, from one gravel-pit to another, I could think; and amidst the undoubtedly interesting geological work I was carrying on, one idea, which appealed far more strongly to my inner self than geology, persistently worked in my mind.

I saw what an immense amount of labor the Finnish peasant spends in clearing the land and in breaking up the hard boulder-clay, and I said to myself: "I will write the physical geography of this part of Russia, and tell the peasant the best means of cultivating this soil. Here an American stump-extractor would be invaluable; there certain methods of manuring would be indicated by science. . . . But what is the use of talking to this peasant about American machines, when he has barely enough bread to live upon from one crop to the next; when the rent which he has to pay for that boulder-clay grows heavier and heavier in proportion to his success in improving the soil? He gnaws at his hard-as-a-stone rye-flour cake which he bakes twice a year; he has with it a morsel of fearfully salted cod and a drink of skimmed milk. How dare I talk to him of American machines, when all that he can raise must be sold to pay rent and taxes? He needs me to live with him, to help him to become the owner or the free occupier of that land. Then he will read books with profit, but not now."

And my thoughts wandered from Finland to our Nikólskoe peasants, whom I had lately seen. Now they are free, and they value freedom very much. But they have no meadows. In one way or another, the landlords have got all the meadows for themselves. When I was a child, the Savókhins used to send out six horses for night pasture, the Tolkachóvs had seven. Now, these families have only three horses each; other families, which formerly had three horses, have only one, or none. What can be done with one miserable horse? No meadows, no horses, no manure! How can I talk to them of grass-sowing? They are already ruined,—poor as Lazarus,—and in a few years they will be made still poorer by a foolish taxation. How happy they were when I told them that my father gave them permission to mow the grass in the small open spaces in his Kóstino forest! "Your Nikólskoe peasants are *ferocious* for work,"—that is the common saying about them in our neighborhood; but the arable land, which our stepmother has taken out of their allotments in virtue of the "law of minimum,"—that diabolic clause introduced by the serf-owners when they were allowed to revise the emancipation law,—is now a forest of thistles, and the "ferocious" workers are not allowed to till it. And the same sort of thing goes on throughout all Russia. Even at that time it was evident, and official commissioners gave warning of it, that the first serious failure of crops in Middle Russia would result in a terrible famine,—and famine came, in 1876, in 1884, in 1891, in 1895, and again in 1898.

Science is an excellent thing. I knew its joys and valued them,—perhaps more than many of my colleagues did. Even now, as I was looking on the lakes and the hillocks of Finland, new and beautiful generalizations arose before my eyes. I saw in a remote past, at the very dawn of mankind, the ice accumulating from year to year in the northern archipelagoes, over Scandinavia and Finland. An immense growth of ice invaded the north of Europe and slowly spread as far as its middle portions. Life dwindled in that part of the northern hemisphere, and, wretchedly poor, uncertain, it fled further and further south before the icy breath which came from that immense frozen mass. Man—miserable, weak, ignorant—had every difficulty in maintaining a precarious existence. Ages passed away, till the melting of the ice began, and with it came the lake period, when countless lakes were formed in the cavities, and a wretched subpolar vegetation began timidly to invade the unfathomable marshes with which every lake was surrounded. Another series of ages passed before an extremely slow process of drying up set in, and vegetation began its slow invasion from the south. And now we are fully in the period of a rapid desiccation, accompanied by the formation of dry prairies and steppes, and man has to find out the means to put a check to that desiccation to which Central Asia already has fallen a victim, and which menaces Southeastern Europe.

Belief in an ice-cap reaching Middle Europe was at that time rank heresy; but before my eyes a grand picture was rising, and I wanted to draw it, with the thousands of details I saw in it; to use it as a key to the present distribution of floras and faunas; to open new horizons for geology and physical geography.

But what right had I to these highest joys, when all around me was nothing but misery and struggle for a moldy bit of bread; when whatsoever I should spend to enable me to live in that world of higher emotions must needs be taken from the very mouths of those who grew the wheat and had not bread enough for their children? From somebody's mouth it must be taken, because the aggregate production of mankind remains still so low.

Knowledge is an immense power. Man must know. But we already know much! What if that knowledge—and only that—should become the possession of all? Would not science itself progress in leaps, and cause mankind to make strides in production, invention, and social creation, of which we are hardly in a condition now to measure the speed?

The masses want to know: they are willing to learn; they *can* learn. There, on the crest of that immense moraine which runs between the lakes, as if giants had heaped it up in a hurry to connect the two shores, there stands a Finnish peasant plunged in contemplation of the beautiful lakes, studded with islands, which lie before him. Not one of these peasants, poor and downtrodden though they may be, will pass this spot with-

out stopping to admire the scene. Or there, on the shore of a
lake, stands another peasant, and sings something so beautiful
that the best musician would envy him his melody, for its feeling and its meditative power. Both deeply feel, both meditate,
both think; they are ready to widen their knowledge,—only give
it to them, only give them the means of getting leisure.

This is the direction in which, and these are the kind of
people for whom, I must work. All those sonorous phrases
about making mankind progress, while at the same time the
progress-makers stand aloof from those whom they pretend to
push onwards, are mere sophisms made up by minds anxious
to shake off a fretting contradiction.

So I sent my negative reply to the Geographical Society.

IV

St. Petersburg had changed greatly from what it was when I
left it in 1862. "Oh, yes, you knew the St. Petersburg of
Chernyshévsky," the poet Máikov remarked to me once. True,
I knew the St. Petersburg of which Chernyshévsky was the
favorite. But how shall I describe the city which I found on
my return? Perhaps as the St. Petersburg of the *cafés chan-
tants*, of the music halls, if the words "all St. Petersburg" ought
really to mean the upper circles of society which took their
keynote from the court.

At the court, and in its circles, liberal ideas were in sorely
bad repute. All prominent men of the sixties, even such mod-
erates as Count Nicholas Muravióv and Nicholas Miliútin, were
treated as suspects. Only Dmítri Miliútin, the minister of war,
was kept by Alexander II. at his post, because the reform which
he had to accomplish in the army required many years for
its realization. All other active men of the reform period had
been brushed aside.

I spoke once with a high dignitary of the ministry for foreign affairs. He sharply criticized another high functionary, and
I remarked in the latter's defense, "Still, there is this to be
said for him, that he never accepted service under Nicholas I."
"And now he is in service under the reign of Shuválov and

Trépov!" was the reply, which so correctly described the situation that I could say nothing more.

General Shuválov, the chief of the state police, and General Trépov, the chief of the St. Petersburg police, were indeed the real rulers of Russia. Alexander II. was their executive, their tool. And they ruled by fear. Trépov had so frightened Alexander by the specter of a revolution which was going to break out at St. Petersburg, that if the omnipotent chief of the police was a few minutes late in appearing with his daily report at the palace, the Emperor would ask, "Is everything quiet at St. Petersburg?"

Shortly after Alexander had given an "entire dismissal" to Princess X., he conceived a warm friendship for General Fleury, the aide-de-camp of Napoleon III., that sinister man who was the soul of the *coup d'état* of December 2, 1852. They were continually seen together, and Fleury once informed the Parisians of the great honor which was bestowed upon him by the Russian Tsar. As the latter was riding along the Nevsky Prospekt, he saw Fleury, and asked him to mount into his carriage, an *égoïste*, which had a seat only twelve inches wide, for a single person; and the French general recounted at length how the Tsar and he, holding fast to each other, had to leave half of their bodies hanging in the air on account of the narrowness of the seat. It is enough to name this new friend, fresh from Compiègne, to suggest what the friendship meant.

Shuválov took every advantage of the present state of mind of his master. He prepared one reactionary measure after another, and when Alexander showed reluctance to sign any one of them, Shuválov would speak of the coming revolution and the fate of Louis XVI., and, "for the salvation of the dynasty," would implore him to sign the new additions to the laws of repression. For all that, sadness and remorse would from time to time besiege Alexander. He would fall into a gloomy melancholy, and speak in a sad tone of the brilliant beginning of his reign, and of the reactionary character which it was taking. Then Shuválov would organize a bear hunt. Hunters, merry courtiers, and carriages full of ballet girls would go to the forests of Nóvgorod. A couple of bears would be killed by Alexander II., who was a good shot, and used to let the animals approach within a few yards of his rifle; and there, in the excitement of the hunting festivities, Shuválov would obtain his master's signature to any scheme of repression or robbery in the interest of his clients, which he had concocted.

Alexander II. certainly was not a rank-and-file man, but two different men lived in him, both strongly developed, struggling with each other; and this inner struggle became more and more violent as he advanced in age. He could be charming in his behavior, and the next moment display sheer brutality. He was possessed of a calm, reasoned courage in the face of a real danger, but he lived in constant fear of dangers which existed in his brain only. He assuredly was not a coward; he would meet a bear face to face; on one occasion, when the animal was not killed outright by his first bullet, and the man who stood behind him with a lance, rushing forward, was knocked down by the bear, the Tsar came to his rescue, and killed the bear close to the muzzle of his gun (I know this from the man himself); yet he was haunted all his life by the fears of his own imagination and of an uneasy conscience. He was very kind in his manner toward his friends, but that kindness existed side by side with the terrible cold-blooded cruelty—a seventeenth century cruelty—which he displayed in crushing the Polish insurrection, and later on in 1880, when similar measures were taken to put down the revolt of the Russian youth; a cruelty of which no one would have thought him capable. He thus lived a double life, and at the period of which I am speaking, he merrily signed the most reactionary decrees, and afterward became despondent about them. Toward the end of his life this inner struggle, as will be seen later on, became still stronger, and assumed an almost tragical character.

In 1872 Shuválov was nominated ambassador to England, but his friend General Potápov continued the same policy till the beginning of the Turkish war in 1877. During all this time, the most scandalous plundering of the state exchequer, as also of the crown lands, the estates confiscated in Lithuania after the insurrection, the Bashkír lands in Orenbúrg, and so on, was proceeding on a grand scale. Several such affairs were subsequently brought to light and judged publicly by the Senate acting as a high court of justice, after Potápov, who became insane, and Trépov had been dismissed, and their rivals at the palace wanted to show them to Alexander II. in their true light. In one of these judicial inquiries it came out that a friend of Potápov had most shamelessly robbed the peasants of a Lithuanian estate of their lands, and afterward, empowered by his friends at the ministry of the interior, he had caused the peasants, who sought redress, to be imprisoned, subjected to wholesale flogging, and shot down by the troops. This was one of the most revolting stories of the kind even in the annals of Russia, which teem with similar robberies up to the present time. It was only after Véra Zasúlich had shot at Trépov and wounded him (to avenge his having ordered one of the political prisoners to be flogged in prison) that the thefts of Potápov and his clients became widely known and he was dismissed. Thinking that he was going to die, Trépov wrote his will, from which it became known that this man, who made the Tsar believe that he died poor, even though he had occupied for years the lucrative post of chief of the St. Petersburg police, left in reality to his heirs a considerable fortune. Some courtiers reported it to Alexander II. Trépov lost his credit, and it was then that a few of the robberies of the Shuválov-Potápov-and-Trépov party were brought before the Senate.

The pillage which went on in all the ministries, especially in connection with the railways and all sorts of industrial enterprises, was really enormous. Immense fortunes were made at that time. The navy, as Alexander II. himself said to one of his sons, was "in the pockets of So-and-So." The cost of the railways, guaranteed by the state, was simply fabulous. As to commercial enterprises, it was openly known that none could be launched unless a specified percentage of the dividends was promised to different functionaries in the several ministries. A friend of mine, who intended to start some enterprise at St. Petersburg, was frankly told at the ministry of the interior that he would have to pay twenty-five per cent of the net profits to a certain person, fifteen per cent to one man at the ministry of finances, ten per cent to another man in the same ministry, and five per cent to a fourth person. The bargains were made without concealment, and Alexander II. knew it. His own remarks, written on the reports of the comptroller-general, bear testimony to this. But he saw in the thieves his protectors from the revolution, and kept them until their robberies became an open scandal.

The young grand dukes, with the exception of the heir apparent, afterward Alexander III., who always was a good and thrifty *paterfamilias*, followed the example of the head of the family. The orgies which one of them used to arrange in a small restaurant on the Nevsky Prospekt were so degradingly notorious that one night the chief of the police had to interfere, and warned the owner of the restaurant that he would be marched to Siberia if he ever again let his "grand duke's room" to the grand duke. "Imagine my perplexity," this man said to me, on one occasion, when he was showing me that room, the walls and ceiling of which were upholstered with thick satin cushions. "On the one side I had to offend a member of the imperial family, who could do with me what he liked, and on the other side General Trépov menaced me with Siberia! Of course, I obeyed the general; he is, as you know, omnipotent now." Another grand duke became conspicuous for ways belonging to the domain of psychopathy; and a third was exiled to Turkestan, after he had stolen the diamonds of his mother.

The Empress Marie Alexándrovna, abandoned by her husband, and probably horrified at the turn which court life was taking, became more and more a devotee, and soon she was entirely in the hands of the palace priest, a representative of a quite new type in the Russian Church,—the Jesuitic. This new genus of well-combed, depraved, and Jesuitic clergy made rapid progress at that time; already they were working hard and with success to become a power in the state, and to lay hands on the schools.

It has been proved over and over again that the village clergy in Russia are so much taken up by their functions—performing baptisms and marriages, administering communion to the dying, and so on—that they cannot pay due attention to the schools; even when the priest is paid for giving the Scripture lesson at a village school, he usually passes that lesson to some one else, as he has no time to attend to it himself. Nevertheless, the higher clergy, exploiting the hatred of Alexander II. toward the so-called revolutionary spirit, began their campaign for laying their hands upon the schools. "No schools unless clerical ones" became their motto. All Russia wanted education, but even the ridiculously small sum of four million dollars included every year in the state budget for primary schools used *not* to be spent by the ministry of public instruction, while nearly as much was given to the Synod as an aid for establishing schools under the village clergy,—schools most of which existed, and now exist, on paper only.

All Russia wanted technical education, but the ministry opened only classical gymnasia, because formidable courses of Latin and Greek were considered the best means of preventing the pupils from reading and thinking. In these gymnasia, only two or three per cent of the pupils succeeded in completing an eight years' course,—all boys promising to become something and to show some independence of thought being carefully sifted out before they could reach the last form; and all sorts of measures were taken to *reduce* the number of pupils. Education was considered as a sort of luxury, for the few only. At the same time the ministry of education was engaged in a continuous, passionate struggle against all private persons and all institutions—district and county councils, municipalities, and the like—which endeavored to open teachers' seminaries or technical schools, or even simple primary schools. Technical education—in a country which was so much in want of engineers, educated agriculturists, and geologists—was treated as equivalent to revolutionism. It was prohibited, prosecuted; so that up to the present time, every autumn, something like two or three thousand young men are refused admission to the higher technical schools from mere lack of vacancies. A feeling of despair took possession of all those who wished to do anything useful in public life; while the peasantry were ruined at an appalling rate by over-taxation, and by "beating out" of them the arrears of the taxes by means of semi-military executions, which ruined them forever. Only those governors of the provinces were in favor at the capital who managed to beat out the taxes in the most severe way.

Such was the official St. Petersburg. Such was the influence it exercised upon Russia.

V

When we were leaving Siberia, we often talked, my brother
and I, of the intellectual life which we should find at St. Petersburg, and of the interesting acquaintances we should make in
the literary circles. We made such acquaintances, indeed, both
among the radicals and among the moderate Slavophiles; but
I must confess that they were rather disappointing. We found
plenty of excellent men,—Russia is full of excellent men,—but
they did not quite correspond to our ideal of political writers.
The best writers—Chernyshévsky, Mikháilov, Lavróv—were in
exile, or were kept in the fortress of St. Peter and St. Paul,
like Písarev. Others, taking a gloomy view of the situation, had
changed their ideas, and were now leaning toward a sort of
paternal absolutism; while the greater number, though holding still to their beliefs, had become so cautious in expressing
them that their prudence was almost equal to desertion.

At the height of the reform period nearly every one in the
advanced literary circles had had some relations either with
Hérzen or with Turgénev and his friends, or with the Great
Russian or the Land and Freedom secret societies which had
had at that period an ephemeral existence. Now, these same
men were only the more anxious to bury their former sympathies as deep as possible, so as to appear above political
suspicion.

One or two of the liberal reviews which were tolerated at
that time, owing chiefly to the superior diplomatic talents of
their editors, contained excellent material, showing the ever
growing misery and the desperate conditions of the great mass
of the peasants, and making clear enough the obstacles that
were put in the way of every progressive worker. The amount
of such facts was enough to drive one to despair. But no one
dared to suggest any remedy, or to hint at any field of action,
at any outcome from a position which was represented as hopeless. Some writers still cherished the hope that Alexander II.
would once more assume the character of reformer; but with
the majority the fear of seeing their reviews suppressed, and
both editors and contributors marched "to some more or less

remote part of the empire," dominated all other feelings. Fear and hope equally paralyzed them.

The more radical they had been ten years before, the greater were their fears. My brother and I were very well received in one or two literary circles, and we went occasionally to their friendly gatherings; but the moment the conversation began to lose its frivolous character, or my brother, who had a great talent for raising serious questions, directed it toward home affairs, or toward the state of France, where Napoleon III. was hastening to his fall in 1870, some sort of interruption was sure to occur. "What do you think, gentlemen, of the latest performance of *La Belle Hélène?*" or "What is your opinion of that cured fish?" was loudly asked by one of the elder guests, —and the conversation was brought to an end.

Outside the literary circles, things were even worse. In the sixties, Russia, and especially St. Petersburg, was full of men of advanced opinions, who seemed ready at that time to make any sacrifices for their ideas. "What has become of them?" I asked myself. I looked up some of them; but, "Prudence, young man!" was all they had to say. "Iron is stronger than straw," or "One cannot break a stone wall with his forehead," and similar proverbs, unfortunately too numerous in the Russian language, constituted now their code of practical philosophy. "We have done something in our life: ask no more from us;" or "Have patience: this sort of thing will not last," they told us, while we, the youth, were ready to resume the struggle, to act, to risk, to sacrifice everything, if necessary, and only asked them to give us advice, some guidance, and some intellectual support.

Turgénev has depicted in *Smoke* some of the ex-reformers from the upper layers of society, and his picture is disheartening. But it is especially in the heart-rending novels and sketches of Madame Kokhanóvskaia, who wrote under the pseudonym of "V. Krestóvsky" (she must not be confounded with another novel-writer, Vsévolod Krestóvsky), that one can follow the many aspects which the degradation of the "liberals of the sixties" took at that time. "The joy of living"—perhaps the joy of having survived—became their goddess, as soon as the nameless crowd which ten years before made the force of the reform movement refused to hear any more of "all that sentimentalism." They hastened to enjoy the riches which poured into the hands of "practical" men.

Many new ways to fortune had been opened since serfdom had been abolished, and the crowd rushed with eagerness into these channels. Railways were feverishly built in Russia; to the lately opened private banks the landlords went in numbers to mortgage their estates; the newly established private notaries and lawyers at the courts were in possession of large incomes; the shareholders' companies multiplied with an appalling rapidity and the promoters flourished. A class of men who formerly would have lived in the country on the modest income of a small estate cultivated by a hundred serfs, or on the still more modest salary of a functionary in a law court, now made fortunes, or had such yearly incomes as in the times of serfdom were possible only for the land magnates.

The very tastes of "society" sunk lower and lower. The Italian opera, formerly a forum for radical demonstrations, was now deserted; the Russian opera, timidly asserting the rights of its great composers, was frequented by a few enthusiasts only. Both were found "tedious," and the cream of St. Petersburg society crowded to a vulgar theater where the second-rate stars of the Paris small theaters won easy laurels from their Horse Guard admirers, or went to see *La Belle Hélène*, which was played on the Russian stage, while our great dramatists were forgotten. Offenbach's music reigned supreme.

It must be said that the political atmosphere was such that the best men had reasons, or had at least weighty excuses, for keeping quiet. After Karakózov had shot at Alexander II. in April, 1866, the state police had become omnipotent. Every one suspected of "radicalism," no matter what he had done or what he had not done, had to live under the fear of being arrested any night, for the sympathy he might have shown to some one involved in this or that political affair, or for an innocent letter intercepted in a midnight search, or simply for his "dangerous" opinions; and arrest for political reasons might mean anything: years of seclusion in the fortress of St. Peter and St. Paul, transportation to Siberia, or even torture in the casemates of the fortress.

This movement of the circles of Karakózov remains up to this date very imperfectly known, even in Russia. I was at that time in Siberia, and know of it only by hearsay. It appears, however, that two different currents combined in it. One of them was the beginning of that great movement "toward the people," which later took on such formidable dimensions; while the other current was mainly political. Groups of young men, some of whom were on the road to become brilliant university professors, or men of mark as historians and ethnographers, had come together about 1864, with the intention of carrying to the people education and knowledge in spite of the opposition of the government. They went as mere artisans to great industrial towns, and started there coöperative associations, as well as informal schools, hoping that by the exercise of much tact and patience they might be able to educate the people, and thus to create the first centers from which better and higher conceptions would gradually radiate amongst the masses. Their zeal was great; considerable fortunes were brought into the service of the cause; and I am inclined to think that, compared with all similar movements which took place later on, this one stood perhaps on the most practical basis. Its initiators certainly were very near to the working-people.

On the other side, with some of the members of these circles —Karakózov, Ishútin, and their nearest friends—the movement took a political direction. During the years from 1862 to 1866 the policy of Alexander II. had assumed a decidedly reactionary character; he had surrounded himself with men of the most reactionary type, taking them as his nearest advisers; the very reforms which made the glory of the beginning of his reign were now wrecked wholesale by means of by-laws and ministerial circulars; a return to manorial justice and serfdom in a disguised form was openly expected in the old camp; while no one could hope at that time that the main reform—the abolition of serfdom—could withstand the assaults directed against it from the Winter Palace itself. All this must have brought Karakózov and his friends to the idea that a further continuance of Alexander II.'s reign would be a menace even to the little that had been won; that Russia would have to return to the horrors of Nicholas I., if Alexander continued to rule. Great hopes were felt at the same time—this is "an often repeated story, but always new"—as to the liberal inclinations of the heir to the throne and his uncle Constantine. I must also say that before 1866 such fears and such considerations were not unfrequently expressed in much higher circles than those with which Karakózov seems to have been in contact. At any rate, Karakózov shot at Alexander II. one day, as he was coming out of the summer garden to take his carriage. The shot missed, and Karakózov was arrested on the spot.

Katkóv, the leader of the Moscow reactionary party, and a great master for extracting pecuniary profits out of every political disturbance, at once accused of complicity with Karakózov all radicals and liberals,—which was certainly untrue,—and insinuated in his paper, making all Moscow believe it, that Karakózov was a mere instrument in the hands of the Grand Duke Constantine, the leader of the reform party in the highest circles. One can imagine to what an extent the two rulers, Shuválov and Trépov, exploited these accusations, and the consequent fears of Alexander II.

Michael Muraviov, who had won during the Polish insurrection his nickname "the hangman," received orders to make a most searching inquiry, and to discover by every possible means the plot which was supposed to exist. He made arrests in all classes of society, ordered hundreds of searches, and boasted that he "would find the means to render the prisoners more talkative." He certainly was not the man to recoil even before torture,—and public opinion in St. Petersburg was almost unanimous in saying that Karakózov was tortured to obtain avowals, but made none.

State secrets are well kept in fortresses, especially in that huge mass of stone opposite the Winter Palace, which has seen so many horrors, only in recent times disclosed by historians. It still keeps Muraviov's secrets. However, the following may perhaps throw some light on this matter.

In 1866 I was in Siberia. One of our Siberian officers, who traveled from Russia to Irkútsk toward the end of that year, met at a post station two gendarmes. They had accompanied to Siberia a functionary exiled for theft, and were now returning home. Our Irkútsk officer, who was a very amiable man, finding the gendarmes at the tea table on a cold winter night,

joined them and chatted with them, while the horses were
being changed. One of the men knew Karakózov.

"He was cunning, he was," he said. "When he was in the
fortress, we were ordered, two of us,—we were relieved every
two hours,—not to let him sleep. So we kept him sitting on a
small stool, and as soon as he began to doze, we shook him
to keep him awake. . . . What will you?—we were ordered to
do so! . . . Well, see how cunning he was: he would sit with
crossed legs, swinging one of his legs to make us believe that
he was awake, and himself, in the meantime, would get a nap,
continuing to swing his leg. But we soon made it out and told
those who relieved us, so that he was shaken and waked up
every few minutes, whether he swung his leg or not." "And
how long did that last?" my friend asked. "Oh, many days,—
more than one week."

The naïve character of this description is in itself a proof
of veracity: it could not have been invented; and that Karakózov was tortured to this degree may be taken for granted.

When Karakózov was hanged, one of my comrades from the
Corps of Pages was present at the execution with his regiment
of cuirassiers. "When he was taken out of the fortress," my
comrade told me, "sitting on the high platform of the cart
which was jolting on the rough glacis of the fortress, my first
impression was that they were bringing out an india-rubber
doll to be hanged; that Karakózov was already dead. Imagine
that the head, the hands, the whole body were absolutely loose,
as if there were no bones in the body, or as if the bones had
all been broken. It was a terrible thing to see, and to think
what it meant. However, when two soldiers took him down
from the cart, I saw that he moved his legs and made strenuous
endeavors to walk by himself and to ascend the steps of the
scaffold. So it was not a doll, nor could he have been in a
swoon. All the officers were very much puzzled at the circumstance and could not explain it." When, however, I suggested
to my comrade that perhaps Karakózov had been tortured, the
color came into his face and he replied, "So we all thought."

Absence of sleep for weeks would alone be sufficient to explain the state in which that morally very strong man was at
the time of the execution. I may add that I am absolutely certain that—at least in one case—drugs were administered to a

prisoner in the fortress, namely, Adrián Sabúrov, in 1879. Did
Muravióv limit the torture to this only? Was he prevented from
going any further, or not? I do not know. But this much I
know: that I often heard from high officials at St. Petersburg
that torture had been resorted to in this case.

Muravióv had promised to root out all radical elements in
St. Petersburg, and all those who had had in any degree a
radical past now lived under the fear of falling into the despot's clutches. Above all, they kept aloof from the younger
people, from fear of being involved with them in some perilous
political associations. In this way a chasm was opened not only
between the "fathers" and the "sons," as Turgénev described
it in his novel,—not only between the two generations, but also
between all men who had passed the age of thirty and those
who were in their early twenties. Russian youth stood consequently in the position not only of having to fight in their
fathers the defenders of serfdom, but of being left entirely to
themselves by their elder brothers, who were unwilling to join
them in their leanings toward Socialism, and were afraid to
give them support even in their struggle for more political freedom. Was there ever before in history, I ask myself, a youthful band engaging in a fight against so formidable a foe, so
deserted by fathers and even by elder brothers, although those
young men had merely taken to heart, and had tried to realize
in life, the intellectual inheritance of these same fathers and
brothers? Was there ever a struggle undertaken in more tragical conditions than these?

VI

The only bright point which I saw in the life of St. Petersburg
was the movement which was going on amongst the youth of
both sexes. Various currents joined to produce the mighty agitation which soon took an underground and revolutionary character, and engrossed the attention of Russia for the next fifteen
years. I shall speak of it in a subsequent chapter; but I must
mention in this place the movement which was carried on,
quite openly, by our women for obtaining access to higher ed-

ucation. St. Petersburg was at that time its main center.

Every afternoon the young wife of my brother, on her return from the women's pedagogical courses which she followed, had something new to tell us about the animation which prevailed there. Schemes were laid for opening a medical academy and universities for women; debates upon schools or upon different methods of education were organized in connection with the courses, and hundreds of women took a passionate interest in these questions, discussing them over and over again in private. Societies of translators, publishers, printers, and bookbinders were started in order that work might be provided for the poorest members of the sisterhood who flocked to St. Petersburg, ready to do any sort of work, only to live in the hope that they, too, would some day have their share of higher education. A vigorous, exuberant life reigned in those feminine centers, in striking contrast to what I met elsewhere.

Since the government had shown its determined intention not to admit women to the existing universities, they had directed all their efforts toward opening universities of their own. They were told at the ministry of education that the girls who had passed through the girls' gymnasia (the high schools) were not prepared to follow university lectures. "Very well," they replied, "permit us to open intermediate courses, preparatory to the university, and impose upon us any program you like. We ask no grants from the state. Only give us the permission, and it will be done." Of course, the permission was not given.

Then they started private courses and drawing-room lectures in all parts of St. Petersburg. Many university professors, in sympathy with the new movement, volunteered to give lectures. Poor men themselves, they warned the organizers that any mention of remuneration would be taken as a personal offense. Natural science excursions used to be made every summer in the neighborhood of St. Petersburg, under the guidance of university professors, and women constituted the bulk of the excursionists. In the courses for midwives they forced the professors to treat each subject in a far more exhaustive way than was required by the program, or to open additional courses. They took advantage of every possibility, of every breach in

the fortress, to storm it. They gained admission to the ana-
tomical laboratory of old Dr. Gruber, and by their admirable
work they won this enthusiast of anatomy entirely to their side.
If they learned that a professor had no objection to letting them
work in his laboratory on Sundays and at night on week days,
they took advantage of the opportunity.

At last, notwithstanding all the opposition of the ministry,
they opened the intermediate courses, only giving them the
name of pedagogical courses. Was it possible, indeed, to forbid
future mothers studying the methods of education? But as the
methods of teaching botany or mathematics could not be
taught in the abstract, botany, mathematics, and the rest were
soon introduced into the curriculum of the pedagogical courses,
which became preparatory for the university.

Step by step the women thus widened their rights. As soon
as it became known that at some German university a certain
professor might open his lecture-room to a few women, they
knocked at his door and were admitted. They studied law and
history at Heidelberg, and mathematics at Berlin; at Zürich,
more than a hundred girls and women worked at the university
and the polytechnicum. There they won something more valuable than the degree of Doctor of Medicine; they won the
esteem of the most learned professors, who expressed it publicly several times. When I came to Zürich in 1872, and became acquainted with some of the students, I was astonished
to see quite young girls, who were studying at the polytechnicum, solving intricate problems of the theory of heat, with
the aid of the differential calculus, as easily as if they had had
years of mathematical training. One of the Russian girls who
studied mathematics under Weierstrass at Berlin, Sophia Ko-
valévskaia, became a mathematician of high repute, and was
invited to a professorship at Stockholm; she was, I believe, the
first woman in our century to hold a professorship in a university for men. She was so young that in Sweden no one
wanted to call her by anything but her diminutive name of
Sónia.

In spite of the open hatred of Alexander II. for educated
women,—when he met in his walks a girl wearing spectacles
and a round Garibaldian cap, he began to tremble, thinking
that she must be a nihilist bent on shooting at him; in spite

of the bitter opposition of the state police, who represented every woman student as a revolutionist; in spite of the thunders and the vile accusations which Katkóv directed against the whole of the movement in almost every number of his venomous gazette, the women succeeded, in the teeth of the government, in opening a series of educational institutions. When several of them had obtained medical degrees abroad, they forced the government, in 1872, to let them open a medical academy with their own private means. And when the Russian women were recalled by their government from Zürich, to prevent their intercourse with the revolutionist refugees, they forced the government to let them open in Russia four universities of their own, which soon had nearly a thousand pupils. It seems almost incredible, but it is a fact that notwithstanding all the prosecutions which the Women's Medical Academy had to live through, and its temporary closure, there are now in Russia more than six hundred and seventy women practicing as physicians.

It was certainly a grand movement, astounding in its success and instructive in a high degree. Above all, it was through the unlimited devotion of a mass of women in all possible capacities that they gained their successes. They had already worked as sisters of charity during the Crimean war; as organizers of schools later on; as the most devoted schoolmistresses in the villages; as educated midwives and doctors' assistants amongst the peasants. They went afterward as nurses and doctors in the fever-stricken hospitals during the Turkish war of 1878, and won the admiration of the military commanders and of Alexander II. himself. I know two ladies, both very eagerly "wanted" by the state police, who served as nurses during the war, under assumed names which were guaranteed by false passports; one of them, the greater "criminal" of the two, who had taken a prominent part in my escape, was even appointed head nurse of a large hospital for wounded soldiers, while her friend nearly died from typhoid fever. In short, women took any position, no matter how low in the social scale, and no matter what privations it involved, if only they could be in any way useful to the people; not a few of them, but hundreds

and thousands. They have *conquered* their rights in the true
sense of the word.

Another feature of this movement was that in it the chasm
between the two generations—the older and the younger sisters
—did not exist; or, at least, it was bridged over to a great extent. Those who were the leaders of the movement from its
origin never broke the link which connected them with their
younger sisters, even though the latter were far more advanced
in their ideals than the older women were.

They pursued their aims in the higher spheres; they kept
strictly aloof from any political agitation; but they never committed the fault of forgetting that their true force was in the
masses of younger women, of whom a great number finally
joined the radical or revolutionary circles. These leaders were
correctness itself,—I considered them too correct; but they did
not break with those younger students who went about as
typical nihilists, with short-cropped hair, disdaining crinoline,
and betraying their democratic spirit in all their behavior. The
leaders did not mix with them, and occasionally there was
friction, but they never repudiated them,—a great thing, I believe, in those times of madly raging prosecutions.

They seemed to say to the younger and more democratic
people: "We shall wear our velvet dresses and chignons, because we have to deal with fools who see in a velvet dress and
a chignon the tokens of 'political reliability;' but you, girls, remain free in your tastes and inclinations." When the women
who studied at Zürich were ordered by the Russian government to return, these correct ladies did not turn against the
rebels. They simply said to the government: "You don't like
it? Well, then, open women's universities at home; otherwise
our girls will go abroad in still greater numbers, and of course
will enter into relations with the political refugees." When they
were reproached with breeding revolutionists, and were menaced with the closing of their academy and universities, they
retorted, "Yes, many students become revolutionists; but is
that a reason for closing all universities?" How few political
leaders have the moral courage not to turn against the more
advanced wing of their own party!

The real secret of their wise and fully successful attitude
was that none of the women who were the soul of that move-

ment were mere "feminists," desirous to get their share of the
privileged positions in society and the state. Far from that. The
sympathies of most of them went with the masses. I remember
the lively part which Miss Stásova, the veteran leader of the
agitation, took in the Sunday schools in 1861, the friendships
she and her friends made among the factory girls, the interest
they manifested in the hard life of these girls outside the school,
the fights they fought against their greedy employers. I recall the keen interest which the women showed, at their
pedagogical courses, in the village schools, and in the work of
those few who, like Baron Korf, were permitted for some time
to do something in that direction, and the social spirit which
permeated those courses. The rights they strove for—both the
leaders and the great bulk of the women—were not only the
individual right to higher instruction, but much more, far more,
the right to be useful workers among the people, the masses.
This is why they succeeded to such an extent.

VII

For the last few years the health of my father had been going
from bad to worse, and when my brother Alexander and I
came to see him, in the spring of 1871, we were told by the
doctors that with the first frosts of autumn he would be gone.
He had continued to live in the old style, in the Stáraia
Konúshennaia, but around him everything in this aristocratic
quarter had changed. The rich serf-owners, who once were
so prominent there, had gone. After having spent in a reckless
way the redemption money which they had received at the
emancipation of the serfs, and after having mortgaged and
remortgaged their estates in the new land banks which preyed
upon their helplessness, they had withdrawn at last to the country or to provincial towns, there to sink into oblivion. Their
houses had been taken by "the intruders,"—rich merchants,
railway builders, and the like,—while in nearly every one of
the old families which remained in the Old Equerries' Quarter
a young life struggled to assert its rights upon the ruins of
the old one. A couple of retired generals, who cursed the
new ways, and relieved their griefs by predicting for Russia

a certain and speedy ruin under the new order, or some relative
occasionally dropping in, were all the company my father
had now. Out of our many relatives, numbering nearly a score
of families at Moscow alone in my childhood, two families
only had remained in the capital, and these had joined the
current of the new life, the mothers discussing with their girls
and boys such matters as schools for the people and women's
universities. My father looked upon them with contempt. My
stepmother and my younger sister, Pauline, who had not
changed, did their best to comfort him; but they themselves
felt strange in their unwonted surroundings.

My father had always been unkind and most unjust toward my brother Alexander, but Alexander was utterly incapable of holding a grudge against any one. When he entered
our father's sick-room, with the deep, kind look of his large
blue eyes and with a smile revealing his infinite kindness, and
when he immediately found out what could be done to render
the sufferer more comfortable in his sick-chair, and did it as
naturally as if he had left the sick-room only an hour before,
my father was simply bewildered; he stared at him without
being able to understand. Our visit brought life into the dull,
gloomy house; the nursing became brighter; my stepmother,
Pauline, the servants themselves, grew more animated, and my
father felt the change.

One thing worried him, however. He had expected to see
us come as repentant sons, imploring his support. But when
he tried to direct conversation into that channel, we stopped
him with such a cheerful "Don't bother about that; we get on
very nicely," that he was still more bewildered. He looked for a
scene in the old style,—his sons begging pardon—and money;
perhaps he even regretted for a moment that this did not happen; but he regarded us with a greater esteem. We were all
three affected at parting. He seemed almost to dread returning
to his gloomy loneliness amidst the wreckage of a system
he had lived to maintain. But Alexander had to go back to
his service, and I was leaving for Finland.

When I was called home again from Finland, I hurried to
Moscow, to find the burial ceremony just beginning, in that
same old red church where my father had been baptized, and
where the last prayers had been said over his mother. As the

funeral procession passed along the streets, of which every
house was so familiar to me in my childhood, I noticed that the
houses had changed little, but I knew that in all of them a new
life had begun.

In the house which had formerly belonged to my father's
mother and then to Princess Drútskaia, and which now was the
property of General Durnovo, an old inhabitant of the quarter, the only daughter of the family maintained for a couple
of years a painful struggle against her good-natured but ob-
stinate parents, who worshiped her, but would not allow her
to study at the university courses which had been opened for
ladies at Moscow. At last she was allowed to join these
courses, but was taken to them in an elegant carriage, under
the close supervision of her mother, who courageously sat for
hours on the benches amongst the students, by the side of her
beloved daughter; and yet, notwithstanding all this care and
watchfulness, a couple of years later the daughter joined the
revolutionary party, was arrested, and spent one year in the
fortress of St. Peter and St. Paul.

In the house opposite, the despotic heads of the family,
Count and Countess Z——, were in a bitter struggle against
their two daughters, who were sick of the idle and useless
existence their parents forced them to lead, and wanted to join
those other girls who, free and happy, flocked to the university courses. The struggle lasted for years; the parents did not
yield in this case, and the result was that the elder girl ended
her life by poisoning herself, whereupon her younger sister was
allowed to follow her own inclinations.

In the house next door, which had been our family residence for a year, when I entered it with Chaikóvsky to hold
in it the first secret meeting of a circle which we founded at
Moscow, I at once recognized the rooms which had been so
familiar to me in such a different atmosphere in my childhood.
It now belonged to the family of Nathalie Armfeld,—that
highly sympathetic Kára "convict," whom George Kennan
has so touchingly described in his book on Siberia. And in a
house within a stone's throw of that in which my father had
died, and only a few months after his death, I received
Stepniák, clothed as a peasant, he having escaped from a

country village where he had been arrested for spreading socialist ideas among the peasants.

Such were the changes which the Old Equerries' Quarter had undergone within the last fifteen years. The last stronghold of the old nobility was now invaded by the new spirit.

VIII

The next year, early in the spring, I made my first journey to Western Europe. In crossing the Russian frontier, I experienced what every Russian feels on leaving his mother country. So long as the train runs on Russian ground, through the thinly populated northwestern provinces, one has the feeling of crossing a desert. Hundreds of miles are covered with low growths which hardly deserve the name of forests. Here and there the eye discovers a small, miserably poor village buried in the snow, or an impracticable, muddy, narrow, and winding village road. Then everything—scenery and surroundings— changes all of a sudden, as soon as the train enters Prussia, with its clean-looking villages and farms, its gardens, and its paved roads; and the sense of contrast grows stronger and stronger as one penetrates further into Germany. Even dull Berlin seemed animated, after our Russian towns.

And the contrast of climate! Two days before, I had left St. Petersburg thickly covered with snow, and now, in middle Germany, I walked without an overcoat along the railway platform, in warm sunshine, admiring the budding flowers. Then came the Rhine, and further on Switzerland bathed in the rays of a bright sun, with its small, clean hotels, where breakfast was served out of doors, in view of the snow-clad mountains. I never before had realized so vividly what Russia's northern position meant, and how the history of the Russian nation had been influenced by the fact that the main centers of its life had to develop in high latitudes, as far north as the shores of the Gulf of Finland. Only then I fully understood the uncontrollable attraction which southern lands have exercised on the Russians, the colossal efforts which they have made to reach the Black Sea, and the steady pressure of the Siberian colonists southward, further into Manchuria.

At that time Zürich was full of Russian students, both women and men. The famous Oberstrass, near the Polytechnic, was a corner of Russia, where the Russian language prevailed over all others. The students lived as most Russian students do, especially the women; that is, upon very little. Tea and bread, some milk, and a thin slice of meat cooked over a spirit lamp, amidst animated discussions of the latest news from the socialistic world or the last book read,—that was their regular fare. Those who had more money than was needed for such a mode of living gave it for the common cause,—the library, the Russian review which was going to be published, the support of the Swiss labor papers. As to their dress, the most parsimonious economy reigned in that direction. Púshkin has written in a well-known verse, "What hat may not suit a girl of sixteen?" Our girls at Zürich seemed defiantly to throw this question at the population of the old Zwinglian city: "Can there be a simplicity in dress which does not become a girl, when she is young, intelligent, and full of energy?"

With all this, the busy little community worked harder than any other students have ever worked since there were universities in existence, and the Zürich professors were never tired of showing the progress accomplished by the women at the university, as an example to the male students.

For many years I had longed to learn all about the International Workingmen's Association. Russian papers mentioned it pretty frequently in their columns, but they were not allowed to speak of its principles or of what it was doing. I felt that it must be a great movement, full of consequences, but I could not grasp its aims and tendencies. Now that I was in Switzerland, I determined to satisfy my longings.

When I came to Zürich, I joined one of the local sections of the International Workingmen's Association. I also asked my Russian friends where I could learn more about the great movement which was going on in other countries. "Read," was their reply, and my sister-in-law, who was then studying at Zürich, brought me large numbers of books and collections of newspapers for the last two years. I spent days and nights in reading, and received a deep impression which nothing will efface; the flood of new thoughts awakened is associated in my

mind with a tiny clean room in the Oberstrass, commanding
from a window a view of the blue lake, with the mountains
beyond it, where the Swiss fought for their independence, and
the high spires of the old town,—that scene of so many religious
struggles.

Socialistic literature has never been rich in books. It is written for workers, for whom one penny is money, and its main
force lies in its small pamphlets and its newspapers. Moreover,
he who seeks for information about socialism finds in books
little of what he requires most. They contain the theories or
the scientific arguments in favor of socialist aspirations, but
they give no idea how the workers accept socialist ideals, and
how the latter could be put into practice. There remains nothing but to take collections of papers and read them all through,
—the news as well as the leading articles, the former perhaps
even more than the latter. Quite a new world of social relations
and methods of thought and action is revealed by this reading,
which gives an insight into what cannot be found anywhere
else,—namely, the depth and the moral force of the movement,
the degree to which men are imbued with the new theories,
their readiness to carry them out in their daily life and to suffer
for them. All discussions about the impracticability of socialism and the necessary slowness of evolution are of little value,
because the speed of evolution can only be judged from a
close knowledge of the human beings of whose evolution we
are speaking. What estimate of a sum can be made without
knowing its components?

The more I read, the more I saw that there was before me
a new world, unknown to me, and totally unknown to the
learned makers of sociological theories,—a world that I could
know only by living in the Workingmen's Association and by
meeting the workers in their every-day life. I decided, accordingly, to spend a couple of months in such a life. My Russian
friends encouraged me, and after a few days' stay at Zürich
I left for Geneva, which was then a great center of the international movement.

The place where the Geneva sections used to meet was the
spacious Masonic Temple Unique. More than two thousand
men could come together in its large hall, at the general meet-

ings, while every evening all sorts of committee and section
meetings took place in the side rooms, or classes in history,
physics, engineering, and so on were held. Free instruction
was given there to the workers by the few, very few, middle-
class men who had joined the movement, mainly French refugees of the Paris Commune. It was a people's university as
well as a people's forum.

One of the chief leaders of the movement at the Temple
Unique was a Russian, Nicholas Utin,—a bright, clever, and
active man; and the real soul of it was a most sympathetic
Russian lady, who was known far and wide amongst the workers as Madame Olga. She was the working force in all the
committees. Both Utin and Madame Olga received me cordially, made me acquainted with all the men of mark in the
sections of the different trades, and invited me to be present at
the committee meetings. So I went, but I preferred being with
the workers themselves. Taking a glass of sour wine at one
of the tables in the hall, I used to sit there every evening amid
the workers, and soon became friendly with several of them,
especially with a stone-mason from Alsace, who had left
France after the insurrection of the Commune. He had children, just about the age of the two whom my brother had so
suddenly lost a few months before, and through the children
I was soon on good terms with the family and their friends.
I could thus follow the movement from the inside, and know
the workers' view of it.

The workers had built all their hopes on the international
movement. Young and old flocked to the Temple Unique after
their long day's work, to get hold of the scraps of instruction
which they could obtain there, or to listen to the speakers
who promised them a grand future, based upon the common
possession of all that man requires for the production of wealth,
and upon a brotherhood of men, without distinction of caste,
race, or nationality. All hoped that a great social revolution,
peaceful or not, would soon come and totally change the economic conditions. No one desired class war, but all said that
if the ruling classes rendered it unavoidable through their
blind obstinacy, the war must be fought, provided it would
bring with it well-being and liberty to the downtrodden masses.

One must have lived among the workers at that time to

realize the effect which the sudden growth of the association had upon their minds,—the trust they put in it, the love with which they spoke of it, the sacrifices they made for it. Every day, week after week and year after year, thousands of workers gave their time and their money, even went hungry, in order to support the life of each group, to secure the appearance of the papers, to defray the expenses of the congresses, to support the comrades who had suffered for the association,—nay, even to be present at the meetings and the manifestations. Another thing that impressed me deeply was the elevating influence which the International exercised. Most of the Paris Internationalists were almost total abstainers from drink, and all had abandoned smoking. "Why should I nurture in myself that weakness?" they said. The mean, the trivial disappeared to leave room for the grand, the elevating inspirations.

Outsiders never realize the sacrifices which are made by the workers in order to keep their labor movements alive. No small amount of moral courage was required to join openly a section of the International Association, and to face the discontent of the master and a probable dismissal at the first opportunity, with the long months out of work which usually followed. But even under the best circumstances, belonging to a trade union, or to any advanced party, requires a series of uninterrupted sacrifices. Even a few pence given for the common cause represent a burden on the meager budget of the European worker, and many pence had to be disbursed every week. Frequent attendance at the meetings means a sacrifice, too. For us it may be a pleasure to spend a couple of hours at a meeting, but for men whose working day begins at five or six in the morning those hours have to be stolen from necessary rest.

I felt this devotion as a standing reproach. I saw how eager the workers were to gain instruction, and despairingly few were those who volunteered to aid them. I saw how much the toiling masses needed to be helped by men possessed of education and leisure, in their endeavors to spread and to develop the organization; but few were those who came to assist without the intention of making political capital out of this very helplessness of the people! More and more I began to feel that I was bound to cast in my lot with them. Stepniák says, in his

Career of a Nihilist, that every revolutionist has had a moment in his life when some circumstance, maybe unimportant in itself, has brought him to pronounce his oath of giving himself to the cause of revolution. I know that moment; I lived through it after one of the meetings at the Temple Unique, when I felt more acutely than ever before how cowardly are the educated men who hesitate to put their education, their knowledge, their energy, at the service of those who are so much in need of that education and that energy. "Here are men," I said to myself, "who are conscious of their servitude, who work to get rid of it; but where are the helpers? Where are those who will come to serve the masses—not to utilize them for their own ambitions?"

Gradually, however, some doubts began to creep into my mind as to the soundness of the agitation which was carried on at the Temple Unique. One night, a well-known Geneva lawyer, Monsieur A., came to the meeting, and stated that if he had not hitherto joined the association, it was because he had first to settle his own business affairs; having now succeeded in that direction, he came to join the labor movement. I felt shocked at this cynical avowal, and when I communicated my reflections to my stone-mason friend, he explained to me that this gentleman, having been defeated at the previous election, when he sought the support of the radical party, now hoped to be elected by the support of the labor vote. "We accept their services for the present," my friend concluded, "but when the revolution comes, our first move will be to throw all of them overboard."

Then came a great meeting, hastily convoked, to protest, as it was said, against "the calumnies" of the *Journal de Genève*. This organ of the moneyed classes of Geneva had ventured to suggest that mischief was brewing at the Temple Unique, and that the building trades were going once more to make a general strike, such as they had made in 1869. The leaders at the Temple Unique called the meeting. Thousands of workers filled the hall, and Utin asked them to pass a resolution, the wording of which seemed to me very strange,—an indignant protest was expressed in it against the inoffensive suggestion that the workers were going to strike. "Why should this suggestion be described as a calumny?" I asked myself. "Is it then a crime to strike?" Utin concluded a hurried speech with the words, "If you agree, citizens, to this resolution, I will send it at once to the press." He was going to leave the platform, when somebody in the hall suggested that discussion would not be out of place; and then the representatives of all branches of the building trades stood up in succession, saying that the wages had lately been so low that they could hardly live upon them; that with the opening of the spring there was plenty of work in view, of which they intended to take advantage to increase their wages; and that if an increase were refused they intended to begin a general strike.

I was furious, and next day hotly reproached Utin for his behavior. "As a leader," I told him, "you were bound to know that a strike had really been spoken of." In my innocence I did not suspect the real motives of the leaders, and it was Utin himself who made me understand that a strike at that time would be disastrous for the election of the lawyer, Monsieur A.

I could not reconcile this wire-pulling by the leaders with the burning speeches I had heard them pronounce from the platform. I felt disheartened, and spoke to Utin of my intention to make myself acquainted with the other section of the International Association at Geneva, which was known as the Bakúnists; the name "anarchist" was not much in use then. Utin gave me at once a word of introduction to another Russian, Nicholas Zhukhóvsky, who belonged to that section, and, looking straight into my face, he added, with a sigh, "Well, you won't return to us; you will remain with them." He had guessed right.

IX

I went first to Neuchâtel, and then spent a week or so among the watchmakers in the Jura Mountains. I thus made my first acquaintance with that famous Jura Federation which for the next few years played an important part in the development of socialism, introducing into it the no-government, or anarchist, tendency.

In 1872 the Jura Federation was becoming a rebel against

the authority of the general council of the International Work-ingmen's Association. The association was essentially a work-ingmen's movement, the workers understanding it as such and not as a political party. In east Belgium, for instance, they had introduced into the statutes a clause in virtue of which no one could be a member of a section unless employed in a manual trade; even foremen were excluded.

The workers were, moreover, federalist in principle. Each nation, each separate region, and even each local section had to be left free to develop on its own lines. But the middle-class revolutionists of the old school who had entered the Inter-national, imbued as they were with the notions of the central-ized, pyramidal secret organizations of earlier times, had intro-duced the same notions into the Workingmen's Association. Beside the federal and national councils, a general council was nominated at London, to act as a sort of intermediary between the councils of the different nations. Marx[7] and Engels were its leading spirits. It soon appeared, however, that the mere fact of having such a central body became a source of substantial inconvenience. The general council was not satis-fied with playing the part of a correspondence bureau; it strove to govern the movement, to approve or to censure the action of the local federations and sections, and even of indi-vidual members. When the Commune insurrection began in Paris,—and "the leaders had only to follow," without being able to say whereto they would be led within the next twenty-four hours,—the general council insisted upon directing the insurrection from London. It required daily reports about the events, gave orders, favored this and hampered that, and thus put in evidence the disadvantage of having a governing body, even within the association. The disadvantage became still more evident when, at a secret conference held in 1871, the general council, supported by a few delegates, decided to di-rect the forces of the association toward electoral agitation. It set people thinking about the evils of any government, how-ever democratic its origin. This was the first spark of anarch-ism. The Jura Federation became the center of opposition to the general council.

The separation between leaders and workers which I had

noticed at Geneva in the Temple Unique did not exist in the Jura Mountains. There were a number of men who were more intelligent, and especially more active than the others; but that was all. James Guillaume, one of the most intelligent and broadly educated men I ever met, was a proof-reader and the manager of a small printing-office. His earnings in this capacity were so small that he had to give his nights to translating novels from German into French, for which he was paid eight francs—one dollar and sixty cents—for sixteen pages!

When I came to Neuchâtel, he told me that unfortunately he could not give even as much as a couple of hours for a friendly chat. The printing-office was just issuing that afternoon the first number of a local paper, and in addition to his usual duties of proof-reader and co-editor, he had to write the addresses of a thousand persons to whom the first three numbers were to be sent, and to put on the wrappers himself.

I offered to aid him in writing the addresses, but that was not practicable because they were either kept in memory, or written on scraps of paper in an unreadable hand. "Well, then," said I, "I will come in the afternoon to the office and put on the wrappers, and you will give me the time which you may thus save."

We understood each other. Guillaume warmly shook my hand, and that was the beginning of a standing friendship. We spent all the afternoon in the office, he writing the addresses, I fastening the wrappers, and a French communard, who was a compositor, chatting with us all the while as he rapidly set up a novel, intermingling his conversation with the sentences which he was putting in type and which he read aloud.

"The fight in the streets," he would say, "became very sharp" . . . "Dear Mary, I love you" . . . "The workers were furious and fought like lions at Montmartre" . . . "and he fell on his knees before her" . . . "and that lasted for four days. We knew that Gallifet was shooting all prisoners,—the more terrible still was the fight,"—and so on he went, rapidly lifting the type from the case.

It was late in the evening when Guillaume took off his working blouse, and we went out for a friendly chat for a couple of hours; then he had to resume his work as editor of the *Bulletin* of the Jura Federation.

From Neuchâtel I went to Sonvilliers. In a little valley in the Jura hills there is a succession of small towns and villages, of which the French-speaking population was at that time entirely employed in the various branches of watchmaking; whole families used to work in small workshops. In one of them I found another leader, Adhémar Schwitzguébel, with whom, also, I afterward became very closely connected. He sat among a dozen young men who were engraving lids of gold and silver watches. I was asked to take a seat on a bench, or table, and soon we were all engaged in a lively conversation upon socialism, government or no government, and the coming congresses.

In the evening a heavy snowstorm raged; it blinded us and froze the blood in our veins, as we struggled to the next village. But, notwithstanding the storm, about fifty watchmakers, chiefly old people, came from the neighboring towns and villages,—some of them as far as seven miles distant,—to join a small informal meeting that was called for that evening.

The very organization of the watch trade, which permits men to know one another thoroughly and to work in their own houses, where they are free to talk, explains why the level of intellectual development in this population is higher than that of workers who spend all their life from early childhood in the factories. There is more independence and more originality among the petty trades' workers. But the absence of a division between the leaders and the masses in the Jura Federation was also the reason why there was not a question upon which every member of the federation would not strive to form his own independent opinion. Here I saw that the workers were not a mass that was being led and made subservient to the political ends of a few men; their leaders were simply their more active comrades,—initiators rather than leaders. The clearness of insight, the soundness of judgment, the capacity for disentangling complex social questions, which I noticed amongst these workers, especially the middle-aged ones, deeply impressed me; and I am firmly persuaded that if the Jura Federation has played a prominent part in the development of socialism, it is not only on account of the importance of the no-government and federalist ideas of which it was the champion, but also on account of the expression which was given to these ideas by the good sense of the Jura watchmakers. Without their aid, these conceptions might have remained mere abstractions for a long time.

The theoretical aspects of anarchism, as they were then beginning to be expressed in the Jura Federation, especially by Bakúnin; the criticisms of state socialism—the fear of an economic despotism, far more dangerous than the merely political despotism—which I heard formulated there; and the revolutionary character of the agitation, appealed strongly to my mind. But the equalitarian relations which I found in the Jura Mountains, the independence of thought and expression which I saw developing in the workers, and their unlimited devotion to the cause appealed far more strongly to my feelings; and when I came away from the mountains, after a week's stay with the watchmakers, my views upon socialism were settled. I was an anarchist.

X

Bakúnin was at that time at Locarno. I did not see him, and now regret it very much, because he was dead when I returned four years later to Switzerland. It was he who had helped the Jura friends to clear up their ideas and to formulate their aspirations; he who had inspired them with his powerful, burning, irresistible revolutionary enthusiasm. As soon as he saw that a small newspaper, which Guillaume began to edit in the Jura hills (at Locle) was sounding a new note of independent thought in the socialist movement, he came to Locle, talked for whole days and whole nights also to his new friends about the historical necessity of a new move in the direction of anarchy; he wrote for that paper a series of profound and brilliant articles on the historical progress of mankind towards freedom; he infused enthusiasm into his new friends, and he created that center of propaganda, from which anarchism spread later on to other parts of Europe.

After he had moved to Locarno,—whence he started a similar movement in Italy, and, through his sympathetic and gifted emissary, Fanelli, also in Spain,—the work that he had

begun in the Jura hills was continued independently by the
Jurassians themselves. The name of "Michel" often recurred
in their conversations,—not, however, as that of an absent chief
whose opinions were law, but as that of a personal friend of
whom every one spoke with love, in a spirit of comradeship.
What struck me most was that Bakúnin's influence was felt
much less as the influence of an intellectual authority than as
the influence of a moral personality. In conversations about
anarchism, or about the attitude of the federation, I never
heard it said, "Bakúnin says so," or "Bakúnin thinks so," as if
it settled the question. His writings and his sayings were not
regarded as laws,—as is unfortunately often the case in political
parties. In all such matters, in which intellect is the supreme
judge, every one in discussion used his own arguments. Their
general drift and tenor might have been suggested by Bakúnin,
or Bakúnin might have borrowed them from his Jura friends;
at any rate, in each individual the arguments retained their
own individual character. I only once heard Bakúnin's name
invoked as an authority in itself, and that impressed me so
deeply that I even now remember the spot where the conversation took place and all the surroundings. Some young men
were indulging in talk that was not very respectful toward the
other sex, when one of the women who were present put a
sudden stop to it by exclaiming: "Pity that Michel is not here:
he would put you in your place!" The colossal figure of the
revolutionist who had given up everything for the sake of the
revolution, and lived for it alone, borrowing from his conception of it the highest and the purest views of life, continued
to inspire them.

I returned from this journey with distinct sociological ideas
which I have retained since, doing my best to develop them
in more and more definite, concrete forms.

There was, however, one point which I did not accept without having given to it a great deal of thinking and many hours
of my nights. I clearly saw that the immense change which
would deliver everything that is necessary for life and production into the hands of society—be it the Folk State of the social
democrats or the unions of freely associated groups, which
the anarchists advocate—would imply a revolution far more

profound than any of the revolutions which history had on record. Moreover, in such a revolution the workers would have against them, not the rotten generation of aristocrats against whom the French peasants and republicans had to fight in the last century,—and even that fight was a desperate one,—but the middle classes, which are far more powerful, intellectually and physically, and have at their service all the potent machinery of the modern state. However, I soon noticed that no revolution, whether peaceful or violent, had ever taken place without the new ideals having deeply penetrated into the very class whose economical and political privileges were to be assailed. I had witnessed the abolition of serfdom in Russia, and I knew that if a consciousness of the injustice of their privileges had not spread widely within the serf-owners' class itself (as a consequence of the previous evolution and revolutions accomplished in Western Europe), the emancipation of the serfs would never have been accomplished as easily as it was accomplished in 1861. And I saw that the idea of emancipating the workers from the present wage-system was making headway amongst the middle classes themselves. The most ardent defenders of the present economical conditions had already abandoned the idea of *right* in defending their present privileges,—questions as to the *opportuneness* of such a change having already taken its place. They did not deny the desirability of some such change, they only asked whether the new economical organization advocated by the socialists would really be better than the present one; whether a society in which the workers would have a dominant voice would be able to manage production better than the individual capitalists actuated by mere considerations of self-interest manage it at the present time.

Besides, I began gradually to understand that revolutions —that is, periods of accelerated rapid evolution and rapid changes—are as much in the nature of human society as the slow evolution which incessantly goes on now among the civilized races of mankind. And each time that such a period of accelerated evolution and reconstruction on a grand scale begins, civil war is liable to break out on a small or large scale. The question is, then, not so much how to avoid revolutions, as how to attain the greatest results with the most limited

amount of civil war, the smallest number of victims, and a
minimum of mutual embitterment. For that end there is only
one means; namely, that the oppressed part of society should
obtain the clearest possible conception of what they intend to
achieve, and how, and that they should be imbued with the
enthusiasm which is necessary for that achievement; in that
case they will be sure to attach to their cause the best and the
freshest intellectual forces of the privileged class.

With these ideas I returned to Russia.

XI

During my journey I had bought a number of books and collections of socialist newspapers. In Russia, such books were
"unconditionally prohibited" by censorship; and some of the
collections of newspapers and reports of international congresses could not be bought for any amount of money, even
in Belgium. "Shall I part with them, while my brother and
my friends would be so glad to have them at St. Petersburg?"
I asked myself; and I decided that by all means I must get
them into Russia.

I returned to St. Petersburg via Vienna and Warsaw. Thousands of Jews live by smuggling on the Polish frontier, and I
thought that if I could succeed in discovering only one of them,
my books would be carried in safety across the border. However, to alight at a small railway station near the frontier,
while every other passenger went on, and to hunt there for
smugglers, would hardly have been reasonable; so I took a
side branch of the railway and went to Cracow. "The capital
of old Poland is near to the frontier," I thought, "and I shall
find there some Jew who will lead me to the men I seek."

I reached the once renowned and brilliant city in the evening, and early next morning went out from the hotel on my
search. To my bewilderment I saw, however, at every street
corner and wherever I turned my eyes in the otherwise deserted market-place, a Jew, wearing the traditional long dress
and locks of his forefathers, and watching there for some Polish
nobleman or tradesman who might send him on an errand and
pay him a few coppers for the service. I wanted to find *one*

Jew; and now there were too many of them. Whom should I approach? I made the round of the town, and then, in my despair, I decided to accost the Jew who stood at the entrance gate of my hotel,—an immense old palace, of which, in former days, every hall was filled with elegant crowds of gayly dressed dancers, but which now fulfilled the more prosaic function of giving food and shelter to a few occasional travelers. I explained to the man my desire of smuggling into Russia a rather heavy bundle of books and newspapers.

"Very easily done, sir," he replied. "I will just bring to you the representative of the Universal Company for the International Exchange of (let me say) Rags and Bones. They carry on the largest smuggling business in the world, and he is sure to oblige you." Half an hour later he really returned with the representative of the company,—a most elegant young man, who spoke in perfection Russian, German, and Polish.

He looked at my bundle, weighed it with his hands, and asked what sort of books were in it.

"All severely prohibited by Russian censorship: that is why they must be smuggled in."

"Books," he said, "are not exactly in our line of trade; our business lies in costly silks. If I were going to pay my men by weight, according to our silk tariff, I should have to ask you a quite extravagant price. And then, to tell the truth, I don't much like meddling with books. The slightest mishap, and 'they' would make of it a political affair, and then it would cost the Universal Rags and Bones Company a tremendous sum of money to get clear of it."

I probably looked very sad, for the elegant young man who represented the Universal Rags and Bones Company immediately added: "Don't be troubled. He, the hotel commissionnaire, will arrange it for you in some other way."

"Oh, yes. There are scores of ways to arrange such a trifle, to oblige the gentleman," jovially remarked the commissionnaire, as he left me.

In an hour's time he came back with another young man. This one took the bundle, put it by the side of the door, and said: "It's all right. If you leave to-morrow, you shall have your books at such a station in Russia," and he explained to me how it would be managed.

"How much will it cost?" I asked.

"How much are you disposed to pay?" was the reply.

I emptied my purse on the table, and said: "That much for my journey. The remainder is yours. I will travel third class!"

"Wai, wai, wai!" exclaimed both men at once. "What are you saying, sir? Such a gentleman travel third class! Never! No, no, no, that won't do. . . . Five dollars will do for us, and then one dollar or so for the commissionnaire, if you are agreeable to it,—just as much as you like. We are not highway robbers, but honest tradesmen." And they bluntly refused to take more money.

I had often heard of the honesty of the Jewish smugglers on the frontier; but I had never expected to have such a proof of it. Later on, when our circle imported many books from abroad, or still later, when so many revolutionists and refugees crossed the frontier in entering or leaving Russia, there was not a case in which the smugglers betrayed any one, or took advantage of circumstances to exact an exorbitant price for their services.

Next day I left Cracow; and at the designated Russian station a porter approached my compartment, and, speaking loudly, so as to be heard by the gendarme who was walking along the platform, said to me, "Here is the bag your highness left the other day," and handed me my precious parcel.

I was so pleased to have it that I did not even stop at Warsaw, but continued my journey directly to St. Petersburg, to show my trophies to my brother.

XII

A formidable movement was developing in the meantime amongst the educated youth of Russia. Serfdom was abolished. But quite a network of habits and customs of domestic slavery, of utter disregard of human individuality, of despotism on the part of the fathers, and of hypocritical submission on that of the wives, the sons, and the daughters, had developed during the two hundred and fifty years that serfdom had existed. Everywhere in Europe, at the beginning of this century, there was a great deal of domestic despotism,—the writings of

Thackeray and Dickens bear ample testimony to it; but no-where else had that tyranny attained such a luxurious development as in Russia. All Russian life, in the family, in the relations between commander and subordinate, military chief and soldier, employer and employee, bore the stamp of it. Quite a world of customs and manners of thinking, of prejudices and moral cowardice, of habits bred by a lazy existence, had grown up. Even the best men of the time paid a large tribute to these products of the serfdom period.

Law could have no grip upon these things. Only a vigorous social movement, which would attack the very roots of the evil, could reform the habits and customs of every-day life; and in Russia this movement—this revolt of the individual—took a far more powerful character, and became far more sweeping in its criticisms, than anywhere in Western Europe or America. "Nihilism" was the name that Turgénev gave it in his epoch-making novel, *Fathers and Sons*.

The movement is misunderstood in Western Europe. In the press, for example, nihilism is continually confused with terrorism. The revolutionary disturbance which broke out in Russia toward the close of the reign of Alexander II., and ended in the tragical death of the Tsar, is constantly described as nihilism. This is, however, a mistake. To confuse nihilism with terrorism is as wrong as to confuse a philosophical movement like stoicism or positivism with a political movement such as, for example, republicanism. Terrorism was called into existence by certain special conditions of the political struggle at a given historical moment. It has lived, and has died. It may revive and die out again. But nihilism has impressed its stamp upon the whole of the life of the educated classes of Russia, and that stamp will be retained for many years to come. It is nihilism, divested of some of its rougher aspects,—which were unavoidable in a young movement of that sort,—which gives now to the life of a great portion of the educated classes of Russia a certain peculiar character which we Russians regret not to find in the life of Western Europe. It is nihilism, again, in its various manifestations, which gives to many of our writers that remarkable sincerity, that habit of "thinking aloud," which astounds Western European readers.

First of all, the nihilist declared war upon what may be

described as "the conventional lies of civilized mankind."
Absolute sincerity was his distinctive feature, and in the name
of that sincerity he gave up, and asked others to give up, those
superstitions, prejudices, habits, and customs which their own
reason could not justify. He refused to bend before any
authority except that of reason, and in the analysis of every
social institution or habit he revolted against any sort of more
or less masked sophism.

He broke, of course, with the superstitions of his fathers, and
in his philosophical conceptions he was a positivist, an
agnostic, a Spencerian evolutionist, or a scientific materialist;
and while he never attacked the simple, sincere religious belief
which is a psychological necessity of feeling, he bitterly fought
against the hypocrisy that leads people to assume the outward
mask of a religion which they repeatedly throw aside as useless
ballast.

The life of civilized people is full of little conventional lies.
Persons who hate each other, meeting in the street, make their
faces radiant with a happy smile; the nihilist remained un-
moved, and smiled only for those whom he was really glad
to meet. All those forms of outward politeness which are mere
hypocrisy were equally repugnant to him, and he assumed a
certain external roughness as a protest against the smooth
amiability of his fathers. He saw them wildly talking as idealist sentimentalists, and at the same time acting as real barbarians toward their wives, their children, and their serfs; and
he rose in revolt against that sort of sentimentalism which,
after all, so nicely accommodated itself to the anything but
ideal conditions of Russian life. Art was involved in the same
sweeping negation. Continual talk about beauty, the ideal, art
for art's sake, æsthetics, and the like, so willingly indulged
in,—while every object of art was bought with money exacted
from starving peasants or from underpaid workers, and the
so-called "worship of the beautiful" was but a mask to cover
the most commonplace dissoluteness,—inspired him with disgust, and the criticisms of art which Tolstóy, one of the greatest artists of the century, has now so powerfully formulated,
the nihilist expressed in the sweeping assertion, "A pair of boots
is more important than all your Madonnas and all your refined
talk about Shakespeare."

Marriage without love, and familiarity without friendship, were equally repudiated. The nihilist girl, compelled by her parents to be a doll in a Doll's House, and to marry for property's sake, preferred to abandon her house and her silk dresses. She put on a black woolen dress of the plainest description, cut off her hair, and went to a high school, in order to win there her personal independence. The woman who saw that her marriage was no longer a marriage, that neither love nor friendship connected those who were legally considered husband and wife, preferred to break a bond which retained none of its essential features. Accordingly she often went with her children to face poverty, preferring loneliness and misery to a life which, under conventional conditions, would have given a perpetual lie to her best self.

The nihilist carried his love of sincerity even into the minutest details of every-day life. He discarded the conventional forms of society talk, and expressed his opinions in a blunt and terse way, even with a certain affectation of outward roughness.

In Irkútsk we used to meet once a week in a club and have some dancing. I was for a time a regular visitor at these soirées, but afterwards, having to work, I abandoned them. One night, when I had not made my appearance for several weeks, a young friend of mine was asked by one of the ladies why I did not appear any more at their gatherings. "He takes a ride now when he wants exercise," was the rather rough reply of my friend. "But he might come and spend a couple of hours with us, without dancing," one of the ladies ventured to say. "What would he do here?" retorted my nihilist friend; "talk with you about fashions and furbelows? He has had enough of that nonsense." "But he sees Miss So-and-So occasionally," timidly remarked one of the young ladies present. "Yes, but she is a studious girl," bluntly replied my friend; "he helps her with her German." I must add that this undoubtedly rough rebuke had its effect, for most of the Irkútsk girls soon began to besiege my brother, my friend, and myself with questions as to what we should advise them to read or to study.

With the same frankness the nihilist spoke to his acquaintances, telling them that all their talk about "this poor people" was sheer hypocrisy so long as they lived upon the underpaid work of these people whom they commiserated at their ease as they chatted together in richly decorated rooms; and with the same frankness a nihilist would declare to a high functionary that the latter cared not a straw for the welfare of those whom he ruled, but was simply a thief, and so on.

With a certain austerity the nihilist would rebuke the woman who indulged in small talk and prided herself on her "womanly" manners and elaborate toilette. He would bluntly say to a pretty young person: "How is it that you are not ashamed to talk this nonsense and to wear that chignon of false hair?" In a woman he wanted to find a comrade, a human personality,—not a doll or a "muslin girl,"—and he absolutely refused to join in those petty tokens of politeness with which men surround those whom they like so much to consider as "the weaker sex." When a lady entered a room a nihilist did not jump from his seat to offer it to her, unless he saw that she looked tired and there was no other seat in the room. He behaved towards her as he would have behaved towards a comrade of his own sex; but if a lady—who might have been a total stranger to him—manifested the desire to learn something which he knew and she did not, he would walk every night to the far end of a large city to help her.

Two great Russian novelists, Turgénev and Goncharóv, have tried to represent this new type in their novels. Goncharóv, in *Precipice*, taking a real but unrepresentative individual of this class, made a caricature of nihilism. Turgénev was too good an artist, and had himself conceived too much admiration for the new type, to let himself be drawn into caricature painting; but even his nihilist, Bazárov, did not satisfy us. We found him too harsh, especially in his relations with his old parents, and, above all, we reproached him with his seeming neglect of his duties as a citizen. Russian youth could not be satisfied with the merely negative attitude of Turgénev's hero. Nihilism, with its affirmation of the rights of the individual and its negation of all hypocrisy, was but a first step toward a higher type of men and women, who are equally free, but live for a great cause. In the nihilists of Chernyshévsky, as they are depicted in his far less artistic novel, *What is to be Done?* they saw better portraits of themselves.

"It is bitter, the bread that has been made by slaves," our poet Nekrásov wrote. The young generation actually refused to eat that bread, and to enjoy the riches that had been accumulated in their fathers' houses by means of servile labor, whether the laborers were actual serfs or slaves of the present industrial system.

All Russia read with astonishment, in the indictment which was produced at the court against Karakózov and his friends, that these young men, owners of considerable fortunes, used to live three or four in the same room, never spending more than five dollars apiece a month for all their needs, and giving at the same time their fortunes for starting coöperative associations, coöperative workshops (where they themselves worked), and the like. Five years later, thousands and thousands of the Russian youth—the best part of it—were doing the same. Their watchword was, "V naród!" (To the people; be the people.) During the years 1860–65, in nearly every wealthy family a bitter struggle was going on between the fathers, who wanted to maintain the old traditions, and the sons and daughters, who defended their right to dispose of their lives according to their own ideals. Young men left the military service, the counter, the shop, and flocked to the university towns. Girls, bred in the most aristocratic families, rushed penniless to St. Petersburg, Moscow, and Kíev, eager to learn a profession which would free them from the domestic yoke, and some day, perhaps, also from the possible yoke of a husband. After hard and bitter struggles, many of them won that personal freedom. Now they wanted to utilize it, not for their own personal enjoyment, but for carrying to the people the knowledge that had emancipated them.

In every town of Russia, in every quarter of St. Petersburg, small groups were formed for self-improvement and self-education; the works of the philosophers, the writings of the economists, the historical researches of the young Russian historical school, were carefully read in these circles, and the reading was followed by endless discussions. The aim of all that reading and discussion was to solve the great question which rose before them. In what way could they be useful to the masses? Gradually, they came to the idea that the only way was to settle amongst the people, and to live the people's life. Young men went into the villages as doctors, doctors' helpers, teachers, village scribes, even as agricultural laborers, blacksmiths, woodcutters, and so on, and tried to live there in close contact with the peasants. Girls passed teachers' examinations, learned midwifery or nursing, and went by the hundred into the villages, devoting themselves entirely to the poorest part of the population.

These people went without any ideal of social reconstruction in their mind, or any thought of revolution. They simply wanted to teach the mass of the peasants to read, to instruct them in other things, to give them medical help, and in any way to aid in raising them from their darkness and misery, and to learn at the same time what were *their* popular ideals of a better social life.

When I returned from Switzerland, I found this movement in full swing.

XIII

I hastened to share with my friends my impressions of the International Workingmen's Association and my books. At the university I had no friends, properly speaking; I was older than most of my companions, and among young people a difference of a few years is always an obstacle to complete comradeship. It must also be said that since the new rules of admission to the university had been introduced in 1861, the best of the young men—the most developed and the most independent in thought—were sifted out of the gymnasia, and did not gain admittance to the university. Consequently, the majority of my comrades were good boys, laborious, but taking no interest in anything besides the examinations. I was friendly with only one of them, Dmítri Klementz. He was born in South Russia, and although his name was German, he hardly spoke German, and his face was South Russian rather than Teutonic. He was very intelligent, had read a great deal, and had seriously thought over what he had read. He loved science and deeply respected it, but, like many of us, he soon came to the conclusion that to follow the career of a scientific man meant to join the camp of the Philistines, and that there was plenty of other and more urgent work that he could do. He attended the university lectures for two years, and then abandoned them, giving himself entirely to social work. He lived somehow; I even doubt if he had a permanent lodging. Sometimes he would come to me and ask, "Have you some paper?" and having taken a supply of it, he would sit at the corner of a table for an hour or two, diligently making a translation. The little that he earned in this way was more than sufficient to satisfy all his limited wants. Then he would hurry to a distant part of the town to see a comrade or to help a needy friend; or he would cross St. Petersburg on foot, to a remote suburb, in order to obtain free admission to a college for some boy in whom the comrades were interested. He was undoubtedly a gifted man. In Western Europe a man far less gifted would have worked his way to a position of political or socialist leadership. No such thought ever entered the brain of Klementz. To lead men was by no means his ambition, and there was no work too insignificant for him to do. This trait, however, was not distinctive of him alone; all those who had lived some years in the students' circles of those times were possessed of it to a high degree.

Soon after my return Klementz invited me to join a circle which was known amongst the youth as "the Circle of Chaikóvsky." Under this name it played an important part in the history of the social movement in Russia, and under this name it will go down to history. "Its members," Klementz said to me, "have hitherto been mostly constitutionalists; but they are excellent men, with minds open to any honest idea; they have plenty of friends all over Russia, and you will see later on what you can do." I already knew Chaikóvsky, and a few other members of this circle. Chaikóvsky had won my heart at our first meeting, and our friendship has remained unshaken for twenty-seven years.

The beginning of this circle was a very small group of young men and women,—one of whom was Sophia Peróvskaia,—who had united for purposes of self-education and self-improvement. Chaikóvsky was of their number. In 1869 Necháev had tried to start a secret revolutionary organization among the youth imbued with the before-mentioned desire of working among the people, and to secure this end he resorted to the ways of old conspirators, without recoiling even before deceit when he wanted to force his associates to follow his lead. Such methods could have no success in Russia, and very soon his society broke down. All the members were arrested, and some of the best and purest of the Russian youth went to Siberia before they had done anything. The circle of self-education of which I am speaking was constituted in opposition to the methods of Necháev. The few friends had judged, quite correctly, that a morally developed individuality must be the foundation of every organization, whatever political character it may take afterward, and whatever program of action it may adopt in the course of future events. This was why the Circle of Chaikóvsky, gradually widening its program, spread so extensively in Russia, achieved such important results, and later on, when the ferocious prosecutions of the government created a revolutionary struggle, produced that remarkable set of men and women who fell in the terrible contest they waged against autocracy.

At that time, however,—that is, in 1872,—the circle had nothing revolutionary in it. If it had remained a mere circle of self-improvement, it would soon have petrified, like a monastery. But the members found a suitable work. They began to spread good books. They bought the works of Lassalle, Bervi (on the condition of the laboring classes in Russia), Marx, Russian historical works, and so on,—whole editions,—and distributed them among students in the provinces. In a few years there was not a town of importance in "thirty-eight provinces of the Russian Empire," to use official language, where this circle did not have a group of comrades engaged in the spreading of that sort of literature. Gradually, following the general drift of the times, and stimulated by the news which came from Western Europe about the rapid growth of the labor movement, the circle became more and more a center of socialistic propaganda among the educated youth, and a natural intermediary between members of provincial circles; and then, one day, the ice between students and workers was broken, and direct relations were established with working-people at St.

Petersburg and in some of the provinces. It was at that juncture that I joined the circle, in the spring of 1872.

All secret societies are fiercely prosecuted in Russia, and
the Western reader will perhaps expect from me a description
of my initiation and of the oath of allegiance which I took. I
must disappoint him, because there was nothing of the sort,
and could not be; we should have been the first to laugh at
such ceremonies, and Klementz would not have missed the
opportunity of putting in one of his sarcastic remarks, which
would have killed any ritual. There was not even a statute. The
circle accepted as members only persons who were well known
and had been tested in various circumstances, and of whom it
was felt that they could be trusted absolutely. Before a new
member was received, his character was discussed with the
frankness and seriousness which were characteristic of the
nihilist. The slightest token of insincerity or conceit would have
barred the way to admission. The circle did not care to make
a show of numbers, and had no tendency to concentrate in
its hands all the activity that was going on amongst the youth,
or to include in one organization the scores of different circles
which existed in the capitals and the provinces. With most of
them friendly relations were maintained; they were helped,
and they helped us, when necessity arose, but no assault was
made on their autonomy.

The circle preferred to remain a closely united group of
friends; and never did I meet elsewhere such a collection of
morally superior men and women as the score of persons whose
acquaintance I made at the first meeting of the Circle of
Chaikóvsky. I still feel proud of having been received into that
family.

XIV

When I joined the Circle of Chaikóvsky, I found its members
hotly discussing the direction to be given to their activity. Some
were in favor of continuing to carry on radical and socialistic
propaganda among the educated youth; but others thought
that the sole aim of this work should be to prepare men who
would be capable of arousing the great inert laboring masses,

and that their chief activity ought to be among the peasants and workmen in the towns. In all the circles and groups which were formed at that time by the hundred, at St. Petersburg and in the provinces, the same discussions went on; and everywhere the second program prevailed over the first.

If our youth had merely taken to socialism in the abstract, they might have felt satisfied with a simple declaration of socialist principles, including as a distant aim "the communistic possession of the instruments of production,"—and in the meantime they might have carried on some sort of political agitation. Many middle-class socialist politicians in Western Europe and America really take this course. But our youth had been drawn to socialism in quite another way. They were not theorists about socialism, but had become socialists by living no better than the workers live, by making no distinction between "mine and thine" in their circles, and by refusing to enjoy for their own satisfaction the riches they had inherited from their fathers. They had done with regard to capitalism what Tolstóy urges should be done with regard to war, when he calls upon the people, instead of criticizing war and continuing to wear the military uniform, to refuse, each one for himself, to be a soldier and to bear arms. In this same way our Russian youth, each one for himself or herself, refused to take personal advantage of the revenues of their fathers. It was, of course, necessary that they should identify themselves with the people. Thousands and thousands of young men and women had already left their houses, and now they tried to live in the villages and the industrial towns in all possible capacities. This was not an organized movement: it was one of those mass movements which occur at certain periods of sudden awakening of human conscience. Now that small organized groups were formed, ready to try a systematic effort for spreading ideas of freedom and revolt in Russia, they were forced to carry on that propaganda among the masses of the peasants and of the workers in the towns. Various writers have tried to explain this movement "to the people" by influences from abroad: "foreign agitators are everywhere," was a favorite explanation. It is certainly true that our youth listened to the mighty voice of Bakúnin, and that the agitation of the International Workingmen's Association had a fascinating effect

upon us. But the movement had a far deeper origin: it began
before "foreign agitators" had spoken to the Russian youth,
and even before the International Association had been
founded. It was beginning in the groups of Karakózov in 1866;
Turgénev saw it coming, and already in 1859 faintly indicated
it. I did my best to promote that movement in the Circle of
Chaikóvsky; but I was only working with the tide which was
infinitely more powerful than any individual efforts.

We often spoke, of course, of the necessity of a political
agitation against our absolute government. We saw already
that the mass of the peasants was being driven to unavoidable
and irremediable ruin by foolish taxation, and by still more
foolish selling off of their cattle to cover the arrears of taxes. We
"visionaries" saw coming that complete ruin of a whole population which by this time, alas, has been accomplished to an appalling extent in Central Russia, and is confessed by the government itself. We knew how, in every direction, Russia was
being plundered in a most scandalous manner. We knew, and
we learned more every day, of the lawlessness of the functionaries, and the almost incredible bestiality of many among
them. We heard continually of friends whose houses were
raided at night by the police, who disappeared in prisons, and
who—we ascertained later on—had been transported without
judgment to hamlets in some remote province of Russia. We
felt, therefore, the necessity of a political struggle against this
terrible power, which was crushing the best intellectual forces
of the nation. But we saw no possible ground, legal or semi-
legal, for such a struggle.

Our elder brothers did not want our socialistic aspirations,
and we could not part with them. Nay, even if some of us
had done so, it would have been of no avail. The young
generation, as a whole, were treated as "suspects," and the
elder generation feared to have anything to do with them. Every young man of democratic tastes, every young woman following a course of higher education, was a suspect in the eyes
of the state police, and was denounced by Katkóv as an enemy
of the state. Cropped hair and blue spectacles worn by a girl,
a Scotch plaid worn in winter by a student, instead of an
overcoat, which were evidences of nihilist simplicity and democracy, were denounced as tokens of "political unreliability."

If any student's lodging came to be frequently visited by other students, it was periodically invaded by the state police and searched. So common were the night raids in certain students' lodgings that Klementz once said, in his mildly humorous way, to the police officer who was searching the rooms: "Why should you go through all our books, each time you come to make a search? You might as well have a list of them, and then come once a month to see if they are all on the shelves; and you might, from time to time, add the titles of the new ones." The slightest suspicion of political unreliability was sufficient ground upon which to take a young man from a high school, to imprison him for several months, and finally to send him to some remote province of the Uráls,—"for an undetermined term," as they used to say in their bureaucratic slang. Even at the time when the Circle of Chaikóvsky did nothing but distribute books, all of which had been printed with the censor's approval, Chaikóvsky was twice arrested and kept some four or six months in prison; on the second occasion at a critical time of his career as a chemist. His researches had recently been published in the *Bulletin of the Academy of Sciences,* and he had come up for his final university examinations. He was released at last, because the police could not discover sufficient evidence against him to warrant his transportation to the Uráls! "But if we arrest you once more," he was told, "we shall send you to Siberia." In fact, it was a favorite dream of Alexander II. to have somewhere in the steppes a special town, guarded night and day by patrols of Cossacks, where all suspected young people could be sent, so as to make of them a city of ten or twenty thousand inhabitants. Only the menace which such a city might some day offer prevented him from carrying out this truly Asiatic scheme.

One of our members, an officer, had belonged to a group of young men whose ambition was to serve in the provincial *Zémstvos* (district and county councils). They regarded work in this direction as a high mission, and prepared themselves for it by serious studies of the economical conditions of Central Russia. Many young people cherished for a time the same hopes; but all these hopes vanished at the first contact with the actual government machinery.

Having granted a very limited form of self-government to certain provinces of Russia, the government immediately directed all its efforts to reducing that reform to nothing by depriving it of all its meaning and vitality. The provincial "self-government" had to content itself with the mere function of state officials who would collect additional local taxes and spend them for the local needs of the state. Every attempt of the county councils to take the initiative in any improvement —schools, teachers' colleges, sanitary measures, agricultural improvements, etc.—was met by the central government with suspicion, with hostility,—and denounced by the *Moscow Gazette* as "separatism," as the creation of "a state within the state," as rebellion against autocracy.

If any one were to tell the true history, for example, of the teachers' college of Tver, or of any similar undertaking of a Zémstvo in those years, with all the petty persecutions, the prohibitions, the suspensions, and what not with which the institution was harassed, no West European, and especially no American reader, would believe it. He would throw the book aside, saying, "It cannot be true; it is too stupid to be true." And yet it was so. Whole groups of the elected representatives of several Zémstvos were deprived of their functions, ordered to leave their province and their estates, or were simply exiled, for having dared to petition the Emperor in the most loyal manner concerning such rights as belonged to the Zémstvos by law. "The elected members of the provincial councils must be simple ministerial functionaries, and obey the minister of the interior:" such was the theory of the St. Petersburg government. As to the less prominent people,—teachers, doctors, and the like, in the service of the local councils,—they were removed and exiled by the state police in twenty-four hours, without further ceremony than an order of the omnipotent Third Section of the imperial chancery. No longer ago than last year, a lady whose husband is a rich landowner and occupies a prominent position in one of the Zémstvos, and who is herself interested in education, invited eight schoolmasters to her birthday party. "Poor men," she said to herself, "they never have the opportunity of seeing any one but the peasants." The day after the party, the village policeman called at the mansion and insisted upon having the names of the eight teachers, in order to report them to the police authorities. The lady refused to give the names. "Very well," he replied, "I will find them out, nevertheless, and make my report. Teachers *must not* come together, and I am bound to report if they do." The high position of the lady sheltered the teachers, in this case; but if they had met in the lodgings of one of their own number, they would have received a visit from the state police, and half of them would have been dismissed by the ministry of education; and if, moreover, an angry word had escaped from one of them during the police raid, he or she would have been sent to some province of the Uráls. This is what happens to-day, thirty-three years after the opening of the county and district councils; but it was far worse in the seventies. What sort of basis for a political struggle could such institutions offer?

When I inherited from my father his Tambóv estate, I thought very seriously for a time of settling on that estate, and devoting my energy to work in the local Zémstvo. Some peasants and the poorer priests of the neighborhood asked me to do so. As for myself, I should have been content with anything I could do, no matter how small it might be, if only it would help to raise the intellectual level and the well-being of the peasants. But one day, when several of my advisers were together, I asked them: "Supposing I were to try to start a school, an experimental farm, a coöperative enterprise, and, at the same time, also took upon myself the defense of that peasant from our village who has lately been wronged,—would the authorities let me do it?" "Never!" was the unanimous reply.

An old gray-haired priest, a man who was held in great esteem in our neighborhood, came to me, a few days later, with two influential dissenting leaders, and said: "Talk with these two men. If you can manage it, go with them and, Bible in hand, preach to the peasants. . . . Well, you know what to preach. . . . No police in the world will find you, if they conceal you. . . . There's nothing to be done besides; that's what I, an old man, advise you."

I told them frankly why I could not assume the part of Wiclif.[8] But the old man was right. A movement similar to that of the Lollards is rapidly growing now amongst the Russian peasants. Such tortures as have been inflicted on the

peace-loving Dukhobórs, and such raids upon the peasant dis-
senters in South Russia as were made in 1897, when children
were kidnapped so that they might be educated in orthodox
monasteries, will only give to that movement a force that it
could not have attained five-and-twenty years ago.

As the question of agitation for a constitution was continually being raised in our discussions, I once proposed to our
circle to take it up seriously, and to choose an appropriate plan
of action. I was always of the opinion that when the circle
decided anything unanimously, each member ought to put
aside his personal feeling and give all his strength to the task.
"If you decide to agitate for a constitution," I said, "this is my
plan: I will separate myself from you, for appearance' sake,
and maintain relations with only one member of the circle,—
for instance, Chaikóvsky,—through whom I shall be kept informed how you succeed in your work, and can communicate
to you in a general way what I am doing. My work will be
among the courtiers and the higher functionaries. I have
among them many acquaintances, and know a number of persons who are disgusted with the present conditions. I will
bring them together and unite them, if possible, into a sort of
organization; and then, some day, there is sure to be an opportunity to direct all these forces toward compelling Alexander II. to give Russia a constitution. There certainly will come
a time when all these people, feeling that they are compromised, will in their own interest take a decisive step. If it is
necessary, some of us, who have been officers, might be very
helpful in extending the propaganda amongst the officers in
the army; but this action must be quite separate from yours,
though parallel with it. I have seriously thought of it. I know
what connections I have and who can be trusted, and I believe some of the discontented already look upon me as a
possible center for some action of this sort. This course is not
the one I should take of my own choice; but if you think that
it is best, I will give myself to it with might and main."

The circle did not accept that proposal. Knowing one another as well as they did, my comrades probably thought that
if I went in this direction I should cease to be true to myself.
For my own personal happiness, for my own personal life, I

cannot feel too grateful now that my proposal was not accepted. I should have gone in a direction which was not the one dictated by my own nature, and I should not have found in it the personal happiness which I have found in other paths. But when, six or seven years later, the terrorists were engaged in their terrible struggle against Alexander II., I regretted that there had not been somebody else to do the sort of work I had proposed to do in the higher circles at St. Petersburg. With some understanding there beforehand, and with the ramifications which such an understanding probably would have taken all over the empire, the holocausts of victims would not have been made in vain. At any rate, the underground work of the executive committee ought by all means to have been supported by a parallel agitation at the Winter Palace.

Over and over again the necessity of a political effort thus came under discussion in our little group, with no result. The apathy and the indifference of the wealthier classes were hopeless, and the irritation among the persecuted youth had not yet been brought to that high pitch which ended, six years later, in the struggle of the terrorists under the executive committee. Nay,—and this is one of the most tragical ironies of history,—it was the same youth whom Alexander II., in his blind fear and fury, ordered to be sent by the hundred to hard labor and condemned to slow death in exile; it was the same youth who protected him in 1871–78. The very teachings of the socialist circles were such as to prevent the repetition of a Karakózov attempt on the Tsar's life. "Prepare in Russia a great socialist mass movement amongst the workers and the peasants," was the watchword in those times. "Don't trouble about the Tsar and his counselors. If such a movement begins, if the peasants join in the mass movement to claim the land and to abolish the serfdom redemption taxes, the imperial power will be the first to seek support in the moneyed classes and the landlords and to convoke a Parliament,—just as the peasant insurrection in France, in 1789, compelled the royal power to convoke the National Assembly; so it will be in Russia."9

But there was more than that. Separate men and groups, seeing that the reign of Alexander II. was hopelessly doomed to sink deeper and deeper in reaction, and entertaining at the same time vague hopes as to the supposed "liberalism" of the heir apparent,—all young heirs to thrones are supposed to be liberal,—persistently reverted to the idea that the example of Karakózov ought to be followed. The organized circles, however, strenuously opposed such an idea, and urged their comrades not to resort to that course of action.[10] I may now divulge the following fact which has never before been made public. When a young man came to St. Petersburg from one of the southern provinces with the firm intention of killing Alexander II., and some members of the Chaikóvsky circle learned of his plan, they not only applied all the weight of their arguments to dissuade the young man, but, when he would not be dissuaded, they informed him that they would keep a watch over him and prevent him by force from making any such attempt. Knowing well how loosely guarded the Winter Palace was at that time, I can positively say that they saved the life of Alexander II. So firmly were the youth opposed at that time to the war in which later, when the cup of their sufferings was filled to overflowing, they took part.

XV

The two years that I worked with the Circle of Chaikóvsky, before I was arrested, left a deep impression upon all my subsequent life and thought. During these two years it was life under high pressure,—that exuberance of life when one feels at every moment the full throbbing of all the fibers of the inner self, and when life is really worth living. I was in a family of men and women so closely united by their common object, and so broadly and delicately humane in their mutual relations, that I cannot now recall a single moment of even temporary friction marring the life of our circle. Those who have had any experience of political agitation will appreciate the value of this statement.[11]

Before abandoning entirely my scientific career, I considered myself bound to complete the report of my journey to Finland for the Geographical Society, as well as some other work that I had in hand for the same society; and my new friends were the first to confirm me in that decision. It would not be fair, they said, to do otherwise. Consequently, I worked hard to finish my geographical and geological books.

Meetings of our circle were frequent, and I never missed them. We used to meet then in a suburban part of St. Petersburg, in a small house of which Sophia Peróvskaia, under the assumed name and the fabricated passport of an artisan's wife, was the supposed tenant. She was born of a very aristocratic family, and her father had been for some time the military governor of St. Petersburg; but, with the approval of her mother, who adored her, she had left her home to join a high school, and with the three Kornílov sisters—daughters of a rich manufacturer—she had founded that little circle of self-education which later on became our circle. Now, in the capacity of an artisan's wife, in her cotton dress and men's boots, her head covered with a cotton kerchief, as she carried on her shoulders her two pails of water from the Nevá, no one would have recognized in her the girl who a few years before shone in one of the most fashionable drawing-rooms of the capital. She was a general favorite, and every one of us, on entering the house, had a specially friendly smile for her,—even when she, making a point of honor of keeping the house relatively clean, quarreled with us about the dirt which we, dressed in peasant top-boots and sheepskins, brought in, after walking the muddy streets of the suburbs. She tried then to give to her girlish, innocent, and very intelligent little face the most severe expression possible to it. In her moral conceptions she was a "rigorist," but not in the least of the sermon-preaching type. When she was dissatisfied with some one's conduct, she would cast a severe glance at him from beneath her brows; but in that glance one saw her open-minded, generous nature, which understood all that is human. On one point only she was inexorable. "A women's man," she once said, speaking of some one, and the expression and the manner in which she said it, without interrupting her work, are engraved forever in my memory.

Peróvskaia was a "popularist" to the very bottom of her heart, and at the same time a revolutionist, a fighter of the truest steel. She had no need to embellish the workers and the peasants with imaginary virtues, in order to love them and to work for them. She took them as they were, and said to me once: "We have begun a great thing. Two generations, perhaps, will succumb in the task, and yet it must be done." None of the women of our circle would have given way before the certainty of death on the scaffold. Each would have looked death straight in the face. But none of them, at that stage of our propaganda, thought of such a fate. Peróvskaia's well-known portrait is exceptionally good; it records so well her earnest courage, her bright intelligence, and her loving nature. The letter she wrote to her mother a few hours before she went to the scaffold is one of the best expressions of a loving soul that a woman's heart ever dictated.

The following incident will show what the other women of our circle were. One night, Kupriiánov and I went to Varvára Bátiushkova, to whom we had to make an urgent communication. It was past midnight, but, seeing a light in her window, we went upstairs. She sat in her tiny room, at a table, copying a program of our circle. We knew how resolute she was, and the idea came to us to make one of those stupid jokes which men sometimes think funny. "Bátiushkova," I said, "we came to fetch you: we are going to try a rather mad attempt to liberate our friends from the fortress." She asked not one question. She quietly laid down her pen, rose from the chair, and said only, "Let us go." She spoke in so simple, so unaffected a voice that I felt at once how foolishly I had acted, and told her the truth. She dropped back into her chair, with tears in her eyes, and in a despairing voice asked: "It was only a joke? Why do you make *such* jokes?" I fully realized then the cruelty of what I had done.

Another general favorite in our circle was Sergéi Kravchínsky, who became so well known, both in England and in the United States, under the name of Stepniák. He was often called "the Baby," so unconcerned was he about his own security; but this carelessness about himself was merely the result of a complete absence of fear, which, after all, is often the best policy for one who is hunted by the police. He soon became well known for his propaganda in the circles of workers, under his real Christian name of Sergéi, and consequently was very much wanted by the police; notwithstanding that, he took no precautions whatever to conceal himself, and I remember that one day he was severely scolded at one of our meetings for what was described as a gross imprudence. Being late for the meeting, as he often was, and having a long distance to cover in order to reach our house, he, dressed as a peasant in his sheepskin, ran the whole length of a great main thoroughfare at full speed in the middle of the street. "How could you do it?" he was reproachfully asked. "You might have aroused suspicion and have been arrested as a common thief." But I wish that every one had been as cautious as he was in affairs where other people could be compromised.

We made our first intimate acquaintance over Stanley's book, *How I Discovered Livingstone*. One night our meeting had lasted till twelve, and as we were about to leave, one of the Kornílovs entered with a book in her hand, and asked who among us could undertake to translate by the next morning at eight o'clock sixteen printed pages of Stanley's book. I looked at the size of the pages, and said that if somebody would help me, the work could be done during the night. Sergéi volunteered, and by four o'clock the sixteen pages were done. We read to each other our translations, one of us following the English text; then we emptied a jar of Russian porridge which had been left on the table for us, and went out together to return home. We became close friends from that night.

I have always liked people capable of working, and doing their work properly. So Sergéi's translation and his capacity of working rapidly had already influenced me in his favor. But when I came to know more of him, I felt real love for his honest, frank nature, for his youthful energy and good sense, for his superior intelligence, simplicity, and truthfulness, and for his courage and tenacity. He had read and thought a great deal, and upon the revolutionary character of the struggle which he had undertaken, it appeared we had similar views. He was ten years younger than I was, and perhaps did not quite realize what a hard contest the coming revolution would be. He told us later on, with much humor, how he once worked among the peasants in the country. "One day," he said, "I was walking along the road with a comrade, when we were overtaken by a peasant in a sleigh. I began to tell the peasant that

he must not pay taxes, that the functionaries plunder the people, and I tried to convince him by quotations from the Bible
that they must revolt. The peasant whipped up his horse, but
we followed rapidly; he made his horse trot, and we began to
trot behind him; all the time I continued to talk to him about
taxes and revolt. Finally he made his horse gallop; but the
animal was not worth much,—an underfed peasant pony,—so
my comrade and I did not fall behind, but kept up our propaganda till we were quite out of breath."

For some time Sergéi stayed in Kazán, and I had to correspond with him. He always hated writing letters in cipher, so
I proposed a means of correspondence which had often been
used before in conspiracies. You write an ordinary letter about
all sorts of things, but in this letter it is only certain words—
let us say every fifth word—which has a sense. You write, for
instance: "Excuse my hurried letter. Come to-night to see me;
to-morrow I shall go away to my sister. My brother Nicholas
is worse; it was late to perform an operation." Reading each
fifth word, you find, "Come to-morrow to Nicholas, late." We
had to write letters of six or seven pages to transmit one page
of information, and we had to cultivate our imagination in
order to fill the letters with all sorts of things by way of introducing the words that were required. Sergéi, from whom it
was impossible to obtain a cipher letter, took to this kind of
correspondence, and used to send me letters containing stories
with thrilling incidents and dramatic endings. He said to me
afterward that this correspondence helped to develop his literary talent. When one has talent, everything contributes to its
development.

In January or February, 1874, I was at Moscow, in one of
the houses in which I had spent my childhood. Early in the
morning I was told that a peasant desired to see me. I went
out and found it was Sergéi, who had just escaped from
Tver. He was strongly built, and he and another ex-officer,
Rogachóv, endowed with equal physical force, went traveling
about the country as lumber sawyers. The work was very
hard, especially for inexperienced hands, but both of them
liked it; and no one would have thought to look for disguised
officers in these two strong sawyers. They wandered in this
capacity for about a fortnight without arousing suspicion, and

made revolutionary propaganda right and left without fear. Sometimes Sergéi, who knew the New Testament almost by heart, spoke to the peasants as a religious preacher, proving to them by quotations from the Bible that they ought to start a revolution. Sometimes he formed his arguments of quotations from the economists. The peasants listened to the two men as to real apostles, took them from one house to another, and refused to be paid for food. In a fortnight they had produced quite a stir in a number of villages. Their fame was spreading far and wide. The peasants, young and old, began to whisper to one another in the barns about the "delegates;" they began to speak out more loudly than they usually did that the land would soon be taken from the landlords, who would receive pensions from the Tsar. The younger people became more aggressive toward the police officers, saying: "Wait a little; our turn will soon come; you Herods will not rule long now." But the fame of the sawyers reached the ears of one of the police authorities, and they were arrested. An order was given to take them to the next police official, ten miles away.

They were taken under the guard of several peasants, and on their way had to pass through a village which was holding its festival. "Prisoners? All right! Come on here, my uncle," said the peasants, who were all drinking in honor of the occasion. They were kept nearly the whole day in that village, the peasants taking them from one house to another, and treating them to home-made beer. The guards did not have to be asked twice. They drank, and insisted that the prisoners should drink, too. "Happily," Sergéi said, "they passed round the beer in such large wooden bowls that I could put my mouth to the rim of the bowl as if I were drinking, but no one could see how much beer I had imbibed." The guards were all drunk toward night, and preferred not to appear in this state before the police officer, so they decided to stay in the village till morning. Sergéi kept talking to them; and all listened to him, regretting that such a good man had been caught. As they were going to sleep, a young peasant whispered to Sergéi, "When I go to shut the gate, I will leave it unbolted." Sergéi and his comrade understood the hint, and as soon as all fell asleep, they went out into the street. They started at a fast pace, and at five o'clock in the morning were twenty miles away from the village, at a small railway station, where they took the first train, and went to Moscow. Sergéi remained there, and later, when all of us at St. Petersburg had been arrested, the Moscow circle, under his and Voinarálsky's inspiration, became the main center of the agitation.

Here and there, small groups of propagandists had settled in towns and villages in various capacities. Blacksmiths' shops and small farms had been started, and young men of the wealthier classes worked in the shops or on the farms, to be in daily contact with the toiling masses. At Moscow, a number of young girls, of rich families, who had studied at the Zürich University and had started a separate organization, went even so far as to enter cotton factories, where they worked from fourteen to sixteen hours a day, and lived in the factory barracks the miserable life of the Russian factory girls. It was a grand movement, in which, at the lowest estimate, from two to three thousand persons took an active part, while twice or thrice as many sympathizers and supporters helped the active vanguard in various ways. With a good half of that army our St. Petersburg circle was in regular correspondence,—always, of course, in cipher.

The literature which could be published in Russia under a rigorous censorship—the faintest hint of socialism being prohibited—was soon found insufficient, and we started a printing-office of our own abroad. Pamphlets for the workers and the peasants had to be written, and our small "literary committee," of which I was a member, had its hands full of work. Sergéi wrote two such pamphlets, one in the Lamennais style and another containing an exposition of socialism in a fairy tale, and both had a wide circulation. The books and pamphlets which were printed abroad were smuggled into Russia by thousands, stored at certain spots, and sent out to the local circles, which distributed them amongst the peasants and the workers.[12] All this required a vast organization as well as much traveling about, and a colossal correspondence, particularly for protecting our helpers and our bookstores from the police. We had special ciphers for different provincial circles, and often, after six or seven hours had been passed in discussing all details, the women, who did not trust to our accuracy in the cipher correspondence, spent all the night in covering sheets of paper with cabalistic figures and fractions.

The utmost cordiality always prevailed at our meetings. Chairmen and all sorts of formalism are so utterly repugnant to the Russian mind that we had none; and although our debates were sometimes extremely hot, especially when "program questions" were under discussion, we always managed very well without resorting to Western formalities. An absolute sincerity, a general desire to settle the difficulties for the best, and a frankly expressed contempt for all that in the least degree approached theatrical affectation were quite sufficient. If any one of us had ventured to attempt oratorical effects by a speech, friendly jokes would have shown him at once that speech-making was out of place. Often we had to take our meals during these meetings, and they invariably consisted of rye bread, with cucumbers, a bit of cheese, and plenty of weak tea to quench the thirst. Not that money was lacking; there was always enough, and yet there was never too much to cover the steadily growing expenses for printing, transportation of books, concealing friends wanted by the police, and starting new enterprises.

At St. Petersburg, it was not long before we had wide acquaintance amongst the workers. Serdiukóv, a young man of splendid education, had made a number of friends amongst the engineers, most of them employed in a state factory of the artillery department, and he had organized a circle of about thirty members, which used to meet for reading and discussion. The engineers are pretty well paid at St. Petersburg, and those who were not married were fairly well off. They soon became quite familiar with the current radical and socialist literature,—Buckle, Lassalle, Mill, Draper, Spielhagen, were familiar names to them; and in their aspect these engineers differed little from students. When Klementz, Sergéi, and I joined the circle, we frequently visited their group, and gave them informal lectures upon all sorts of things. Our hopes, however, that these young men would grow into ardent propagandists amidst less privileged classes of workers were not fully realized. In a free country they would have been the habitual speakers at public meetings; but, like the privileged workers of the watch trade in Geneva, they treated the mass of the factory

hands with a sort of contempt, and were in no haste to become martyrs to the socialist cause. It was only after they had
been arrested and kept three or four years in prison for having
dared to *think* as socialists, and had sounded the full depth of
Russian absolutism, that several of them developed into ardent
propagandists, chiefly of a political revolution.[13]

My sympathies went especially toward the weavers and the
workers in the cotton factories. There are many thousands of
them at St. Petersburg, who work there during the winter, and
return for the three summer months to their native villages to
cultivate the land. Half peasants and half town workers, they
had generally retained the social spirit of the Russian villager.
The movement spread like wildfire among them. We had to
restrain the zeal of our new friends; otherwise they would have
brought to our lodgings hundreds at a time, young and old.
Most of them lived in small associations, or *artéls*, ten or
twelve persons hiring a common apartment and taking their
meals together, each one paying every month his share of the
general expenses. It was to these lodgings that we used to go,
and the weavers soon brought us in contact with other artéls,
of stone-masons, carpenters, and the like. In some of these
artéls Sergéi, Klementz, and two more of our friends were
quite at home, and spent whole nights talking about socialism.
Besides, we had in different parts of St. Petersburg special
apartments, kept by some of our people, to which ten or twelve
workers would come every night, to learn reading and writing,
and after that to have a talk. From time to time one of us went
to the native villages of our town friends, and spent a couple
of weeks in almost open propaganda amongst the peasants.

Of course, all of us who had to deal with this class of workers
had to dress like the workers themselves; that is, to wear the
peasant garb. The gap between the peasants and the educated
people is so great in Russia, and contact between them is so
rare, that not only does the appearance in a village of a man
who wears the town dress awaken general attention, but even
in town, if one whose talk and dress reveal that he is not a
worker is seen to go about with workers, the suspicion of the
police is aroused at once. "Why should he go about with 'low
people,' if he has not a bad intention?" Often, after a dinner

in a rich mansion, or even in the Winter Palace, where I went frequently to see a friend, I took a cab, hurried to a poor student's lodging in a remote suburb, exchanged my fine clothes for a cotton shirt, peasant top-boots, and a sheepskin, and, joking with peasants on the way, went to meet my worker friends in some slum. I told them what I had seen of the labor movement abroad. They listened eagerly; they lost not a word of what was said; and then came the question, "What can we do in Russia?" "Agitate, organize," was our reply; "there is no royal road;" and we read them a popular story of the French Revolution, an adaptation of Erckmann-Chatrian's admirable *Histoire d'un Paysan*. Every one admired M. Chovel, who went as a propagandist through the villages, distributing prohibited books, and all burned to follow in his footsteps. "Speak to others," we said; "bring men together; and when we become more numerous, we shall see what we can attain." They fully understood, and we had only to moderate their zeal.

Amongst them I passed my happiest hours. New Year's Day of 1874, the last I spent in Russia at liberty, is especially memorable to me. The previous evening I had been in a choice company. Inspiring, noble words were spoken that night about the citizen's duties, the well-being of the country, and the like. But underneath all the thrilling speeches one note sounded: How could each of the speakers preserve his own personal well-being? Yet no one had the courage to say, frankly and openly, that he was ready to do only that which would not endanger his own dovecote. Sophisms—no end of sophisms— about the slowness of evolution, the inertia of the lower classes, the uselessness of sacrifice, were uttered to justify the unspoken words, all intermingled with assurances of each one's willingness to make sacrifices. I returned home, seized suddenly with profound sadness amid all this talk.

Next morning I went to one of our weavers' meetings. It took place in an underground dark room. I was dressed as a peasant, and was lost in the crowd of other sheepskins. My comrade, who was known to the workers, simply introduced me: "Borodín, a friend." "Tell us, Borodín," he said, "what you have seen abroad." And I spoke of the labor movement in Western Europe, its struggles, its difficulties, and its hopes.

The audience consisted mostly of middle-aged people. They

were intensely interested. They asked me questions, all to the point, about the minute details of the workingmen's unions, the aims of the International Association and its chances of success. And then came questions about what could be done in Russia and the prospects of our propaganda. I never minimized the dangers of our agitation, and frankly said what I thought. "We shall probably be sent to Siberia, one of these days; and you—part of you—will be kept long months in prison for having listened to us." This gloomy prospect did not frighten them. "After all, there are men in Siberia, too,—not bears only." "Where men are living others can live." "The devil is not so terrible as they paint him." "If you are afraid of wolves, never go into the wood," they said, as we parted. And when, afterward, several of them were arrested, they nearly all behaved bravely, sheltering us and betraying no one.

XVI

During the two years of which I am now speaking many arrests were made, both at St. Petersburg and in the provinces. Not a month passed without our losing some one, or learning that members of this or that provincial group had disappeared. Toward the end of 1873 the arrests became more and more frequent. In November one of our main settlements in a suburb of St. Petersburg was raided by the police. We lost Peróvskaia and three other friends, and all our relations with the workers in this suburb had to be suspended. We founded a new settlement, further away from the town, but it had soon to be abandoned. The police became very vigilant, and the appearance of a student in the workmen's quarters was noticed at once; spies circulated among the workers, who were watched closely. Dmítri Klementz, Sergéi, and myself, in our sheepskins and with our peasant looks, passed unnoticed, and continued to visit the haunted ground. But Dmítri and Sergéi, whose names had acquired a wide notoriety in the workmen's quarters, were eagerly wanted by the police; and if they had been found accidentally during a nocturnal raid at a friend's lodgings, they would have been arrested at once. There were periods when Dmítri had to hunt every day for a place where he could spend the night in relative safety. "Can I spend the night with you?" he would ask, entering some comrade's room at ten o'clock. "Impossible! my lodgings have been closely watched lately. Better go to N." "I have just come from him, and he says spies swarm his neighborhood." "Then go to M.; he is a great friend of mine and above suspicion. But it is far from here, and you must take a cab. Here is the money." But on principle Dmítri would not take a cab, and would walk to the other end of the town to find a refuge, or at last go to a friend whose rooms might be searched at any moment.

Early in January, 1874, another settlement, our main stronghold for propaganda amongst the weavers, was lost. Some of our best propagandists disappeared behind the gates of the mysterious Third Section. Our circle became narrower, general meetings were increasingly difficult, and we made strenuous efforts to form new circles of young men who might continue our work when we should all be arrested. Chaikóvsky was in the south, and we forced Dmítri and Sergéi to leave St. Petersburg,—actually forced them, imperiously ordering them to leave. Only five or six of us remained to transact all the business of our circle. I intended, as soon as I should have delivered my report to the Geographical Society, to go to the southwest of Russia, and there to start a sort of land league, similar to the league which became so powerful in Ireland at the end of the seventies.

After two months of relative quiet, we learned in the middle of March that nearly all the circle of the engineers had been arrested, and with them a young man named Nízovkin, an ex-student, who unfortunately had their confidence, and, we were sure, would soon try to clear himself by telling all he knew about us. Besides Dmítri and Sergéi he knew Serdiukóv, the founder of the circle, and myself, and he would certainly name us as soon as he was pressed with questions. A few days later, two weavers—most unreliable fellows, who had even embezzled some money from their comrades, and who knew me under the name of Borodín—were arrested. These two would surely set the police at once upon the track of Borodín, the man dressed as a peasant, who spoke at the weavers' meetings. Within a week's time all the members of our circle, excepting Serdiukóv and myself, were arrested.

There was nothing left us but to fly from St. Petersburg: this was exactly what we did not want to do. All our immense organization for printing pamphlets abroad and for smuggling them into Russia; all the network of circles, farms, and country settlements with which we were in correspondence in nearly forty (out of fifty) provinces of European Russia, and which had been slowly built up during the last two years; and finally, our workers' groups at St. Petersburg and our four different centers for propaganda amongst workers of the capital,—how could we abandon all these without having found men to maintain our relations and correspondence? Serdiukóv and I decided to admit to our circle two new members, and to transfer the business to them. We met every evening in different parts of the town, and as we never kept any addresses or names in writing,—the smuggling addresses alone had been deposited in a secure place, in cipher,—we had to teach our new members hundreds of names and addresses and a dozen ciphers, repeating them over and over, until our friends had learned them by heart. Every evening we went over the whole map of Russia in this way, dwelling especially on its western frontier, which was studded with men and women engaged in receiving books from the smugglers, and on the eastern provinces, where we had our main settlements. Then, always in disguise, we had to take the new members to our sympathizers in the town, and introduce them to those workers who had not yet been arrested.

The thing to be done in such a case was to disappear from one's apartments, and to reappear somewhere else under an assumed name. Serdiukóv had abandoned his lodging, but, having no passport, he concealed himself in the houses of friends. I ought to have done the same, but a strange circumstance prevented me. I had just finished my report upon the glacial formations in Finland and Russia, and this report had to be read at a meeting of the Geographical Society. The invitations were already issued, but it happened that on the appointed day the two geological societies of St. Petersburg had a joint meeting, and they asked the Geographical Society to postpone the reading of my report for a week. It was known that I would present certain ideas about the extension of the ice cap as far as Middle Russia, and our geologists, with the exception of my friend and teacher, Friedrich Schmidt, considered this a speculation of too far-reaching character, and wanted to have it thoroughly discussed. For one week more, consequently, I could not go away.

Strangers prowled about my house and called upon me under all sorts of fantastical pretexts: one of them wanted to buy a forest on my Tambóv estate, which was situated in absolutely treeless prairies. I noticed in my street—the fashionable Morskáia—one of the two arrested weavers whom I have mentioned, and thus learned that my house was watched. Yet I had to act as if nothing extraordinary had happened, because I was to appear at the meeting of the Geographical Society the following Friday night.

The meeting came. The discussions were very animated, and one point, at least, was won. It was recognized that all old theories concerning the diluvial period in Russia were totally baseless, and that a new departure must be made in the investigation of the whole question. I had the satisfaction of hearing our leading geologist, Barbot-de-Marny, say, "Ice cap or not, we must acknowledge, gentlemen, that all we have hitherto said about the action of floating ice had no foundation whatever in actual exploration." And I was proposed at that meeting to be nominated president of the physical geography section, while I was asking myself whether I should not spend that very night in the prison of the Third Section.

It would have been best not to return at all to my apartment, but I was broken down with fatigue, after the exertion of the last few days, and went home. There was no police raid during that night. I looked through the heaps of my papers, destroyed everything that might be compromising for any one, packed all my things, and prepared to leave. I knew that my apartment was watched, but I hoped that the police would not pay me a visit before late in the night, and that at dusk I could slip out of the house without being noticed. Dusk came, and, as I was starting, one of the servant girls said to me, "You had better go by the service staircase." I understood what she meant, and went quickly down the staircase and out of the house. One cab only stood at the gate; I jumped into it. The driver took me to the great Nevsky Prospekt. There was no pursuit at first, and I thought myself safe; but presently I noticed another cab running full speed after us; our horse was delayed somehow, and the other cab passed ours.

To my astonishment, I saw in it one of the two arrested weavers, accompanied by some one else. He waved his hand as if he had something to tell me. I told my cabman to stop. "Perhaps," I thought, "he has been released from arrest, and has an important communication to make to me." But as soon as we stopped, the man who was with the weaver—he was a detective—shouted loudly, "Mr. Borodín, Prince Kropótkin, I arrest you!" He made a signal to the policemen, of whom there are hosts along the main thoroughfare of St. Petersburg, and at the same time jumped into my cab and showed me a paper which bore the stamp of the St. Petersburg police. "I have an order to take you before the governor-general for an explanation," he said. Resistance was impossible,—a couple of policemen were already close by,—and I told my cabman to turn round and drive to the governor-general's house. The weaver remained in his cab and followed us.

It was now evident that the police had hesitated for ten days to arrest me, because they were not sure that Borodín and I were the same person. My response to the weaver's call had settled their doubts.

It so happened that just as I was leaving my house a young man came from Moscow, bringing me a letter from a friend, Voinarálsky, and another from Dmítri addressed to our friend Poliakóv. The former announced the establishment of a secret printing-office at Moscow, and was full of cheerful news concerning the activity in that city. I read it and destroyed it. As the second letter contained nothing but innocent friendly chat, I took it with me. Now that I was arrested, I thought it would be better to destroy it, and, asking the detective to show me his paper again, I took advantage of the time that he was fumbling in his pocket to drop the letter on the pavement without his noticing it. However, as we reached the governor-general's house the weaver handed it to the detective, saying, "I saw the gentleman drop this letter on the pavement, so I picked it up."

Now came tedious hours of waiting for the representative of the judicial authorities, the procureur or public prosecutor. This functionary plays the part of a straw man, who is paraded by the state police during their searches: he gives an aspect of legality to their proceedings. It was many hours before that gentleman was found and brought to perform his functions as a sham representative of Justice. I was taken back to my house, and a most thorough search of all my papers was made; this lasted till three in the morning, but did not reveal a scrap of paper that could tell against me or any one else.

From my house I was taken to the Third Section, that omnipotent institution which has ruled in Russia from the beginning of the reign of Nicholas I. down to the present time,—a true "state in the state." It began under Peter I. in the Secret Department, where the adversaries of the founder of the Russian military empire were subject to the most abominable tortures, under which they expired; it was continued in the Secret Chancelry during the reigns of the Empresses, when the Torture Chamber of the powerful Minich inspired all Russia with terror; and it received its present organization from the iron despot, Nicholas I., who attached to it the corps of gendarmes, —the chief of the gendarmes becoming a person far more dreaded in the Russian Empire than the Emperor himself.

In every province of Russia, in every populous town, nay, at every railway station, there are gendarmes who report directly to their own generals or colonels, who in turn correspond with the chief of the gendarmes; and the latter, seeing the Emperor every day, reports to him what he finds necessary to report. All functionaries of the empire are under gendarme supervision; it is the duty of the generals and colonels to keep an eye upon the public and private life of every subject of the Tsar,—even upon the governors of the provinces, the ministers, and the grand dukes. The Emperor himself is under their close watch, and as they are well informed of the petty chronicle of the palace, and know every step that the Emperor takes outside his palace, the chief of the gendarmes becomes, so to speak, a confidant of the most intimate affairs of the rulers of Russia.

At this period of the reign of Alexander II. the Third Section was absolutely all-powerful. The gendarme colonels made searches by the thousand without troubling themselves in the least about the existence of laws and law courts in Russia. They arrested whom they liked, kept people imprisoned as long as they pleased, and transported hundreds to Northeast Russia or Siberia according to the fancy of general or colonel; the signature of the minister of the interior was a mere formality, because he had no control over them and no knowledge of their doings.

It was four o'clock in the morning when my examination began. "You are accused," I was solemnly told, "of having belonged to a secret society which has for its object the overthrow of the existing form of government, and of conspiracy against the sacred person of his Imperial Majesty. Are you guilty of this crime?"

"Till I am brought before a court where I can speak publicly, I will give you no replies whatever."

"Write," the procureur dictated to a scribe: " 'Does not acknowledge himself guilty.' Still," he continued, after a pause, "I must ask you certain questions. Do you know a person of the name of Nikolái Chaikóvsky?"

"If you persist in your questions, then write 'No' to any question whatsoever that you are pleased to ask me."

"But if we ask you whether you know, for instance, Mr. Poliakóv, whom you spoke about awhile ago?"

"The moment *you* ask me such a question, don't hesitate: write 'No.' And if you ask me whether I know my brother, or my sister, or my stepmother, write 'No.' You will not receive from me another reply: because if I answered 'Yes' with regard to any person, you would at once plan some evil against him, making a raid or something worse, and saying next that I named him."

A long list of questions was read, to which I patiently replied each time, "Write 'No.' " That lasted for an hour, during which I learned that all who had been arrested, with the exception of the two weavers, had behaved very well. The weavers knew only that I had twice met a dozen workers, and the gendarmes knew nothing about our circle.

"What are you doing, prince?" a gendarme officer said, as he took me to my cell. "Your refusal to answer questions will be made a terrible weapon against you."

"It is my right, is it not?"

"Yes, but—you know. . . . I hope you will find this room comfortable. It has been kept warm since your arrest."

I found it quite comfortable, and fell sound asleep. I was
waked the next morning by a gendarme, who brought me the
morning tea. He was soon followed by somebody else, who
whispered to me in the most unconcerned way, "Here's a
scrap of paper and a pencil: write your letter." It was a sym-
pathizer, whom I knew by name; he used to transmit our correspondence with the prisoners of the Third Section.

From all sides I heard knocks on the walls, following in
rapid succession. It was the prisoners communicating with one
another by means of light taps; but, being a newcomer, I could
make nothing out of the noise, which seemed to come from all
parts of the building at once.

One thing worried me. During the search in my house, I
overheard the procureur whispering to the gendarme officer
about going to make a search at the apartment of my friend
Poliakóv, to whom the letter of Dmítri was addressed.
Poliakóv was a young student, a very gifted zoölogist and bota-
nist, with whom I had made my Vitím expedition in Siberia.
He was born of a poor Cossack family on the frontier of Mon-
golia, and, after having surmounted all sorts of difficulties, he
had come to St. Petersburg, entered the university, where he
had won the reputation of a most promising zoölogist, and was
then passing his final examinations. We had been great friends
since our long journey, and had even lived together for a time
at St. Petersburg, but he took no interest in my political activity.

I spoke of him to the procureur. "I give you my word of
honor," I said, "that Poliakóv has never taken part in any
political affair. To-morrow he has to pass an examination, and
you will spoil forever the scientific career of a young man who
has gone through great hardships, and has struggled for years
against all sorts of obstacles, to attain his present position. I
know that you do not much care for it, but he is looked upon
at the university as one of the future glories of Russian science."

The search was made, nevertheless, but a respite of three
days was given for the examinations. A little later I was called
before the procureur, who triumphantly showed me an envelope addressed in my handwriting, and in it a note, also
in my handwriting, which said, "Please take this packet to
V. E., and ask that it be kept until demand in due form is

made." The person to whom the note was addressed was not mentioned in the note. "This letter," the procureur said, "was found at Mr. Poliakóv's; and now, prince, his fate is in your hands. If you tell me who V. E. is, Mr. Poliakóv will be released; but if you refuse to do so, he will be kept as long as he does not make up his mind to give us the name of that person."

Looking at the envelope, which was addressed in black chalk, and the letter, which was written in common lead pencil, I immediately remembered the circumstances under which the two had been written. "I am positive," I exclaimed at once, "that the note and the envelope were not found together! It is *you* who have put the letter in the envelope."

The procureur blushed. "Would you have me believe," I continued, "that you, a practical man, did not notice that the two were written with different pencils? And now you are trying to make people think that the two belong to each other! Well, sir, then I tell you that the letter was not to Poliakóv."

He hesitated for some time, but then, regaining his audacity, he said, "Poliakóv has admitted that this letter of yours was written to him."

Now I knew he was lying. Poliakóv would have admitted everything concerning himself; but he would have preferred to be marched to Siberia rather than to involve another person. So, looking straight in the face of the procureur, I replied, "No, sir, he has *never* said that, and you know perfectly well that your words are not true."

He became furious, or pretended to be so. "Well, then," he said, "if you wait here a moment, I will bring you Poliakóv's written statement to that effect. He is in the next room under examination."

"Ready to wait as long as you like."

I sat on a sofa, smoking countless cigarettes. The statement did not come, and never came.

Of course there was no such statement. I met Poliakóv in 1878 at Geneva, whence we made a delightful excursion to the Aletsch glacier. I need not say that his answers were what I expected them to be: he denied having any knowledge of the letter or of the person the letters V. E. represented. Scores of books used to be taken from me to him, and back to me, and the letter was found in a book, while the envelope was discovered in the pocket of an old coat. He was kept several weeks under arrest, and then released, owing to the intervention of his scientific friends. V. E. was not molested, and delivered my papers in due time.

I was not taken back to my cell, but half an hour later the procureur came in, accompanied by a gendarme officer. "Our examination," he announced to me, "is now terminated; you will be removed to another place."

Later on, each time I saw him I teased him with the question: "And what about Poliakóv's statement?"

A four-wheeled cab stood at the gate. I was asked to enter it, and a stout gendarme officer, of Circassian origin, sat by my side. I spoke to him, but he only snored. The cab crossed the Chain Bridge, then passed the parade grounds and ran along the canals, as if avoiding the more frequented thoroughfares. "Are we going to the Litóvsky prison?" I asked the officer, as I knew that many of my comrades were already there. He made no reply. The system of absolute silence which was maintained toward me for the next two years began in this four-wheeled cab; but when we went rolling over the Palace Bridge, I understood that I was on the way to the fortress of St. Peter and St. Paul.

I admired the beautiful river, knowing that I should not soon see it again. The sun was going down. Thick gray clouds were hanging in the west above the Gulf of Finland, while light clouds floated over my head, showing here and there patches of blue sky. Then the carriage turned to the left and entered a dark arched passage, the gate of the fortress.

"Now I shall have to remain here for a couple of years," I remarked to the officer.

"No, why so long?" replied the Circassian, who now that we were within the fortress had regained the power of speech. "Your affair is almost terminated, and may be brought into court in a fortnight."

"My affair," I replied, "is very simple; but before bringing me to a court you will try to arrest all the socialists in Russia, and they are many, very many; in two years you will not have done." I did not then realize how prophetic my remark was.

The carriage stopped at the door of the military commander

of the fortress, and we entered his reception hall. General Korsákov, a thin old man, came in, with a peevish expression on his face. The officer spoke to him in a subdued voice, and the old man answered, "All right," looking at him with a sort of scorn, and then turned his eyes toward me. It was evident that he was not at all pleased to receive a new inmate, and that he felt slightly ashamed of his rôle; but he seemed to add, "I am a soldier, and only do my duty." Presently we got into the carriage again, but soon stopped before another gate, where we were kept a long time until a detachment of soldiers opened it from the inside. Proceeding on foot through narrow passages we came to a third iron gate, opening into a dark arched passage, from which we entered a small room where darkness and dampness prevailed.

Several noncommissioned officers of the fortress troops moved noiselessly about in their soft felt boots, without speaking a word, while the governor signed the Circassian's book acknowledging the reception of a new prisoner. I was required to take off all my clothes, and to put on the prison dress,— a green flannel dressing-gown, immense woolen stockings of an incredible thickness, and boat-shaped yellow slippers, so big that I could hardly keep them on my feet when I tried to walk. I always hated dressing-gowns and slippers, and the thick stockings inspired me with disgust. I had to take off even a silk undergarment, which in the damp fortress it would have been especially desirable to retain, but that could not be allowed. I naturally began to protest and to make a noise about this, and after an hour or so it was restored to me by order of General Korsákov.

Then I was taken through a dark passage, where I saw armed sentries walking about, and was put into a cell. A heavy oak door was shut behind me, a key turned in the lock, and I was alone in a half-dark room.

❋ ❋ ❋ ❋ ❋ ❋ ❋ ❋ ❋ ❋ ❋ ❋ ❋ ❋ ❋ ❋ ❋ ❋

PART FIVE

THE FORTRESS; THE ESCAPE

I

This was, then, the terrible fortress where so much of the true strength of Russia had perished during the last two centuries, and the very name of which is uttered in St. Petersburg in a hushed voice.

Here Peter I. tortured his son Alexis and killed him with his own hand; here the Princess Tarakánova was kept in a cell which filled with water during an inundation,—the rats climbing upon her to save themselves from drowning; here the terrible Minich tortured his enemies, and Catherine II. buried alive those who objected to her having murdered her husband. And from the times of Peter I. for a hundred and seventy years, the annals of this mass of stone which rises from the Nevá in front of the Winter Palace were annals of murder and torture, of men buried alive, condemned to a slow death, or driven to insanity in the loneliness of the dark and damp dungeons.

Here the Decembrists, who were the first to unfurl in Russia the banner of republican rule and the abolition of serfdom, underwent their first experiences of martyrdom, and traces of them may still be found in the Russian Bastille. Here were imprisoned the poets Ryléev and Shevchénko, Dostoévsky, Bakúnin, Chernyshévsky, Písarev, and so many others of our best contemporary writers. Here Karakózov was tortured and hanged.

Here, somewhere in the Alexis ravelin, is still kept Necháev, who was given up to Russia by Switzerland as a common-law criminal, but is treated as a dangerous political prisoner, and will never again see the light. In the same ravelin are also two or three men whom, rumor says, Alexander II., because of what they knew, and others must not know, about some palace mystery, ordered imprisoned for life. One of them, adorned with a long gray beard, was lately seen by an acquaintance of mine in the mysterious fortress.

All these shadows rose before my imagination. But my thoughts fixed especially on Bakúnin, who, though he had been shut up in an Austrian fortress, after 1848, for two years, chained to the wall, and then handed over to Nicholas I., who kept him in the fortress for six years longer, yet came out, when the Iron Tsar's death released him, fresher and fuller of vigor than his comrades who had remained at liberty. "He has lived it through," I said to myself, "and I must, too: I will *not* succumb here!"

My first movement was to approach the window, which was placed so high that I could hardly reach it with my lifted hand. It was a long, low opening, cut in a wall five feet thick, and protected by an iron grating and a double iron window frame. At a distance of a dozen yards from this window I saw the outer wall of the fortress, of immense thickness, on the top of which I could make out a gray sentry box. Only by looking upward could I perceive a bit of the sky.

I made a minute inspection of the room where I had now to spend no one could say how many years. From the position of the high chimney of the Mint I guessed that I was in the southwestern corner of the fortress, in a bastion overlooking the Nevá. The building in which I was incarcerated, however, was not the bastion itself, but what is called in a fortification a *réduit;* that is, an inner two-storied pentagonal piece of masonry which rises a little higher than the walls of the bastion, and is meant to contain two tiers of guns. This room of mine was a casemate destined for a big gun, and the window was an embrasure. The rays of the sun could never penetrate it; even in summer they were lost in the thickness of the wall. The room held an iron bed, a small oak table, and an oak stool. The floor was covered with painted felt, and the walls with yellow paper. However, in order to deaden sounds, the paper was not put on the wall itself; it was pasted upon canvas, and behind the canvas I discovered a wire grating, back of which was a layer of felt; only beyond the felt could I reach the stone wall. At the inner side of the room there was a washstand, and a thick oak door in which I made out a locked opening, for passing food through, and a little slit, protected by glass and by a shutter from the outside: this was the "Judas," through which the prisoner could be spied upon at every moment. The sentry who stood in the passage frequently lifted the shutter and looked inside,—his boots squeaking as he crept toward the door. I tried to speak to him; then the eye which I could see through the slit assumed an expression of terror and the shutter was immediately let down, only to be furtively opened a minute or two later; but I could not get a word of response from the sentry.

Absolute silence reigned all round. I dragged my stool to the window and looked upon the little bit of sky that I could see; I tried to catch any sound from the Nevá or from the town on the opposite side of the river, but I could not. This dead silence began to oppress me, and I tried to sing, softly at first, and louder and louder afterwards.

"Have I then to say farewell to love forever?" I caught myself singing from my favorite opera, Glínka's *Ruslán and Ludmíla.*

"Sir, do not sing, please," a bass voice said through the food-window in my door.

"I *will* sing."

"You must not."

"I will sing nevertheless."

Then came the governor, who tried to persuade me that I must not sing, as it would have to be reported to the commander of the fortress, and so on.

"But my throat will become blocked and my lungs become useless if I do not speak and cannot sing," I tried to argue.

"Better try to sing in a lower tone, more or less to yourself," said the old governor in a supplicatory manner.

But all this was useless. A few days later I had lost all desire to sing. I tried to do it on principle, but it was of no avail.

"The main thing," I said to myself, "is to preserve my physical vigor. I *will* not fall ill. Let me imagine myself compelled to spend a couple of years in a hut in the far north, during an arctic expedition. I will take plenty of exercise, practice gymnastics, and not let myself be broken down by my surroundings. Ten steps from one corner to the other is already something.

If I repeat them one hundred and fifty times, I shall have walked one verst" (two thirds of a mile). I determined to walk every day seven versts,—about five miles: two versts in the morning, two before dinner, two after dinner, and one before going to sleep. "If I put on the table ten cigarettes, and move one of them each time that I pass the table, I shall easily count the three hundred times that I must walk up and down. I must walk rapidly, but turn slowly in the corner to avoid becoming giddy, and turn each time a different way. Then, twice a day I shall practice gymnastics with my heavy stool." I lifted it by one leg, holding it at arm's length. I turned it like a wheel, and soon learned to throw it from one hand to the other, over my head, behind my back, and across my legs.

A few hours after I had been brought into the prison the governor came to offer me some books, and among them was an old acquaintance and friend of mine, the first volume of George Lewes's *Physiology*, in a Russian translation; but the second volume, which I especially wanted to read again, was missing. I asked, of course, to have paper, pen, and ink, but was absolutely refused. Pen and ink are never allowed in the fortress, unless special permission is obtained from the Emperor himself. I suffered very much from this forced inactivity, and began to compose in my imagination a series of novels for popular reading, taken from Russian history,—something like Eugène Sue's *Mystères du Peuple*. I made up the plot, the descriptions, the dialogues, and tried to commit the whole to memory from the beginning to the end. One can easily imagine how exhausting such a work would have been if I had had to continue it for more than two or three months.

But my brother Alexander obtained pen and ink for me. One day I was asked to enter a four-wheeled cab, in company with the same speechless Georgian gendarme officer of whom I have spoken before. I was taken to the Third Section, where I was allowed an interview with my brother, in the presence of two gendarme officers.

Alexander was at Zürich when I was arrested. From early youth he had longed to go abroad, where men think as they like, read what they like, and openly express their thoughts. Russian life was hateful to him. Veracity—absolute veracity— and the most open-hearted frankness were the dominating features of his character. He could not bear deceit or even conceit in any form. The absence of free speech in Russia, the Russian readiness to submit to oppression, the veiled words to which our writers resort, were utterly repulsive to his frank and open nature. Soon after my return from Western Europe he removed to Switzerland, and decided to settle there. After he had lost his two children—one from cholera in a few hours, and the other from consumption—St. Petersburg became doubly repugnant to him.

My brother did not take part in our work of agitation. He did not believe in the possibility of a popular uprising, and he conceived a revolution only as the action of a representative body, like the National Assembly of France in 1789. As for the socialist agitation, he knew it only by means of public meetings and public speeches,—not as the secret, minute work of personal propaganda which we were carrying on. In England he would have sided with John Bright or with the Chartists. If he had been in Paris during the uprising of June, 1848, he would surely have fought with the last handful of workers behind the last barricade; but in the preparatory period he would have followed Louis Blanc or Ledru Rollin.

In Switzerland he settled at Zürich, and his sympathies went with the moderate wing of the International. Socialist on principle, he carried out his principles in his most frugal and laborious mode of living, toiling on passionately at his great scientific work,—the main purpose of his life,—a work which was to be a nineteenth-century counterpart to the famous *Tableau de la Nature* of the Encyclopædists. He soon became a close personal friend of the old refugee Colonel P. L. Lavróv, with whom he had very much in common in his Kantian philosophical views.

When he learned about my arrest, Alexander immediately left everything,—the work of his life, the life itself of freedom which was as necessary for him as free air is necessary for a bird,—and returned to St. Petersburg, which he disliked, only to help me through my imprisonment.

We were both very much affected at this interview. My brother was extremely excited. He hated the very sight of the blue uniforms of the gendarmes,—those executioners of all independent thought in Russia,—and expressed his feeling frankly in their presence. As for me, the sight of him at St. Petersburg filled me with the most dismal apprehensions. I was happy to see his honest face, his eyes full of love, and to hear that I should see them once a month; and yet I wished him hundreds of miles away from that place to which he came free that day, but to which he would inevitably be brought some night under an escort of gendarmes. "Why did you come into the lion's den? Go back at once!" my whole inner self cried; and yet I knew that he would remain as long as I was in prison.

He understood better than any one else that inactivity would kill me, and had already made application to obtain for me permission to resume work. The Geographical Society wanted me to finish my book on the glacial period, and my brother turned the whole scientific world in St. Petersburg upside down to move it to support his application. The Academy of Sciences was interested in the matter; and finally, two or three months after my imprisonment, the governor entered my cell and announced to me that I was permitted by the Emperor to complete my report to the Geographical Society, and that I should be allowed pen and ink for that purpose. "Till sunset only," he added. Sunset, at St. Petersburg, is at three in the afternoon, in winter time; but that could not be helped. "Till sunset" were the words used by Alexander II. when he granted the permission.

II

So I could work!

I could hardly express now the immensity of relief I then felt at being enabled to resume writing. I would have consented to live on nothing but bread and water, in the dampest of cellars, if only permitted to work.

I was, however, the only prisoner to whom writing materials were allowed. Several of my comrades spent three years and more in confinement before the famous trial of "the hundred and ninety-three" took place, and all they had was a slate. Of course, even the slate was welcome in that dreary loneliness, and they used it to write exercises in the languages they were learning, or to work out mathematical problems; but what was jotted down on the slate could last only a few hours.

My prison life now took on a more regular character. There was something immediate to live for. At nine in the morning I had already made the first three hundred pacings across my cell, and was waiting for my pencils and pens to be delivered to me. The work which I had prepared for the Geographical Society contained, beside a report of my explorations in Finland, a discussion of the bases upon which the glacial hypothesis ought to rest. Now, knowing that I had plenty of time before me, I decided to rewrite and enlarge that part of my work. The Academy of Sciences put its admirable library at my service, and a corner of my cell soon filled up with books and maps, including the whole of the Swedish Geological Survey publications, a nearly complete collection of reports of all arctic travels, and whole sets of the *Quarterly Journal* of the London Geological Society. My book grew in the fortress to the size of two large volumes. The first of them was printed by my brother and Poliakóv (in the Geographical Society's *Memoirs*); while the second, not quite finished, remained in the hands of the Third Section when I ran away. The manuscript was found only in 1895, and given to the Russian Geographical Society, by whom it was forwarded to me in London.

At five in the afternoon,—at three in the winter,—as soon as the tiny lamp was brought in, my pencils and pens were taken away, and I had to stop work. Then I used to read, mostly books of history. Quite a library had been formed in the fortress by the generations of political prisoners who had been confined there. I was allowed to add to the library a number of staple works on Russian history, and with the books which were brought to me by my relatives I was enabled to read almost every work and collection of acts and documents bearing on the Moscow period of the history of Russia. I relished, in reading, not only the Russian annals, especially the admirable annals of the democratic mediæval republic of Pskov,— the best, perhaps, in Europe for the history of that type of mediæval cities,—but all sorts of dry documents, and even the Lives of the Saints, which occasionally contain facts of the real life of the masses which cannot be found elsewhere. I also read during this time a great number of novels, and even arranged for myself a treat on Christmas Eve. My relatives managed to send me then the Christmas stories of Dickens, and I spent the festival laughing and crying over those beautiful creations of the great novelist.

III

The worst was the silence, as of the grave, which reigned about me. In vain I knocked on the walls and struck the floor with my foot, listening for the faintest sound in reply. None was to be heard. One month passed, then two, three, fifteen months, but there was no reply to my knocks. We were only six then, scattered among thirty-six casemates,—all my arrested comrades being kept in the Litóvsky Zámok prison. When the non-commissioned officer entered my cell to take me out for a walk, and I asked him, "What kind of weather have we? Does it rain?" he cast a furtive side glance at me, and without saying a word promptly retired behind the door, where a sentry and another noncommissioned officer kept watch upon him. The only living being from whom I could hear even a few words was the governor, who came to my cell every morning to say "good-morning" and ask whether I wanted to buy tobacco or paper. I tried to engage him in conversation; but he also cast furtive glances at the noncommissioned officers who stood in the half-opened door, as if to say, "You see, I am watched, too." Only the pigeons were not afraid to hold intercourse with me. Every morning and afternoon they came to my window to receive their food through the grating.

There were no sounds whatever except the squeak of the sentry's boots, the hardly perceptible noise of the shutter of the Judas, and the ringing of the bells on the fortress cathedral. They rang a "Lord save me" ("Góspodi pomílui") every quarter of an hour,—one, two, three, four times. Then, each hour, the big bell struck slowly, with long intervals between successive strokes. A lugubrious canticle followed, chimed by the bells, which at every sudden change of temperature went out of tune, making at such times a horrible cacophony which sounded like the ringing of bells at a burial. At the gloomy hour of midnight, the canticle, moreover, was followed by the discordant notes of a "God save the Tsar." The ringing lasted a full quarter of an hour; and no sooner had it come to an end than a new "Lord save me" announced to the sleepless prisoner that a quarter of an hour of his uselessly spent life had gone in the meantime, and that many quarters of an hour, and hours, and days, and months of the same vegetative life would pass, before his keepers, or maybe death, would release him.

Every morning I was taken out for a half-hour's walk in the prison yard. This yard was a small pentagon with a narrow pavement round it, and a little building—the bath house—in the middle. But I liked those walks.

The need of new impressions is so great in prison that, when I walked in our narrow yard, I always kept my eyes fixed upon the high gilt spire of the fortress cathedral. This was the only thing in my surroundings which changed its aspect, and I liked to see it glittering like pure gold when the sun shone from a clear blue sky, or assuming a fairy aspect when a light bluish haze lay upon the town, or becoming steel gray when dark clouds obscured the sky.

During these walks I occasionally saw the daughter of the governor, a girl of eighteen or nineteen, as she came out from her father's apartment and had to walk a few steps in our yard in order to reach the entrance gate, the only issue from the building. She always hurried along, with her eyes cast down, as if she felt ashamed of being the daughter of a jailer. Her younger brother, on the contrary, a cadet whom I also saw once or twice in the yard, always looked straight in my face with such a frank expression of sympathy that I was struck with it and even mentioned it to some one after my release. Four or five years later, when he was already an officer, he was exiled to Siberia. He had joined the revolutionary party, and must have helped, I suppose, to carry on correspondence with prisoners in the fortress.

Winter is gloomy at St. Petersburg for those who cannot be out in the brightly lighted streets. It was still gloomier, of course, in a casemate. But dampness was even worse than darkness. The casemates are so damp that in order to drive away moisture they must be overheated, and I felt almost suf-

focated; but when at last I obtained my request, that the temperature should be kept lower than before, the outer wall became dripping with moisture, and the paper was as if a pail
of water had been poured upon it every day,—the consequence being that I suffered a great deal from rheumatism.

With all that I was cheerful, continuing to write and to draw
maps in the darkness, sharpening my lead pencils with a
broken piece of glass which I had managed to get hold of in
the yard; I faithfully walked my five miles a day in the cell,
and performed gymnastic feats with my oak stool. Time went
on. But then sorrow crept into my cell and nearly broke me
down. My brother Alexander was arrested.

Toward the end of December, 1874, I was allowed an interview with him and our sister Hélène, in the fortress, in the
presence of a gendarme officer. Interviews, granted at long
intervals, always bring both the prisoner and his relatives into
a state of excitement. One sees beloved faces and hears beloved
voices, knowing that the vision will last but a few moments;
one feels so near to the other, and yet so far off, as there
can be no intimate conversation before a stranger, an enemy
and a spy. Besides, my brother and sister felt anxious for my
health, upon which the dark, gloomy winter days and the
dampness had already marked their first effects. We parted
with heavy hearts.

A week after that interview I received, instead of an expected letter from my brother concerning the printing of my
book, a short note from Poliakóv. He informed me that hence-
forward he would read the proofs, and that I should have to
address to him everything relative to the printing. From the
very tone of the note I understood at once that something
must be wrong with my brother. If it were only illness, Poliakóv
would have mentioned it. Days of fearful anxiety came upon
me. Alexander must have been arrested, and I must have been
the cause of it! Life suddenly ceased to have any meaning for
me. My walks, my gymnastics, my work, lost interest. All the
day long I went ceaselessly up and down my cell, thinking of
nothing but Alexander's arrest. For me, an unmarried man, imprisonment was only personal inconvenience; but he was married, he passionately loved his wife, and they now had a boy,

upon whom they had concentrated all the love that they had felt for their first two children.

Worst of all was the incertitude. What could he have done? For what reason had he been arrested? What were they going to do with him? Weeks passed; my anxiety became deeper and deeper; but there was no news, till at last I heard in a roundabout way that he had been arrested for a letter written to P. L. Lavróv.

I learned the details much later. After his last interview with me he wrote to his old friend, who at that time was editing a Russian socialist review, *Forward!*, in London. He mentioned in this letter his fears about my health; he spoke of the many arrests which were then being made in Russia; and he freely expressed his hatred of the despotic rule. The letter was intercepted at the post-office by the Third Section, and they came on Christmas Eve to search his apartments. They carried out their search in an even more brutal manner than usual. After midnight half a dozen men made an irruption into his flat, and turned everything upside down. The very walls were examined; the sick child was taken out of its bed, that the bedding and the mattresses might be inspected. They found nothing,—there was nothing to find.

My brother very much resented this search. With his customary frankness, he said to the gendarme officer who conducted it: "Against you, captain, I have no grievance. You have received little education, and you hardly understand what you are doing. But you, sir," he continued, turning towards the procureur, "you know what part you are playing in these proceedings. You have received a university education. You know the law, and you know that you are trampling all law, such as it is, under your feet, and covering the lawlessness of these men by your presence; you are simply—a scoundrel!"

They swore hatred against him. They kept him imprisoned in the Third Section till May. My brother's child—a charming boy, whom illness had rendered still more affectionate and intelligent—was dying from consumption. The doctors said he had only a few days more to live. Alexander, who had never asked any favor of his enemies, asked them this time to permit him to see his child for the last time. He begged to be allowed to go home for one hour, upon his word of honor to return, or to be taken there under escort. They refused. They could not deny themselves that vengeance.

The child died, and its mother was thrown once more into a state bordering on insanity when my brother was told that he was to be transported to East Siberia, to a small town, Minusínsk. He would travel in a cart between two gendarmes, and his wife might follow later, but could not travel with him.

"Tell me, at least, what is my crime," he demanded; but there was no accusation of any sort against him beyond the letter.[14] This transportation appeared so arbitrary, so much an act of mere revenge on the part of the Third Section, that none of our relatives could believe that the exile would last more than a few months. My brother lodged a complaint with the minister of the interior. The reply was that the minister could not interfere with the will of the chief of the gendarmes. Another complaint was lodged with the Senate. It was of no avail.

A couple of years later our sister Hélène, acting on her own initiative, wrote a petition to the Tsar. Our cousin Dmítri, governor-general of Khárkov, aide-de-camp of the Emperor, and a favorite at the court, also deeply incensed at this treatment by the Third Section, handed the petition personally to the Tsar, and in so doing added a few words in support of it. But the vindictiveness of the Románovs was a family trait strongly developed in Alexander II. He wrote upon the petition, "Pust posidít" (Let him remain some time more). My brother stayed in Siberia twelve years, and never returned to Russia.

IV

The countless arrests which were made in the summer of 1874, and the serious turn which was given by the police to the prosecution of our circle, produced a deep change in the opinions of Russian youth. Up to that time the prevailing idea had been to pick out among the workers, and eventually the peasants, a number of men who should be prepared to become socialistic agitators. But the factories were now flooded with spies, and it was evident that, do what they might, both propagandists and workers would very soon be arrested and hidden forever in Siberia. Then began a great movement "to the people" in a new form, when several hundred young men and women, disregarding all precautions hitherto taken, rushed to the country, and, traveling through the towns and villages, incited the masses to revolution, almost openly distributing pamphlets, songs, and proclamations. In our circles this summer received the name of "the mad summer."

The gendarmes lost their heads. They had not hands enough to make the arrest nor eyes enough to trace the steps of every propagandist. Yet not less than fifteen hundred persons were arrested during this hunt, and half of them were kept in prison for years.

One day in the summer of 1875, in the cell that was next to mine, I distinctly heard the light steps of heeled boots, and a few minutes later I caught fragments of a conversation. A feminine voice spoke from the cell, and a deep bass voice— evidently that of the sentry—grunted something in reply. Then I recognized the sound of the colonel's spurs, his rapid steps, his swearing at the sentry, and the click of the key in the lock. He said something, and a feminine voice loudly replied: "We did not talk. I only asked him to call the noncommissioned officer." Then the door was locked, and I heard the colonel swearing in whispers at the sentry.

So I was alone no more. I had a lady neighbor, who at once broke down the severe discipline which had hitherto reigned amongst the soldiers. From that day the walls of the fortress, which had been mute during the last fifteen months, became animated. From all sides I heard knocks with the foot on the floor: one, two, three, four, . . . eleven knocks, twenty-four knocks, fifteen knocks; then an interruption, followed by three knocks and a long succession of thirty-three knocks. Over and over again these knocks were repeated in the same succession, until the neighbor would guess at last that they were meant for "Kto vy?" (Who are you?) the letter *v* being the third letter in our alphabet. Thereupon conversation was soon established, and usually was conducted in the abridged alphabet; that is, the alphabet being divided into six rows of five letters, each letter is marked by its row and its place in the row.

I discovered with great pleasure that I had at my left my friend Serdiukóv, with whom I could soon talk about everything, especially when we used our cipher. But intercourse with men brought its sufferings as well as its joys. Underneath me was lodged a peasant, whom Serdiukóv knew. He talked to him by means of knocks; and even against my will, often unconsciously during my work, I followed their conversations. I also spoke to him. Now, if solitary confinement without any sort of work is hard for educated men, it is infinitely harder for a peasant who is accustomed to physical work, and not at all wont to spend years in reading. Our peasant friend felt quite miserable, and having been kept for nearly two years in another prison before he was brought to the fortress,—his crime was that he had listened to socialists,—he was already broken down. Soon I began to notice, to my terror, that from time to time his mind wandered. Gradually his thoughts grew more and more confused, and we two perceived, step by step, day by day, evidences that his reason was failing, until his talk became at last that of a lunatic. Frightful noises and wild cries came next from the lower story; our neighbor was mad, but was still kept for several months in the casemate before he was removed to an asylum, from which he never emerged. To witness the destruction of a man's mind, under such conditions, was terrible. I am sure it must have contributed to increase the nervous irritability of my good and true friend Serdiukóv. When, after four years of imprisonment, he was acquitted by the court and released, he shot himself.

One day I received a quite unexpected visit. The Grand Duke Nicholas, brother of Alexander II., who was inspecting the fortress, entered my cell, followed only by his aide-de-camp. The door was shut behind him. He rapidly approached me, saying, "Good-day, Kropótkin." He knew me personally, and spoke in a familiar, good-natured tone, as to an old acquaintance. "How is it possible, Kropótkin, that you, a page de chambre, a sergeant of the corps of pages, should be mixed up in this business, and now be here in this horrible casemate?"

"Every one has his own opinions," was my reply.

"Opinions! So your opinions were that you must stir up a revolution?"

What was I to reply? Yes? Then the construction which would be put upon my answer would be that I, who had refused to give any answers to the gendarmes, "avowed everything" before the brother of the Tsar. His tone was that of a commander of a military school when trying to obtain "avowals" from a cadet. Yet I could not say No: it would have been a lie. I did not know what to say, and stood without saying anything.

"You see! You feel ashamed of it now"—

This remark angered me, and I at once said in a rather sharp way, "I have given my replies to the examining magistrate, and have nothing to add."

"But understand, Kropótkin, please," he said then, in the most familiar tone, "that I don't speak to you as an examining magistrate. I speak quite as a private person,—quite as a private man," he repeated, lowering his voice.

Thoughts went whirling in my head. To play the part of Marquis Posa? To tell the Emperor through the grand duke of the desolation of Russia, the ruin of the peasantry, the arbitrariness of the officials, the terrible famines in prospect? To say that we wanted to help the peasants out of their desperate condition, to make them raise their heads, and by all this try to influence Alexander II.? These thoughts followed one another in rapid succession, till at last I said to myself: "Never! Nonsense! They know all that. They are enemies of the nation, and such talk would not change them."

I replied that he always remained an official person, and that I could not look upon him as a private man.

He then began to ask me indifferent questions. "Was it not in Siberia, with the Decembrists, that you began to entertain such ideas?"

"No; I knew only one Decembrist, and with him I had no talks worth speaking of."

"Was it then at St. Petersburg that you got them?"

"I was always the same."

"Why! Were you such in the Corps of Pages?" he asked me with terror.

"In the corps I was a boy, and what is indefinite in boyhood grows definite in manhood."

He asked me some other similar questions, and as he spoke I distinctly saw what he was driving at. He was trying to obtain avowals, and my imagination vividly pictured him saying to his brother: "All these examining magistrates are imbeciles. He gave them no replies, but I talked to him ten minutes, and he told me everything." That began to annoy me; and when he said to me something to this effect, "How could you have anything to do with all these people,—peasants and people with no names?"—I sharply turned upon him and said, "I have told you already that I have given my replies to the examining magistrate." Then he abruptly left the cell.

Later, the soldiers of the guard made quite a legend of that visit. The person who came in a carriage to carry me away at the time of my escape wore a military cap, and, having sandy whiskers, bore a faint resemblance to the Grand Duke Nicholas. So a tradition grew up amongst the soldiers of the St. Petersburg garrison that it was the grand duke himself who came to rescue me and kidnapped me. Thus are legends created even in times of newspapers and biographical dictionaries.

V

Two years had passed. Several of my comrades had died, several had become insane, but nothing was heard yet of our case coming before a court.

My health gave way before the end of the second year. The oak stool now seemed heavy in my hand, and the five miles became an endless distance. As there were about sixty of us in the fortress, and the winter days were short, we were taken out for a walk in the yard for twenty minutes only every third day. I did my best to maintain my energy, but the "arctic wintering" without an interruption in the summer got the better of me. I had brought back from my Siberian journeys slight symptoms of scurvy; now, in the darkness and dampness of the casemate, they developed more distinctly; that scourge of the prisons had got hold of me.

In March or April, 1876, we were at last told that the Third Section had completed the preliminary inquest. The "case" had been transmitted to the judicial authorities, and consequently we were removed to a prison attached to the court of justice,—the house of detention.

It was an immense show prison, recently built on the model of the French and Belgian prisons, consisting of four stories of small cells, each of which had a window overlooking an inner yard and a door opening on an iron balcony; the balconies of the several stories were connected by iron staircases.

For most of my comrades the transfer to this prison was a great relief. There was much more life in it than in the fortress; more opportunity for correspondence, for seeing one's relatives, and for mutual intercourse. Tapping on the walls continued all day long undisturbed, and I was able in this way to relate to a young neighbor the history of the Paris Commune from the beginning to the end. It took, however, a whole week's tapping.

As to my health, it grew even worse than it had lately been in the fortress. I could not bear the close atmosphere of the tiny cell, which measured only four steps from one corner to another, and where, as soon as the steampipes were set to work, the temperature changed from a glacial cold to an unbearable heat. Having to turn so often, I became giddy after a few minutes' walk, and ten minutes of outdoor exercise, in the corner of a yard inclosed between high brick walls, did not refresh me in the least. As to the prison doctor, who did not want to hear the word "scurvy" pronounced "in his prison," the less said of him the better.

I was allowed to receive food from home, it so happening that one of my relatives, married to a lawyer, lived a few doors from the court. But my digestion had become so bad that I was soon able to eat nothing but a small piece of bread and one or two eggs a day. My strength rapidly failed, and the general opinion was that I should not live more than a few months. When climbing the staircase which led to my cell in the second story, I had to stop two or three times to rest, and I remember an elderly soldier from the escort once commiserating me and saying, "Poor man, you won't live till the end of the summer."

My relatives now became very much alarmed. My sister Hélène tried to obtain my release on bail, but the procureur, Shúbin, replied to her, with a sardonic smile, "If you bring me a doctor's certificate that he will die in ten days, I will release him." He had the satisfaction of seeing my sister fall into a chair and sob aloud in his presence. She succeeded, however, in gaining her request that I should be visited by a good physician,—the chief doctor of the military hospital of the St. Petersburg garrison. He was a bright, intelligent, aged general, who examined me in the most scrupulous manner, and concluded that I had no organic disease, but was suffering simply from a want of oxidation of the blood. "Air is all that you want," he said. Then he stood a few moments in hesitation, and added in a decided manner, "No use talking, you cannot remain here; you must be transferred."

Some ten days later I was transferred to the military hospital, which is situated on the outskirts of St. Petersburg, and has a special small prison for the officers and soldiers who fall ill when they are under trial. Two of my comrades had already been removed to this hospital prison, when it was certain that they would soon die of consumption.

In the hospital I began at once to recover. I was given a spacious room on the ground floor, close by the room of the military guard. It had an immense grated window looking south, which opened on a small boulevard with two rows of trees; and beyond the boulevard there was a wide space where two hundred carpenters were engaged in building wooden shanties for typhoid patients. Every evening they gave an hour or so to singing in chorus,—such a chorus as is formed only in large carpenters' artéls. A sentry marched up and down the boulevard, his box standing opposite my room.

My window was kept open all the day, and I battened in the rays of the sun, which I had missed for such a long time. I breathed the balmy air of May with a full chest, and my health improved rapidly,—too rapidly, I began to think. I was soon able to digest light food, gained strength, and resumed my work with renewed energy. Seeing no way in which I could finish the second volume of my work, I wrote a résumé of it, which was printed in the first volume.

In the fortress I had heard from a comrade who had been in the hospital prison that it would not be hard for me to escape from it, and I made my presence there known to my friends. However, escape proved far more difficult than I had been led to believe. A stricter supervision than had ever before been heard of was exercised over me. The sentry in the passage was placed at my door, and I was never let out of my room. The hospital soldiers and the officers of the guard who occasionally entered it seemed to be afraid to stay more than a minute or two.

Various plans were made by my friends to liberate me,—some of them very amusing. I was, for instance, to file through the iron bars of my window. Then, on a rainy night, when the sentry on the boulevard was dozing in his box, two friends were to creep up from behind and overturn the box, so that it would fall upon the sentry and catch him like a mouse in a trap, without hurting him. In the meantime, I was to jump out of the window. But a better solution came in an unexpected way.

"Ask to be let out for a walk," one of the soldiers whispered to me one day. I did so. The doctor supported my demand, and every afternoon, at four, I was allowed to take an hour's walk in the prison yard. I had to keep on the green flannel dressing-gown which is worn by the hospital patients, but my boots, my vest, and my trousers were delivered to me every day.

I shall never forget my first walk. When I was taken out, I saw before me a yard full three hundred paces long and more than two hundred paces wide, all covered with grass. The gate was open, and through it I could see the street, the immense hospital opposite, and the people who passed by. I stopped on the doorsteps of the prison, unable for a moment to move when I saw that yard and that gate.

At one end of the yard stood the prison,—a narrow building, about one hundred and fifty paces long,—at each end of which was a sentry box. The two sentries paced up and down in front of the building, and had tramped out a footpath in the green. Along this footpath I was told to walk, and the two sentries continued to walk up and down,—so that I was never more than ten or fifteen paces from the one or the other. Three hospital soldiers took their seats on the doorsteps.

At the opposite end of this spacious yard wood for fuel was being unloaded from a dozen carts, and piled up along the wall by a dozen peasants. The whole yard was inclosed by a high fence made of thick boards. Its gate was open to let the carts in and out.

This open gate fascinated me. "I must not stare at it," I said to myself; and yet I looked at it all the time. As soon as I was taken back to my cell I wrote to my friends to communicate to them the welcome news. "I feel well-nigh unable to use the cipher," I wrote with a tremulous hand, tracing almost illegible signs instead of figures. "This nearness of liberty makes me tremble as if I were in a fever. They took me out to-day in the yard; its gate was open, and no sentry near it. Through this unguarded gate I will run out; my sentries will not catch me,"—and I gave the plan of the escape. "A lady is to come in an open carriage to the hospital. She is to alight, and the carriage to wait for her in the street, some fifty paces from the gate. When I am taken out, at four, I shall walk for a while with my hat in my hand, and somebody who passes by the gate will take it as the signal that all is right within the prison. Then you must return a signal: 'The street is clear.' Without it I shall not start; once beyond the gate I must not be recaptured. Light or sound only can be used for your signal. The coachman may send a flash of light,—the sun's rays reflected from his lacquered hat upon the main hospital building; or, still better, the sound of a song continued as long as the street is clear; unless you can occupy the little gray bungalow which I see from the yard, and signal to me from its window. The sentry will run after me like a dog after a hare, describing a curve, while I run in a straight line, and I *will* keep five or ten paces in advance of him. In the street, I shall spring into the carriage and we shall gallop away. If the sentry shoots—well, that cannot be helped; it lies beyond our foresight; and then, against a certain death in prison, the thing is well worth the risk."

Counter proposals were made, but that plan was ultimately adopted. The matter was taken in hand by our circle; people who never had known me entered into it, as if it were the release of the dearest of their brothers. However, the attempt was beset with difficulties, and time went with terrible rapidity. I worked hard, writing late at night; but my health improved, nevertheless, at a speed which I found appalling. When I was let out into the yard for the first time, I could only creep like a tortoise along the footpath; now I felt strong enough to run. True, I continued to go at the same tortoise pace, lest my walks should be stopped; but my natural vivacity might betray me at any moment. And my comrades, in the meantime, had to enlist more than a score of people in the affair, to find a reliable horse and an experienced coachman, and to arrange hundreds of unforeseen details which always spring up around such conspiracies. The preparations took a month or so, and any day I might be moved back to the house of detention.

At last the day of the escape was settled. June 29, Old Style, is the day of St. Peter and St. Paul. My friends, throwing a touch of sentimentalism into their enterprise, wanted to set me free on that day. They had let me know that in reply to my signal "All right within" they would signal "All right outside" by sending up a red toy balloon. Then the carriage would come, and a song would be sung to let me know when the street was open.

I went out on the 29th, took off my hat, and waited for the balloon. But nothing of the kind was to be seen. Half an hour passed. I heard the rumble of a carriage in the street; I heard a man's voice singing a song unknown to me; but there was no balloon.

The hour was over, and with a broken heart I returned to my room. "Something must have gone wrong," I said to myself.

The impossible had happened that day. Hundreds of children's balloons are always on sale in St. Petersburg, near the Gostínoi Dvor. That morning there were none; not a single balloon was to be found. One was discovered at last, in the possession of a child, but it was old and would not fly. My friends rushed then to an optician's shop, bought an apparatus for making hydrogen, and filled the balloon with it; but it would not fly any better: the hydrogen had not been dried. Time pressed. Then a lady attached the balloon to her umbrella, and, holding the umbrella high over her head, walked up and down in the street along the high wall of our yard; but I saw nothing of it,—the wall being too high, and the lady too short.

As it turned out, nothing could have been better than that accident with the balloon. When the hour of my walk had passed, the carriage was driven along the streets which it was intended to follow after the escape; and there, in a narrow street, it was stopped by a dozen or more carts which were carrying wood to the hospital. The horses of the carts got into disorder,—some of them on the right side of the street, and some on the left,—and the carriage had to make its way at a slow pace amongst them; at a turning it was actually blocked. If I had been in it, we should have been caught.

Now a whole system of signals was established along the streets through which we should have to go after the escape, in order to give notice if the streets were not clear. For a couple of miles from the hospital my comrades took the position of sentries. One was to walk up and down with a handkerchief in his hand, which at the approach of the carts he was to put into his pocket; another was to sit on a stone and eat cherries, stopping when the carts came near; and so on. All these signals, transmitted along the streets, were finally to reach the carriage. My friends had also hired the gray bungalow that I had seen from the yard, and at an open window of that little house a violinist stood with his violin, ready to play when the signal "Street clear" reached him.

The attempt had been settled for the next day. Further postponement would have been dangerous. In fact, the carriage had been taken notice of by the hospital people, and something suspicious must have reached the ears of the authorities, as on the night before my escape I heard the patrol officer ask the sentry who stood opposite my window, "Where are your ball cartridges?" The soldier began to take them in a clumsy way out of his cartridge pouch, spending a couple of minutes before he got them. The patrol officer swore at him. "Have you not been told to-night to keep four ball cartridges in the pocket of your coat?" And he stood by the sentry till the latter put four cartridges into his pocket. "Look sharp!" he said as he turned away.

The new arrangements concerning the signals had to be communicated to me at once; and at two on the next day a lady—a dear relative of mine[15]—came to the prison, asking that a watch might be transmitted to me. Everything had to go through the hands of the procureur; but as this was simply a watch, without a box, it was passed along. In it was a tiny cipher note which contained the whole plan. When I read it I was seized with terror, so daring was the feat. The lady, herself under pursuit by the police for political reasons, would have been arrested on the spot, if any one had chanced to open the lid of the watch. But I saw her calmly leave the prison and move slowly along the boulevard.

I came out at four, as usual, and gave my signal. I heard next the rumble of the carriage, and a few minutes later the tones of the violin in the gray house sounded through our yard. But I was then at the other end of the building. When I got back to the end of my path which was nearest the gate,— about a hundred paces from it,—the sentry was close upon my heels. "One turn more," I thought—but before I reached the farther end of the path the violin suddenly ceased playing.

More than a quarter of an hour passed, full of anxiety, be- fore I understood the cause of the interruption. Then a dozen heavily loaded carts entered the gate and moved to the other end of the yard.

Immediately, the violinist—a good one, I must say—began a wildly exciting mazurka from Kontsky, as if to say, "Straight on now,—this is your time!" I moved slowly to the nearer end of the footpath, trembling at the thought that the mazurka might stop before I reached it.

When I was there I turned round. The sentry had stopped five or six paces behind me; he was looking the other way. "Now or never!" I remember that thought flashing through my head. I flung off my green flannel dressing-gown and began to run.

For many days in succession I had practiced how to get rid of that immeasurably long and cumbrous garment. It was so long that I carried the lower part on my left arm, as ladies carry the trains of their riding habits. Do what I might, it would not come off in one movement. I cut the seams under the armpits, but that did not help. Then I decided to learn to throw it off in two movements: one casting the end from my arm, the other dropping the gown on the floor. I practiced patiently in my room until I could do it as neatly as soldiers handle their rifles. "One, two," and it was on the ground.

I did not trust much to my vigor, and began to run rather slowly, to economize my strength. But no sooner had I taken a few steps than the peasants who were piling the wood at the other end shouted, "He runs! Stop him! Catch him!" and they hastened to intercept me at the gate. Then I flew for my life. I thought of nothing but running,—not even of the pit which the carts had dug out at the gate. Run! run! full speed!

The sentry, I was told later by the friends who witnessed the scene from the gray house, ran after me, followed by three soldiers who had been sitting on the doorsteps. The sentry was so near to me that he felt sure of catching me. Several times he flung his rifle forward, trying to give me a blow in the back with the bayonet. One moment my friends in the window thought he had me. He was so convinced that he could stop me in this way that he did not fire. But I kept my distance, and he had to give up at the gate.

Safe out of the gate, I perceived, to my terror, that the carriage was occupied by a civilian who wore a military cap. He sat without turning his head to me. "Sold!" was my first thought. The comrades had written in their last letter, "Once in the street, don't give yourself up: there will be friends to defend you in case of need," and I did not want to jump into the carriage if it was occupied by an enemy. However, as I got nearer to the carriage I noticed that the man in it had sandy whiskers which seemed to be those of a warm friend of mine. He did not belong to our circle, but we were personal friends, and on more than one occasion I had learned to know his admirable, daring courage, and how his strength suddenly became herculean when there was danger at hand. "Why should he be there? Is it possible?" I reflected, and was going to shout out his name, when I caught myself in good time, and instead clapped my hands, while still running, to attract his attention. He turned his face to me—and I knew who it was.[16]

"Jump in, quick, quick!" he shouted in a terrible voice, calling me and the coachman all sorts of names, a revolver in his hand and ready to shoot. "Gallop! gallop! I will kill you!" he cried to the coachman. The horse—a beautiful racing trotter, which had been bought on purpose—started at full gallop. Scores of voices yelling, "Hold them! Get them!" resounded behind us, my friend meanwhile helping me to put on an elegant overcoat and an opera hat. But the real danger was not

so much in the pursuers as in a soldier who was posted at the
gate of the hospital, about opposite to the spot where the carriage had to wait. He could have prevented my jumping into
the carriage, or could have stopped the horse, by simply rushing a few steps forward. A friend was consequently commis-
sioned to divert this soldier by talking. He did this most successfully. The soldier having been employed at one time in the
laboratory of the hospital, my friend gave a scientific turn to
their chat, speaking about the microscope and the wonderful
things one sees through it. Referring to a certain parasite of the
human body, he asked, "Did you ever see what a formidable
tail it has?" "What, man, a tail?" "Yes, it has; under the
microscope it is as big as that." "Don't tell me any of your
tales!" retorted the soldier. "I know better. It was the first thing
I looked at under the microscope." This animated discussion
took place just as I ran past them and sprang into the carriage.
It sounds like fable, but it is fact.

The carriage turned sharply into a narrow lane, past the
same wall of the yard where the peasants had been piling
wood, and which all of them had now deserted in their run
after me. The turn was so sharp that the carriage was nearly
upset, when I flung myself inward, dragging toward me my
friend; this sudden movement righted the carriage.

We trotted through the narrow lane and then turned to the
left. Two gendarmes were standing there at the door of a
public house, and gave to the military cap of my companion
the military salute. "Hush! hush!" I said to him, for he was
still terribly excited. "All goes well; the gendarmes salute us!"
The coachman thereupon turned his face toward me, and I
recognized in him another friend, who smiled with happiness.

Everywhere we saw friends, who winked to us or gave us a
Godspeed as we passed at the full trot of our beautiful horse.
Then we entered the large Nevsky Prospekt, turned into a side
street, and alighted at a door, sending away the coachman. I
ran up a staircase, and at its top fell into the arms of my
sister-in-law, who had been waiting in painful anxiety. She
laughed and cried at the same time, bidding me hurry to put
on another dress and to crop my conspicuous beard. Ten minutes later my friend and I left the house and took a cab.

In the meantime, the officer of the guard at the prison and

the hospital soldiers had rushed out into the street, doubtful
as to what measures they should take. There was not a cab for
a mile round, every one having been hired by my friends. An
old peasant woman from the crowd was wiser than all the lot.
"Poor people," she said, as if talking to herself, "they are sure
to come out on the Prospekt, and there they will be caught if
somebody runs along that lane, which leads straight to the
Prospekt." She was quite right, and the officer ran to the tram-
way car that stood close by, and asked the men to let them
have their horses to send somebody on horseback to intercept
us. But the men obstinately refused to give up their horses,
and the officer did not use force.

As to the violinist and the lady who had taken the gray
house, they too rushed out and joined the crowd with the
old woman, whom they heard giving advice, and when the
crowd dispersed they went away also.

It was a fine afternoon. We drove to the islands where all
the St. Petersburg aristocracy goes on bright spring days to
see the sunset, and called on the way, in a remote street, at a
barber's shop to shave off my beard, which operation changed
me, of course, but not very much. We drove aimlessly up and
down the islands, but, having been told not to reach our night
quarters till late in the evening, did not know where to go.
"What shall we do in the meantime?" I asked my friend. He
also pondered over that question. "To Donon!" he suddenly
called out to the cabman, naming one of the best St. Petersburg
restaurants. "No one will ever think of looking for you at
Donon," he calmly remarked. "They will hunt for you everywhere else, but not there; and we shall have a dinner, and a
drink too, in honor of the success of your escape."

What could I reply to so reasonable a suggestion? So we
went to Donon, passed the halls flooded with light and
crowded with visitors at the dinner hour, and took a separate
room, where we spent the evening till the time came when we
were expected. The house where we had first alighted was
searched less than two hours after we left, as were also the
apartments of nearly all our friends. Nobody thought of making a search at Donon.

A couple of days later I was to take possession of an apartment which had been engaged for me, and which I could

occupy under a false passport. But the lady who was to accompany me there in a carriage took the precaution of visiting the house first by herself. It was thickly surrounded by spies. So many of my friends had come to inquire whether I was safe there that the suspicions of the police had been aroused. Moreover, my portrait had been printed by the Third Section, and hundreds of copies had been distributed to policemen and watchmen. All the detectives who knew me by sight were looking for me in the streets; while those who did not were accompanied by soldiers and warders who had seen me during my imprisonment. The Tsar was furious that such an escape should have taken place in his capital in full daylight, and had given the order, "He *must* be found."

It was impossible to remain at St. Petersburg, and I concealed myself in country houses in its neighborhood. In company with half a dozen friends, I stayed at a village frequented at this time of the year by St. Petersburg people bent on picnicking. Then it was decided that I should go abroad. But from a foreign paper we had learned that all the frontier stations and railway termini in the Baltic provinces and Finland were closely watched by detectives who knew me by sight. So I determined to travel in a direction where I should be least expected. Armed with the passport of a friend, and accompanied by another friend, I crossed Finland, and went northward to a remote port on the Gulf of Bothnia, whence I crossed to Sweden.

After I had gone on board the steamer, and it was about to sail, the friend who was to accompany me to the frontier told me the St. Petersburg news, which he had promised our friends not to tell me before. My sister Hélène had been arrested, as well as the sister of my brother's wife, who had visited me in prison once a month after my brother and his wife went to Siberia.

My sister knew absolutely nothing of the preparations for my escape. Only after I had escaped a friend had hurried to her, to tell her the welcome news. She protested her ignorance in vain: she was taken from her children, and was kept imprisoned for a fortnight. As to the sister of my brother's wife, she had known vaguely that something was to be attempted, but she had had no part in the preparations. Common sense

ought to have shown the authorities that a person who had
officially visited me in prison would not be involved in such an
affair. Nevertheless, she was kept in prison for over two
months. Her husband, a well-known lawyer, vainly endeavored
to obtain her release. "We are aware now," he was told by the
gendarme officers, "that she has had nothing to do with the
escape; but, you see, we reported to the Emperor, on the day
we arrested her, that the person who had organized the escape
was discovered and arrested. It will now take some time to
prepare the Emperor to accept the idea that she is not the
real culprit."

I crossed Sweden without stopping anywhere, and went to
Christiania, where I waited a few days for a steamer to sail
for Hull, gathering information in the meantime about the
peasant party of the Norwegian Storthing. As I went to the
steamer I asked myself with anxiety, "Under which flag does
she sail,—Norwegian, German, English?" Then I saw floating
above the stern the union jack,—the flag under which so many
refugees, Russian, Italian, French, Hungarian, and of all nations, have found an asylum. I greeted that flag from the depth
of my heart.

❖　❖　❖　❖　❖　❖　❖　❖　❖　❖　❖　❖　❖　❖　❖　❖

PART SIX

WESTERN EUROPE

I

A storm raged in the North Sea, as we approached the coasts
of England. But I met the storm with delight. I enjoyed the
struggle of our steamer against the furiously rolling waves,
and sat for hours on the stem, the foam of the waves dashing
into my face. After the two years that I had spent in a gloomy
casemate, every fiber of my inner self seemed to be throbbing
and eager to enjoy the full intensity of life.

My intention was not to stay abroad more than a few weeks
or months: just enough time to allow the hue and cry caused
by my escape to subside, and also to restore my health a little.
I landed under the name of Levashóv, the name which I had
used in leaving Russia; and avoiding London, where the spies
of the Russian embassy would soon have been at my heels, I
went first to Edinburgh.

It has so happened, however, that I have never returned to
Russia. I was soon taken up by the wave of the anarchist movement, which was just then rising in Western Europe; and I
felt that I should be more useful in helping that movement to
find its proper expression than I could possibly be in Russia.
In my mother country I was too well known to carry on an
open propaganda, especially among the workers and the peasants; and later on, when the Russian movement became a conspiracy and an armed struggle against the representative of
autocracy, all thought of a popular movement was necessarily
abandoned; while my own inclinations drew me more and
more intensely toward casting in my lot with the laboring and
toiling masses. To bring to them such conceptions as would
aid them to direct their efforts to the best advantage of all the
workers; to deepen and to widen the ideals and principles

which will underlie the coming social revolution; to develop these ideals and principles before the workers, not as an order coming from their leaders, but as a result of their own reason; and so to awaken their own initiative, now that they were called upon to appear in the historical arena as the builders of a new, equitable mode of organization of society,—this seemed to me as necessary for the development of mankind as anything I could accomplish in Russia at that time. Accordingly, I joined the few men who were working in that direction in Western Europe, relieving those of them who had been broken down by years of hard struggle.[17]

When I landed at Hull and went to Edinburgh, I informed but a few friends in Russia and in the Jura Federation of my safe arrival in England. A socialist must always rely upon his own work for his living, and consequently, as soon as I was settled in the Scotch capital, in a small room in the suburbs, I tried to find some work.

Among the passengers on board our steamer there was a Norwegian professor, with whom I talked, trying to remember the little that I formerly had known of the Swedish language. He spoke German. "But as you speak some Norwegian," he said to me, "and are trying to learn it, let us both speak it."

"You mean Swedish?" I ventured to ask. "I speak Swedish, don't I?"

"Well, I should say it is rather Norwegian; surely not Swedish," was his reply.

Thus happened to me what happened to one of Jules Verne's heroes, who had learned by mistake Portuguese instead of Spanish. At any rate, I talked a good deal with the professor,— let it be in Norwegian,—and he gave me a Christiania paper, which contained the reports of the Norwegian North Atlantic deep-sea expedition, just returned home.

As soon as I was at Edinburgh I wrote a note in English about these explorations, and sent it to *Nature*, which my brother and I used regularly to read at St. Petersburg from its first appearance. The sub-editor acknowledged the note with thanks, remarking with an extreme leniency, which I have often met with since in England, that my English was "all right," and only required to be made "a little more idiomatic."

I may say that I had learned English in Russia, and, with my brother, had translated Page's *Philosophy of Geology* and Herbert Spencer's *Principles of Biology*. But I had learned it from books, and pronounced it very badly, so that I had the greatest difficulty in making myself understood by my Scotch landlady; her daughter and I used to write on scraps of paper what we had to say to each other; and as I had no idea of idiomatic English, I must have made the most amusing mistakes. I remember, at any rate, protesting once to her, in writing, that it was not a "cup of tea" that I expected at tea time, but many cups. I am afraid my landlady took me for a glutton, but I must say, by way of apology, that neither in the geological books I had read in English nor in Spencer's *Biology* was there any allusion to such an important matter as tea-drinking.

I got from Russia the *Journal* of the Russian Geographical Society, and soon began to supply the *Times* also with occasional paragraphs about Russian geographical explorations. Przheválsky was at that time in Central Asia, and his progress was followed in England with interest.

However, the money I had brought with me was rapidly disappearing, and all my letters to Russia being intercepted, I could not succeed in making my address known to my relatives. So I moved in a few weeks to London, thinking I could find more regular work there. The old refugee, P. L. Lavróv, continued to edit at London his newspaper *Forward!*; but as I hoped soon to return to Russia, and the editorial office of the Russian paper must have been closely watched by spies, I did not go there.[18]

I went, very naturally, to the office of *Nature*, where I was most cordially received by the sub-editor, Mr. J. Scott Keltie. The editor wanted to increase the column of Notes, and found that I wrote them exactly as they were required. A table was consequently assigned me in the office, and scientific reviews in all possible languages were piled upon it. "Come every Monday, Mr. Levashóv," I was told, "look over these reviews, and if there is any article that strikes you as worthy of notice, write a note, or mark the article; we will send it to a specialist." Mr. Keltie did not know, of course, that I used to rewrite each note three or four times before I dared to submit my English to him; but taking the scientific reviews home, I soon managed very nicely, with my *Nature* notes and my *Times* paragraphs, to get a living. I found that the weekly payment, on Thursday, of the paragraph contributors to the *Times* was an excellent institution. To be sure, there were weeks when there was no interesting news from Przheválsky, and news from other parts of Russia was not found interesting; in such cases my fare was bread and tea only.

One day, however, Mr. Keltie took from the shelves several Russian books, asking me to review them for *Nature*. I looked at the books, and, to my embarrassment, saw that they were my own works on the *Glacial Period* and the *Orography of Asia*. My brother had not failed to send them to our favorite *Nature*. I was in great perplexity, and, putting the books into my bag, took them home, to reflect upon the matter. "What shall I do with them?" I asked myself. "I cannot praise them, because they are mine; and I cannot be too sharp on the author, as I hold the views expressed in them." I decided to take them back next day, and explain to Mr. Keltie that, although I had introduced myself under the name of Levashóv, I was the author of these books, and could not review them.

Mr. Keltie knew from the papers about Kropótkin's escape, and was very much pleased to discover the refugee safe in England. As to my scruples, he remarked wisely that I need neither scold nor praise the author, but could simply tell the readers what the books were about. From that day a friendship, which still continues, grew up between us.

In November or December, 1876, seeing in the letter-box of P. L. Lavróv's paper an invitation for "K." to call at the editorial office to receive a letter from Russia, and thinking that the invitation was for me, I called at the office, and soon established friendship with the editor and the younger people who printed the paper.

When I called for the first time at the office—my beard shaved and my "top" hat on—and asked the lady who opened the door, in my very best English, "Is Mr. Lavróv in?" I imagined that no one would ever know who I was, as I had not mentioned my name. It appeared, however, that the lady, who did not know me at all, but well knew my brother while he stayed at Zürich, at once recognized me and ran upstairs to say who the visitor was. "I knew you immediately," she said afterwards, "by your eyes, which have much in common with those of your brother."

That time I did not stay long in England. I had been in lively correspondence with my friend James Guillaume, of the Jura Federation, and as soon as I found some permanent geographical work, which I could do in Switzerland as well as in London, I removed to Switzerland. The letters that I got at last from home told me that I might as well stay abroad, as there was nothing in particular to be done in Russia. A wave of enthusiasm was rolling over the country, at that time, in favor of the Slavonians who had revolted against the age-long Turkish oppression, and my best friends, Sergéi (Stepniák), Klementz, and several others, had gone to the Balkan peninsula to join the insurgents. "We read," my friends wrote, "the correspondence of the *Daily News* about the horrors in Bulgaria; we weep at the reading, and go next to enlist either as volunteers in the Balkan insurgents' bands or as nurses."

II

During a stay at Paris I made my first acquaintance with Turgénev. He had expressed to our common friend P. L. Lavróv the desire to see me, and, as a true Russian, to celebrate my escape by a small friendly dinner. It was with a feeling almost of worship that I crossed the threshold of his room. If by his *Sportsman's Notebook* he rendered to Russia the immense service of throwing odium upon serfdom (I did not know at that time that he took a leading part in Hérzen's powerful *Bell*), he has rendered no less service through his later novels. He has shown what the Russian woman is, what treasuries of mind and heart she possesses, what she may be as an inspirer of men; and he has taught us how men who have a real claim to superiority look upon women, how they love. Upon me, and upon thousands of my contemporaries, this part of his teaching made an indelible impression, far more powerful than the best articles upon women's rights.

His appearance is well known. Tall, strongly built, the head covered with soft and thick gray hair, he was certainly beautiful; his eyes gleamed with intelligence, not devoid of a touch of humor, and his whole manner testified to that simplicity and absence of affectation which are characteristic of the best Russian writers. His fine head revealed a vast development of brain power, and when he died, and Paul Bert, with Paul Reclus (the surgeon), weighed his brain, it so much surpassed the heaviest brain then known,—that of Cuvier,—reaching something over two thousand gram, that they would not trust to their scales, but got new ones, to repeat the weighing.

His talk was especially remarkable. He spoke, as he wrote, in images. When he wanted to develop an idea, he did not resort to arguments, although he was a master in philosophical discussions; he illustrated his idea by a scene presented in a form as beautiful as if it had been taken out of one of his novels.[19]

"You must have had a great deal of experience in your life amongst Frenchmen, Germans, and other peoples," he said to me once. "Have you not remarked that there is a deep, unfathomable chasm between many of their conceptions and the views which we Russians hold on the same subjects,—that there are points upon which we can never agree?"

I replied that I had not noticed such points.

"Yes, there are some. Here is one of them. One night we were at the first representation of a new play. I was in a box with Flaubert, Daudet, Zola. (I am not quite sure whether he named both Daudet and Zola, but he certainly named one of the two.) All were men of advanced opinions. The subject of the play was this: A woman had separated from her husband. She had loved again, and now lived with another man. This man was represented in the play as an excellent person. For years they had been quite happy. Her two children—a girl and a boy—were babies at the time of the separation; now they had grown, and throughout all these years they had supposed the man to be their real father. The girl was about eighteen and the boy about seventeen. The man treated them quite as a father; they loved him, and he loved them. The scene represented the family meeting at breakfast. The girl comes in and approaches her supposed father, and he is going to kiss her, when the boy, who has learned in some way the true state of affairs, rushes forward and shouts, 'Don't dare!' (N'osez pas!)

"This exclamation brought down the house. There was an outburst of frantic applause. Flaubert and the others joined in it. I was disgusted.

"'Why,' I said, 'this family was happy; the man was a better father to these children than their real father, . . . their mother loved him and was happy with him. . . . This mischievous, perverted boy ought simply to be whipped for what he has said.' . . . It was of no use. I discussed for hours with them afterwards; none of them could understand me!"

I was, of course, fully in accordance with Turgénev's point of view. I remarked, however, that his acquaintances were chiefly amongst the middle classes. There, the difference between nation and nation is immense indeed. But my acquaintances were exclusively amongst the workers, and there is an immense resemblance between the workers, and especially amongst the peasants, of all nations.

In so saying, I was quite wrong, however. After I had had the opportunity of making a closer acquaintance with French workers, I often thought of the truth of Turgénev's remark. There is a real chasm indeed between Russian conceptions of marriage relations and those which prevail in France, amongst the workers as well as in the middle classes; and in many other things there is a similar difference between the Russian point of view and that of other nations.

It was said somewhere, after Turgénev's death, that he had intended to write a novel upon this subject. If he had begun it, the above-mentioned scene must be in his manuscript. What a pity that he did not write it! He, a thorough "Occidental" in his ways of thinking, could have said very deep things upon a subject which must have so profoundly affected him personally throughout his life.

Of all novel-writers of our century, Turgénev has certainly attained the greatest perfection as an artist, and his prose sounds to the Russian ear like music,—music as deep as that of Beethoven. His principal novels—the series of *Dmítri Rúdin, A Nobelman's Retreat, On the Eve, Fathers and Sons, Smoke,* and *Virgin Soil*—represent the leading "history-making" types of the educated classes of Russia, which evolved in rapid succession after 1848; all sketched with a fullness of philosophical conception and humanitarian understanding and an artistic beauty which have no parallel in any other literature. Yet *Fathers and Sons*—a novel which he rightly considered his profoundest work—was received by the young people of Russia with a loud protest. Our youth declared that the nihilist Bazárov was by no means a true representation of his class; many described him even as a caricature of nihilism. This misunderstanding deeply affected Turgénev, and, although a reconciliation between him and the young generation took place later on at St. Petersburg, after he had written *Virgin Soil,* the wound inflicted upon him by these attacks was never healed.

He knew from Lavróv that I was an enthusiastic admirer of his writings; and one day, as we were returning in a carriage from a visit to Antokólsky's studio,[20] he asked me what I thought of Bazárov. I frankly replied, "Bazárov is an admirable painting of the nihilist, but one feels that you did not love him as much as you did your other heroes."

"On the contrary, I loved him, intensely loved him," Turgénev replied, with an unexpected vigor. "When we get home I will show you my diary, in which I have noted how I wept when I had ended the novel with Bazárov's death."

Turgénev certainly loved the intellectual aspect of Bazárov. He so identified himself with the nihilist philosophy of his hero that he even kept a diary in his name, appreciating the current events from Bazárov's point of view. But I think that he admired him more than he loved him. In a brilliant lecture on Hamlet and Don Quixote, he divided the history makers of mankind into two classes, represented by one or the other of these characters. "Analysis first of all, and then egotism, and therefore no faith,—an egotist cannot even believe in himself:" so he characterized Hamlet. "Therefore he is a skeptic, and never will achieve anything; while Don Quixote, who fights against windmills, and takes a barber's plate for the magic helmet of Mambrino (who of us has never made the same mistake?), is a leader of the masses, because the masses always follow those who, taking no heed of the sarcasms of the majority, or even of persecutions, march straight forward, keeping their eyes fixed upon a goal which is seen, perhaps, by no one but themselves. They search, they fall, but they rise again, and find it,—and by right, too. Yet, although Hamlet is a skeptic, and disbelieves in Good, he does not disbelieve in Evil. He hates it; Evil and Deceit are his enemies; and his skepticism is not indifferentism, but only negation and doubt, which finally consume his will."

These thoughts of Turgénev give, I think, the true key for understanding his relations to his heroes. He himself and several of his best friends belonged more or less to the Hamlets. He loved Hamlet, and admired Don Quixote. So he admired also Bazárov. He represented his superiority admirably well, he understood the tragic character of his isolated position, but he could not surround him with that tender, poetical love which he bestowed as on a sick friend, when his heroes approached the Hamlet type. It would have been out of place.

"Did you know Mýshkin?" he once asked me, in 1878. At the trial of our circles Mýshkin revealed himself as the most powerful personality. "I should like to know all about him," he continued. "That *is* a man; not the slightest trace of Hamletism." And in so saying he was obviously meditating on this new type in the Russian movement, which did not exist in the phase that Turgénev described in *Virgin Soil*, but was to appear two years later.

I saw him for the last time in the autumn of 1881. He was very ill, and worried by the thought that it was his duty to write to Alexander III.,—who had just come to the throne, and hesitated as to the policy he should follow,—asking him to give Russia a constitution, and proving to him by solid arguments the necessity of that step. With evident grief he said to me: "I feel that I must do it, but I feel that I shall not be able to do it." In fact, he was already suffering awful pains occasioned by a cancer in the spinal cord, and had the greatest difficulty even in sitting up and talking for a few moments. He did not write then, and a few weeks later it would have been useless. Alexander III. had announced in a manifesto his intention to remain the absolute ruler of Russia.

III

In the meantime affairs in Russia took quite a new turn. The war which Russia began against Turkey in 1877 had ended in general disappointment. There was in the country, before the war broke out, a great deal of enthusiasm in favor of the Slavonians. Many believed, also, that a war of liberation in the Balkans would result in a move in the progressive direction in Russia itself. But the liberation of the Slavonian populations was only partly accomplished. The tremendous sacrifices which had been made by the Russians were rendered ineffectual by the blunders of the higher military authorities. Hundreds of thousands of men had been slaughtered in battles which were only half victories, and the concessions wrested from Turkey were brought to naught at the Berlin congress. It was also widely known that the embezzlement of state money went on during this war on almost as large a scale as during the Crimean war.

It was amidst the general dissatisfaction which prevailed in Russia at the end of 1877 that one hundred and ninety-three persons, arrested since 1873, in connection with our agitation, were brought before a high court. The accused, supported by a number of lawyers of talent, won at once the sympathies of the great public. They produced a very favorable impression upon St. Petersburg society; and when it became known that most of them had spent three or four years in prison, waiting for this trial, and that no less than twenty-one of them had either put an end to their lives by suicide or become insane, the feeling grew still stronger in their favor, even among the judges themselves. The court pronounced very heavy sentences upon a few, and relatively lenient ones upon the remainder, saying that the preliminary detention had lasted so long, and was so hard a punishment in itself, that nothing could justly be added to it. It was confidently expected that the Emperor would still further mitigate the sentences. It happened, however, to the astonishment of all, that he revised the sentences only to increase them. Those whom the court had acquitted were sent into exile in remote parts of Russia and Siberia, and

from five to twelve years of hard labor were inflicted upon
those whom the court had condemned to short terms of imprisonment. This was the work of the chief of the Third Section, General Mézentsov.

At the same time, the chief of the St. Petersburg police,
General Trépov, noticing, during a visit to the house of detention, that one of the political prisoners, Bogoliúbov, did not
take off his hat to greet the omnipotent satrap, rushed upon
him, gave him a blow, and, when the prisoner resisted, ordered
him to be flogged. The other prisoners, learning the fact in
their cells, loudly expressed their indignation, and were in consequence fearfully beaten by the warders and the police. The
Russian political prisoners bore without murmuring all hardships inflicted upon them in Siberia or through hard labor,
but they were firmly decided not to tolerate corporal punishment. A young girl, Véra Zasúlich, who did not even personally
know Bogoliúbov, took a revolver, went to the chief of police,
and shot at him. Trépov was only wounded. Alexander II.
came to look at the heroic girl, who must have impressed him
by her extremely sweet face and her modesty. Trépov had
so many enemies at St. Petersburg that they managed to bring
the affair before a common-law jury, and Véra Zasúlich declared in court that she had resorted to arms only when all
means for bringing the affair to public knowledge and obtaining some sort of redress had been exhausted. Even the St.
Petersburg correspondent of the London *Times* had been asked
to mention the affair in his paper, but had not done so, perhaps
thinking it improbable. Then, without telling any one her intentions, she went to shoot Trépov. Now that the affair had
become public, she was quite happy to know that he was but
slightly wounded. The jury acquitted her unanimously; and
when the police tried to rearrest her, as she was leaving the
court house, the young men of St. Petersburg, who stood in
crowds at the gates, saved her from their clutches. She went
abroad, and soon was among us in Switzerland.

This affair produced quite a sensation throughout Europe.
I was at Paris when the news of the acquittal came, and had
to call that day on business at the offices of several newspapers.
I found the editors fired with enthusiasm, and writing powerful articles to glorify the girl. Even the serious *Revue des Deux*

Mondes wrote, in its review of the year, that the two persons who had most impressed public opinion in Europe during 1878 were Prince Gorchakóv at the Berlin congress and Véra Zasúlich. Their portraits were given side by side in several almanacs. Upon the workers in Europe the devotion of Véra Zasúlich produced a tremendous impression.

In Russia the struggle for freedom was taking on a more and more acute character. Several political trials had been brought before high courts,—the trial of "the hundred and ninety-three," of "the fifty," of "the Dolgúshin circle," and so on,—and in all of them the same thing was apparent. The youth had gone to the peasants and the factory workers, preaching socialism to them; socialist pamphlets, printed abroad, had been distributed; appeals had been made to revolt—in some vague, indeterminate way—against the oppressive economical conditions. In short, nothing was done that does not occur in socialist agitations in every other country of the world. No traces of conspiracy against the Tsar, or even of preparations for revolutionary action, were found; in fact, there were none. The great majority of our youth were at that time hostile to such action. Nay, looking now over that movement of the years 1870–78, I can say in full confidence that most of them would have felt satisfied if they had been simply allowed to live by the side of the peasants and the workers, to teach them, to collaborate in any of the thousand capacities—private or as a part of the local self-government—in which an educated and earnest man or woman can be useful to the masses of the people. I knew the men, and say so with full knowledge of them.

Yet the sentences were ferocious,—stupidly ferocious, because the movement, which had grown out of the previous state of Russia, was too deeply rooted to be crushed down by mere brutality. Hard labor for six, ten, twelve years in the mines, with subsequent exile to Siberia for life, was a common sentence. There were such cases as that of a girl who got nine years' hard labor and life exile to Siberia, for giving one socialist pamphlet to a worker; that was all her crime. Another girl of fourteen, Miss Gukóvskaia, was transported for life to a remote village of Siberia, for having tried, like Goethe's Klärchen, to excite an indifferent crowd to deliver Koválsky and

his friends when they were going to be hanged,—an act the
more natural in Russia, even from the authorities' standpoint,
as there is no capital punishment in our country for common-
law crimes, and the application of the death penalty to "po-
liticals" was then a novelty, a return to almost forgotten traditions. Thrown into the wilderness, this young girl soon drowned
herself in the Yeniséi. Even those who were acquitted by the
courts were banished by the gendarmes to little hamlets in
Siberia and Northeast Russia, where they had to starve on the
government's monthly allowance, one dollar and fifty cents
(three rubles). There are no industries in such hamlets, and
the exiles were strictly prohibited from teaching.

As if to exasperate the youth still more, their condemned
friends were not sent direct to Siberia. They were locked up,
first, for a number of years, in central prisons, which made
them envy the convict's life in Siberia. These prisons were awful indeed. In one of them—"a den of typhoid fever," as a priest
of that particular jail said in a sermon—the mortality reached
twenty per cent in twelve months. In the central prisons, in
the hard-labor prisons of Siberia, in the fortress, the prisoners
had to resort to the strike of death, the famine strike, to protect
themselves from the brutality of the warders, or to obtain conditions—some sort of work, or reading, in their cells—that would
save them from being driven into insanity in a few months.
The horror of such strikes, during which men and women refused to take any food for seven or eight days in succession,
and then lay motionless, their minds wandering, seemed not
to appeal to the gendarmes. At Khárkov, the prostrated prisoners were tied up with ropes and fed by force, artificially.

Information of these horrors leaked out from the prisons,
crossed the boundless distances of Siberia, and spread far and
wide among the youth. There was a time when not a week
passed without disclosing some new infamy of that sort, or
even worse.

Sheer exasperation took hold of our young people. "In other
countries," they began to say, "men have the courage to resist.
An Englishman, a Frenchman, would not tolerate such out-
rages. How can we tolerate them? Let us resist, arms in hands,
the nocturnal raids of the gendarmes; let them know, at least,
that since arrest means a slow and infamous death at their

hands, they will have to take us in a mortal struggle." At Odéssa, Koválsky and his friends met with revolver shots the gendarmes who came one night to arrest them.

The reply of Alexander II. to this new move was the proclamation of a state of siege. Russia was divided into a number of districts, each of them under a governor-general, who received the order to hang offenders pitilessly. Koválsky and his friends—who, by the way, had killed no one by their shots—were executed. Hanging became the order of the day. Twenty-three persons perished in two years, including a boy of nineteen, who was caught posting a revolutionary proclamation at a railway station; this act—I say it deliberately—was the only charge against him. He was a boy, but he died like a man.

Then the watchword of the revolutionists became "self-defense": self-defense against the spies who introduced themselves into the circles under the mask of friendship, and denounced members right and left, simply because they would not be paid if they did not accuse large numbers of persons; self-defense against those who ill-treated prisoners; self-defense against the omnipotent chiefs of the state police.

Three functionaries of mark and two or three small spies fell in that new phase of the struggle. General Mézentsov, who had induced the Tsar to double the sentences after the trial of the hundred and ninety-three, was killed in broad daylight at St. Petersburg; a gendarme colonel, guilty of something worse than that, had the same fate at Kíev; and the governor-general of Khárkov—my cousin, Dmítri Kropótkin—was shot as he was returning home from a theater. The central prison, in which the first famine strike and artificial feeding took place, was under his orders. In reality, he was not a bad man,—I know that his personal feelings were somewhat favorable to the political prisoners; but he was a weak man and a courtier, and he hesitated to interfere. One word from him would have stopped the ill-treatment of the prisoners. Alexander II. liked him so much, and his position at the court was so strong, that his interference very probably would have been approved. "Thank you; you have acted according to my own wishes," the Tsar said to him, a couple of years before that date, when he came to St. Petersburg to report that he had taken a peaceful attitude in a riot of the poorer population of Khárkov, and had treated the rioters very leniently. But this time he gave his approval to the jailers, and the young men of Khárkov were so exasperated at the treatment of their friends that one of them shot him.

However, the personality of the Emperor was kept out of the struggle, and down to the year 1879 no attempt was made on his life. The person of the Liberator of the serfs was surrounded by an aureole which protected him infinitely better than the swarms of police officials. If Alexander II. had shown at this juncture the least desire to improve the state of affairs in Russia; if he had only called in one or two of those men with whom he had collaborated during the reform period, and had ordered them to make an inquiry into the conditions of the country, or merely of the peasantry; if he had shown any intention of limiting the powers of the secret police, his steps would have been hailed with enthusiasm. A word would have made him "the Liberator" again, and once more the youth would have repeated Hérzen's words: "Thou hast conquered, Galilean." But just as during the Polish insurrection the despot awoke in him, and, inspired by Katkóv, he resorted to hanging, so now again, following the advice of his evil genius, Katkóv, he found nothing to do but to nominate special military governors—for hanging.

Then, and then only, a handful of revolutionists,—the Executive Committee,—supported, I must say, by the growing discontent in the educated classes, and even in the Tsar's immediate surroundings, declared that war against absolutism which, after several attempts, ended in 1881 in the death of Alexander II.

Two men, I have said already, lived in Alexander II., and now the conflict between the two, which had grown during all his life, assumed a really tragic aspect. When he met Solovióv, who shot at him and missed the first shot, he had the presence of mind to run to the nearest door, not in a straight line, but in zigzags, while Solovióv continued to fire; and he thus escaped with but a slight tearing of his overcoat. On the day of his death, too, he gave a proof of his undoubted courage. In the face of real danger he was courageous; but he continually trembled before the phantasms of his own imagination. Once he shot at an aide-de-camp, when the latter had made an abrupt movement, and Alexander thought he was going to attempt his life. Merely to save his life, he surrendered entirely all his imperial powers into the hands of those who cared nothing for him, but only for their lucrative positions.

He undoubtedly retained an attachment to the mother of his children, even though he was then with the Princess Iurievsko-Dolgorúkaia, whom he married immediately after the death of the Empress. "Don't speak to me of the Empress; it makes me suffer too much," he more than once said to Lorís-Mélikov. And yet he entirely abandoned the Empress Marie, who had stood faithfully by his side while he was the Liberator; he let her die in the palace in neglect. A well-known Russian doctor, now dead, told his friends that he, a stranger, felt shocked at the neglect with which the Empress was treated during her last illness,—deserted, of course, by the ladies of the court, having by her side but two ladies, deeply devoted to her, and receiving every day but a short official visit from her husband, who stayed in another palace in the meantime.

When the Executive Committee made the daring attempt to blow up the Winter Palace itself, Alexander II. took a step which had no precedent. He created a sort of dictatorship, vesting unlimited powers in Lorís-Mélikov. This general was an Armenian, to whom Alexander II. had once before given similar dictatorial powers, when the bubonic plague broke out on the Lower Vólga, and Germany threatened to mobilize her troops and put Russia under quarantine if the plague were not stopped. Now that Alexander II. saw that he could not have confidence in the vigilance of even the palace police, he gave dictatorial powers to Lorís-Mélikov, and as Mélikov had the reputation of being a Liberal, this new move was interpreted as indicating that the convocation of a National Assembly would soon follow. As, however, no new attempts upon his life were made immediately after that explosion, the Tsar regained confidence, and a few months later, before Mélikov had been allowed to do anything, he was dictator no longer, but simply minister of the interior. The sudden attacks of sadness of which I have already spoken, during which Alexander II. reproached himself with the reactionary character that his reign had assumed, now took the shape of violent paroxysms of tears. He would sit weeping by the hour, bringing Mélikov to despair. Then he would ask his minister, "When will your constitutional scheme be ready?" If, two days later, Mélikov said that it was now ready, the Emperor seemed to have forgotten all about it. "Did I mention it?" he would ask. "What for? We had better leave it to my successor. That will be his gift to Russia."

When rumors of a new plot reached him, he was ready to undertake something; but when everything seemed to be quiet among the revolutionists, he turned his ear again to his reactionary advisers, and let things go. Every moment Mélikov expected dismissal.

In February, 1881, Mélikov reported that a new plot had been laid by the Executive Committee, but its plan could not be discovered by any amount of searching. Thereupon Alexander II. decided that a sort of deliberative assembly of delegates from the provinces should be called. Always under the idea that he would share the fate of Louis XVI., he described this gathering as an Assemblée des Notables, like the one convoked by Louis XVI. before the National Assembly in 1789. The scheme had to be laid before the council of state, but then again he hesitated. It was only on the morning of March 1 (13), 1881, after a final warning by Lorís-Mélikov, that he ordered it to be brought before the council on the following Thursday. This was on Sunday, and he was asked by Mélikov not to go out to the parade that day, there being danger of an attempt on his life. Nevertheless, he went. He wanted to see the Grand Duchess Catherine (daughter of his aunt, Hélène Pávlovna, who had been one of the leaders of the emancipation party in 1861), and to carry her the welcome news, perhaps as an expiatory offering to the memory of the Empress Marie. He is said to have told her, "Je me suis décidé à convoquer une Assemblée des Notables." However, this belated and half-hearted concession had not been announced, and on his way back to the Winter Palace he was killed.

It is known how it happened. A bomb was thrown under his iron-clad carriage, to stop it. Several Circassians of the escort were wounded. Rysakóv, who flung the bomb, was arrested on the spot. Then, although the coachman of the Tsar earnestly advised him not to get out, saying that he could drive him still in the slightly damaged carriage, he insisted upon alighting. He felt that his military dignity required him to see the wounded Circassians, to condole with them as he had done with the wounded during the Turkish war, when a mad storming of Plevna, doomed to end in a terrible disaster, was made on the day of his fête. He approached Rysakóv and asked him something; and as he passed close by another young man, Grinevítsky, the latter threw a bomb between himself and Alexander II., so that both of them should be killed. They both lived but a few hours.

There Alexander II. lay upon the snow, profusely bleeding, abandoned by every one of his followers! All had disappeared. It was cadets, returning from the parade, who lifted the suffering Tsar from the snow and put him in a sledge, covering his shivering body with a cadet mantle and his bare head with a cadet cap. And it was one of the terrorists, Emeliánov, with a bomb wrapped in a paper under his arm, who, at the risk of being arrested on the spot and hanged, rushed with the cadets to the help of the wounded man. Human nature is full of these contrasts.

Thus ended the tragedy of Alexander II.'s life. People could not understand how it was possible that a Tsar who had done so much for Russia should have met his death at the hands of revolutionists. To me, who had the chance of witnessing the first reactionary steps of Alexander II. and his gradual deterioration, who had caught a glimpse of his complex personality, —that of a born autocrat, whose violence was but partially mitigated by education, of a man possessed of military gallantry, but devoid of the courage of the statesman, of a man of strong passions and weak will,—it seemed that the tragedy developed with the unavoidable fatality of one of Shakespeare's dramas. Its last act was already written for me on the day when I heard him address us, the promoted officers, on June 13, 1862, immediately after he had ordered the first executions in Poland.

IV

A wild panic seized the court circles at St. Petersburg. Alexander III., who, notwithstanding his colossal stature and force, was not a very courageous man, refused to move to the Winter Palace, and retired to the palace of his grandfather, Paul I., at Gatchina. I know that old building, planned as a Vauban fortress, surrounded by moats and protected by watchtowers, from the tops of which secret staircases lead to the Emperor's study. I have seen the trap-doors in the study, for suddenly throwing an enemy on the sharp rocks in the water underneath, and the secret staircase leading to underground prisons and to an underground passage which opens on a lake. All the palaces of Paul I. had been built on a similar plan. In the meantime, an underground gallery, supplied with automatic electric appliances to protect it from being undermined by the revolutionists, was dug round the Anichkov palace, in which Alexander III. resided when he was heir apparent.

A secret league for the protection of the Tsar was started. Officers of all grades were induced by triple salaries to join it, and to undertake voluntary spying in all classes of society. Comical scenes followed, of course. Two officers, without knowing that they both belonged to the league, would entice each other into a disloyal conversation, during a railway journey, and then proceed to arrest each other, only to discover at the last moment that their pains had been labor lost. This league still exists in a more official shape, under the name of Okhrána (Protection), and from time to time frightens the present Tsar with all sorts of concocted "dangers," in order to maintain its existence.

A still more secret organization, the Holy League, was formed at the same time, under the leadership of the brother of the Tsar, Vladímir, for the purpose of opposing the revolutionists in different ways, one of which was to kill those of the refugees who were supposed to have been the leaders of the late conspiracies. I was of this number. The grand duke violently reproached the officers of the league for their cowardice, regretting that there were none among them who would undertake to kill such refugees; and an officer, who had been a page de chambre at the time I was in the Corps of Pages, was appointed by the league to carry out this particular work.

The fact is that the refugees abroad did not interfere with the work of the Executive Committee at St. Petersburg. To pretend to direct conspiracies from Switzerland, while those who were at St. Petersburg acted under a permanent menace of death, would have been sheer nonsense; and as Stepniák and I wrote several times, none of us would have accepted the doubtful task of forming plans of action without being on the spot. But of course it suited the plans of the St. Petersburg police to maintain that they were powerless to protect the Tsar because all plots were devised abroad, and their spies—I know it well—amply supplied them with the desired reports.

Skóbelev, the hero of the Turkish war, was also asked to join this league, but he blankly refused. It appears from Loris-Mélikov's posthumous papers, part of which were published by a friend of his in London, that when Alexander III. came to the throne, and hesitated to convoke the Assembly of Notables, Skóbelev even made an offer to Loris-Mélikov and Count Ignátiev ("the lying Pasha," as the Constantinople diplomatists used to nickname him), to arrest Alexander III., and compel him to sign a constitutional manifesto; whereupon Ignátiev is said to have denounced the scheme to the Tsar, and thus to have obtained his nomination as prime minister, in which capacity he resorted, with the advice of M. Andrieux, the ex-prefect of police at Paris, to various stratagems in order to paralyze the revolutionists.

If the Russian Liberals had shown anything like a modest courage and some power of organized action, at that time, a National Assembly would have been convoked. From the same posthumous papers of Loris-Mélikov it appears that Alexander III. was willing for a time to call one. He had made up his mind to do so, and had announced it to his brother. Old Wilhelm I. supported him in this intention. It was only when he saw that the Liberals undertook nothing, while the Katkóv party was busy in the opposite direction,—M. Andrieux advising him to crush the nihilists, and indicating how it ought to be done (his letter to this effect is in the pamphlet referred to),—that Alexander III. finally resolved to declare that he would continue to be absolute ruler of the empire.

I was expelled from Switzerland by order of the federal council a few months after the death of Alexander II. I did not take umbrage at this. Assailed by the monarchical powers on account of the asylum which Switzerland offered to refugees, and menaced by the Russian official press with a wholesale expulsion of all Swiss governesses and ladies' maids, who are numerous in Russia, the rulers of Switzerland, by banishing me, gave some sort of satisfaction to the Russian police. But I very much regret, for the sake of Switzerland itself, that that step was taken. It was a sanction given to the theory of "conspiracies concocted in Switzerland," and it was an acknowledgment of weakness, of which Italy and France took advantage at once. Two years later, when Jules Ferry proposed to Italy and Germany the partition of Switzerland, his argument must have been that the Swiss government itself had admitted that Switzerland was "a hotbed of international conspiracies." This first concession led to more arrogant demands, and has certainly placed Switzerland in a far less independent position than it might otherwise have occupied.

The decree of expulsion was delivered to me immediately after I had returned from London, where I was present at an anarchist congress in July, 1881. After that congress I had stayed for a few weeks in England, writing the first articles on Russian affairs from our standpoint for the *Newcastle Chronicle*. The English press, at that time, was an echo of the opinions of Madame Novikóva,—that is, of Katkóv and the Russian state police,—and I was most happy when Mr. Joseph Cowen agreed to give me the hospitality of his paper in order to state our point of view.

I had just joined my wife in the high mountains where she was staying, near the abode of Elisée Reclus, when I was asked to leave Switzerland. We sent the little luggage we had to the next railway station and went on foot to Aigle, enjoying for the last time the sight of the mountains that we loved so much. We crossed the hills by taking short cuts over them, and laughed when we discovered that the short cuts led to long windings; and when we reached the bottom of the valley, we tramped along the dusty road. The comical incident which always comes in such cases was supplied by an English lady. A richly dressed dame, reclining by the side of a gentleman in a hired carriage, threw several tracts to the two poorly dressed tramps, as she passed them. I lifted the tracts from the dust. She was evidently one of those ladies who believe themselves to be Christians, and consider it their duty to distribute religious tracts among "dissolute foreigners." Thinking we were sure to overtake the lady at the railway station, I wrote on one of the pamphlets the well-known verse relative to the rich in the kingdom of God, and similarly appropriate quotations about the Pharisees being the worst enemies of Christianity. When we came to Aigle, the lady was taking refreshments in her carriage. She evidently preferred to continue the journey in this vehicle along the lovely valley, rather than to be shut up in a stuffy railway car. I returned her the pamphlets with politeness, saying that I had added to them something that she might find useful for her own instruction. The lady did not know whether to fly at me, or to accept the lesson with Christian patience. Her eyes expressed both impulses in rapid succession.

My wife was about to pass her examination for the degree of Bachelor of Science at the Geneva University, and we settled, therefore, in a tiny town of France, Thonon, situated on the Savoy coast of the Lake of Geneva, and stayed there a couple of months.

As to the death sentence of the Holy League, a warning reached me from one of the highest quarters of Russia. Even the name of the lady who was sent from St. Petersburg to Geneva to be the head center of the conspiracy became known to me. So I simply communicated the fact and the names to the Geneva correspondent of the *Times,* asking him to publish them if anything should happen, and I put a note to that effect in *Le Révolté*. After that I did not trouble myself more about it. My wife did not take it so lightly, and the good peasant woman, Madame Sansaux, who gave us board and lodgings at Thonon, and who had learned of the plot in a different way (through her sister, who was a nurse in the family of a Russian agent), bestowed the most touching care upon me. Her cottage was out of town, and whenever I went to town at night—some-

times to meet my wife at the railway station—she always found
a pretext to have me accompanied by her husband with a
lantern. "Wait only a moment, Monsieur Kropótkin," she
would say; "my husband is going that way for purchases, and
you know he always carries a lantern!" Or else she would
send her brother to follow me at a distance, without my noticing it.

I never saw such numbers of Russian spies as during the two
months that I remained at Thonon. To begin with, as soon as
we had engaged lodgings, a suspicious character, who gave
himself out for an Englishman, took the other part of the
house. Flocks, literally flocks of Russian spies besieged the
house, seeking admission under all possible pretexts, or simply
tramping in pairs, trios, and quartettes in front of the house. I
can imagine what wonderful reports they wrote. A spy must
report. If he should merely say that he has stood for a week
in the street without noticing anything mysterious, he would
soon be put on the half-pay list or dismissed.

It was then the golden age of the Russian secret police.
Ignátiev's policy had borne fruit. There were two or three
bodies of police competing with one another, each having any
amount of money at their disposal, and carrying on the bold-
est intrigues. Colonel Sudéikin, for instance, chief of one of
the branches,—plotting with a certain Degáev, who after all
killed him,—denounced Ignátiev's agents to the revolutionists
at Geneva, and offered to the terrorists in Russia all facilities
for killing the minister of the interior, Count Tolstóy, and the
Grand Duke Vladímir; adding that he himself would then be
nominated minister of the interior, with dictatorial powers, and
the Tsar would be entirely in his hands. This activity of the
Russian police culminated, later on, in the kidnapping of the
Prince of Battenberg from Bulgaria.

The French police, also, were on the alert. The question,
"What is he doing at Thonon?" worried them. I continued to
edit *Le Révolté*, and wrote articles for the *Encyclopædia Britannica* and the *Newcastle Chronicle*. But what reports could
be made out of that? One day the local gendarme paid a visit
to my landlady. He had heard from the street the rattling of
some machine, and wished to report that I had in my house
a secret printing-press. So he came in my absence and asked

the lady to show him the press. She replied that there was none and suggested that perhaps the gendarme had overheard the noise of her sewing-machine. But he would not be convinced by so prosaic an explanation, and actually compelled the landlady to sew on her machine, while he listened inside the house and outside to make sure that the rattling he had heard was the same.

"What is he doing all day?" he asked the landlady.

"He writes."

"He cannot write all day long."

"He saws wood in the garden at midday, and he takes walks every afternoon between four and five." It was in November.

"Ah, that's it! When the dusk is coming on?" (A la tombée de la nuit?) And he wrote in his notebook, "Never goes out except at dusk."

I could not well explain at that time this special attention of the Russian spies; but it must have had some connection with the following. When Ignátiev was nominated prime minister, advised by the ex-prefect of Paris, Andrieux, he hit on a new plan. He sent a swarm of his agents into Switzerland, and one of them undertook the publication of a paper which slightly advocated the extension of provincial self-government in Russia, but whose chief purpose was to combat the revolutionists, and to rally to its standard those of the refugees who did not sympathize with terrorism. This was certainly a means of sowing division. Then, when nearly all the members of the Executive Committee had been arrested in Russia, and a couple of them had taken refuge at Paris, Ignátiev sent an agent to Paris to offer an armistice. He promised that there should be no further executions on account of the plots during the reign of Alexander II., even if those who had escaped arrest fell into the hands of the government; that Chernyshévsky should be released from Siberia; and that a commission should be nominated to review the cases of all those who had been exiled to Siberia without trial. On the other side, he asked the Executive Committee to promise to make no attempts against the Tsar's life until his coronation was over. Perhaps the reforms in favor of the peasants, which Alexander III. intended to make, were also mentioned. The agreement was made at Paris, and was kept on both sides. The terrorists suspended hostilities. Nobody was executed for complicity in the former conspiracies; those who were arrested later on under this indictment were immured in the Russian Bastille at Schlüsselburg, where nothing was heard of them for fifteen years, and where most of them still are. Chernyshévsky was brought back from Siberia, and ordered to stay at Astrakhan, where he was severed from all connection with the intellectual world of Russia, and soon died. A commission went through Siberia, releasing some of the exiles, and specifying terms of exile for the remainder. My brother Alexander received from it an additional five years.

While I was at London, in 1882, I was told one day that a man who pretended to be a *bona fide* agent of the Russian government, and could prove it, wanted to enter into negotiations with me. "Tell him that if he comes to my house I will throw him down the staircase," was my reply. Probably the result was that while Ignátiev considered the Tsar guaranteed from the attacks of the Executive Committee, he was afraid that the anarchists might make some attempt, and wanted to have me out of the way.

v

The anarchist movement had undergone a considerable development in France during the years 1881 and 1882. When I crossed France in 1881, on my way from Thonon to London, I visited Lyons, St. Etienne, and Vienne, lecturing there, and I found in these cities a considerable number of workers ready to accept our ideas.

By the end of 1882 a terrible crisis prevailed in the Lyons region. The silk industry was paralyzed, and the misery among the weavers was so great that crowds of children stood every morning at the gates of the barracks, where the soldiers gave away what they could spare of their bread and soup. This was the beginning of the popularity of General Boulanger, who had permitted this distribution of food. The miners of the region were also in a very precarious state.

I knew that there was a great deal of fermentation, but during the eleven months I had stayed at London I had lost close contact with the French movement. A few weeks after I returned to Thonon I learned from the papers that the miners of Monceau-les-Mines, incensed at the vexations of the ultra-Catholic owners of the mines, had begun a sort of movement; they were holding secret meetings, talking of a general strike; the stone crosses erected on all the roads round the mines were thrown down or blown up by dynamite cartridges, which are largely used by the miners in underground work, and often remain in their possession. The agitation at Lyons also took on a more violent character. The anarchists, who were rather numerous in the city, allowed no meeting of the opportunist politicians to be held without obtaining a hearing for themselves,—storming the platform, as a last resource. They brought forward resolutions to the effect that the mines and all necessaries for production, as well as the dwelling-houses, ought to be owned by the nation; and these resolutions were carried with enthusiasm, to the horror of the middle classes.

The feeling among the workers was growing every day against the opportunist town councilors and political leaders, as also against the press, which made light of a very acute crisis, while nothing was undertaken to relieve the widespread misery. As is usual at such times, the fury of the poorer people turned especially against the places of amusement and debauch, which become only the more conspicuous in times of desolation and misery, as they impersonate for the worker the egotism and dissoluteness of the wealthier classes. A place particularly hated by the workers was the underground café at the Théâtre Bellecour, which remained open all night, and where, in the small hours of the morning, one could see newspaper men and politicians feasting and drinking in company with gay women. Not a meeting was held but some menacing allusion was made to that café, and one night a dynamite cartridge was exploded in it by an unknown hand. A worker who was occasionally there, a socialist, jumped to blow out the lighted fuse of the cartridge, and was killed, while a few of the feasting politicians were slightly wounded. Next day a dynamite cartridge was exploded at the doors of a recruiting bureau, and it was said that the anarchists intended to blow up the huge statue of the Virgin which stands on one of the hills of Lyons. One must have lived at Lyons or in its neighborhood to realize the extent to which the population and the schools are still in the hands of the Catholic clergy, and to understand the hatred that the male portion of the population feel toward the clergy.

A panic now seized the wealthier classes of Lyons. Some sixty anarchists—all workers, and only one middle-class man, Emile Gautier, who was on a lecturing tour in the region— were arrested. The Lyons papers undertook at the same time to incite the government to arrest me, representing me as the leader of the agitation, who had come on purpose from England to direct the movement. Russian spies began to parade again in conspicuous numbers in our small town. Almost every day I received letters, evidently written by spies of the international police, mentioning some dynamite plot, or mysteriously announcing that consignments of dynamite had been shipped to me. I made quite a collection of these letters, writing on each of them "Police Internationale," and they were taken away by the French police when they made a search in my house. But they did not dare to produce these letters in court, nor did they ever restore them to me.

Not only was the house searched, but my wife, who was going to Geneva, was arrested at the station in Thonon, and searched. But of course absolutely nothing was found to compromise me or any one else.

Ten days passed, during which I was quite free to go away, if I wished to do so. I received several letters advising me to disappear,—one of them from an unknown Russian friend, perhaps a member of the diplomatic staff, who seemed to have known me, and wrote that I must leave at once, because otherwise I should be the first victim of the extradition treaty which was about to be concluded between France and Russia. I remained where I was; and when the *Times* inserted a telegram saying that I had disappeared from Thonon, I wrote a letter to the paper, giving my address. Since so many of my friends were arrested, I had no intention of leaving.

In the night of December 21 my brother-in-law died in my arms. We knew that his illness was incurable, but it is terrible to see a young life extinguished in your presence after a brave struggle against death. Both my wife and I were broken down. Three or four hours later, as the dull winter morning was dawning, gendarmes came to my house to arrest me. Seeing in what a state my wife was, I asked permission to remain with her till the burial was over, promising upon my word of honor to be at the prison door at a given hour; but it was refused, and the same night I was taken to Lyons. Elisée Reclus, notified by telegraph, came at once, bestowing on my wife all the gentleness of his golden heart; friends came from Geneva; and although the funeral was absolutely civil, which was a novelty in that little town, half of the population was at the burial, to show my wife that the hearts of the poorer classes and the simple Savoy peasants were with us, and not with their rulers. When my trial was going on, the peasants used to come from the mountain villages to town to get the papers, and to see how my affair stood before the court.

Another incident which profoundly touched me was the arrival at Lyons of an English friend. He came on behalf of a gentleman, well-known and esteemed in the English political world, in whose family I had spent many happy hours at London, in 1882. He was the bearer of a considerable sum of money for the purpose of obtaining my release on bail, and he transmitted me at the same time the message of my London friend that I need not care in the least about the bail, but must leave France immediately. In some mysterious way he had managed to see me freely,—not in the double-grated iron cage in which I was allowed interviews with my wife,—and he was as much affected by my refusal to accept the offer as I was by that touching token of friendship on the part of one whom, with his excellent wife, I had already learned to esteem so highly.

The French government wanted to have one of those great trials which produce an impression upon the population, but there was no possibility of prosecuting the arrested anarchists for the explosions. It would have required bringing us before a jury, which in all probability would have acquitted us. Consequently, the government adopted the Machiavellian course of prosecuting us for having belonged to the International Workingmen's Association. There is in France a law, passed immediately after the fall of the Commune, under which men can be brought before a simple police court for having belonged to that association. The maximum penalty is five years' imprisonment; and a police court is always sure to pronounce the sentences which are wanted by the government.

The trial began at Lyons in the first days of January, 1883, and lasted about a fortnight. The accusation was ridiculous, as every one knew that none of the Lyons workers had ever joined the International, and it entirely fell through, as may be seen from the following episode. The only witness for the prosecution was the chief of the secret police at Lyons, an elderly man, who was treated at the court with the utmost respect. His report, I must say, was quite correct as concerns the facts. The anarchists, he said, had taken hold of the population; they had rendered opportunist meetings impossible, because they spoke at each meeting, preaching communism and anarchism, and carrying with them the audiences. Seeing that so far he had been fair in his testimony, I ventured to ask him a question: "Did you ever hear the International Workingmen's Association spoken of at Lyons?"

"Never," he replied sulkily.

"When I returned from the London congress of 1881, and did all I could to have the International reconstituted in France, did I succeed?"

"No. They did not find it revolutionary enough."

"Thank you," I said, and turning toward the procureur added, "There's all your prosecution overthrown by your own witness!"

Nevertheless, we were all condemned for having belonged to the International. Four of us got the maximum sentence, five years' imprisonment and four hundred dollars' fine; the remainder got from four years to one year. In fact, they never tried to prove anything concerning the International. It was quite forgotten. We were simply asked to speak about anarchism, and so we did. Not a word was said about the explosions; and when one or two of the Lyons comrades wanted to clear this point, they were bluntly told that they were not prosecuted for that, but for having belonged to the International, —to which I alone belonged.

There is always some comical incident in such trials, and this time it was supplied by a letter of mine. There was nothing upon which to base the accusation. Scores of searches had been made at the houses of French anarchists, but only two letters of mine had been found. The prosecution tried to make the best of them. One was written to a French worker when he was despondent. I spoke to him in my letter about the great times we were living in, the great changes coming, the birth and spreading of new ideas, and so on. The letter was not long, and little capital was made out of it by the procureur. As to the other letter, it was twelve pages long. I had written it to another French friend, a young shoemaker. He earned his living by making shoes in his own room. On his left side he used to have a small iron stove, upon which he himself cooked his daily meal, and upon his right a small stool upon which he wrote long letters to the comrades, without leaving his shoe-maker's low bench. After he had made just as many pairs of shoes as were required to cover the expenses of his extremely modest living, and to send a few francs to his old mother in the country, he would spend long hours in writing letters in which he developed the theoretical principles of anarchism with admirable good sense and intelligence. He is now a writer well known in France and generally respected for the integrity of his character. Unfortunately, at that time he would cover eight or twelve pages of note paper without one single full stop, or even a comma. I once sat down and wrote a long letter in which I explained to him how our written thoughts sub-divide into sentences, clauses, and phrases, each of which should end with its appropriate period, semicolon, or comma, and so on,—in short, gave him a little lesson in the elements of punctuation. I told him how much it would improve his writings if he adopted this simple plan.

This letter was read by the prosecutor before the court and elicited from him most pathetic comments. "You have heard, gentlemen, this letter"—he went on, addressing the Court. "You have listened to it. There is nothing particular in it at first sight. He gives a lesson in grammar to a worker. . . . But"—and here his voice vibrated with accents of a deep emotion—"it was not in order to help a poor worker in getting instruction which he, owing probably to laziness, failed to get at school. It was not to help him to earn an honest living. No! gentlemen, it was written in order to inspire him with hatred for our grand and beautiful institutions, in order only the better to infuse into him the venom of anarchism, in order to make of him only a more terrible enemy of society. Cursed be the day when Kropótkin set his foot upon the soil of France!"

We could not help laughing like boys all the time he was delivering that speech; the judges stared at him as if to tell him that he was overdoing his rôle, but he seemed not to notice anything, and, carried by his eloquence, went on speaking with more and more theatrical gestures and intonations. He really did his best to obtain his reward from the Russian government.

Very soon after the condemnation the presiding magistrate was promoted to the magistracy of an assize court. As to the procureur and another magistrate,—one would hardly believe it,—the Russian government offered them the Russian cross of Sainte-Anne, and they were allowed by the republic to accept it! The famous Russian alliance thus had its origin in the Lyons trial.

This trial—during which most brilliant anarchist speeches, reported by all the papers, were made by such first-rate speakers as the worker Bernard and Emile Gautier, and during which all the accused took a very firm attitude, preaching our doctrines for a fortnight—had a powerful influence in clearing away false ideas about anarchism in France, and surely contributed to some extent to the revival of socialism in other countries. As to the condemnation, it was so little justified by the proceedings that the French press—with the exception of the papers devoted to the government—openly blamed the magistrates. Even the moderate *Journal des Economistes* found fault with the verdict, which "nothing in the proceedings before the court could have made one foresee." The contest between the accusers and ourselves was won by us, in the public opinion. Immediately a proposition of amnesty was brought before the Chamber, and received about a hundred votes in support of it. It came up regularly every year, each time securing more and more voices, until we were released.

VI

In the middle of March, 1883, twenty-two of us, who had been condemned to more than one year of imprisonment, were removed in great secrecy to the central prison of Clairvaux.

It was formerly an abbey of St. Bernard, of which the great Revolution had made a house for the poor. Subsequently it became a house of detention and correction, which went among the prisoners and the officials themselves under the well-deserved nickname of "house of detention and corruption."

So long as we were kept at Lyons we were treated as the prisoners under preliminary arrest are treated in France; that is, we had our own clothes, we could get our own food from a restaurant, and one could hire for a few francs per month a larger cell, a pistole. I took advantage of this for working hard upon my articles for the *Encyclopædia Britannica* and the *Nineteenth Century*. Now, the treatment we should have at Clairvaux was an open question. However, in France it is generally understood that, for political prisoners, the loss of liberty and the forced inactivity are in themselves so hard that there is no need to inflict additional hardships. Consequently, we were told that we should remain under the same régime that we had had at Lyons. We should have separate quarters, retain our own clothes, be free of compulsory work, and be allowed to smoke. "Those of you," the governor said, "who wish to earn something by manual work will be enabled to do so by sewing stays or engraving small things in mother of pearl. This work is poorly paid; but you could not be employed in the prison workshops for the fabrication of iron beds, picture frames, and so on, because that would require your lodging with the common-law prisoners." Like the other prisoners, we were allowed to buy from the prison canteen some additional food and a pint of claret every day, both being supplied at a very low price and of good quality.

The first impression which Clairvaux produced upon me was most favorable. We had been locked up and had been traveling all the day, from two or three o'clock in the morning, in those tiny cupboards into which the railway carriages used for the transportation of prisoners are usually divided. When we reached the central prison, we were taken temporarily to the penal quarters, and were introduced into extremely clean cells. Hot food, plain but of excellent quality, had been served to us notwithstanding the late hour of the night, and we had been offered the opportunity of having a half-pint each of the very good *vin du pays*, which was sold at the prison canteen at the extremely modest price of twenty-four centimes (less than five cents) per quart. The governor and all the warders were most polite to us.

Next day the governor of the prison took me to see the rooms which he intended to give us, and when I remarked that they were all right, only a little too small for such a number,—we were twenty-two,—and that overcrowding might result in illness, he gave us another set of rooms in what had been in olden times the house of the superintendent of the abbey, and was now the hospital. Our windows looked down upon a little garden and off upon beautiful views of the surrounding country. In another room, on the same landing, old Blanqui had been kept the last three or four years before his release. Before that he was confined in one of the cells in the cellular house.

We obtained thus three spacious rooms, and a smaller room was spared for Gautier and myself, so that we could pursue our literary work. We probably owed this last favor to the intervention of a considerable number of English men of science, who, as soon as I was condemned, had signed a petition asking for my release. Many contributors to the *Encyclopædia Britannica*, Herbert Spencer, and Swinburne were among the signers, while Victor Hugo had added to his signature a few warm words. Altogether, public opinion in France received our condemnation very unfavorably; and when my wife had mentioned at Paris that I required books, the Academy of Sciences offered its library, and Ernest Renan, in a charming letter, put his private library at her service.

We had a small garden, where we could play ninepins or *jeu de boules,* and soon we managed to cultivate a narrow bed along the building's wall, in which, on a surface of some eighty square yards, we grew almost incredible quantities of lettuce and radishes, as well as some flowers. I need not say that at once we organized classes, and during the three years that we remained at Clairvaux I gave my comrades lessons in cosmography, geometry, or physics, also aiding them in the study of languages. Nearly every one learned at least one language,— English, German, Italian, or Spanish,—while a few learned two. We also managed to do some bookbinding, having learned how from one of those excellent Encyclopédie Roret booklets.

At the end of the first year, however, my health again gave way. Clairvaux is built on marshy ground, upon which malaria is endemic, and malaria, with scurvy, laid hold of me. Then my wife, who was studying at Paris, working in Würtz's laboratory and preparing to take an examination for the degree of Doctor of Science, abandoned everything, and came to the tiny hamlet of Clairvaux, which consists of less than a dozen houses grouped at the foot of an immense high wall which encircles the prison. Of course, her life in that hamlet, with the prison wall opposite, was anything but gay; yet she stayed there till I was released. During the first year she was allowed to see me only once in two months, and all interviews were held in the presence of a warder, who sat between us. But when she settled at Clairvaux, declaring her firm intention to remain there, she was soon permitted to see me every day, in one of the small houses within the prison walls where a post of warders was kept, and food was brought me from the inn where she stayed. Later, we were even allowed to take a walk in the governor's garden, closely watched all the time, and usually one of my comrades joined us in the walk.

I was quite astonished to discover that the central prison of Clairvaux had all the aspects of a small manufacturing town, surrounded by orchards and cornfields, all encircled by an outer wall. The fact is, that if in a French central prison the inmates are perhaps more dependent upon the fancies and caprices of the governor and the warders than they seem to be in English prisons, the treatment of the prisoners is far more humane than it is in the corresponding institutions on the other side of the Channel. The mediæval revengeful system which still prevails in English prisons has been given up long since in France. The imprisoned man is not compelled to sleep on planks, or to have a mattress on alternate days only; the day he comes to prison he gets a decent bed, and retains it. He is not compelled, either, to degrading work, such as to climb a wheel, or to pick oakum; he is employed, on the contrary, in useful work, and this is why the Clairvaux prison has the aspect of a manufacturing town, iron furniture, picture frames, looking-glasses, metric measures, velvet, linen, ladies' stays, small things in mother of pearl, wooden shoes, and so on, being made by the nearly sixteen hundred men who are kept there.

Moreover, if the punishment for insubordination is very cruel, there is, at least, none of the flogging which goes on still in English prisons. Such a punishment would be absolutely impossible in France. Altogether, the central prison at Clairvaux may be described as one of the best penal institutions in Europe. And, with all that, the results obtained at Clairvaux are as bad as in any of the prisons of the old type. "The watchword nowadays is that convicts are reformed in our prisons," one of the members of the prison administration once said to me. "This is all nonsense, and I shall never be induced to tell such a lie."

I will not repeat here what I have said in a book, *In Russian and French Prisons,* which I published in England in 1886, soon after my release from Clairvaux, upon the moral influence of prisoners upon prisoners. But there is one thing which must be said. The prison population consists of heterogeneous elements; but, taking only those who are usually described as "the criminals" proper, and of whom we have heard so much lately from Lombroso and his followers, what struck me most as regards them was that the prisons, which are considered as preventive of anti-social deeds, are exactly the institutions for breeding them. Every one knows that absence of education, dislike of regular work, physical incapability of sustained effort, misdirected love of adventure, gambling propensities, absence of energy, an untrained will, and carelessness about the happiness of others are the causes which bring this class of people before the courts. Now I was deeply impressed during my imprisonment by the fact that it is exactly these defects of human nature—each one of them—which the prison breeds in its inmates; and it is bound to breed them because it is a prison, and will breed them so long as it exists. Incarceration in a prison of necessity entirely destroys the energy of a man and annihilates his will. In prison life there is no room for exercising one's will; to possess one's own will in prison means surely to get into trouble. The will of the prisoner *must* be killed, and it is killed. Still less room is there for exercising one's natural sympathies, everything being done to prevent free contact with all those, outside and inside, with whom the prisoner may have feelings of sympathy. Physically and mentally he is rendered less and less capable of sustained effort, and if he has had already a dislike for regular work, this dislike is only the more increased during his prison years. If, before he first came to the prison, he was easily wearied by monotonous work which he could not do properly, or had an antipathy to underpaid overwork, his dislike now becomes hatred. If he doubted about the social utility of current rules of morality, now after having cast a critical glance upon the official defenders of these rules, and learned his comrades' opinions of them, he openly throws these rules overboard. And if he has got into trouble in consequence of a morbid development of the passionate, sensual side of his nature, now, after having spent a number of years in prison, this morbid character is still more developed, in many cases to an appalling extent. In this last direction—the most dangerous of all—prison education is most effective.

In Siberia I had seen what sinks of filth and what hotbeds of physical and moral deterioration the dirty, overcrowded, "unreformed" Russian prisons were, and at the age of nineteen I imagined that if there were less overcrowding in the rooms and a certain classification of the prisoners, and if healthy occupations were provided for them, the institution might be substantially improved. Now I had to part with these illusions. I could convince myself that as regards their effects upon the prisoners and their results for society at large, the best "reformed" prisons—whether cellular or not—are as bad as, or even worse than the dirty prisons of old. They do not reform the prisoners. On the contrary, in the immense, overwhelming majority of cases they exercise upon them the most deteriorating effect. The thief, the swindler, the rough, who has spent some years in a prison, comes out of it more ready than ever to resume his former career; he is better prepared for it; he has learned to do it better; he is more embittered against society, and he finds a more solid justification for being in revolt against its laws and customs; necessarily, unavoidably, he is bound to sink deeper and deeper into the anti-social acts which first brought him before a law court. The offenses he will commit after his release will inevitably be graver than those which first got him into trouble; and he is doomed to finish his life in a prison or in a hard-labor colony. In the above-mentioned book I said that prisons are "universities of crime, maintained by the state." And now, thinking of it at fifteen years' distance, in the light of my subsequent experience, I can only confirm that statement of mine.

VII

Demands for our release were continually raised, both in the press and in the Chamber of Deputies. However, Alexander III. objected to it; and one day the prime minister, M. Freycinet, answering an interpellation in the Chamber, said that "diplomatic difficulties stood in the way of Kropótkin's release." Strange words in the mouth of the prime minister of an independent country; but still stranger words have been heard since in connection with that ill-omened alliance of France with imperial Russia.

In the middle of January, 1886, the four of us who were still at Clairvaux were set free.

My release meant also the release of my wife from her voluntary imprisonment in the little village at the prison gates, which began to tell upon her health, and we went to Paris to stay there for a few weeks. From Paris we went to London, where I found once more my two old friends, Stepniák and Chaikóvsky. Near the end of the summer [1886] a heavy blow fell upon me. I learned that my brother Alexander was no longer living.

During the years that I had been abroad before my imprisonment in France we had never corresponded with each other. In the eyes of the Russian government, to love a brother who is persecuted for his political opinions is itself a sin. To maintain relations with him after he has become a refugee is a crime. A subject of the Tsar must hate all the rebels against the supreme ruler's authority,—and Alexander was in the clutches of the Russian police. I persistently refused, therefore, to write to him or to any other of my relatives. After the Tsar had written on the petition of our sister Hélène, "Let him remain there," there was no hope of a speedy release for my brother. Two years after that a committee was nominated to settle terms for those who had been exiled to Siberia without judgment, for an undetermined time, and my brother got five years.

That made seven, with the two which he had already been
kept there. Then a new committee was nominated under Lorís-
Mélikov, and added another five years. My brother was thus
to be liberated in October, 1886. That made twelve years of
exile, first in a tiny town of East Siberia, and afterwards at
Tomsk,—that is, in the lowlands of West Siberia, where he had
not even the dry and healthy climate of the high prairies further east.

When I was imprisoned at Clairvaux he wrote to me, and
we exchanged a few letters. He wrote that though our letters
would be read by the Russian police in Siberia, and by the
French prison authorities in France, we might as well write to
each other even under this double supervision. He spoke of his
family life, of his three children, whom he described interest-
ingly, and of his work. He earnestly advised me to keep a
watchful eye upon the development of science in Italy, where
excellent and original researches are conducted, but remain
unknown in the scientific world until they have been exploited
in Germany; and he gave me his opinions about the probable
progress of political life in Russia. He did not believe in the
possibility with us, in a near future, of constitutional rule on
the pattern of the West European parliaments; but he looked
forward—and found it quite sufficient for the moment—to
the convocation of a sort of deliberative National Assembly
(*Zémsky Sobór* or *Etats Généraux*). It would not make laws,
but would only work out the schemes of laws, to which the
imperial power and the Council of State would give definitive
form and final sanction.

Above all he wrote to me about his scientific work. He had
always had a decided leaning towards astronomy, and when
we were at St. Petersburg he had published in Russian an
excellent summary of all our knowledge of the shooting stars.
With his fine critical mind he soon saw the strong or the weak
points of different hypotheses; and without sufficient knowledge of mathematics, but endowed with a powerful imagination, he succeeded in grasping the results of the most intricate
mathematical researches. Living with his imagination amongst
the moving celestial bodies, he realized their complex movements often better than some mathematicians,—especially the
pure algebraists,—who are apt to lose sight of the realities of

the physical world and see nothing but their own formulæ. Our St. Petersburg astronomers spoke to me with great appreciation of that work of my brother's. Now, he undertook to study the structure of the universe; to analyze the data and the hypotheses about the worlds of suns, star-clusters, and nebulæ in the infinite space, and to work out the problems of their grouping, their life, and the laws of their evolution and decay. The Púlkova astronomer, Gyldén, spoke highly of this new work of Alexander's, and introduced him by correspondence to Mr. Holden in the United States, from whom, while at Washington lately, I had the pleasure of hearing an appreciative estimate of the value of these researches. Science is greatly in need, from time to time, of such scientific speculations of a higher standard, made by a scrupulously laborious, critical, and, at the same time, imaginative mind.

But in a small town of Siberia, far away from all the libraries, unable to follow the progress of science, he had only succeeded in embodying in his work the researches which had been made up to the date of his exile. Some capital work had been done since. He knew it, but how could he get access to the necessary books, so long as he remained in Siberia? The approach of the time of his liberation did not inspire him with hope either. He knew that he would not be allowed to stay in any of the university towns of Russia, or of Western Europe, but that his exile to Siberia would be followed by a second exile, perhaps even worse than the first, to some hamlet of Eastern Russia.

"A despair like Faust's takes hold of me at times," he wrote to me. When the time of his liberation was at hand, he sent his wife and children to Russia, taking advantage of one of the last steamers before the close of navigation, and, on a gloomy night, this despair put an end to his life.

A dark cloud hung upon our cottage for many months,— until a flash of light pierced it, when, the next spring, a tiny being, a girl who bears my brother's name, came into the world, and with her helpless cry set new strings vibrating in my heart.

VIII

In 1886 the socialist movement in England was in full swing. I took a lively part in this movement, and with a few English comrades I started, in addition to the three socialist papers already in existence, an anarchist-communist monthly, *Freedom*, which continues to live up to the present hour. At the same time I resumed my work on anarchism where I had had to interrupt it at the time of my arrest. The critical part of it was published by Elisée Reclus, during my Clairvaux imprisonment, under the title, *Paroles d'un Révolté*.[21] Now I began to work out the constructive part of an anarchist-communist society,—so far as it could be forecast,—in a series of articles published at Paris in *La Révolte*. "Our boy," prosecuted for anti-militarist propaganda, had been compelled to change its title-page, and now appeared under a feminine name. Later on these articles were published in a more elaborate form in a book, *La Conquête du Pain*.

These researches caused me to study more thoroughly certain points in the economic life of the civilized nations of to-day. Most socialists had hitherto said that in our present civilized societies we actually produce much more than is necessary for guaranteeing full well-being to all; that it was only the distribution which was defective; and, if a social revolution took place, all that was required would be for every one to return to his factory or workshop,—society taking possession for itself of the "surplus value," or benefits, which now went to the capitalist. I thought, on the contrary, that under the present conditions of private ownership production itself had taken a wrong turn, and was entirely inadequate even as regards the very necessaries of life. None of these necessaries are produced in greater quantities than would be required to secure well-being for all; and the over-production, so often spoken of, means nothing but that the masses are too poor to buy even what is now considered as necessary for a decent existence. But in all civilized countries the production, both agricultural and industrial, ought to and easily might be immensely increased, so as to secure a reign of plenty for all. This brought me to consider the possibilities of modern agriculture, as well as those of an education which would give to every one the possibility of carrying on at the same time both enjoyable manual work and brain work. I developed these ideas in a series of articles in the *Nineteenth Century*, which are now published as a book under the title of *Fields, Factories, and Workshops*.

Another great question also engrossed my attention. It is known to what conclusions Darwin's formula, the "struggle for existence," had been developed by his followers generally, even the most intelligent of them, such as Huxley. There is no infamy in civilized society, or in the relations of the whites towards the so-called lower races, or of the strong towards the weak, which would not have found its excuse in this formula.

Even during my stay at Clairvaux I saw the necessity of completely revising the formula itself and its applications to human affairs. The attempts which had been made by a few socialists in this direction did not satisfy me, but I found in a lecture by a Russian zoölogist, Professor Kessler, a true expression of the law of struggle for life. "Mutual aid," he said in that lecture, "is as much a law of nature as mutual struggle; but for the *progressive* evolution of the species the former is far more important than the latter." These few words—contained for me the key of the whole problem. When Huxley published in 1888 his atrocious article, "The Struggle for Existence; a Program," I decided to put in a readable form my objections to his way of understanding the struggle for life, among animals as well as among men, the materials for which I had been accumulating for two years. I spoke of it to my friends. However, I found that the interpretation of "struggle for life" in the sense of a war-cry of "Woe to the Weak," raised to the height of a commandment of nature revealed by science, was so deeply rooted in this country that it had become almost a matter of religion. Two persons only supported me in my revolt against this misinterpretation of the facts of nature. The editor of the *Nineteenth Century*, Mr. James Knowles, with his admirable perspicacity, at once seized the gist of the matter, and with a truly youthful energy encouraged me to take it in hand. The other supporter was the regretted H. W. Bates, whom Darwin, in his *Autobiography*, de-

scribed as one of the most intelligent men he ever met. He was
secretary of the Geographical Society, and I knew him; so I
spoke to him of my intention. He was delighted with it. "Yes,
most assuredly write it," he said. "That is true Darwinism. It
is a shame to think of what they have made of Darwin's ideas.
Write it, and when you have published it, I will write you a
letter of commendation which you may publish." I could not
have had better encouragement, and I began the work, which
was published in the *Nineteenth Century* under the titles of
"Mutual Aid among Animals," "Among Savages," "Among
Barbarians," "In the Mediæval City," and "Amongst Ourselves." Unfortunately I neglected to submit to Bates the first
two articles of this series, dealing with animals, which were
published during his lifetime; I hoped to be soon ready with
the second part of the work, "Mutual Aid among Men;" but it
took me several years to complete it, and in the meantime Bates
passed from among us.

The researches which I had to make during these studies,
in order to acquaint myself with the institutions of the bar-
barian period and with those of the mediæval free cities, led
me to another important research: the part played in history
by the state during its latest manifestation in Europe, in the
last three centuries. And on the other hand, the study of the
mutual support institutions at different stages of civilization led
me to examine the evolutionist bases of the senses of justice
and morality in man.[22]

When I think of the vague, confused, timid ideas which
were expressed by the workers at the first congresses of the
International Workingmen's Association, or which were current
at Paris during the Commune insurrection, even among the
most thoughtful of the leaders, and compare them with those
which have been arrived at to-day by a vast number of workers, I must say that they seem to me to belong to two entirely
different worlds.

There is no period in history—with the exception, perhaps,
of the period of the insurrections in the twelfth and thirteenth
centuries, which led to the birth of the mediæval Communes
—during which a similarly deep change has taken place in the
current conceptions of society. And now, in my fifty-seventh
year, I am even more deeply convinced than I was twenty-five

years ago that a chance combination of accidental circumstances may bring about in Europe a revolution as wide-spread
as that of 1848, and far more important; not in the sense of
mere fighting between different parties, but in the sense of a
profound and rapid social reconstruction; and I am convinced
that whatever character such a movement may take in different countries, there will be displayed everywhere a far deeper
comprehension of the required changes than has ever been
displayed within the last six centuries; while the resistance
which the movement will meet in the privileged classes will
hardly have the character of obtuse obstinacy which made the
revolutions of times past so violent.

To obtain this great result is well worth the efforts which
so many thousands of men and women of all nations and all
classes have made within the last thirty years.

EPILOGUE

After the publication of his Memoirs, *Kropótkin received an invitation from the Lowell Institute of Boston to lecture on Russian literature.*[23] *He gave a large part of his discussion to the works of Tolstóy. Although Kropótkin and Tolstóy had never met, they had corresponded indirectly through Tolstóy's disciple, Vladímir Chertkóv.*

"Kropótkin's letter has pleased me very much," Tolstóy wrote to Chertkóv in the spring of 1897. "His arguments in favor of violence do not seem to me the expression of his opinion but only of his fidelity to the banner under which he has served so honestly all his life. He cannot fail to see that the protest against violence, in order to be strong, must have a solid foundation and for this very reason is destined to failure."

In order to comprehend how much I sympathize with the ideas of Tolstóy, *Kropótkin replied to Chertkóv,* it suffices to say that I have written a whole volume to demonstrate that life is created not by the struggle for existence but only by mutual aid.

While Kropótkin admired Tolstóy's literary genius and his spirit, he privately told a friend, I am not in sympathy with Tolstóy's asceticism, nor with his doctrine of nonresistance to evil, nor with his New Testament literalism. *But when Tolstóy attempted to retire from the world just before his death in 1910, Kropótkin came indirectly to the defense of Tolstóy's religion:*

. . . I am sure that, having devoted the last thirty years of his life to the working out of a universal rationalist religion, divested of all the mystical elements of modern Christianity, a

religion which, he says, would be equally acceptable to the
Christian, the Buddhist, the Hebrew, the Musulman, the fol-
lower of Lao-Tse and to every ethical philosopher, and after
having so passionately proclaimed in his latest writings the supreme decisive right of reason in religious matters, Tolstóy will
certainly not return to the teachings of the Greek Orthodox
Church.

I am not astonished to learn that Tolstóy had decided to
retire to a peasant house where he might continue his teachings without having to rely upon anyone else's labor for supplying himself or his family with the luxuries of life. It is the
necessary outcome of the terrible inner drama he had been
living through the last thirty years—the drama, by the way,
of thousands upon thousands of intellectuals in our present
society.

*To his audience at the Lowell Institute in Boston, Kropótkin
described Tolstóy as the most loved man—the most touchingly
loved man—in the world.*[24]

*During this same period, the Royal Geographic Society of
London asked Kropótkin to publish his scientific work on the
orography of Asia.*[25] *He was also offered membership in the
society, which he refused, because the society was under royal
patronage. Kropótkin attended, however, a banquet of the society and gave its embarrassing consequences as an excuse for
refusing to speak at a Danish banquet:*

I cannot come. Doubtless they will toast the King of England. In conformity with my convictions, I could not rise and
this would scandalize the assembly. A month ago I was invited to a banquet of the Royal Geographic Society of London.
The chairman proposed, "The King!" Everybody rose, and I
alone remained seated. It was a painful moment. And I was
thunderstruck when immediately afterward the same chairman cried, "Long live Prince Kropótkin!" and everybody,
without exception, rose.

*Kropótkin had always considered France and England as
the two nations which offered the greatest possibility for a
social revolution. When the Russian Revolution of 1905 (despite its failure) appeared to place his own country on that
same path, he wanted no European crisis to alter the status*

quo in favor of Germany, whose defeat of France in 1871 he blamed for the lack of a social revolution in Europe.

I consider that the duty of everyone who cherishes the ideals of human progress . . . is to do everything in one's power to crush down the invasion of the Germans into Western Europe, *Kropótkin wrote his friend, Professor Gustav Steffens in Sweden, after war began in 1914.* The cause of the present war lies in the consequences of the war of 1870–71. . . . Since 1871 Germany has become a standing menace to European progress. All countries have been compelled to introduce obligatory military service on the lines that had been introduced in Germany, and to keep immense standing armies. All lived under the menace of a sudden invasion. More than that, for Eastern Europe, and especially for Russia, Germany was the chief support and protection of reaction.

Kropótkin saw in the war a great lesson for all nations: it would teach them that war cannot be fought by pacifist dreams. Nor can it be combated, *he added,* by that sort of antimilitarist propaganda which has been carried on till now.

Kropótkin himself had written anarchist antiwar propaganda until the eve of the war, but after 1914 he found the anarchist attitude toward the war incomprehensible:

I have just received your letter, *Kropótkin wrote in September of 1914 to Jean Grave, the editor of the anarchist* Les Temps Nouveaux *in Paris.* My heart was wrung with pain in reading it. In what world of illusions do you live to speak of peace. The conditions of peace will be imposed by the victor. . . . Arm yourself! Make a superhuman effort—this is the only way that France will reconquer the right and the strength to inspire the people of Europe with her civilization and her ideas of liberty, communism and fraternity. At least wake up! . . . I am quite aware that socialism exists in Germany, but it consists of only a handful, who, if they tried to rise, would be crushed as the Russian revolution was crushed in 1905. It is the military clique which rules. What would happen if they were victorious? Please pass this letter on to our friends. We are better informed here and better placed than you to see where we are in this war.

Kropótkin's stand on the war sharply separated him from the international anarchist movement which condemned his views and reprinted from that time on only his earlier antiwar articles. His support of the Entente was no more welcome to those Russian radicals who stood apart from the war. "I recently read Kropótkin's article," Stalin wrote to Lenin in 1915, "the old fool must have completely lost his mind." Trotsky noted that the "superannuated anarchist Kropótkin, who had a weakness ever since youth for the populists, made use of the war to disavow everything he had been teaching for almost half a century."[26]

From the beginning of the war, Kropótkin took it as his personal duty to encourage his countrymen to defend their country and then to set it free. Some Russians, such as S. Melgounóff, feared this type of appeal and warned Kropótkin that the Russian people were not psychologically prepared for the war and that any patriotism or enthusiasm was only a façade which Kropótkin might influence toward more undesirable goals.

If my opinions have taken this form, *Kropótkin replied,* it is because, having lived nearly forty years in close contact with the workers of Western Europe, I have been able to have an idea of what Western, Latin culture represents in the development of socialist thought. . . .

All this has led me to believe that the destruction or even the retarding (as happened after 1870) of Latin culture and particularly of French culture in the fields of social thought and the natural sciences would be an enormous loss for Europe. . . .

Like many others you fear that Russian chauvinism would be developed to the point of becoming more dangerous than Germany's imperialism and thirst for conquest.

I consider for my part—and all of history is in evidence—that the tendencies which prevail in Russian life depend entirely upon the influences which are dominant in the life of Western Europe.

. . . I now ask myself with fear: "What will happen if the Germans triumph?" And I think of the consequences, especially for Russia.

The fall of the Russian autocracy in February of 1917 delighted Kropótkin, although he feared it might raise hopes for a premature peace among the weary Russian people. He immediately telegraphed an open letter to his countrymen:

It is absurd to speak of the peace-loving intentions of Germany when it finds itself under the rule of the Hohenzollerns. Men, women and children of Russia, save our country and civilization from the black hordes of the Central Powers! We must not lose an hour. Present a united front to them. Now, when you have so heroically dealt with internal enemies, every effort that you make for the expulsion of the invading enemies will strengthen the further development of our freedom and a stable peace.

Before leaving for Russia, Kropótkin wrote The Times *of London to thank publicly the English people for the kindness he had found in their country during his long years of exile:*

Those of us who have lived through it will not forget the energy with which our friends and the Labor organizations altogether took the defense of every Russian refugee whose extradition the Tsar's Government tried to obtain, in order to establish a precedent, nor the contempt with which the British nation as a whole treated all attempts at obtaining an extradition treaty.

And we shall not forget the friendly support which we found each time we appealed, be it for the relief of a famine (especially in 1891), the relief of exiles in Siberia, the expression of sympathy with the attempt at throwing off the yoke of autocracy in 1905, or a vigorous protest against the atrocious repression that followed this attempt. . . . I can only say how happy I am to see my mother country standing in one camp with the Western democracies against the Central Empires.

Kropótkin arrived in Russia in June of 1917 where he was greeted by Alexander Kérensky and a crowd of sixty thousand. To a Russian friend living in England, Professor S. P. Turin, Kropótkin wrote a series of letters giving his impressions of the new Russia:

We are now staying at Kámmenny Óstrov and nonetheless certain days we have visits all day long, for the most part useful people, *Kropótkin wrote in July of 1917.* Evening comes and still more visits, and when the last one has left, I no longer have the strength to write.

. . . We arrived at Petrograd at two in the morning rather

than eleven at night. My niece Polovseva and the Russian correspondents came to meet us at Beloóstrov; but at Petrograd there was such an enormous crowd that they nearly crushed Sophia, Sasha [*Kropótkin's wife and daughter*], and me. The soldiers and officers of the Semenov Regiment had the idea of making a chain and they led us into the hall where we waited for our friends.

. . . If I could tell you, dear Sergéi Petróvich, what I felt at this arrival when the train slowly entered the station to the sound of the *Marseillaise* and the sight of this boundless sea of heads in the dawn of a St. Petersburg morning; the dear faces of my nieces, their hair already touched with gray, whom I did not even know for certain, and particularly this crowd of intelligent, audacious and proud faces celebrating the triumph of light over darkness, of truth over falsehood and of freedom over slavery. And then there were the welcoming speeches of the young people upon whom is placed the heavy responsibility of carrying through successfully all that has begun. Their speeches were courageous and bold and like their faces full of hope. Among old friends there was Chaikóvsky.

The next day I had to speak in the Bolshóoi Theátre. I spoke in a high-sounding voice, very loud, surprised at the range of my voice, and I grew hoarse. And then several things indicated something was wrong with my lungs. I had to go to bed, the doctor—with a cupping glass to the lungs—fixed it in time.

. . . I will not describe to you the state of mind here. You know it by the newspapers: they report accurately the variety of opinions in Petrograd; things are definitely better in Moscow. I know this from friends on the way back. Here the great outburst of heroism mixes or rather clashes with Bolshevism, which, however, is in decline these days.

This is already the second—no, the third time—that I have tried to write to you and have been unable to finish, *Kropótkin wrote in August of 1917.* First of all my illness (I took cold the day of my arrival) and then the innumerable people who come to see me, then the mass of impressions which heap themselves up one on the other, sometimes marvelously beautiful, sometimes profoundly sad, and always new, beyond anything I have ever encountered or lived through either in life or in books. Then the events of the first days of July and, during the course of the past two weeks, what is called "the crisis of power," that is, the patched-up settlement of the Provisional Government with all its consequences for the present.

This last week I saw many people both here and at Petrograd. You certainly already know from the newspapers of the offer which has been made to me.

The new Prime Minister, Alexander Kérensky, had called on Kropótkin to offer him a cabinet post. "Petr Alexséevich, you must be my Minister of Education," Kérensky had told him. What! cried Kropótkin in surprise, his face turning red with anger. You are asking me—an anarchist—to enter your government? *He gave his answer immediately punctuated with pounding on the table:* No! No! No!

I naturally immediately refused the offer, *Kropótkin continued in his letter to Turin,* but to the full extent of my strength I will help the people to agree on a program and to direct their strength toward the reconstruction of the internal life of the country which is moving toward an enormous debacle.

. . . I have naturally been to see Prince Lvov since my arrival. I saw him four times: once on June 18, to be exact, then during the ministerial crisis; on the eve of his departure for Moscow he came to see me in the country. We liked each other, and I am sorry he left the government. He and those who were helping him in the Union of Zémstvos worked seriously to organize complete administrative autonomy of the Zémstvos according to fundamentally democratic principles.

Life marches on at such a pace, *Kropótkin wrote in September of 1917,* that even in good health I would not have the time to write my friends. Moreover, I am still ill.

. . . As I do not belong to any organization, I would have been unable to take part in the Moscow Conference, but Kérensky and the others decided to invite [Catherine] Breshkóvskaia, [George] Plekhánov, Morózov, Pankrátov [*two famous prisoners of Schlüsselburg*] and me, besides the members of various organizations. That is how I finally landed in Moscow.

In his speech to the Moscow Conference, Kropótkin called for a national rally to the defense of Russia against the German armies: You must know, comrades, that there is something

worse than all this, that is the psychology of a defeated nation.[27] *Besides advocating a continuation of the war, Kropót-*
kin also proposed that the future Russian government take the
form of a federal republic:

I had proposed it in an extremely moderate form (up till
then no one had pronounced the word "republic"), notably
in order to avoid encroaching in advance upon the rights of
the supreme Constituent Assembly and simply to facilitate its
task. I asked the Conference to express its wish in favor of the
Republic. The entire hall arose and gave a tumultuous ovation.
It lasted a long time: one to one and a half minutes. I looked
around the hall: the entire floor was standing, the Left in its
boxes, and, to my amazement, all the Right also. What struck
me particularly was the balcony (industrialists, financiers)
who had maintained an aloofness and a significant silence during the democratic ovations of the Left.

Kérensky was right to say in his speech that the Republic
had been accepted by the Conference unanimously. Unfortunately because of the principle laid down in advance, the Conference did not have the right to take any decision. That is
why I had expressed myself in such a moderate fashion.

. . . At St. Petersburg I became closely acquainted with
Kérensky and I took a liking to him. His position is most
tragic. Here I often see George Evgénevich [*Prince Lvov*]
and we have taken a great liking to him. At this tragic moment
he has gone to St. Petersburg in order to help Kérensky, and I
would have gone with him if I had not been in bed with a high
fever. I am still in bed.

. . . I believe very firmly that Russia will overcome this
present debacle. But she will have to pass through difficult
times. I spoke with George Evgénevich and asked him if it
would not be possible to find the strength for the necessary
reconstruction in the Zémstvos, and to organize a Russia of
Zémstvos for the inevitable reconstruction in the same way he
organized the Union of Zémstvos for the war, as well as for a
serious political force. But there are no more Zémstvos.

There is such a mess here, *Kropótkin wrote two months*
after the Bolshevik Revolution of October 1917, that all work
is impossible. It is scarcely possible to get permission to write
in [*the journal*] *Russkie vedomosti* and I have given it up

entirely. After we settled here, I intended to occupy myself with a large work with some of your friends on demobilization and on Social reconstruction which are inevitably linked. But what is the use of that now? Life goes on at much too rapid a pace.

. . . I would have liked to have written you of many things, but what we are living through is too difficult to write and it is useless to describe the follies.

I counted a great deal, *Kropótkin wrote in January of 1918*, for the indispensable work of reconstruction, on the people who had gathered together in the Union of Zémstvos and the Union of Cities. It is they . . . who could have produced a thoughtful and sensible plan which is so necessary now for the reorganization of our life. The conversation I had with some of their members before the departure of George Evgénevich for the South led me to believe that they had the actual strength that could effectively help the people to emerge from this really frightful situation. But I learn today that even this last center is destroyed, dispersed, annihilated without the faintest hope that those who now dominate this organization are capable of rebuilding anything vital and capable of working.

. . . At this moment we are trying to develop the federative element. I see in it the only counterweight to the monarchical appetites which are developed assiduously by the propaganda of the two camps, the Prussian and the Holstein-Gottorp. But even here one meets a pile of obstacles, internal and external. The faith in centralism is still strong. But, at any rate, there are clear horizons.

. . . That Russia will emerge from this debacle I do not doubt for a second. But she will have to go through two or three very hard years. Afterward I foresee years of vigorous, healthy and intelligent development. The elements are there, of an extreme richness. If only we were finished with the threat of restoration, if only we could prevent the Germans from advancing farther. . . .

I see many good people, *Kropótkin wrote in May of 1918*. We have undertaken a large work at our League of Federalists: we shall publish four volumes . . . on federalism in all its aspects: geographical, ethnographical, economic, political, historical, etc. Each volume consists of a dozen articles, all by

specialists. The contributors to each volume examine minutely
the contents of each article. It promises to be a sound and
indispensable work. We meet at my house and I am the editor-
in-chief. (The contributors are for the most part professors,
Privatdocents, etc.)

At my age it is physically impossible to take part in public
affairs during a revolution, and to take part as an amateur is
not in my nature, *Kropótkin wrote to another friend, Georg
Brandes, the Danish literary critic, nearly a year later, in April
of 1919.* During the past winter, which we spent at Moscow,
I worked with a group of collaborators in outlining the elements of a federal republic. But the group had to break up,
and I have returned to a work on ethics which I began fifteen
years ago in England.

All that I can do now is to give you a general idea of the
situation in Russia, which in my opinion is not correctly understood in the West. An analogy will perhaps explain what
I mean.

We are at this moment going through what France experienced during the Jacobin revolution, from September 1792
to July 1794, with this addition, that now it is a social revolution that seeks its way.

The dictatorial method of the Jacobins was false. It was not
able to create a stable organization and it necessarily led to the
reaction. And yet the Jacobins accomplished in June 1793 the
abolition of the feudal rights begun in 1789, which neither the
Constituent Assembly nor the Legislative Assembly had been
able to achieve. And they nobly proclaimed the political
equality of all citizens. Two immense fundamental changes
which in the course of the nineteenth century were accomplished all over Europe.

An analogous thing has happened in Russia. The Bolsheviki
strive to introduce by the dictatorship of a fraction of the Social Democratic party the socialization of the soil, of industry,
and of commerce. This change which they labor to accomplish is the fundamental principle of socialism. Unhappily, the
method by which they seek to impose, in a strongly centralized
state, a communism resembling that of Babeuf—and thereby
paralyzing the constructive work of the people—that method

makes success absolutely impossible, and is paving the way to a furious and vicious reaction.

. . . They speak in the West of restoring "order" in Russia by an armed intervention of the Allies. . . . I protest with all my strength against every kind of armed intervention of the Allies in Russian affairs. That intervention would result in an increase of Russian chauvinism. It would restore over us a chauvinist monarchy—we see the signs of it already—and, note this well, it produces in the mass of Russian people a hostile attitude towards Western Europe—an attitude which will have the saddest consequences. The Americans have already grasped this very well.

. . . Instead of playing the role which Austria, Prussia, and Russia played in 1793 towards France, the Allies should do everything to aid the Russian people to emerge from this terrible situation. Besides, oceans of blood would have to be spilled to make the Russian people return to the past—it could never be accomplished.

That Kropótkin was concerned with the welfare of Russia rather than the preservation of Bolshevik rule became obvious when he had a meeting with Lenin in the following month of May 1919. Kropótkin went to Moscow to plead for the life of an old friend scheduled for execution by the Bolsheviks. Lenin received Kropótkin with respect and listened to his arguments condemning the taking of hostages as a threat against counterrevolutionary activities. The discussion soon turned to the future of Russia.

You and I have different points of view, *Kropótkin frankly remarked.* Our aims seem to be the same, but as to a number of questions about means, actions and organization, I differ with you greatly. Neither I, nor any of my friends, will refuse to help you; but our help will consist only in that we will report to you all the injustices taking place everywhere from which the people are groaning.

Lenin accepted Kropótkin's offer and received several letters criticizing the rule of the Bolsheviks: At every point, people who don't know actual life are making awful mistakes for which we have to pay in hundreds of thousands of human lives and the ruination of whole regions. Without the participation of the local population in construction—the participation of the peasants and workers themselves—it is impossible to build a new life. . . .

Russia has become a Soviet Republic only in name. . . . At present it is ruled not by Soviets but by party committees. . . . If the present situation should continue much longer, the very word "socialism" will turn into a curse, as did the slogan of "equality" for forty years after the rule of Jacobins.

When Kropótkin read in Pravda *that the Council of People's Commissars had decided to hold as hostages several officers of Wrangel's army, he wrote vehemently to Lenin in protest:*

Is it possible that you do not know what a hostage really is —a man imprisoned not because of a crime committed but only because it suits his enemies to exert blackmail on his companions? . . . If you admit such methods, one can foresee that one day you will use torture, as was done in the Middle Ages.

I hope you will not answer me that power is for political men a professional duty, and that any attack against that power must be considered a threat against which one must guard oneself at any price. This opinion is no longer held even by kings; the rulers of countries where monarchy still exists have abandoned long ago the means of defense now introduced into Russia with the seizure of hostages.

How can you, Vladimir Ilyich, you who want to be the apostle of new truths and the builder of a new state, give your consent to the use of such repulsive conduct, of such unacceptable methods? . . . What future lies in store for Communism when one of its most important defenders tramples in this way on every honest feeling?

Lenin soon became tired of these letters. "I am sick of this old fogy," he told one of his associates. "He doesn't understand a thing about politics and intrudes with his advice, most of which is very stupid."[28]

While Kropótkin was not in agreement with the Bolsheviks, he found the interference of outside powers in the internal affairs of Russia equally unacceptable: The working men of the civilized world and their friends in the other classes ought to induce their Governments to abandon entirely the idea of an armed intervention in the affairs of Russia—whether open or disguised, whether military or in the shape of subventions to different nations, *Kropótkin wrote in the summer of 1920 in an open letter to the workers of the Western world.*

Russia is now living through a revolution of the same depth and the same importance as the British nation underwent in 1639–1648 and France in 1789–1794. Every nation ought to refuse to play the shameful role which abased England, Prussia, Austria and Russia during the French Revolution.

This did not mean, Kropótkin explained at length, that there was nothing to oppose in the methods of the Bolshevik government. But he believed that every armed intervention of a foreign government necessarily resulted in a reinforcement of the dictatorial tendencies of the Bolshevik rulers and paralyzed those Russians who were trying to aid in the reconstruction of Russia independently of the Bolshevik government:

I must point out, moreover, that if the Allies' military intervention is continued, it will certainly develop a bitter feeling against the Western nations in Russia, a sentiment that will someday be utilized by their enemies in possible future conflicts. Such a bitterness is already developing.

Kropótkin's move from Moscow to Dmítrov (a small village sixty kilometers northwest of Moscow) symbolized the spiritual isolation in which the Bolshevik Revolution had left him. In his solitude Kropótkin sought an answer to the perennial Russian question of what is to be done.

The revolution we have gone through is not the sum total of the efforts of separate individuals, but a natural phenomenon, independent of the human will, *he wrote in a private memorandum of 1920.* The revolution will advance in its own way, in the direction of least resistance, without paying the slightest attention to our efforts.

What is then to be done? To prevent the revolution? Absurd! Too late. . . . It must wear itself out.

And then? Then—inevitably a reaction will come. Such is the law of history. . . . Therefore the only thing we can do is to use our energy to lessen the fury and force of the approaching reaction.

Kropótkin attempted to make his contribution by returning to his work on ethics: I have undertaken to write on *Ethics* because I regard that work as absolutely necessary, *he wrote* in May of 1920. I know well that intellectual movements are not created by books, and that just the reverse is true. But I also know that for clarifying an idea the help of a book is needed, a book that expresses the bases of thought in their complete form.

Kropótkin's work on ethics was never completed.[29] In the middle of January, 1921, while playing the piano in an unheated room of the house at Dmítrov, he became chilled. It aggravated the bronchitis from which he suffered and soon developed into pneumonia. On receiving the news of Kropótkin's illness, Lenin sent a special train with doctors and medical supplies to Dmítrov. But despite medical care, Kropótkin's condition worsened. He died in the early hours of the morning of February 8, 1921.

BIBLIOGRAPHY

The following bibliography lists the major works of Kropótkin which are available in English, as well as two small anthologies of his writings.

The Conquest of Bread (New York and London, 1906).
Ethics, Origin and Development, tr. by L. Friedland and J. Piroshnikoff (New York, 1924).
Fields, Factories and Workshops (New York, 1901).
The Great French Revolution, 1789–1793, tr. by N. F. Dryhurst (New York, 1909).
Ideals and Realities in Russian Literature (New York, 1915).
In Russian and French Prisons (London, 1887).
Modern Science and Anarchism, revised edition (London, 1923).
Mutual Aid, A Factor of Evolution (London, 1902, reprinted Boston, 1955).
Kropotkin's Revolutionary Pamphlets, edited by Roger Nash Baldwin (New York, 1927).
Kropotkin, Selections from his Writings, edited by Herbert Read (London, 1924).

NOTES

1. Russian editions of Kropótkin's *Memoirs* based upon the 1902 translation from English were published in Russia itself from 1906 to 1933. The later editions made use of various parts of Kropótkin's additional notes in Russian. Of these, the most complete was edited by N. K. Lebedev in two volumes and published in Moscow in 1929 as *Zapiski Revoliutsionera*.

2. Kropótkin carried this emphasis so far in the latter half of his *Memoirs* that the reader learns only incidentally that Kropótkin had married, although his letters of the period show that he loved his wife deeply: "I have met in Geneva a Russian girl, young, quiet, good, very gentle, with one of those wonderful dispositions which, after an austere youth, becomes still better," Kropótkin wrote a friend shortly after his marriage in 1878. "She loves me and I love her." A visitor to the Kropótkins a quarter of a century after their marriage remarked that Kropótkin courted his wife as if they were just married, speaking to her with particular tenderness and often kissing her hand. (Ivan Knizhnik, *"Vospominaniia o P.A. Kropotkine i ob odnoi anarkhistskoi emigrantskoi gruppe,"* [Memoirs of P. A. Kropotkin and an Anarchist Emigrant Group] *Krasnaia letopis'*, no. 4 (1922), pp. 28–51.

3. Kropótkin developed his idea of mutual aid in a series of articles later published in book form as *Mutual Aid, A Factor of Evolution* (London, 1902 and reprinted Boston, 1955). A brief description of Kropótkin's philosophy of anarchism is given in the following note.

4. Kropótkin's attempt to develop a theory of anarchism is expressed in *Paroles d'un révolté* (Paris, 1885) and in *An-*

archist Communism, Its Basis and Principles (London, 1895). He began with an analysis of contemporary society in which he saw an individualistic ethic predominating at the cost of the broad mass of people. But instead of condemning this attitude, Kropótkin found it a natural result of the efforts of the individual to protect himself from the "tyranny of Capital and the State."

In the formulas of contemporary socialism, Kropótkin saw no solution, since they would merely prolong the tyranny under another form. To the socialist suggestion that the "tyranny of Capital" could be lifted if the individual received only according to his contribution to society, Kropótkin replied that such an assessment was impossible and that under a real socialism the individual would receive according to his needs. Moreover, in the power to make such an assessment, Kropótkin saw reimposed the "tyranny of the State." For this reason, he stood against the use of the State to implement socialism whether under the form of parliamentary socialism or the dictatorship of the proletariat as a class.

Kropótkin proposed anarchism as the most advanced form of socialism or communism (he used the concepts interchangeably in a non-Marxist sense) because it avoided, according to his interpretation, the "tyranny of Capital and the State" by distributing the goods of society according to individual need under a "no-government" society.

How such a society could be brought into existence and how it could be made to function, Kropótkin attempted to explain in *Conquest of Bread* (New York and London, 1906) and *Fields, Factories and Workshops* (New York, 1901). But since he left so many explanations dependent on the "goodwill of the people," he presented in effect only his ideal of the anarchist society. In brief, he described a society where there was no division between manual and intellectual workers (everyone doing both kinds of work), where everyone received according to need, and where all decisions were made directly by all those affected. This society was to be composed of small and fairly self-sufficient units voluntarily federated into larger and larger organizations.

In his efforts to prove that his theory of anarchism was in accord with the "historical progress of culture," Kropótkin brought together his political and scientific ideas in his book, *Mutual Aid.* Here he implied that the essence of an anarchist society is that it is governed by the principle of mutual aid rather than by the "tyranny of Capital and the State." Tracing the growth of mutual aid in history, Kropótkin interpreted the eras of individual city-states as the high points of civilization where the principle of mutual aid had flourished most fully. He concluded that the rise of the State (meaning here empires or nation-states, which he saw as the antithesis of the city-state) marked always a period of decline in history: "The absorption of all social functions by the State necessarily favors the development of an unbridled, narrow-minded individualism. In proportion as the obligations toward the State grow in number, the citizens are evidently relieved of their obligations toward each other."

5. The letters were actually preserved by Alexander Kropótkin, who in 1872 had reclaimed his letters from Peter, numbered the entire collection and carried it with him to Zürich. He left the letters there in the safekeeping of P. L. Lavróv when he returned to Russia in 1874. After Alexander's suicide, Lavróv returned the letters to Alexander's family, who in turn forwarded them to Peter in England. When Kropótkin returned to Russia in 1917 he carried the letters with him. They have since been published in Russian as *Petr i Aleksandr Kropotkini, Perepiska,* edited by N. Lebedev, 2 vols. (Moscow, 1932).

6. George Kennan (1845–1924), an American writer, published the results of his investigations of Russian prisons in a book which was very famous in its time, *Siberia and the Exile System* (New York, 1891).

7. In an addition to his *Memoirs,* Kropótkin gave his opinion of Marx's *Das Kapital:* "I read this book while still in St. Petersburg where it appeared in 1872 in Herman Lopatin's translation. The pretentiousness of the book, together with its unscientific nature (the theory of value, for example, is not proven scientifically at all and must be taken on faith) and its abuse of scientific jargon I did not like at all. The excursions of Marx into the realm of quantitative expression and algebraic formula were ridiculous. They prove his complete incompetence to think concretely quantitatively. I laughed a great deal

with N. Tsinger (the astronomer) at the "formulas" of Marx which he so importantly wrote out, not even suspecting how ridiculous they would appear to mathematicians who are accustomed to the idea of units of measure. To express by formulas what a formula does not express is indeed ridiculous."

8. Kropótkin inserted the following speech by himself at this point in a later addition to his *Memoirs:* "I could not speak *from the Bible* when it is for me a book like any other. For the success of religious propaganda *faith* is necessary and I am unable to believe in the divinity of Christ or the authority of God." Then, as a digression, Kropótkin added, "So I spoke then, and now after a lifetime of experience I still say that if religious propaganda in the name of religion effectively grips the masses whom socialist propaganda does not touch, this religious propaganda in return also carries within itself a sort of evil which overcomes the good. It teaches *obedience;* it teaches *submission to authority;* it pulls to the front those who are despotic and want *to rule.* Because of this, religious propaganda in the end inevitably produces a church, that is, the organized submission of the people to some authority. It has been so with all religious movements even when they began by revolutionary teachings such as the Anabaptists. . . ."

9. At this point Kropótkin made the following addition later: "But generally, what would the peasants gain if Alexander II. granted a constitution? . . . If, in the conditions of that time, 1871–74, there had been any evidence to presuppose the possibility of political reform in the sense of political freedom, the reasoning cited above [the quotation in the text] would have lost all influence. The majority would have been longing to get into political agitation and would have carried along all the rest. But with the meekness of our liberal older brothers, there did not appear to be any hope for a change in political conditions. What is now written sometimes in Russian emigrant political literature about that period insists that because of theoretical considerations an indifference to the political form of government reigned at that time. That is completely mistaken. The theoretical opinions of the majority, of the large majority of the Chaikóvsky Circle as well as the other circles, were not at all so dogmatic. They even vascillated between two trends: the constitutional (or constitutional-revolutionary if it can be

so expressed) and the socialist-revolutionary. If the latter opinion, which I among others supported, prevailed in 1872–77, that was only because there was no hope then for a peaceful or a revolutionary-constitutional agitation. But the feeling of bitterness had not yet spread so much that the youth was resolved to take the way of terror and to kill their tyrants and torturers wherever and however they could."

10. "The assassination of Alexander II. had even then been proposed from time to time," Kropótkin wrote in a new version of the chapter on the Chaikóvsky Circle. "To expect that he would at some time take a turn for the better would have been ridiculous. Up to the end of his reign the reaction *had* to go on, always growing stronger. 'The Heir' always took advantage of his reputation as a liberal; as usual it was said without the slightest foundation that the heir would take the way of the liberals. . . . It was reported, for example, that when they set him to study at the death of his brother, Nicholas Alexándrovich, he replied to his teachers: 'What is this for? I will have responsible (i.e., constitutional) Ministers!'

"I remember well what Alexander Alexándrovich was in his youth when I saw him at court. Knowing the vile way in which he had treated the Finnish officer [Part II, Chapter IX of the *Memoirs*] I placed absolutely no hope in the heir, but said both then and later in Geneva to the members of the Executive Committee [of the People's Will—*Narodnaia Volia*] that it was impossible to place *any* hope in his liberalism, that they must expect a worse reaction from him than from his father. Even if he had been taken by the most liberal aspirations, the fact that he comes to the throne by stepping across the dead body of his father will force him, because of human character in general, to be a worse reactionary than his father. *Inevitably* he must reason, 'Here is the end to which his liberal reforms brought Father.' I understand regicide as a means of obtaining vengeance for the ruin of our lives, but regicide as a means of obtaining political freedom I could never understand."

11. The lack of friction Kropótkin mentions was not so obvious in 1872–74. Kropótkin himself often stood at the center of the conflict. When Dmítri Klementz first proposed to the Chaikóvsky Circle that they invite Kropótkin to enter their circle, they replied, "What prince have you now? He perhaps

wishes to amuse himself under the mask of democracy, later he will become a dignitary and cause us to be hanged." But when the circle became acquainted with the true nature of Kropótkin's thought, they warmly welcomed him. (*Kropotkiné II*, Paris, 1921, p. 8).

But difficulties soon arose because Kropótkin's views were so pronounced and uncompromising. He is "wanting in that flexibility of mind and that faculty of adapting himself to the conditions of the moment and of practical life which are indispensable to a conspirator," his close friend, Sergéi Kravchínsky, felt it necessary to write. "He endeavors to make certain ideas prevail at all costs . . . He is too exclusive and rigid in his theoretical convictions. He admits no departure from the ultra-anarchical program. . . ." (*Underground Russia*, New York, 1885, p. 89).

This combination of rigidity and anarchism led Dmítri Klementz to say to Kropótkin in jest: "Here it comes out at last, we are more anarchic than you." Kropótkin replied somewhat irritably, "On the other hand, I am more revolutionary than you." (Lev Tikhomírov, *Vospominaniia*, Moscow, 1927, p. 79). They were both correct.

Kropótkin later noted in an addition to his *Memoirs:* "We discussed warmly in the circle the question of propaganda among the people and of the militant or non-militant character of agitation. When the circle entrusted to me the drawing up of a program and I brought out a militant program setting forth as a goal peasant uprisings and the seizure of land and all property (which would have to be accomplished in the uprising if it were to be successful), strong arguments began in the circle. In these arguments, [Sophia] Peróvskaia, [Sergéi] Kravchínsky, [Nicholas] Charúshin and I always stood on one side; the majority were on the other but several wavered between."

According to Chaikóvsky, Kropótkin referred disparagingly to his opposition as "socialist-statists and constitutionalists" which did not please them at all. (*Kropotkiné II*, p. 5.)

12. In addition to printing pamphlets for the people, the Chaikóvsky Circle, which had its own press in Zürich, wanted to support an emigrant journal. "In Zürich at that time there was a hard battle going on between the adherents of Lavróv

and those of Bakúnin," Kropótkin wrote later in an addition to his *Memoirs*. "To remain neutral in this struggle was impossible. . . .

"Lavróv wanted in the beginning to publish a constitutional journal, quite moderate, whose program I had seen in St. Petersburg before my entry into the Chaikóvsky Circle and before my trip abroad if I am not mistaken. Knowing neither Lavróv nor any movement in St. Petersburg at that time, I remember that I was completely indifferent to this program. It did not have, as far as I can remember, even a hint of the working-class and socialist movement.

"Lavróv later strengthened his program in a socialist sense.

"When I returned from abroad and described my impressions of the International to the Chaikóvsky Circle, of which I was then a member, the circle decided to send its own delegate to Zürich, who would visit both Lavróv and Bakúnin and decide which of the two journals would be more in accord with our program. I suggested that they send Dmítri [Klementz], but the circle decided to send [M. V.] Kupriiánov, whose intellect the circle regarded with awe.

"I do not know how Kupriiánov fulfilled his commission, but the Bakúnists said that he did not visit any of them but went straight to Lavróv and pointed out to him the necessity of a more socialist program (the third program of Lavróv), if he wanted to work for the new movement which was beginning among the youth. When Kupriiánov returned from abroad (I had given him my passport and I lived that summer without a passport in Obiralovka with Lenochka), the circle recognized *Forward!* (*Vpered!*) as its organ and gave financial support to Lavróv's journal. The majority of the members of the circle, although they knew *very* little about Social Democracy and about anarchism, were by their ties and by their convictions more Social Democratic than anarchist.

"Sergéi, Dmítri, and Charúshin in part and I unreservedly would have preferred to support the Bakúnist organ or both journals, but the Kornílov sisters fiercely defended the Social Democratic organ and we did not begin to quarrel. We all knew nothing would come of that. When the journal came out, if we liked it, then we would import it. If another journal were printed and if we liked it, then we would also bring it in and the reading public itself would decide which was better. In general we had our own affairs to attend to and we were able to treat dispassionately the struggle in Zürich. . . .

"But the first number of *Forward!* with its article about the necessity of studying in the universities (when the youth had gone to learn among the people, as there was nothing about the social sciences to be learned from the professors) made almost everyone indignant even in our circle. It was as though a wind had blown over us from the grave. In general everyone remained dissatisfied with the first number. The leader of the youth himself had to be led or dragged behind.

"We did not, however, attach particular significance to this journal. We distributed it, but our affairs went on by themselves and the exhortations of Lavróv did not produce any kind of impression upon any of us. I remember that at one of our meetings I announced that if, for example, the circle would send me to bring in *Forward!*, I would do so, but I could not put my heart into it. The majority of active members in our circle, particularly those who carried on their activities in working-class surroundings, was of the same opinion. The journal of Lavróv was simply boring when we led such an exuberant life."

13. Kropótkin later elaborated on the somewhat disheartening experiences of the Chaikóvsky Circle with the engineers: "Relations with the workers were established, both with the engineers and with the factory hands. The goal of the circle at that time was to develop several individuals among the workers and from these to form separate and completely independent circles which would carry on by themselves (independent of us but with our help if needed) propaganda and organization among the workers in the towns and among the peasants in the villages. The engineers, having already read something and being able to carry on propaganda, would become valuable propagandists and organizers among the urban workers. The factory hands, having not yet broken their ties with the country since close to a majority of them returned in the summer to their villages to cultivate their strips, would serve as connecting links between town and country, between the city workers and the peasants.

". . . [Anatoly] Serdiukóv was occupied with the engineers,

but when Klementz, Kravchínsky and I joined the circle, we
three also carried on propaganda among them. Kravchínsky
gave them lectures on history and political economy. I told
them about the International and its history, goals and development and about the Paris Commune, whose meaning has
been so little understood even by its contemporaries. We later
brought into our circle a young worker from the engineers,
Orlóv, distinguished from the others by his intelligence and
energy. The rest, about fifteen, formed their own circle, re-
cruited their own members and planned their own activities.
We visited them only to maintain ties and to give them a series
of lectures on various subjects on Sundays.

"It is necessary to say, unfortunately, that our propaganda
among the engineers was not notable for any particular success.
Individuals were developed. The majority of our engineers
were able to carry on conversations no worse than those of
many students on various questions concerning socialism,
capitalism, etc. But with the exception of Orlóv, and not entirely even with him, all this knowledge did not touch them
to the quick. They themselves admired their own 'development,' their 'radicalism,' but to get them to put it into action
was impossible. They openly neglected the factory hands and
carried on only a very weak propaganda in their own surroundings, particularly after they became emancipated from
Serdiukóv and the rest of us.

". . . At the same time they had a sort of envy of the 'students.' Once they became acquainted with the international
socialist point of view so that they could express their opinion
'according to Lassalle' or 'according to Draper,' they did not
try to go deeper into the heart of things. They no longer
needed their guides, the 'students,' i.e., Serdiukóv and Klementz, who were more poorly dressed than they, and who in
giving their lives for the movement appeared only as an un-
necessary and unpleasant reproach to the engineers.

"They liked the lectures of Kravchínsky and they liked him
very much as an interesting speaker. But when Klementz
called them to task or turned with contempt on their talk
about their Saturday-night adventures in all sorts of filthy
places, or insisted that they take their turn in leading small
circles of colleagues instead of spending Sunday morning talk-

ing about their adventures and walking after lunch, they became quite angry with him and told him not to visit them anymore. At this time Sergéi was not in St. Petersburg and Serdiukóv began to visit them less punctually. They endured me probably because of the difference in age as I was much older than they. But generally their relations with the 'students' became hostile. 'We do not need these bourgeoisie as leaders,' they would say. 'We ourselves know what to do.'"

14. Alexander Kropótkin indignantly told George Kennan later in Siberia: "I am not a nihilist nor a revolutionary and I never have been. I was exiled simply because I dared to think, and to say what I thought about the things that happened around me, and because I was the brother of a man whom the Russian Government hated." (George Kennan, *Siberia and the Exile System*, New York, 1891, p. 326.)

15. Sophia Nikolaevna Lavróva, a sister-in-law of Peter Kropótkin.

16. Dr. Orest Edward Weimar.

17. "I could never feel comfortable with the Russian view on propaganda abroad," Kropótkin wrote in an addition to his *Memoirs*. "Russian comrades considered me almost a traitor because I devoted my strength to agitation in Western Europe. But I think, on the contrary, that by working for Western Europe I also work for Russia, perhaps more than if I had remained in Russia. All movements in Russia are conceived under the influence of Western Europe and carry the imprint of the trends of thought prevailing in Europe: Petrashévsky was a child of Fourierism, Chernyshévsky of Fourierism and St.-Simonism. Our movement of the 1870s and the present movement are the children of the International and of the Communes, of the *European* Bakúnin and of the equally European Marxism.

"But if I were in Western Europe simply to strengthen the ranks of the existing parties which are growing in power, then I hardly would have remained there. I would have gone somewhere else where it is necessary to plow anew. But in 1878–79, just at the time when a new movement of a really revolutionary character began in Russia after the crushing defeat of our movement of 1873–76, a new disintegration took place in the Jura Federation, the only remaining stronghold of anarchism in Europe. Out of all our groups, which had worked together in a friendly spirit until then, I remained alone with several comrade-workers. I had to stay alone with them two years to carry on all the work.

"The main point, however, is that in Russia I could see no field of activity for myself. In 1876, when I escaped, nothing was being accomplished in the revolutionary circles, or rather, in the fragments of our circles. All the active people were in prison. After escaping, I spent nearly a week in the environs of St. Petersburg, seeing several of our former comrades. All were out of spirits from idleness. And what was there to undertake?

"There was no one to go to the people. Whoever had been able to go had already gone and had been caught. Besides, it was obviously impossible to carry on peaceful propaganda. It was necessary to take a militant position, and this our youth did not want to do. Even later, when, under the influence of the gallows, of the shooting by Véra Zasúlich and the armed resistance of the Jacobins in Odéssa, a small band of the youth decided to go the way of terror, theoretically giving due attention to the rural revolution, they in fact thought about only one thing: political terror for the elimination of the tsar. I always believed that revolutionary agitation ought to be carried out mainly among the peasants for the preparation of a peasant uprising. Not that I did not understand that a struggle with the tsar was necessary, that it would produce a *revolutionary* spirit. But, in my opinion, it ought to be only a *part* of the agitation being carried on in the country and by no means *all*, and even less should it be the exclusive affair of a revolutionary party.

"I could not convince myself that even the successful assassination of the tsar could have any significant direct results, even in the sense of political freedom. Indirect results I knew would come without question, such as a blow to the idea of autocracy and the development of a militant spirit. But to give oneself wholly to a terroristic struggle against the tsar, it is necessary to believe in the significance of the *direct* results that can be obtained by this path. I cannot believe in this until the terroristic struggle against the autocracy and its satraps goes hand in hand with an armed struggle against the *nearest* enemies of the peasants and workers and is carried on with the goal of a revolution by the people.

"No one, with the exception of three or four persons such as [Sergéi] Koválik and [Porfíry] Voinarálsky, wants to be occupied even with the sort of agitation which is spoken of in the programs, particularly that of Land and Freedom [*Zemlia i Volia*]. The Executive Committee and its partisans even considered such agitation harmful. They dreamt of inspiring the liberals to bold deeds, which would consist of wresting a constitution from the tsar, but any kind of *popular* movement which would inevitably be accompanied by the seizure of land, assassination and arson, would in their opinion only frighten the liberals and alienate them from the revolutionary party.

"So the matter has remained until the present time. However difficult it would be at my age and with a family to be in Russia and to be completely absorbed in illegal revolutionary activity, hiding myself as an agitator, even now if I felt the necessity of my presence there, I would go into the lion's den. I write this quite deliberately since I have often thought about it. But no one needs me in Russia. If I happened to be in Russia now, I would be in the position of a man who is hindering those who are doing something, raising doubts and at the same time feeling that those around him do not have the strength to do anything better. For the same reason I have not begun to publish any kind of journal for Russia.

"I am deeply convinced that at the present time [the summer of 1899] *a peasant uprising* is necessary for Russia as the only way out of her present situation. But even now, as twenty-five years ago, there is no one among the intelligent youth who is imbued with the same thoughts. Today all attention is turned to the German Social Democrats whose success has been greatly exaggerated in Russia. If a popular uprising on a large scale should begin in Italy, and if it should lead to a republican *revolution* like the French Revolution of 1789–93, then that would be a different matter. Or if a popular uprising should begin again in France which would lead to the proclamation of Communes in all of France, and in every Commune to expropriation, then again that would be something else. Our youth would then understand the significance of a peasant, a people's uprising and would throw themselves into the preparation of such an uprising in Russia.

"This is why I think that to work for the preparation of a popular uprising in Europe and for the theoretical basis of the coming movement is still the best way to work for the preparation of the same in Russia."

18. This statement was only a polite pretext. Kropótkin had already been greatly disappointed by the moderate socialist position of Lavróv's paper, *Forward!* (See Note 12). When he landed in England, he found in the issue of July 1876 a very short (and it seemed to Kropótkin very inadequate) obituary of Michael Bakúnin. "When I read it," Kropótkin later wrote, "I had even less reason to visit the editor of *Forward!*" Subsequently, however, Kropótkin did call on Lavróv and they became good friends.

19. "Turgénev once spoke with me about those pamphlets that our circle had published for the people," Kropótkin wrote in a 1920 addition to his *Memoirs*. " 'This is not exactly what is needed,' Turgénev had remarked, thinking about something, and to my surprise there and then mentioned how our people deal with horse stealers. His exact works I cannot recall, but the sense of his remarks engraved itself in my memory. Unfortunately, someone coming into the room interrupted our conversation, and consequently I have time and again asked myself: 'What exactly did he want to say?'

"Some time after his death his story dictated by him to Madame Viardot in French and translated into Russian by Grigoróvich appeared in which he described how the peasants dealt with one landowner-horse stealer."

20. "It is well known how Turgénev loved art," wrote Kropótkin in a note to his *Memoirs*. "When he saw in Antokólsky a really great artist, he talked with enthusiasm about him. 'I do not know whether I have ever met a *genius*, but if I have, it was Antokólsky,' Turgénev told me. Then he added, laughing, 'And, you know, he does not speak one language correctly. He speaks both Russian and French horribly, but on the other hand his sculpture is magnificent.'

"When I told Turgénev that while I was still a youth I had been delighted with Antokólsky's 'Ivan the Terrible' and that

I particularly liked his model in wax of a group of Jews reading a book while the inquisitors are lowering them into a vault, Turgénev insisted that I see without fail his statue, 'Christ Before the People,' then just completed. I did not want to visit Antokólsky for fear of disturbing him, but Turgénev was resolved that on a certain day he would take P. L. Lavróv and me into the studio of Antokólsky.

"And so he did. The striking beauty of the statue of Christ is well known. Particularly impressive is the unusual sadness with which the face of Christ is imbued as he stands before the crowd howling 'Crucify him!' At the same time the might of the whole figure of Christ is striking; particularly if one looks from behind, it seems that one is seeing a healthy, powerful peasant bound by cords.

" 'Now look from above,' Turgénev said to me. 'You will see such might, such defiance in this head.'

"And Turgénev went to ask Antokólsky for a ladder so that I could see the head from above. Antokólsky began to make excuses, but Turgénev insisted: 'He must see it—he is a revolutionary.'

"When they brought a ladder and I looked on this head from above, I understood all the *intellectual* might of this Christ, his profound contempt for the stupidity of the howling crowd, his abhorrence of his executioners. Standing before this statue, one wishes that Christ would tear apart the cords that bind him and begin to drive the executioners away."

21. *Les Paroles d'un Révolté* were later translated into Italian by a young Italian of twenty-one, Benito Mussolini, who wrote: "Twenty years have passed by but the *Paroles* seem quite recent so alive are they with present-day interests. On reading them, one has a first impression that grips one, quite apart from the theories enunciated. They overflow with a great love for oppressed mankind and with infinite kindness." (*Opera Omnia di Benito Mussolini,* Florence, 1951, I, p. 50.)

22. This research resulted in *The State, Its Historic Role* (London, 1898), and *Ethics, Origin and Development* (New York, 1924).

23. These eight lectures formed the basis of a later book, *Ideals and Realities in Russian Literature* (New York, 1915).

24. "You know that I have always loved Tolstóy very much," commented the French writer, Romain Rolland. "But I have often had the impression that Kropótkin has *been* what Tolstóy has *written*. He has realized simply and naturally in his life that ideal of moral purity, of serene abnegation and of perfect love for mankind which the tormented genius of Tolstóy wanted all his life. . . ." (*Les Temps Nouveaux*, March, 1921.)

25. Kropótkin's fame as a geographer was such that his close friend, Robertson Smith, editor of the *Encyclopædia Brittanica* and Lord Almoner, Professor of Arabic at Cambridge University, had long been trying to secure Kropótkin for Cambridge as Professor of Geography. Kropótkin was reportedly offered this position in 1896 with the implied condition that he refrain from any further anarchist activity. He declined the offer, explaining that he could not accept any position which would compromise his freedom. (James Mavor, *My Windows on the Street of the World*, London, 1923, 2 vols., I, p. 75.)

26. Stalin's remark of February 27, 1915, is given in Leon Trotsky, *Stalin* (London, 1947), pp. 175–76. Trotsky's comment appeared in his *History of the Russian Revolution*, translated by Max Eastman (New York, 1932), I, p. 75.

27. In his history of the Russian Revolution, Trotsky added, "The ancient internationalist prefers to see the psychology of a defeated nation on the other side of the border." (*Ibid.*, II, 178–79.)

28. The above material on Kropótkin and Lenin came from an article by Mr. David Shub, "Kropotkin and Lenin," *The Russian Review* (1953), XII, pp. 227–34.

The fundamental differences between the anarchists and Marxists which Kropótkin mentioned in his talk with Lenin had already been summarized by Lenin in his *Letters From Afar:* "The revolutionary Marxists differ from the anarchists not only by the fact that the former stand for centralized large-scale communist production and the latter stand for scattered, small production. No, the difference between us on the problem of government, of the state is that we are *for* the revolutionary utilization of the revolutionary forms of the state in the struggle for socialism, while the anarchists are *against* it."

29. Kropótkin's work on ethics was published in the unfinished form in which he left it. The English version is entitled *Ethics, Origin and Development,* translated by L. S. Friedland and J. R. Piroshnikoff (New York, 1924).

INDEX

A NOTE TO READERS

We hope you have enjoyed this Cresset Library edition and would like to take this opportunity to invite you to put forward your suggestions about books that might be included in the series.

The Cresset Library was conceived as a forum for bringing back books that we felt should be widely available in attractively designed and priced paperback editions. The series themes can be loosely described as social, cultural, and intellectual history though, as you can see from the list of published titles at the front of this book, these themes cover a broad range of interest areas.

If you have read or know of books that fall into this category which are no longer available or not available in paperback, please write and tell us about them. Should we publish a book that you have suggested we will send you a free copy upon publication together with three other Cresset Library titles of your choice.

Please address your letter to Claire L'Enfant at:-

Century Hutchinson
FREEPOST
London
WC2N 4BR

There is no need to stamp your envelope.

We look forward to hearing from you.

THE CRESSET LIBRARY